MY GIRLS

A Story of Survival and Togetherness in the Inner City

Graham Danzer

NASW PRESS

National Association of Social Workers
Washington, DC

Jeane W. Anastas, PhD, LMSW, President
Elizabeth J. Clark, PhD, ACSW, MPH, Executive Director

Cheryl Y. Bradley, *Publisher*
Sarah Lowman, *Project Manager*
Mary Killion, *Copyeditor*
Rebecca Tippets, *Proofreader*
Becky Hornyak, *Indexer*

Cover by Eye to Eye Design Studio
Interior design by Rick Soldin
Printed and bound by Victor Graphics

© 2011 by the NASW Press

First impression: October 2011

Library of Congress Cataloging-in-Publication Data

Danzer, Graham.
  My girls : a story of survival and togetherness in the inner city /
Graham Danzer.
    p. cm.
  Includes bibliographical references and index.
  ISBN 978-0-87101-423-8
  1. African American girls—Conduct of life. 2. Group counseling
for girls—United States. I. Title.

  BJ1581.2.D334 2011
  155.5'3308996073—dc22

                                        2011010000

Printed in the United States of America

Contents

Acknowledgment

I want to acknowledge Debra Stevens, my mother, for helping with the editing. Thanks, Mom.

About the Author

Graham Danzer, ASW PPSC RASi, has over 12 years of clinical social work experience. His primary areas of expertise are working with at-risk adolescents and their families, substance abuse, and crisis. He has undertaken extensive research on cross-cultural issues in therapy and has had his work published in the following peer-reviewed journals: The *Journal of Aggression, Maltreatment, and Trauma* and the *Journal of Social Work in Public Health.* He is also pursuing a PhD in clinical social work at Sanville Institute in Berkeley, CA.

ONE

Introduction

When people are overwhelmed by life, they often need to talk about what is bothering them. This can help them experience some relief from painful emotions, which may be what they need to get through hard times. I have often heard people say that they do not want to talk about their problems because "talking won't change anything." Their argument is that talking about their problems will not change the external circumstances.

In my experience, the external circumstances are not as much of a problem as the feeling of being overwhelmed. It is this feeling that makes external problems seem worse than they are, which results in paralysis. When people are unable to take corrective action, their problems seem all the more unsolvable. I have found that intense feelings often inhibit a person's ability to think clearly, and this confusion can make problem solving impossible. Talking things out will usually help people calm down and experience some relief, which helps them think more clearly so that they can better decide what to do next.

I relearned this when I counseled six young teenage African American girls in a group setting at an inner-city public school where I was interning as part of my graduate training program. I will present a narrative of the more clinically significant weeks of the school year and will describe the events as they actually happened, with as little interpretation or censure as possible. In this way, readers can gain a deeper understanding and appreciation for how overwhelming the circumstances were for these girls and how talking about their problems helped them to hold themselves together.

These girls were called names, put down, threatened, and even attacked practically every day. The East Bay Community Recovery Project hosted an African American women's panel in 2009; one of the guest speakers stated that these traumas tend to be routine experiences for African American women.[1]

I often felt frustrated that all I could do was to sit and listen to these girls' stories. Long after my work with the girls ended, I realized that the group may have been one of their only experiences of feeling truly safe, listened to, understood, and cared about. S. Zemmelman (personal communication, November 16, 2009) stated that when patients feel this way about their therapy, they are most likely to achieve therapeutic outcome.[2] Although the group experience could not begin to compensate for their difficult circumstances, the girls at least had one hour a week to talk and feel and relate.

Many of the girls were already friends and supported each other as much as they could. The only consistent and reliable support that they had was each other, yet each of their lives was so overwhelming that they only had so much of themselves that they could give to each other. Lum (2003) noted that one of the strengths of low-income, urban African Americans is their large extended family and social support networks; this is a surrogate form of clanship that originated in tribal Africa. Lum also noted that these support networks are often worn down by the extreme poverty that low-income, urban African Americans have endured throughout history.

The girls tried to take care of each other, but they often had to bury their feelings and remain prepared and ready to protect themselves. When they experienced feelings that made them vulnerable, adult men or people who were looking for a fight would often try to take advantage of their moments of weakness. The girls tended to protect themselves by being loud, aggressive, obnoxious, trouble-making, and hypersexualized. By listening to the girls and trying to keep an open mind about why they might be "acting out," I learned that they did not have much reliable, supportive guidance from adults, and so they ended up doing whatever they had to do to survive. The group environment provided them with a safe space to explore what this was like in the company of others who knew what they were going through. Ellensweig-Tepper (2000) noted that small groups can help trauma survivors feel safe and understood.

My involvement with this group may have given the girls their first experience of a positive, reliable, nonabusive, nonsexual relationship with a man. K Siegel (1980) and Harwood (2003) recommended that an adolescent girls'

---

[1] The East Bay Community Recovery Project is one of the leading co-occurring disorder-focused outpatient clinics in Northern California.

[2] S. Zemmelman, PhD, is a practicing Jungian analyst and is a faculty member of the Sanville Institute, which has a doctoral program in clinical social work.

group be facilitated by a male and a female therapist so that the girls can experience healthy male and female interactions in a way that resembles a mother–father dyad.

How Did the Group Get Going?

Once the girls were brought together, it did not take long for the group to begin running itself. Initially, the girls were anxious and excited and often tried to talk over each other. They tended to communicate this way outside of group as well. They may have developed this habit because they had learned through experience that this was the only way that people would listen to them. At one point in the group, three or four voices were going all at once until one of the girls called a virtual point of order and suggested that the 60 minutes of group time be divided up equally so that each girl could get her fair share of group time. For example, if there were five members present, each girl would get roughly 12 minutes of group time to share at length without much interruption. The rest of the girls readily agreed. Most of the time, my co-facilitator and I sat back and listened.

I learned a lot about the girls by doing everything I could to plug myself into their community. In addition to my more standard clinical duties, I spent a lot of time visiting and observing the classrooms, playing tag and kick ball with the kids before school, and talking to their teachers and other interested community members. In fact, these more casual interactions yielded a majority of the information I will present about the girls.

When it was time for the group to meet, I would go to the girls' classrooms and escort them to the counseling office so that they would not get in trouble along the way. While my co-facilitator set chairs into a circle in preparation for group, I would let her know I was going to get "the girls" from class. Somewhere over the course of the year, I started to say that I was going to get *My Girls*. The name has stuck ever since.

Many clinicians might view my more casual interactions as a breach of therapeutic boundaries. My analytic training taught me that therapy should be bound by the beginning and end of the therapeutic hour and there should not be any extra dimensions to the therapeutic relationship, which would be created by collateral contact. Through my work with the girls and their community, *The X* (as I am pseudo-naming it), I learned that this was not necessarily the case. When I interacted with them in a less formal, getting-to-know-you way, the girls' community began to consider that I might be part of the solution rather than the problem. This was important, because people in this community overwhelmingly looked upon white clinical staff with suspicion and distrust. The result was that the kids did not want to go to therapy, the parents were often reluctant to consent to their children being in counseling, and interested community members were reluctant to refer youths for clinical services. It was the experience of many community members that clinical staff who met with the children were secretive about what they were doing until Child Protective Services or the police suddenly showed up and started asking questions.

J. Kirk (personal communication, November 9, 2010) believes that collateral contact is absolutely vital to working effectively with highly traumatized, highly disorganized, social work clients and that the more analytic way of working exclusively with the unconscious without "interference" is more appropriate for relatively higher functioning clients.[3] I instinctively knew that I needed to be collaborative and supportive, if the concerned adults in the girls' larger community were going to refer children to me for counseling and provide me with the information I needed to be able to work more effectively with them. In effect, the girls were my clients and so were the members of their larger community. Lum (2003) noted that this more systemic method is the best practice for working with highly traumatized, low-income, urban African American clients.

I protected the girls' confidentiality by not relaying their information to interested community members, but I did sometimes professionally self-disclose to concerned adults and receive information from them about what was going on with the girls. Interested community members often asked about my work with the girls. I let them know that my sessions with the girls had to be kept confidential; if the sessions were not confidential, the girls would not want to say anything in the group. (Clinicians often respond to inquiries about session content by explaining the legality of confidentiality, which low-income, urban African American community members experience as off-putting.) I would also let the community members know that, although I could not share information about the girls with them, they could tell me what they knew about the girls and this would help me work more effectively. These community members tended to see my point and appreciated my being open about what I was doing and why. I have protected the girls' confidentiality in this book by disguising everything that is not directly relevant to the case.

---

[3] J. Kirk, LCSW, is the former director of a Kaiser Hospital teenage substance abuse program and is a practicing family therapist with more than 30 years of clinical experience.

Gender and Cultural Considerations

Duncan and Johnson (2007) found that African American female undergraduate college students expressed a strong preference for a fellow African American woman counselor. When African Americans have been paired with white counselors, their retention in treatment and their corresponding level of satisfaction has tended to be much lower (Gregory & Leslie, 1996; Sykes, 1987). I have sometimes been effective with my low-income, urban African American clients, but it has taken me considerable time to build relationships with them. Even when some trust is built over the course of a long-term relationship, these clients have still tended to tell me only part of their stories.

I have often found that highly traumatized women who are of a stronger, more dominant personality type (like the girls) will often engage more readily with male therapists. J. Kirk (personal communication, December 2, 2010) acknowledged this point but added that women may engage more with male therapists because they are "performing"; thus they may be engaging with male therapists in seductive ways that help them avoid doing the real therapeutic work that they would do with a female therapist. Harwood (2003) noted that women who have been traumatized by men may display avoidant reactions to male therapists. Women who are in therapy with female therapists may be better able to observe feminine gender role modeling and to have their experiences of being oppressed related to and understood at a deeper level (Wood & Roche, 2001). In my experience as a man working clinically with women, I often overlooked how their presenting symptoms might be the result of gender-based oppression until consulting with a female colleague. Evans, Kincade, Marbley, and Seem (2005) noted that gender-based oppression may be the root cause of many women's mental health issues. This speaks to S. Zemmelman's (personal communication, November 16, 2009) statement about the difference in the clinical work when the therapist has had similar experiences and can relate on a deeper, empathic level. Without having had similar experiences, it is likely that the therapist will only be able to understand the client in a more cerebral, superficial way.

It might have been better if the girls were paired with younger, licensed African American female therapists, but none were available. African American therapists are a rarity; in African American communities, one must take what resources are available and make the most out of them. It is typical for public schools in low-income, urban, predominantly African American communities to be woefully understaffed and underfunded (Kozol, 2005). I dealt with these limitations by managing a huge caseload and maximizing the yield from what resources were available. This is why the co-facilitator and I elected to see the girls in a group rather than individually: individual therapy hours were scarce, and a group setting provided a programmatically viable alternative. The girls and officials at their school witnessed my efforts to come up with solutions, and this helped me to engage with them. My high-energy approach to working with the girls also helped to get the group going. Ellensweig-Tepper (2000) noted that an assertive, active, engaging role model is often a good candidate for a group leader for adolescent girls.

Before presenting the girls' stories, I will first describe two theories that help clarify the girls' external circumstances in a more general way. Attachment theory emphasizes how development may be affected by trauma. A theory of trauma will point up the fact that low-income, urban, young teenage African American girls are a particularly at-risk group for experiencing trauma and developing posttraumatic symptoms (Kimmerling, Ouimette, & Wolfe, 2002). These theories helped me to conceptualize the girls' often erratic and chaotic ways of behaving in an empathic, relational way, which helped me build relationships with them.

TWO

Attachment Theory

Attachment theory developed out of the Freudian schools of psychoanalysis, so I will begin with an overview of Freudian theory. Then, I will discuss the attachment theories of development and psychotherapy. I will emphasize the parts of these theories that have the strongest implications for my work with the girls.

Freudian Schools

S. Freud theorized that human development occurred through a series of psychosexual stages (Mitchell & Black, 1995). The infant grew up instinctively competing with the parent of the same gender for the affections of the parent of the opposite gender. Infants were pushed by the sexual and aggressive drives in the id—the most primitive part of Freud's tripartite psyche. These drives urge individuals to try to gratify their sexual and aggressive needs and fantasies, which may not always be socially appropriate. This is why the ego and super-ego, together, try to control the id (G. Bellows, personal communication, June 4, 2010).[1] The superego tries to morally repress the drives (Mitchell & Black, 1995). The ego is where compromises are reached in the form of the defenses, which allow the drives to be discharged in socially appropriate ways (A. Freud, 1966). It has been my experience that those clients who repress their deepest desires tend to suffer from the most severe depression and psychosomatic symptoms. This speaks to the core principle of Freudian analytic treatment:

---

[1] G. Bellows, PhD, is a practicing Freudian analyst and a faculty member of The Sanville Institute.

Clients should freely explore their unconscious to get in touch with their deepest desires, let them out in session, and have a cathartic experience that will resolve their presenting symptoms (S. Freud, 2007; Mitchell & Black, 1995). This theory coincides with the point I made in the beginning of this book about how talking at length can often lead to a feeling of relief.

Freud developed his model of therapy through working with adults, and he applied it to children without ever having directly observed them (Mitchell & Black, 1995). This gap was partially closed in the 1930s and 1940s by ego psychologists, who were interested in human development and directly observed relational behavior. Wolf and Spitz (as cited in Mitchell & Black, 1995) were among the first analytic researchers to study children and expanded theories about children's emotional needs for relationships with their mothers. Spitz (1951) was particularly interested in how children were affected by the loss of a core love object and how children who did not have their emotional needs met developed severe emotional problems.

Whereas S. Freud focused primarily on the drives, his daughter Anna and his other followers were more interested in the ego and elaborated on the theories of the defenses. They founded ego psychology and focused on human development. They theorized that the ego is both an adaptive and a survival strategy (Mitchell & Black, 1995). A. Freud (1966) noted that infants are born with immature egos and need their parents' help to adapt successfully to various stressors in their immediate environments. The parents provide the infants with auxiliary ego strength when the infants cannot adapt successfully on their own. When infants adapt successfully, whether by using their own ego strength or the auxiliary strength of their caregivers, they will grow internally stronger. In the girls' stories, it is clear that they often used each other as auxiliary support, which was vital to their psychic survival.

Relational Development

John Bowlby is the founder of attachment theory. Bowlby was psychoanalytically trained, though he diverged markedly from his predecessors. Whereas the Freudian psychoanalysts conceptualized human behavior as a manifestation of unconscious conflict, Bowlby (1960) theorized that behavioral patterns were learned based on life experience. He took ego psychological research a step further by looking more deeply at how early life experiences facilitate a system of relating to the self and others (Bowlby, 1960; Mitchell & Black, 1995).

In short, infants learn how to relate to others on the basis of how they are raised by their mothers, as their mothers learned through their own early life experiences (Cassidy & Shaver, 2008). If the mother–child relationship is based on consistent and reliable love, affection, nurturing, and trust, the infants will tend to relate to others in this more secure way. If the mothers are emotionally unavailable, unreliable, or otherwise raise the child insecurely, the children will go through a process of grief and mourning that eventually leads them to "give up" (Bowlby, 1960, 1969). This giving up is traumatic and causes these children to grow up feeling bad about themselves and distrusting others (Bowlby, 1969).

Mary Ainsworth, a former student and follower of Bowlby, researched reunion behavior in her Strange Situation study (Ainsworth, Blehar, Waters, & Wall, 1978). In this study, researchers observed the relational behavior between 12- to 18-month-old infants and their mothers and how the infants behaved around strangers. Ainsworth was particularly interested in how infants were affected by being separated from their mothers and how they behaved once they were reunited. Data were categorized on the basis of the infants' observed desire for proximity and their capacity to be soothed by self and others and whether their responses suggested internal security or insecurity. Their way of relating to their mothers was also compared with how they related to strangers. Researchers particularly noted the infants' levels of preoccupation; dismissing responses; crying and fussing; proximity to mother and strangers; and amount of exploration, smiling, and vocalization.

Ainsworth et al. (1978) found that observed relational behavior tended to fall into three distinct attachment styles: secure, anxious-ambivalent, and anxious-avoidant.

Children raised by caregivers who are consistently and reliably nuturing, soothing, responsive, and emotionally available develop generally positive views of themselves (Bowlby, 1960, 1963, 1969). This translates into healthy senses of trust in themselves and in others and facilitates the development of securely attached children.

Anxious-ambivalent children were anxious regardless of whether or not their mothers were in the observation room. When their mothers were with them, they were clingy. When their mothers left the observation room, these infants grew severely deregulated. They tended to cry and fuss loudly. Some-times, they would go to strangers for comfort. When their mothers came back, they were difficult to soothe and would engage in contradictory attachment behaviors such as reaching out in request for proximity and then leaning away or hitting their mothers when their mothers picked them up. Ainsworth et al. (1978) theorized that anxious-ambivalent children behaved this way because their mothers were inconsistently available. They were difficult to soothe and continued to engage in attachment-seeking behaviors even after their mothers came into proximity, because they had learned through experience that their mothers could become physically or emotionally unavailable at any time. Thus they remained hyperactivated in an attempt to keep their mothers in proximity, but they could not use the proximity to regulate. Wallin (2007) stated that one out of 10 contemporary middle-class Americans exhibits the preoccupied attachment style, the adult version of the anxious-ambivalent style.

Avoidant children ignored their mothers both when they were present and when they left the consulting room. When these children's levels of arousal were tested immediately following separation, it was found that they were as emotionally affected by their mothers' departures as were other infants, although they seemed to be making a considerable effort to hide it. These infants were raised by caregivers who were emotionally unavailable and unresponsive, and they dealt with it by trying to fend for themselves.

A fourth style, disorganized, a variant of insecure attachment, was identified later by Main and Solomon (1986). This attachment style is brought on by severe abuse or neglect, which breaks down the attachment system to the point that relational behavior is no longer coherent. Children who are disorganized are most often raised by caregivers with major psychological problems. They tend to be very aggressive or detached, and they may dissociate. When I met with the girls in the group, I noticed that they sometimes seemed to be a little "checked out" when their peers were telling their stories. Teenagers often have wandering minds, but I wonder whether the girls' behavior might be consistent with low-grade dissociation. Wallin (2007) noted that even the most severely traumatized and unsupported children do not relate in a disorganized way all the time; they may sometimes relate to others more coherently. This latter point is consistent with my observations of the girls' relational behavior.

Theory in Practice

Attachment theory remains, primarily, a research-based theory. Bowlby and his followers studied human development and did not construct attachment theory as a model from which to prescribe treatment. This gap was closed by contemporary attachment theorists. Their research showed that attachment not only applies to the mother–infant relationship, but also to father–child, adult, and romantic relationships (Hughes, 2006; Lieberman & Van Horn, 2008; Sable, 2000; Wallin, 2007).

Wallin (2007) theorized about how attachment styles manifest in the therapeutic relationship. He noted that clients often come to therapy lacking the abilities to behave effectively in relationships, perhaps because they were raised insecurely. To behave more effectively in relationships, they need to be in a long-term therapeutic relationship that gives them the relational experiences that they lacked in early life. For example, a preoccupied client needs the therapist to be consistently reliable and emotionally stable despite the client's often frantic, draining relational behavior. If the therapist can hold a more secure position over the long term, the anxious-ambivalent client will eventually learn that he or she can have a close, meaningful relationship without having to hyperactivate the attachment system. The avoidant client will tend to resist emotionally connecting with the therapist and needs the therapist to reach out and make this connection happen. The disorganized client needs the therapist to be particularly secure and dependable during the client's intense periods of chaos. If the therapist can be the person the client never had, the client will learn to relate to the therapist more securely, which will result in the client being more capable of relating more securely to others (Wallin, 2007; J. Nelson, personal communication, September 28, 2009).[2]

Now that I have explained the core principles of attachment theory, I will discuss how the attachment system is built and how it can be affected by trauma or abuse. J. Nelson (personal communication, May 25, 2009) stated that secure attachment develops neurobiologically when children experience positive and negative arousals and have their underlying emotional states correctly read and responded to by their primary caregivers. This is called *attunement*, and it helps children build a neurobiological capacity for affect regulation. J. Schore (personal communication, June 10, 2009) stated that, when a consistent state of regulation is maintained, other neurobiological and relational capacities develop properly.[3] Attunement also occurs when children and their primary caregivers regularly engage in play or soothing touch, make eye contact, share mutual smiles, and otherwise experience a deeper level of emotional connection and intimacy. These intersubjective experiences teach the children that they are loved and loveable, understood, and capable of connecting with trusted others in meaningful ways (Hughes, 2006). These right-brain to right-brain communications aid in the development of autoregulatory capacities in the brain (J. Schore, personal communication, June 10, 2009).

When infants are regularly attuned to, they will tend to seek proximity with their mothers when they are distressed and will be better able to use this proximity to regulate (Cassidy & Shaver, 2008; J. Nelson, personal communication, November 1, 2009). Infants who have consistently been attuned learn that, when they are distressed, their mothers will respond to their distress and resolve it.

---

[2] J. Nelson, PhD, is a faculty member at the Sanville Institute, Berkeley, California. She is also one of the leading attachment researchers on crying as an attachment behavior.

[3] J. Schore, PhD, is a faculty member of the Sanville Institute, Berkeley, California. She is also one of the leading researchers on the neurobiology of attachment.

Misattunements are inevitable, because even the most attuned mothers will often misperceive what their infants need (J. Nelson, personal communication, November 15, 2009). Sensitive mothers will keep trying to find the source of their infants' distress and will eventually resolve it. J. Schore (personal communication, June 11, 2009) stated that these rupture and repair experiences contribute to the child's development of affect regulatory capacities. Rocking, touching, making eye contact, and other calming experiences help to soothe the infant and repair misattunements (Bowlby, 1969). When ruptures occur and are not repaired, such as when children are abused, the attachment system may break down.

When maltreatment is sufficiently severe, children may be removed from their primary caregiver's custody. Bowlby (1963) noted that permanent separation from the primary caregiver is an irreversible trauma for the child, even though removal from the home of the primary caregiver is sometimes necessary. I have heard from child welfare workers that this is why separating a child from his or her parents is the child welfare system's plan of last resort and why attachment theory remains a strong influence on child welfare practice.

Bowlby (1963) wrote about infants who were severely emotionally deprived and were raised in orphanages. He noted that they were often unable to form lasting attachment bonds with others. Bowlby also theorized that a lack of nurturing and soothing in early life lead to attachment deficits, which were the root cause of why out-of-home placements for severely deprived children tended to fail. In foster care placements, these children were often difficult or demanding. Each time they were too ill-behaved in a new placement, they would be sent to another out-of-home placement, only to act out again and be removed again. Hughes (2006) noted that severely maltreated children act out to gain a feeling of power and control. Under that feeling of control, abused children have a core sense of shame and unlovability, which they may reinforce by preemptively striking out at people who they expect will abandon them.

Insecure strategies are somewhat pathological, but I would add that they are also survival strategies. When I present the girls' stories, I will show that their often chaotic behaviors in relationships were their best efforts to acquire support and protection. For example, they were often hypersexualized, not necessarily out of anxiety but because this is what the world around them taught them that they were worth. When the girls were safe and in each other's company, they often related to each other more securely. When I was working with them, I often tried to come up with theoretical explanations for their behavior, but I consistently found that no one particular theory fully encapsulated the complexity of their lives. Their lives were difficult and dangerous, and they rarely had anyone that they could go to for reliable support. The end result was that they did what they had to do to survive.

THREE

Trauma

In the previous chapter, I outlined attachment theory and how trauma or abuse can influence relational development. In this chapter, I will address trauma itself. First, I will present a general overview of trauma and then move into the theory of trauma treatment. I will present some of the sociocultural realities that make trauma treatment difficult and heighten the likelihood of post-traumatic symptomology. Young teenage, inner-city African American girls are a particularly at-risk group for being traumatized and experiencing related problems (Kimmerling et al., 2002). I hope that the girls' stories that I present later in this book will raise awareness of this issue and why it is so important for this population of adolescents to have access to preventive services.

An event is considered a trauma when the survivor is threatened with serious injury or death or perceives the threat to be of that magnitude (Kimmerling et al., 2002). Lester, Wong, and Hendren (2003) noted that the precise effects of trauma on the brain are not yet fully understood, but there is a general consensus that trauma severely damages neurobiological systems. Trauma can be so severe that it overwhelms the systems that would normally allow for environmental stimulus to be taken in, processed, and responded to in ways that keep the mind, body, and surrounding environment in relative equilibrium (Briere & Scott, 2006; Herman, 1996). If trauma overwhelms the survivor's neurobiological systems, he or she may remain in a high state of arousal, which is expressed through fear, panic, and other anxiety-driven emotions (American Psychiatric Association [APA], 2000; Briere & Scott, 2006; Kimmerling et al., 2002). A pervasively high state of arousal can lead to problems with health, employment, sleeping, affect regulatory, mood, relationships, and substance abuse (Kimmerling et al., 2002).

Lieberman and Van Horn (2008) noted that children who are abused by their primary caregivers tend to remain in high states of arousal; because their home lives are often chaotic, they need to stay ready to fight or flee at any time. To protect themselves, they are very sensitive to changes in their immediate, surrounding environment. They are particularly sensitive to subtle changes in their abusive caregiver's behavior and may be quick to preemptively respond to negative affect or a raised voice (Lieberman & Van Horn, 2008). When I was researching trauma, I reflected on the girls' behaviors and wondered whether their emotionally charged responses were the result of their having been abused.

My clients with the most severe trauma histories tend to be the most isolated from or in conflict with the people they care about. This makes their recovery from trauma challenging, because, as noted by Herman (1996), re-establishing a sense of trust and safety is the first step in the healing process. Trauma survivors can often re-establish trust and safety by talking about their experiences with trusted others. For many of the trauma survivors I have worked with, the people who they were supposed to be able to trust were often the people who hurt them the most. Herman noted that the survivors' core sense of trust may be severely damaged when they are traumatized by someone with whom they are intimately acquainted. This is why it is often a good idea to treat trauma survivors in a group setting, where they can explore these difficulties with others who may feel the same way; this may help them feel comfortable enough to open up and gradually re-establish the trust and safety that may help them to tell their stories (Herman, 1996). When trauma survivors tell their stories, they begin to "make sense" out of what happened to them so that new meaning can be attributed to their experiences (T. Tabancura, personal communication, November 10, 2006). This refers to the trauma treatment principle of cognitive restructuring (Briere & Scott, 2006).

J. Schore (personal communication, June 10, 2009) stated that emotional needs must be addressed in early life and in therapy before cognitive development can occur. When I attempted cognitive interventions early in the school year before I had much of a relationship with this group of girls, my interventions tended to be less effective than when I let the girls talk freely. S. Zemmelman (personal communication, October 18, 2010) stated that cognitive work can help clients, but the therapist should first help clients explore their feelings.

My work with the girls helped them to experience some relief from the emotional pain of their traumas, but I was not doing trauma treatment. To treat their traumas effectively, I would have needed to more thoroughly assess their traumas, have more expertise in this area, and have more than one school year to work with them. Furthermore, the girls remained in unsafe living conditions; just when they seemed to experience some relief by talking about one trauma, they would be traumatized again. My goal was to help them talk about their problems and to deepen their existing bond with each other. My hope was that, if they had a positive experience in the group, they might be more likely to go to trusted others in times of future crisis, including possibly returning to therapy at some point.

As I listened to the girls' stories and heard them relate to each other, I began to suspect that their suffering was well-known to other young African American women in their community. This inspired my research on the subject. Kimmerling, Ouimette, and Wolfe (2002) noted that young teenage, inner-city African American girls are the demographic group that is most at-risk for being traumatized repeatedly and for being traumatized by someone with whom they are intimately acquainted. Because they often live in abject poverty, they lack the social support networks to mitigate the effects of the trauma (Barak, Flavin, & Leighton, 2001; Kimmerling et al., 2002). This population is also particularly at risk for developing posttraumatic stress disorder (PTSD) (Barak et al., 2001; Davis, Ressler, Schwartz, Stephens, & Bradley, 2008; Kimmerling et al., 2002; Springer & Padgett, 2000; U.S. Department of Justice, 1998).

PTSD

When I worked with the girls, I often wondered if their behavior suggested posttraumatic symptomology. PTSD is an anxiety disorder caused by trauma (APA, 2000). When people have been sufficiently traumatized, they may remain in a posttraumatic state of hyperarousal (Kimmerling et al., 2002). With PTSD, the mind and body are essentially maintaining a flight-or-fight response (T. Tabancura, personal communication, November 15, 2006). The survivors are mentally prepared to preemptively respond the next time they are threatened or they sense that they may be threatened. The survivors may reexperience the trauma in nightmares or may recreate traumatic dynamics in their relationships (Kimmerling et al., 2002). Other symptoms of PTSD include avoidance of the reminders of the trauma, detachment, substance abuse, numbing, irritability, and problems with sleeping (APA, 2000; Briere & Scott, 2006; Kimmerling et al., 2002; T. Tabancura, personal communication, November 10, 2007).

I did not have enough information or expertise in PTSD to diagnose the girls. Nevertheless, this diagnosis kept coming to mind when I saw the girls consistently maintain high levels of arousal and respond preemptively when they felt threatened. At the end of the school year, I considered my work with the girls, their lengthy histories of being hurt by men, their different responses to men and women, and their often hypersexualized and anxiety-driven responses to me. The girls' often flirtatious and otherwise nervous-excited energies could be attributed to typical adolescence. Nevertheless, I often wondered whether their behaviors suggested posttraumatic symptomology triggered by the male gender. I also wondered whether to heal from their abuse, they needed at least one positive, nonabusive, nonsexual relationship with a man.

I will now tell the story of what happened in both the girls' lives and my life in the more prominent weeks of time together, tell what happened in the groups, and assess what happened clinically. I will also describe the characters' thoughts in italics so as to give readers a sense of the characters' inner experiences. In the story, I will refer to myself in the third person so as establish a more objective, third-person narrative. In the clinical assessments, I will resume my first-person tone so as to reassert my role as the analyst.

FOUR

Week 1

Shantel and Porsche

CREEEAAKKK...Shantel winced as she gingerly slid her window open to an exhilarating, cool breeze. She paused for a moment and listened to the peaceful snoring of her father in the bedroom adjacent to hers. Once satisfied that she was safe, she cautiously stepped out over the ledge and onto the soft grass outside her bedroom window, sliding her window shut and latching it behind her. Breathing a heavy sigh half of relief, she thought, *Yaya!!! I'm outtie!!!* Her eyes were already twinkling in expectation. Looking briefly and with satisfaction into her reflection in her bedroom window, she pulled a little on each of her long, dyed-blue braids. She spun around quickly, eyeing her back over her shoulder. *These pants make my ass look big? Dey do. Okay. Good, dem boys ain't gonna know what hit 'em.*

Shantel was just beginning her transition into growing up, no longer as much of a child. Over the last year she had noticed a few not-so-subtle changes in her body and mind, new curves and curiosities. With four older sisters, she had watched growing up happen in others and was anxious with envy. *Can't wait 'til I'm grown and can do what I wawn't,* she would sometimes think, watching her sisters fix their hair and makeup and then run out the door or bound out their own bedroom windows to get with older guys, talk about the latest fashions, and trade news of the biggest parties. Shantel could only watch and wait; the suspense of it was terrible. *Someday...* and someday came before she knew it.

As her body grew, the world began to take notice. As she would climb on the bus to school in the morning, she would scan through the rows of seats, looking for an empty one. Her eyes would sometimes connect with those of older adult men, and she would see their eyes combing over her body. It was frightening and yet thrilling in a kind of dark, forbidden way. *Dem mutha fuckas nasty, but its coo' knowin' dey all like me like dat!* The attention was at times intoxicating. It was nice to know that she mattered, even if only in that way. The youngest among five women (including her mother), she often felt invisible. At times, men's lustful desires reminded her that she was alive.

So it was this feeling that led her out of her room that nightaway from, her warm bed with its thick blankets and multicolored sheets, the big vanity mirror over her desk, the clothes piled in heaps on the floor, and the pictures of Little Wayne and Pretty Ricky plastered on the walls. Her bedroom was her sanctuary, but the streets were where she was at home. The night life, the police sirens, helicopter search lights, her girls, the boys, the parties, never knowing what would happen next. The thrill of it all.

Feeling it all in this moment's reflection, she began smiling to herself. *Time ta get dis pa'ty started up in here!* She crept over her family's withered front lawn in timid steps, onto the sidewalk just beyond, then quickening her pace, she headed toward Maully Boulevard. *Dat party's tonight, and is 'bout ta be on and crackin'!* A mile or so away, her friends would have already begun their night of drinking, smoking weed, and flirting with men. She had done this many times before and knew what to expect. It would be like a roller coaster ride. The evening would get louder, and people would get high, float, hang at the top for a while, and then begin to look down. She tore down the tracks at breakneck speed, through the desolate streets with sirens in the distance, a helicopter overhead, and dilapidated housing projects all around.

Despite her leisurely stroll through the night air, the barred windows and trash-littered streets seemed to fly past, time accelerated by teenage excitement. *Da party ain't far now.*

Soon she found herself on Maully Boulevard.

"Hey girl!" called a familiar voice.

Shantel looked up to the house on the corner, its walls vibrating from rap music, thumping like her heartbeat. A graceful form from within the shadows was coming her way. Long-legged strides, swaying hips, purposeful intensity.

"Whassup, Porsche?!?!" Shantel greeted. Smiling slightly. *Das my girl!*

Porsche nodded her head upward in answer, her attention already half pulled back into the house behind her, looking slightly back over her shoulder in expectation. Shantel noted her long neck, the off-center ponytail dangling behind her, and the glow of her light, caramel skin.

"You lookin' good tonight girl!" Shantel admired. Porsche smiled approvingly, a Tootsie Pop bulging in her cheek. *Yeah, I know das right.* There was a long moment's silence, a door opening and slamming abruptly in the distance, and a chorus of teenage laughter ensuing. Shantel and Porsche made their way indoors.

"OOOOHHH it's crackin' tonight!" Shantel cooed with vigor, eyes feverishly scanning in a hundred directions at once, a wide excited smile, her dark eyes twinkling. "Why you ain't inside?" *Betta not be weak up in der. I came all this way fo' nothin'?!*

Porsche, ever perceptive, ponytail swaying behind her, smacked her lips loudly. "Nah don't trip girl. It's tight tonight!" she assured, "I's jus' out hea waitin' on yo' ass! Took you long enough. Sheeitt!" Grinning to show she was only teasing, she left the door open behind her and Shantel could see for herself, chaos was brewing. Every inch of the carpeted floor was covered by someone or some garbage. Empty, plastic red cups, a teenager rolling a marijuana joint, Cheetos and Fritos, soda cans, cigarette butts spilling out of ashtrays. Loud laughter, thuds and booms, breaking glass. Shantel took it all in. *Dayam! Dey off da' hook up in hea!!* she thought, grinning.

Her wandering eyes were now lingering on one young man in particular. A short and well-clipped Afro, tightly combed waves from long hours of forward brushing, a scrubby mustache, flashing gold jewelry, a nice build under dark, baggy clothes, he was a few years older than Shantel, making his stock all the higher. He almost brightened the dark corner of the room where he lounged with several friends. He caught Shantel's eyes watching him. Shantel began looking away first, looking away, a little shy, trailing away, and then returning unmistakably to look at him. His attention never waned. Shantel noticed, smiling slightly, pleased, nervous, hopeful, wondering. Porsche couldn't help but to notice too.

"Not wastin' any time tonight is ya?" she teased, cocking an eyebrow, her head bobbing left at the neck. A balloon popping in a far corner of the room, chortling laughter, several girls in the middle of the room clapping, yelling over one another so that no one's words were any more decipherable than anyone else's. The party roared forward on full blast.

Momentarily running a hand over her long braids, fixing their position, wishing for a mirror, Shantel was listening less to Porsche and listening more to what she herself was thinking. Feeling her admirer's eyes bearing down on her, zeroing in, hungry, her mind racing. *These jeans make me look fat? I brush ma' teeth? Can't have no kickin' breath. Fuck! I didn't brush my shit and I had some chicken!* Questions she couldn't answer. The top of the roller coaster. A thud and boom on the far side of the room, several oohs and encouraging remarks.

"Oooohh dey fightin'?!?!" Porsche observed excitedly. *We need to go check dis out!!!*

But Shantel was still somewhere else. The outside world was somehow far beyond. Panic, ecstasy. *He still lookin' at me too.* Now she didn't have to look to know; she could feel it. Watching him watch her out of a corner of her curious eye. Watching him roll a marijuana cigarette into a green leaf Garcia Vega cigar or "blunt." Watching his hoop earring slightly twinkling as he worked it. Rolling, licking, picking at it with his fingers—all the precision of a jeweler with a priceless diamond. Finally finished. *Kind of sexy how he do that.* In essence, he could do no wrong.

The music thump-thumping louder now. The front door slamming, banging. A flurry of excited yells all at once. Shantel had only had two good looks and had already memorized his every curve, every spoken word, every movement—the subtle corner of her eye taking it all in. The music was really loud, thumping Dr. Dre's latest jam, but the world that Shantel knew had the volume turned down a few notches. It was just she and her guy, even though they had never met. As if the lights were off in the rest of the room, a slow jam was crooning overhead, Shantel and her guy, center stage with an audience only for themselves. He just seemed to appear before her in the next instant.

"Whas' yo' name sweet thang?" his raspy purr invited. Shantel's heart dropped into her stomach. She was fighting for her voice.

"Sha-Shaa-ntel..." she uttered. Weak in the knees, she was still getting used to this whole boy-meets-girl thing. He didn't respond but just stayed there, slouching alongside her, leaning on the wall in his blue baggies, marijuana blunt dangling out of the corner of his mouth. *I'm just speculatin' about dis dude fo' now, ain't like I'm on him like that,* she told herself. *He cute, though.* Fighting back a smile. Trying to play it cool. *Don't wanna look like I'm sprung.* The latest 2Pac song suddenly rolled through the crowd, resounded in long waves through and past the smokers, drinkers, make-out partners, bringing a sudden rush of energy to a scene already vibrating with it.

"Awww das my song! You wanna dance?" Shantel's admirer invited, wide smile betraying his expectations. The herd around them was already rumbling past to the living room dance floor, fairly doubling over one another, eager to get moving. Shantel obliged, her hand, still plump with baby fat, accepting his. They began making their way past four young boys and their improvisation of new lyrics to 2Pac's sound. They stepped over a heavily breathing older boy, passed out on the floor, mouth agape, listless. Others around him were placing garbage on top of him, giggling, snickering as the pile grew higher and higher. Porsche's shrill voice rose above the crowd and failed to reach Shantel, a couple steps toward the dance floor too late.

"Go on girl!" Porsche hollered, watching her friend in earnest, oblivious to a drunken young man babbling an unintelligible pick-up line to the side of her head. The boys in the corner were clapping and cheering in approval of their own, improvised lyrics. A couple who were making out leaning against the kitchen wall had landed with a thud after having slid down toward the floor without realizing it. Another loud raucous cacophony of laughter burst from the center of the room. The party surged ahead in full blast.

Shantel was smiling approvingly. *Hell's yeah!! It's on and crackin' tonight!* But her new admirer was stumbling slightly, having trouble looking like he was dancing, a hit or two too many of marijuana beginning to take its toll. He went down to the floor, but he quickly recovered, picking himself back up, pulling his sagging pants slightly up, transitioning into a too-cool bobbing of the head, a slight dip and rise of his hips, sticking his chest out, keeping up appearances. Shantel followed him in kind, keeping time with the music but still not wanting to draw too much attention to herself. Enough to be noticed, but not so much as to command center stage. Briefly stealing looks at some of the other young women who were dropping it like it was hot, walking it out, all the latest moves. Shantel was ever so slightly jealous in a way, but critical all the same. *Damn deez some skank ass hoes!*

Her dance partner was leading the way, still holding her hand. For Shantel, it was a nice feeling. *He cute and he flauntin' like I be his lady o' somethin'!* Stopping suddenly, closer to center stage, never breaking time with the music, an inviting twinkle in his eyes, and that hungry kind of teenage boy grin they get when they are after something. "You smoke weed?" he invited. Shantel eyed the blunt, looked away, and gathered her thoughts. Tempting, and yet something told her no. *I gotta get home soon, got schoo' tomorrow and shit.* But it was something else that told her not to—a little voice in the back of her head that kept her eyes open.

"Nah, I'm coo'," she replied meekly, not wanting to look square, eager to change the subject. "So whas' yo' name?"

"Oh, my bad," he answered, smiling sheepishly, and licking his lips, quick to recover, "like I ain't got no manners! My name Darrell, o' big D, you know."

"Mmmm-hhhmmm," Shantel replied, smacking her lips. *Too much information.* Still, she couldn't help but to be curious, maybe even a little intrigued. Porsche was watching from behind the scenes, eyeballing their every move, smiles, shifting weight, subtle and not so subtle cues.

Damn! Dey sure all up on it! Sensing that she was falling into the background, never one to go without a fight, she felt that it was time to assert herself, to make her presence known. *Time to let all deez mutha fuckas know who the real queen B is up in here!* And with that, she hit the dance floor in full force, a flash in her eyes, double timing the music, arms and long legs dropping to the floor with a fierce swivel in her hips. The boys were watching closely, captivated, intimidated, desiring. Shantel's eyes caught Darrell's eyes wandering. Sulking only momentarily, she was soon scowling as her competitive side took over. *Oh no she didn't!!!*

Shantel answered with some hip, slick, and cool moves of her own. Taking a step further out into the crowd, leading Darrell in her shadow, arms up over her head and then dragging her hands seductively over the front of her body and down her hip line, she spun inward, pressing her backside ever so slightly into Darrell's front, arching her back. Feeling his immediate reaction, she smiled in satisfaction. *Don't neva fa'get it neitha boy!*

"Damn shorty!" Darrell crooned, his attention refocused. Shantel giggled, her territory having been marked. Meanwhile, Porsche had gone to work on the rest of the room. Dropping low, swiveling her delicate hips, shaking her rear, gracefully sidestepping the drunken young man who had been blubbering about something to the side of her head earlier. *Damn dat foo' don't get a hint?!* He repulsed her so much that he was getting on her nerves. *Man! Era' time I come out to get busy and shake my thang-thang, da ugliest most drunk stank ass mutha fucka gotta be da most all up on me!* Her pursuer, who was still blubbering, made off and on attempts at conversation, one eye almost all the way closed, the other lazily following Porsche's but a half second behind hers. Marijuana and alcohol were taking their toll. He reeked with a dank smell of marijuana mixed with beer. Porsche wrinkled her nose. He was thoroughly disgusting. But he was not put off in the slightest.

Porsche had found a way to almost make a game out of it; he would step in and she would spin away, obviously sending go-away signals but in a way that almost made them seem to be part of her dance steps. He stepped in, she spun away. Her audience cheered and clapped, the boys watching earnestly with bugging eyes, licking their lips. Porsche owned the show, was taking it by storm, bucking at the knees, throwing her arms high overhead, brilliantly beaming that bright smile with her eyes closed as she threw in a couple of steps she had seen the previous night on a J-Lo video.

Marijuana smoke swept through the air, the walls of the room vibrating like an earthquake had hit. There were sounds of choking and gasping for breath. Then someone was throwing up. A loud thud in a back room followed by laughter and oohs and ahhs. Maybe a fight, maybe a body fallen from drunkenness. Who knew? But one thing was for sure, the party had only just begun. Fifty or so teenagers, laughing uproariously, toasting beer bottles, falling over one another in a mix of aggressive shoves, drunken stupors, and sloppy kisses.

Shantel, feeling Darrell's hand move up from her hip toward her shirt, recoiled, pushed his hand down, subtly moved away, more emotionally than physically. "What's up, you shy o' something?" he half asked, half demanded. Shantel had been having a good time until that point, but now she was beginning to feel uneasy. She had made a deal with herself that she wasn't about to let this stranger, this older boy, go that far right away. She had learned the tricks of the trade from her sisters and from savvy older women on her block. *Gotta give 'em a lil' so dey be thinkin' shit's possible. But ya gotta give an' go. Make 'em come at cha. That's when dey be breakin' you off with cash. Take you shoppin'! Gotta play yo' cards right with niggas out here,* she recited to herself. She knew what her game plan was. She admired his body, the bumps and lumps of his stomach and arms. *Damn! dis boy gotta body 'do!*

"Naw, but we need to kick it firs' you know? I just met choo and all," Shantel answered, regaining a bit of balance. Feeling her pocket vibrate, she pulled out her cell phone. The alarm she had set earlier had gone off. *Damn! Midnight already?!?! Seem like we jus' got here!*

"Shit," she sulked, "I gotta bounce." *We been here two hours?! Feel like two minutes!*

Darrell's spirits fell. "Awright, but can I get your numba?" he inquired, his eyes regaining some of their fervor. Shantel looked away, her eyes lingering on another light-skinned boy with short, tightly combed waves and a white tank top on which two thick, heavy gold chains lay. *Damn he cute too.* Her eyes caught his. Shantel looked back as her shyness returned. She noted Darrell's eyes looking for hers. *Oh yeah.* Then he stepped directly into her line of sight, moving ever so slightly closer. Closer. Her heart began to pound as she felt his presence near. She smiled but was not so sure she was ready to kiss him just yet. *Not yet.*

"Here go my cell phone," she said, giving in to the feeling, scribbling her cell phone number on a piece of paper as nonchalantly as she could muster. *He betta call me!* Stealing a hard look at him she thought, *yaya, he will.*

Darrell took the paper she offered, gazed at it for a long second, deep in thought. In silent reflection, Shantel watched him closely from the corner of her eye. A coiling smile crept over his lips as he seductively moved in, inch by inch. Her skin was tingling, heartbeat echoing in her head. He was getting closer, closer. Now they were face to face, him smelling like marijuana and alcohol, his eyes boring through hers. *Oh shit, he gonna kiss me.*

Her eyes slowly surveyed the floor. Scared. Exhilarated. Fluttering heartbeat thumping louder and louder. Maybe Darrell could even hear it. She could hardly wait, wanting to scream, *He gonna do it!* Their eyes locked and their bodies pressed against one another. *Mmmmmmmm.* The taste of malt liquor lingered on her tongue. *Nasty!* But she didn't care. Shantel used to hate the taste of beer. Now, she couldn't remember anything better. It was a kiss that would last a lifetime.

"B- , Bye," she stammered, stumbling back. Darrell was disappearing into the crowd. Shantel was unsure of where she was going, but she was moving back in the crowd.

All of a sudden at Porsche's side, she was not sure how she got there. The last thing that was on her mind resurfaced. *Darrell, Darrell,* picturing long walks and holding hands, sweet love songs, and starlit nights. *Tonight could last forever.*

"Giiiirrrrllll wha'choo been doin'?" Porsche exclaimed, breaking into her friend's fantasy world. Her eyes were glittering, demanding that Shantel give up the juiciest details. With an itching-for-girl-talk smile, she pressed Shantel who was looking away bashfully, licking her lips, smoothing her face and blouse, brushing an imaginary strand of hair over her ear. She was unsuccessfully trying to regain her composure, to set it all straight. "Tryin' to get up out of here!" she answered with frantic energy, her own thoughts still so jumbled. She wanted to talk about what had just happened, but was reluctant to do so until she herself had it figured out. "C'mon my nigga we got homeroom at eight in the mo'nin'…Let's go."

Urgently she led the way to the door, pulling on the front of Shantel's jacket. Shantel, who was keeping up but with dragging feet, turned half backward, watching the boys and girls fall slackly into one another, hands finding body parts, open mouth kisses, crude passion. *Darrell, Darrell…damn, jus' like, maybe five mo' minutes?*

But she knew she had to be careful; she had learned from her sister's mistakes. She had seen her father's long face and heard her mother's harsh words as her sister stood before them, eyes rolling, head bowing low. *Ain't neva gonna be!* Shantel had promised herself.

Porsche's biggest fan suddenly returned to the room, nearly pitching sideways smack into her and Shantel, tongue hanging out of his mouth, bent over, and hunched at the waistline. *Sheeiit. Look at dis foo'. He gotta be no mo' 'n sixteen years old an' he already look like one a dem ol' winos out on da street and he smell like one too!*

"Damn this mutha fucka nasty," she grimaced at Shantel. "Girl for real!" Shantel agreed. "We need to get our asses outta here and away from these drunk ass motha fuckas!" Porsche side-stepped the drunken boy who had fallen and lay sprawled out on the hardwood floor. Shantel eyed this sorry sight and pronounced judgment. "See, dat's what too much of dat shit does to you. Fo' real das why I'm coo' off dat drank! Shit fucks people up!"

Ducking through a thick cloud of marijuana smoke, threading their way through a crowd of party onlookers, they passed a couple locked at the lips, seemingly tuned out to the world. Shantel and Porsche closed the door behind them. The night's events abruptly fell away as they marched quickly home, hands shoved into jacket pockets, each already mentally tucked into her warm bed. Shantel smiled to herself. *He a call me. Yeah, well, he betta!*

Porsche seemed to hear what Shantel was thinking and stopped and looked at her. "Had a good time tonight didn't ya?" she goaded. Shantel pulled away slightly, just a little embarrassed.

"Who? Darrell?" she answered innocently, "I don't know." Trying to play it cool. "We might be seein' wha's up, but, I don't know. He was all up on me like hella quick!"

Porsche snorted. "So wha' choo complainin' about? He was fine as hell!"

As they stopped and faced each other momentarily there on the corner, they heard sirens and then a few seconds later a couple of police cars rolled passed, heading in the direction of the party. Both girls breathed an inward sigh of relief, taking a fleeting glance over their shoulders at the burly white officer stepping out of his car, muttering obscenities, shining his flashlight over the lawn and onto the porch. *Damn, fo' real! That five minutes woulda been it! My momma woulda killed me too!*

"Giiirrrlll, we got up outta dat party just in time!" Porsche exclaimed. "Somebody gonna get whooped tonight!" Shantel nodded. Her parents had never hit her before, and she wasn't planning on finding out what it was like. *Das why I stays careful! Ain't gonna be tryin' to get away wit too much. I mean, I can have my lil' party an' all, but I'm a always keep it on da down low an' ain't neva fit to get caught up.* "Das neva gonna happen ta me. I keep up on my responsibilities don' do too much." Shantel insisted, letting out another deep sigh that sounded like her mother's. Porsche eyed her friend and crinkled her nose, ignoring a male whistle and some hooting from the house they were passing. *My girl like a fuckin' goody-goody! Always trippin' off a somethin'!* "Sheeit girl, you worry too damn much. I pull Bs and As and that ain't goin' nowhere," she proclaimed in her usual *didn't you know* voice. Shantel exhaled softly through her nose, her eyes on the sky in silent prayer for both of them. *Fo' real, we a always keep it coo'.* Home suddenly appeared before her. The neatly clipped hedges and familiar stained glass windows were a solid, warm sight. Shantel's voice dropped to a whisper while she ducked down like an army commando in the underbrush.

"You know. We a always be awright," she pronounced quietly yet a little too loud in her conviction, "Never all a' dat." She was nodding her head in the direction of the police sirens and imagined the child-to-parent sit-down conversations soon to come.

"Fo' real my nigga!" Porsche agreed with a smile. Shantel smiled back, finally scampering up the side of her house, crawling back through her bedroom window, latching it behind her, and breathing a sigh of relief. Soon after she slid under the covers and burrowed her face into the pillow, she drifted off to a deep sleep; dreams of her and Darrell claimed the rest of the night.

Venus

"*I'm Bossy, I'm the chick that y'all love to hate...*" sang a familiar voice, one sending a thrill through Venus's veins. Now she snapped to attention. *OOOHH der go my phone!* She paused the BET music video that had her hypnotized and took up the cell phone at her bedside.

"*I'm Bossy...*" the ring tone continued. Venus gracefully removed a ring pop from her mouth using her long red fingernails, then sat up Indian-style on her bed's soft white comforter. She looked at the display screen to see who was calling...*Jerome!*

"Hello?" she inquired innocently, putting as much nonchalance into her voice as she could. A part of her insides quivered with excitement.

"Wha's up ma? Wha' choo been doin'?" replied Jerome, adjusting his voice also, trying to play it cool but betraying some eagerness. Venus then tried a slightly deeper voice, trying to sound older.

"Nothin', jus' homework," she answered. *Well, das what I should be doin' anyway.* "Why whas' up?"

"Getting dress' fo' da party up at Da'ron' house!" Jerome replied, a subtle, seductive quality creeping into his voice. Tempting, inviting.

"Oh, yeah. I heard it 'posed to be off da hook!" Venus exclaimed. *Sheeit, I need ta be up in der too! Prob'ly some fine ass boys! People's gettin' fucked up! Sheeit, I need ta be up in der like fo' real!* She rose and drew the curtain away from the window.

"So how 'bout I come swoop you up an' we go do our thang-thang?" Jerome invited. Venus pursed her lips, breathed in deeply. *Damn! Ain't dis about a bitch! Everybody from da hood gonna be up in der too. I need ta go find me a man o' two, take me shoppin'.* She frowned at her bedroom closet, looked on the floor. *Yeah-yeah, my Jordan's fucked up!*

Men, partying, dancing, phone numbers, and shopping trips sounded oh so wonderful. *But, oh hell, so comfy here.* Her bed was so comfortable that she half sunk into her pillowy soft comforter, feeling the temperature just right, just cool enough to be comfortable and warm enough to let her drift off to sleep at any moment. It would take work to get up and go. *Damn, why I feel so lazy? Sheeit. Why go wit' some boy? Den my game be fucked up anyway. I already got dis foo'. I need ta go solo or like don't go at all. Yeah, but I could kick it and see who else up in der!*

"Nah, I'm coo'. Gotta get dis homework done," she declined, an intentional uncertainty finding its way into her reply. *I ain't goin' nowhere, but go on and tell me how bad you want me.* There was a satisfaction that came along with being desired.

"C'mon now girl!" Jerome pleaded on cue, trying not to sound pleading. *Hecka cute when dey try ta act like it ain't no thang!* "You know you could do dat shit. Jus' come on out here and le's do dis!"

Venus smiled to herself. She gazed out the window taking her time, but then a familiar beep and vibration in her palm broke her rhythm. Cocking her head and pulling the phone away from her ear, Jerome was now protesting to the empty air. *He still soun' like a bitch!* Venus smiled to herself at the thought, then shook herself back to attention, gazing into the display screen. A lump lodged in her throat. *Clarence!*

She put the receiver back to her ear. "Hey yo that's my grandmamma on da otha line so I gotta go," she interjected, already half pulling herself away from one conversation and into the next. *Jerome a hecka cute lil' boy, but Clarence a FINE ASS MAN!* She only half heard Jerome's protests grow louder and whinier. She felt somewhat sympathetic, did not want to hurt his feelings, but Clarence and his six-pack abs spoke louder. *Ohhh it been on wit' dat boy since dat basketball game! Dos sweaty muscles and dat chest…ooo he fine!*

"Fo' real," Venus insisted, "ain't tryin' to be fucked or nothin' up, but I gotta see what my granny want."

"Yeah, yeah, let her know you 'bout ta come on ova' fo' a lil' study date, you know what I'm sayin'? I mean, you know black people gots ta learn from each other right?" Jerome offered with as much quiet cool as he could muster.

"Boy I' call you later!" Venus exclaimed, feigning outrage, smiling playfully. *He' cute, but maybe later.* Still, it was nice to know he was available. It made her a little smug.

"Girl I ain't gone' tell ya 'gain, get off dat phone and do yo' homework!" came a roar from beyond two closed doors. Venus hunched over, leaned slightly forward in the direction of the resounding bellow. *Nah, I could talk quiet and mama ain't gonna hear nuttin. Jus' gotta keep it hush-hush.* But this insight came with a grim, guilty feeling. *Hate lyin' ta momma.* Still, Venus couldn't bear the thought of passing up the dance.

"Real girls get down on the floor…," her softly humming ring tone moved from the chorus into the main verse, alerting her that time was running out.

Voice mail soon to come. *Sheeit. I don' answer he gonna call some otha bitch! An' my man ain't about to be gettin' lost!*

"Okay mamma. Hold up, granny on da otha line!" Venus called out, wincing at her lie. Her voice betrayed a lack of certainty, a lack of conviction. Never a convincing liar, Venus was too sensitive to be much good at hiding her true feelings. Although the guilt that followed lying to her mother was not pleasant, the image of six-pack abs overcame it.

Cocking her ear and listening intently for a few long seconds, she mentally scanned for remnants of the booming voice at the end of the hall but detected nothing but the hum of the bathroom fan, a chortled mixture of laughter from the television in the living room, and some slight thudding of bass from rap music coming from her brother's bedroom at the far end of the house. Satisfied and frantic at the thought of missing the call, she answered.

"Who dis?" she inquired sweetly.

"Wha's goin' on, baby girl? You know who dis is?" flowed a deep, bold voice on the other end of the phone. Venus recoiled in playful shyness. *Oooohh he sound sexy! Yes, mmm-hmm.*

"Yeah. Hey, wa-choo doin'?" she replied, winding a tightly knit braid around her index finger. She tried to quell her tumultuous insides. Playing with her hair was comforting.

"Jus' got back from my man' house, picked up some weed and den hey, check dis out, I'm 'bout to swing pas' yo' house, feel me?" When Venus didn't answer right away, he added, "You know, what eva'. Grab a bottle a' Hennessey and go kick it or somethin'." She shivered inwardly. *Oooohh, I don't know about all a dat. Don't know what I do! Weed? Hennessey! An' dat man! Oooohh nu-uh. I be a mamma' dat same night!* She was smiling at her thoughts, twisting her braid. It was going to take more than this. She sat back on her bed and settled in.

"MMMM, HHHMM, sounds tempting," she flirted. There was no way she could get out of the house tonight, but the mouse in her couldn't stop teasing the cat.

"So wha's up then? You gonna...," Clarence persisted in his entreaties. Venus laughed softly to herself, let her head sink into the pillow, her eyes fluttering up, sweeping the ceiling. She popped a piece of gum into her mouth only half listening. *Boys! Dey jus' keep comin' on and on and on. Not like I be wantin' shit to stop though!* The intense noise of her inner thoughts mixed with Clarence's voice had been drowning out the creak of her bedroom door, which was now almost wide open.

"Shhiiit, boy I can't get up outta here, my mama kill me..." Venus murmured, gazing out the window, pouting, longing, wishing, oblivious.

"Damn right yo mama gonna kill you!" Venus nearly fell out of bed, doubling over onto its edge. Long-faced, puppy dog eyes looking up over her eyebrows, she softly replied, "Hi Mama...."

"Don't hi mama me! What I tell you? I...," her mother blared in exasperation. She glared down at her daughter, eyes growing wide in annoyance, her head cocked to the left, right hand pressing hard into her hip.

Venus swallowed hard, her mind scrambling for a suitable answer. "Clarence, I gotta go," she murmured into the receiver, pushing down the off button and tossing the phone across her bed.

"...two minutes ago! You need ta get yo' fat, fast ass off the phone with them nappy headed boys and...," her mother kept on. The sting of her words pierced her daughter's soul and brought up anger, hurt, sorrow. Standing there before her, a few feet away and several feet higher than Venus's cowering form on the edge of the bed, her mother seemed large and imposing. She wished she could disappear, but her mother wasn't done yet.

"Girl you hear what I'm sayin' to ya?!?!" her voice rising louder this time. Venus nodded affirmatively, wishing it could just be over, her shoulders curved inward, head down. "Take care of yo' responsibilities! You gonna end up like all a' deez girls 'round here, kids and welfare, no sense and nothin' worth nothin'. Dat what you waw'nt fo' yo' self?"

"No...," Venus whimpered. *Wish I could jus' get up outta here, like anywhere but dis shit right here.*

"MMM, HHHMMM..." her mother snorted in disdain, shaking her head. Venus receded further still. *She could kill you with those mm-hmmms.* It was such a little thing and yet the worst of all as far as Venus was concerned. Seconds of silence passed. *Maybe it was over...*

"Then you bes' ta start acting like it, 'cause talk is cheap! Girl, you bes' shape up. I ain't havin' none o' dis!" She turned to leave but only closed the door halfway. "I gots ta go fix dinner." For a moment she seemed to be listening for something but then slammed the door loudly, making one of the pictures on Venus's dresser shake. The kitchen phone's shrill ringing broke Venus out of her trance. Her mother snapped it up.

"Who dis?...Oh whassup! Wha' choo doin'...MMMM, HHHMMM, sounds tempting."

"Mama I'm hungry!" came a yelp from Venus' older brother in a far bedroom.

"Boy hold on! Y'all must be thinkin' I'm somebady maid 'round here! I'm on the phone with yo' granny!"

Venus scoffed to herself. Flabbergasted. Resentful. *See man, das why I don't neva be listenin'. All a' them be tellin' me "don't do shit," then they go do somethin' they was tellin' me not ta do.* She sat there fuming for long seconds, her anger gradually subsiding enough to think. *Am I getting fat? And, like, headed nowhere? Damn mama! Who she think she is?!?!* She almost wanted to cry, hating that part of herself that only her mother could get to. She made her feel ugly even on her best days. Fragile. Hurt. Shattered. Wanting to cry. There on the edge of her bed, staring off into nothing with a long and lonely night ahead of her.

Rona

Walking through the door with a slight shiver from the cool evening breeze, Rona felt a warm comfort on arriving home from her day of school. It would be a welcome respite from gossipy friends and constant disruptions during her usual junior high school day. *Man it was crazy up in der!*

"Bitch I ain't tryin' ta hear dis right now!" came a rumble from far beyond the living room. Rona's sense of comfort was dashed almost as quickly as it had arisen. *Sheeit, I don't know why mama mess wit' dat foo'! Drunk ass Tyrone. He don't need to be callin' my mama no bitch neither!*

"Well you bes' hear somethin' that gets you up and on yo' responsibilities 'cause I can't do dis by ma self!" her mother retorted in exasperation, followed by a loud thud of a slamming door. Out came her mother in short, brisk strides, contemptuous but still dutifully headed toward the kitchen to make everyone dinner. Rona followed in her shadow.

"Where you been at?" her mother half-asked, half-demanded, darting her head out from behind the refrigerator door, her mind half on her daughter, half elsewhere. Like her mother often did, Rona smacked her lips and cocked her eyebrow.

"Hi Mama," she answered with a slight touch of annoyance. *Damn momma, I can't jus' get a lil' hello and how are ya type shit?!*

Her mother breathed deeply, apologetic, but still elsewhere. "Hi Baby," she conceded, brushing a wild and unruly strand of hair back through her full-length corn rows. Though somewhere in her thirties, Rona's mother seemed to age significantly second by second. "So where...."

"LE'S GO Y'ALL!!!" came an interrupting yell of teenagers in the nearby street. They laughed gaily with the kind of wildness that could only mean youth unsupervised and intoxicated by freedom. Rona, glancing expectantly out the window, followed their every motion and was right in tune with them.

"OOOOHHH, Mama can I go out for a lil' bit?" Rona pleaded.

"Girl you still ain't even told me where you been all day and here you go again!" she tried to point out to Rona, tilting her head as she stood looking at her daughter, smacking her lips for emphasis. Rona feigned a sigh and rolled her eyes over the plastic-covered polyester sofa at her right to the long hallway leading to the bedrooms at her left.

"I was out with Janet and all a dem!" Rona supplied, bursting with impatience. Her mother's head snapped to attention.

"Oh, no no no! Let me tell you somethin' girl, don't get smart with me…" her mother said, taking a monumental half-step forward.

"I'm a tellin' you," resounded a slurring proclamation from what sounded like it was surfacing from the netherworld, "That girl need to…"

Rona and her mother, each sighing wearily, tried to resume their discussion, but the approaching footsteps that echoed through the house made this almost impossible. Trouble was coming.

"Mama I can't be hearing all dis tanight!" Rona protested, bouncing slightly at the knees in pleading tantrum.

"Hey yo," continued the loud, slurring male voice, approaching from the far end of the hall. "I'm tellin' y'all bitches. Lil' girl need ta shut her damn mouth, go to schoo', and try to lose some weight 'stead a runnin' 'round here wit' alla dem young punks!"

Rona felt his words cut through her like shards of glass. *Fuckin' Tyrone! Bitch ass mutha fucka! Who he think he is? He jus' momma's husband! He ain't my daddy! Momma need ta leave his ass fo' real!*

"Momma, he can't be talkin' ta me like dat!" Rona demanded, looking up at her mother with pleading eyes, speaking just quietly enough for Tyrone not to hear her but loud enough to let her mother know she meant business. Her mother pursed her lips reflectively, eyes bouncing from the bathroom door that thankfully had just closed behind her sauntering husband to her daughter in turmoil and then back to the bathroom door. A war of two worlds, and there she was in between them.

"Yeah, I'm gonna have a talk wit' him about that," her mother responded, frowning deeply, weary, confused, not knowing which way was up. Her mind was going in many directions. Her daughter, ever perceptive, sensed her mother's split attention.

"Mama, I'm serious!" Rona insisted, "Dis ain't coo'!" *Fat? Young punks? What the fuck he know anyway?*

Her mother breathed a heavy sigh of despair. "Baby, I hear you," her mother continued, looking down at the floor at her feet, searching for solace, comfort, answers, finding none. "But, hear me? Like I said…"

"Lemme' tell y'all wha' da problem is wit' deez damn kids is…" rumbled a menacing declaration from down the hallway, growing louder with each ominously approaching footstep. The floorboards squeaked under the force of drunken rage, each footstep heavier than the last and more foreboding. His slurring words and his heavy footfalls reverberated in the hearts of the women.

Rona could stand no more. "LEAVE ME ALONE!" she screamed, racing toward Tyrone's stumbling and bumbling figure like a freight train. Most of Rona wanted to cry and yet she did not want to give him the satisfaction. Every muscle in her body flexed against further onslaught as she stomped down the hall, the space between them growing several degrees colder and deafeningly quiet.

As they passed one another, Tyrone scowled down at her the way the well-to-do look down at a passing beggar on the street. Rona felt his eyes burn through her from behind, the ashes still drifting through the hallway as she slammed the door at her back, wishing that she was anywhere but home. Stomp, stomp, stomp-BAM! went the bedroom door behind her.

"And stop slammin' my god damn door!" Tyrone yelled after her. He always had to have the last word.

The anger in Rona was now boiling as she lay in her bed, staring at the ceiling. She was searching for a clever and hurtful retort, but all the colorful metaphors and other revenge she could think of just died on the tip of her tongue. This was not for lack of ideas, but Rona had lost all of her strength. They had worn her all the way down. Anger was melting away. *Tired a' dat mutha fucka! Man, I ain't even do nothing. T*ears welled up in her eyes and she began hating her tears…*fuck, why I'm cryin' fo'? Son 'a bitch, an' he diss my mama too!*

"Why you gotta be cussing so loud in my god damn house!" she heard her mother yell.

"I do what I want in my house 'cause I'm the man o' dis house!" Tyrone retorted. Their voices were growing louder with each counter attack and drastically stronger in intensity. "See das where she gets dem problems! Bitches ain't got no respect!" His words calcified in Rona's bones. Snapping a pillow over her ears, her eyes shut in muted protest, praying silently that she could just be deaf. *God, if you listenin', I need ya now.*

"Oh, na na na," her mother answered in outrage. "You don't neeeeed to be callin' nobody no kind of bitches! Wha' choo neeeeed to do is…"

Rona's ears perked up in shocking delight. *Oooohhh mamma goin' ghetto?!*

"I don't neeeeed ta have nobody tellin' me what to do up in my own house!" thundered Tyrone. Rona was so weary. *Here dey go again.* She heaved her mother's despairing sigh and tossed the pillow onto the floor.

Damn…I need ta get da fuck outta here. Can't take dis no mo'. Crazy at my mama house! Crazy at daddy house!

"Damn lazy fat ass bitch bes' back yo' ass up! Go cook o' clean up o' do somethin'!!!" Tyrone bellowed. Rona looked at herself in the closet door mirror. Enough was enough.

Swinging her small legs off the bed with all the resolve she could muster, her heart raged with fear as her body found its way. *The fuck I'm doin'?* she asked herself. What was she doing? All she knew was that she could no longer stand to hear her mother being abused.

Stepping hard onto the floor with bare, determined feet, she made long strides for the door, her arm lurching for the knob. *Tired a this mutha fucka! Fo' real. Ain't nobody gonna talk ta my momma like dat. I don't give a fuck who he think he is!!! Watch! I'm a call my daddy an' have him come down an' whoop his ass.* Although she knew deep in her heart that her father would be nowhere to be found when she needed him, still the thought was empowering. She stood and imagined seeing Tyrone cowering, bloody on the floor, pleading for mercy, cowardly as she always knew him to be. *How it feel now you fuckin' punk?!* she would scream at his twisted carcass, his eyes wide with fear, mouth agape, wailing, pleading. Somehow this fantasy propelled Rona out of her bedroom.

The boom of the yelling in the other room was growing ominously louder. As she turned the doorknob, she gazed again at herself in the full-length mirror on the closet door. She had been all set to charge back into the kitchen and to beat Tyrone bloody or die trying, but her reflection stopped her in her tracks, drained the life from her arm as it fell slackly to her side. Between her frowning forehead and bulging, red cheeks, her eyes were almost invisible. Her shapeless form took up the entire mirror while her not-so-stylish barrettes dangled from the knot at the back of her head.

She saw all of this in a moment as if she were seeing herself for the first time. She had never felt more ugly. Depression welled up, and there was no way to hold it in. She began to cry in slow, methodical, heavy tears that burned down her cheeks. She sank down to the floor, sat there before the mirror for quite a while as the arguing continued beyond her bedroom door. When Tyrone and her mother argued like that, she sometimes wished she would grow deaf, but now she wished she were invisible.

Gina

Closing and locking the door behind her, Gina was grateful to return home to the inviting aroma of what smelled like beef stew simmering in the kitchen.

"Gina!?! That you?" called an inquisitive yet inviting voice. Dropping her backpack to the floor behind her, Gina passed the dining room dinner table with its brilliant white tablecloth and art along the walls. Gazing at the pictures atop the redwood cabinet at her side opposite the table, she noted the pictures of her and her foster sisters, each of them smiling, dressed up in exquisite dresses, with ornate hair styles. They were good pictures, lined up one after another as if the pictures themselves were holding hands, each of them with their own, separate frame. Almost a real family. For Gina, the thought was bittersweet. Her foster family, this family, had never felt like her family.

A common inquiry interrupted her thoughts. "Mrs. Gina??? Did I hear ya bag bein' hung up on the coat rack and not on the floor? I know that's what I heard right?"

"Yes, Kendra," Gina conceded. *Damn, she stay on my case.* Dutifully returning to her backpack lying on the glistening hardwood floor, she retrieved it, placing it atop one of the pegged hooks protruding from the towering coat rack alongside the front door. Returning to the kitchen at her foster mother's side, without hesitation she grabbed a sharp knife from the rack alongside the spices and began to chop vegetables in preparation for dinner.

"Thank you, sugar," Kendra exclaimed. *She jus' soooo helpful.*

Gina smiled you're welcome. *Oh, shit. I gots homework fo' English. But, nah, I could do it later.*

"How was school today?" Kendra continued.

Got too much homework. Hate dat math teacher. Dat boy tried to grab my butt. Damn it was fucked up now dat I think 'bout it. "Fine," Gina replied with a tinge of teenage insincerity that would alert an attentive adult that something was out of place. Gina's foster mother had already figured out what she would be saying next.

"Do you know that the checks from foster care still haven't come?" Kendra said more to herself than anyone else. Gina just listened. "I don't know what's wrong with the world today. I have bills to pay, and food to put in all of your stomachs and every day I get nothing but more bills. What am I supposed to do?"

Gina swallowed a guilty lump in her throat, searching for ways that she could be helpful. "Maybe we could go down to the mail office?" she offered.

"Post office honey," Kendra replied matter-of-factly, pressing on without missing a beat. "I mean, you have all a' them people in those fancy offices with all they worldly lifestyles, and they can't get down off they high horses to get a check in on time to folks in need?"

Gina's eyes scanned her foster mother's impressive kitchen and dinette set, the spotless hardwood floors, and the fine china in glass cabinets. Cocking an eyebrow, she held her tongue.

"It will be okay, Kendra. It gonna be here any day now," Gina assured, with as much confidence as she could find. Kendra had begun a return to her monologue when the door flew open and a fury spewed through the living room.

"GIIIRRRLL… You won't believe what fucked up shit happen dis day!"

"What bitch got my brush!"

"Did y'all get da mail?"

"I gotta use the phone!"

"Uh-uh you had the phone in the morning! It's my turn!"

"Stop lying!"

"Bitch you touch that phone I'm gonna punch you in yo' face!"

"STOP ALL THAT GOD DAMN YELLIN' IN MY HOUSE!" Kendra roared, nearly blowing the roof off the house, making Gina's ears ring. "Sugar, keep on with dinner. I need ta go straighten these girls out."

Gina's head inched up in concern, listening for her foster sisters' replies once they got the trouble awaiting them. *Uh-oh, they gonna get it, maybe I could go up and tell Kendra dat, well, no, no . ..damn, I better jus' watch dinner.* But her mind continued to drift. *My science project due, and, oooohhh, dat new boy was cute and I think he like me, well, maybe.*

"Kendra, I..." Gina began to call after her rapidly departing foster mother and then, "OW!!! Fuck," she said quietly so that Kendra wouldn't hear. She had cut her finger with the vegetable knife. Silently scolding herself for her carelessness, she returned without protest or preoccupation to her task. Chop, chop, chop went the vegetable knife against the cutting board.

"I don't know where y'all think y'all are but..." Kendra admonished in disgust and rage. *Yeah, she all da way up da stairs. Her voice sound hollow. Man, dey in truh-ble!!!*

Just then the phone rang. Gina darted over to get it after only one ring. "Hello, Ford residence..." she answered with all the professionalism of a world-class executive secretary.

"Gina? You wouldn't believe dis shit I..." came a pleading and yet demanding voice on the other end of the phone, urgent, not really inviting any kind of conversation. Wincing, she pulled the phone slightly away from her ear to lessen the impact. *Damn dis girl off da hook!!! Why she always gotta be yellin'?*

"Gina? You listenin'?" the voice on the other end of the phone continued. Gina began opening her mouth to answer but a second too late, her other half had beaten her to the punch. "Sheeiit, I can't go out cuz' my father came home and when I was up in the 'frigerator, he come' walkin' up behind me and threw me against the wall by my shoulder and..." Gina listened on in concern. *That hella fucked up. They can't be doin' dat shit to her. Whoopin' on her like dat.* As she listened and commiserated, she lost track of the cooking pot of stew and uncut vegetables in front of her. The steam gradually began to blend with some smoke while Gina immersed herself in her friend's problems.

"...then he call me a bitch! And den he tell me I can't have no food," howled the voice on the other end. Gina was racking her brains for something soothing to say, something reassuring. Unable to find the words, she stood there with her mouth open while just behind her the stove was pouring forth smoke.

"Maybe you could…" she began to suggest frantically, wishing, pleading, racing to make things somehow okay.

"I wanna come live at yo' house Gina. Era' body is nice and they ain't always yellin' and shit and…"

"You girls jus' come in here hollerin' and at each other's throats like you own the damn place…" Kendra hollered from up the stairs, as if on cue. *That's ironic,* Gina mused, pleased at remembering the right word, knowing in her heart that she got it right. *I gotta tell Mrs. Scatz tomorrow!!!*

"Loretta, it might seem like that's whas' up here. But, honestly, you just' don't neva come over here an' see what it's like fo' real," Gina replied matter-of-factly and managing to sound rather motherly.

"Anything better than here!" Loretta protested, "They don't feed me o' nothin'! Maybe you can talk to yo' momma and axe her…"

A gradually strengthening, burning smell was joined by thin wisps of black smoke. Still Gina's senses were elsewhere.

"She's not my mother!" Gina corrected, her voice rising and her grip on the phone becoming more firm. "And besides that…," Gina's words were falling on deaf ears.

"I know. She's yo foster mother but maybe she could adopt me too and then…" Loretta protested, her pleadings becoming desperate as she sensed that she was losing ground.

"Gina!" Kendra exclaimed, suddenly having appeared in the doorway between the kitchen and hallway. Gina was quite startled. *Shit!! Where she come from?!?!*

Kendra stood before her, disapprovingly shaking her head. "Now look what you've done! You have to watch the food!" Gina's eyes fell to the floor in shame. "Look at this mess!" Kendra frantically fanned the thick black smoke, took away the remains of the stew pot, and began bustling back and forth trying to rescue dinner.

"I'm sorry, Kendra," Gina replied meekly. "I'll get the…" "No, no honey, you've done enough for one evenin'," Kendra assured. "Here, set the table." She thrust two hands full of silverware inches from Gina's nose without looking at her, took pots off the stove, filled one with water, fanned smoke away from her face.

"Okay Kendra," Gina agreed obediently. *I need to be mo' careful!* Now with that thought, she sounded not so unlike Kendra herself. Hands full of silverware, she left the kitchen and began to set the table in the dining room, grateful for the smell changing from burning stew to a sweet, lemony furniture polish. The change in her senses brought a sudden change in contemplation. A sudden anger, resentment, bitterness. *Man, I try so hard to take care of shit when Kendra ain't around! If it wasn't fo' my stupid foster sisters, none a dis shit woulda happen'! Bitches! Now Kendra mad at me! Mom would feel what I'm sayin'.* Her mother...her mother...the thought came on too quickly for her to run away from it. Bittersweet memories rushed through her.

Gina recalled the nights they lay together shivering in the wind, dirty faces etched with hard lines of worry. Darkness. Terror. Gina looking up to her mother as a little girl, filthy and frightened. Then later, Gina, still a child, unsure of how to take care of her mother but doing her best.

Gina's mother was always high on crack cocaine, her eyes big as golf balls, teeth chattering, chest heaving while she was hyperventilating. Gina recalled her mother squatting in a bleak alley, sweating profusely while Gina trembled violently next to her, both filled with cold and anxiety.

Gina had a mother and yet she was still alone. She used to wonder, *how I let this happen?* She never doubted it was her duty to care for her mother.

These thoughts now came in streams as Gina fought to compose herself outwardly and tried to pretend everything was okay. She struggled to organize her thoughts, tried to straighten up and fight her way back to the kitchen. These thoughts of her mother were too overwhelming, too frightening, too painful to have in company. Her eyes found the pictures along Kendra's bookshelf, the pictures of each of the girls, smiling and well kempt. She looked at her own picture and then those of her foster sisters. Gazing. Wondering. Wishing.

There she was, wearing a baby blue frilly dress with white trim and freshly straightened hair, smiling brilliantly for the camera. Her foster sisters' pictures were aligned alongside her own, but no picture showed them together. *To each their own.* Each had a Kodak-moment of perfection, never looking more beautiful, content, peaceful, loved, cared for, happy. But they were all alone in their pictures. *Happy all alone...* Gina smiled bitterly, returning to the sad comfort of setting the table for Kendra.

Dalanna

Staring hard into the mirror a foot in front of her face, Dalanna searched deep for where she had gone wrong. The longer she looked, the farther away she got. *Hair? Face? Somethin' ain't right.* Shifting her long, twisting braids over one shoulder, then the other. *Almost right, almost, but not quite there,* she ran two fingers over the front cusp of her long, fine extensions, pulling her part slightly from the right, more to the center. *No, that ain't it.* She scrutinized her cheeks, eyes, nose, looked at herself from the side, stared at her mouth. All this scrutiny gave her a headache. The pain of not knowing was unbearable. Something, something was out of place, not quite there.

BOOM! BOOM! BOOM! came a slapping hand against her door. "Girl, c'mon an' get out da bathroom!" bellowed an angry, demanding voice.

"Awright mama, hold up!!!" Dalanna answered in exasperation, a bit irritated at the intrusion. She sighed impatiently to herself, reluctantly admitting that this might be as good as it would get. *Good enough for now.* Dalanna smoothed her hands over her jet black top and smiled wide in the mirror. *Oh, shoot.* With a silent prayer of thanks for having such good eyesight, she picked a not-so-noticeable speck of what could have been black pepper from that evening's dinner out of a tiny space between her two front teeth. With those final, tiny adjustments, she unlocked the bathroom door with her left hand and reached for the bathroom doorknob. *Mama be trippin' when she gotta be waitin'.* But before Dalanna could open the door on her own, it swung open and with such force that it nearly came off its hinges. Dalanna's mother filled the doorway. Still young and beautiful, with smooth dark skin, wide hips, and those same luminous, bulbous, light brown eyes that Dalanna had just been scrutinizing, she was a head taller than her daughter and much more proud, confident, and stern.

"MMM, HHHMMM, it's about time!" she proclaimed, staring hard as if to burn holes through her. Looking Dalanna up and down, half in surprise, half in suspicion, her demeanor switched from impatience to modest admiration. "Well don't you look somethin' special!"

"Is dat right?" Dalanna cooed, running a glancing hand through her extensions, spinning around in the mirror. Reassured, she mused, *Maybe I ain't, like, jus almost cute afta all.* "Mama? Can I axe' you somethin'?"

"Fa' sho' honey, just move over a lil' while ya do it," her mother replied, assisting Dalanna in sharing the mirror with a slight bump of her curvy hip. Wasting no time in going to work on herself, she began pulling down and up on her face, looking for imperfections, peeking at her hair from various angles, pulling her braids over one shoulder, then the other, lifting them up, then to the left.

"Mama, um, um, well. I'm kind of scared 'cause there dis boy…" Dalanna stammered, twisting a long strand of loose hair around a freshly painted red fingernail. She just stood there frowning for a second as she noted its blotchiness. *Fuck!!! I can't do shit right tonight?*

"Hell, there ain't no reason to be scary ova' no man!" her mother snapped. Spinning around in the mirror, taking a long look at her rear, satisfied that her jeans showed off her best feature, she continued, "Sex an' money what they good for, an' that's all we need from 'em, you hear?"

"Yes mama, but I..." Dalanna insisted pointedly.

"Giiiiirl! Sheeit," her mother went on undaunted. "You wanna axe me somethin', den axe me somethin'. But now you gonna answer it yo' self!?" Her mother clicked her tongue in dismay and shook her head as adults do when they are growing impatient with children. She'd spent enough attention on her daughter for the moment.

"Oooh look at my hair! Ain't it somethin' special? Somebody is fixin' to get some tonight an' let me tell ya!! Uh-huh, girl. He got a lot to give!! Dalanna looked down at the floor, embarrassed, awkward. Her mother didn't notice and carried on, ""Lemme tell ya girl!!! I thought it was his leg o' somethin'!"

"Oh, Mama please!" Dalanna exclaimed. Hurriedly, she excused herself from the bathroom and retreated to the familiar comfort of her bedroom as quick as her long legs would carry her. After gently closing the door, she leaned back on it and jammed her hands into her pockets, wishing to barricade herself in. It was such a violation of her sensitivity, her sense of propriety. *She really think I wanna hear all that?! Always tellin' me about deez men she hookin' up wit'?? Why she can't jus' be my mama?!?! Always tryin' ta be somebady friend.*

The phone rang, interrupting Dalanna's thoughts. She snatched the cordless from atop her nearby dresser. "Hello?!" she answered irritably, part of her still in the bathroom with her mother instead of on this phone call.

"Whaaaassup, girl?" replied a tired and yet endearing voice on the other end.

"Hey. What's happ'nin' Shantel," Dalanna replied, relieved. *Damn my girl got some good timing!* Taking a couple of short, weary steps, she plunked herself down at her desk, cupped her chin in her hand, and began gazing out the window, watching the world outside. *Man, I just need to get da fuck outta here. Don't even matta where.* Gazing longingly out to anywhere, she watched the neighborhood with increasing interest.

A lowrider bike was squeaking and squealing past, just slow enough to be seen by everyone yet fast enough not to cause the teenager riding on the axle to fall. Dalanna watched them trail off, envious of their ability to ride off into eternity. No captivity, no mother, no sense of being stuck with too much information or TMI. In just seconds, the bike was gone, returning the night to a calm array of stars atop a desolate blue sky and an occasional chirping cricket. *Damn, da X kind of peaceful sometimes.* Shantel was explaining something about something that had happened at school. Dalanna listened and gradually started to feel grateful for the shift in tempo and tenor, the space to think. Shantel had just complained about her mother and the way she would never listen. Dalanna's interest grew stronger.

"OOO. Girl, fo' sure. Dey do too much. My mama doin' way toooo much!" she exclaimed.

"Mmmm," Shantel acknowledged. *Leas' you gotta motha. Mine's always out. Talkin' 'bout how she gotta go ta work and shit. Don't neva, like, come talk to me. Yo mama steady tryin' to kick it wit' you.*

"I swear to god she come 'round talkin' 'bout how who she hookin' up with an' how big they is an' all kinda shit! Like I wanna hear all dat, feel me?" Dalanna continued.

Shantel sucked her teeth noisily in disagreement. "Girl leas' yo' mama talk to you and shit. I bounce outta my window and be up outta here fo' like hella long an' sheeit, they ain't even know I was gone." *I coulda neva came back, an' I bet they don' even miss me. I wonder how it be den. Like, if I die. If I die, would they even be cryin' at my funeral?*

"Sheeit!" Dalanna insisted in dismay, bitterly shaking her head and rolling her eyes, both from left to right. "If I got my way? My nigga fo' real, I'd take yo' spot any day. My momma gone crazy! Tryin' ta be my girl or somethin'! And I'm like, 'Who you think you are? You trippin' or something. You need ta be my momma fa' once!' Damn."

Shantel laughed in her most carefree of ways. "I don't know why you even bitchin'. I think yo' momma hella coo'! She take you shoppin', let you do what you wanna do."

Dalanna shook her head. *Man, ain't all is cracked up to be. An' dat make it mo' fucked up! Era' bady think is all coo' havin' my momma tryin' to be my girl!!! Dey don' even know.*

"I barely eva see my mama," Shantel continued sadly. "And den, like, once in while she come around? Sheeit, talkin 'bout *you got in trouble up at schoo' this, o', like, help me wit' dat*...I'm like, hell no! Where you been? Now we supposed ta play family an' all?! My nigga please!!!"

"I feel ya," Dalanna conceded. "Anyway, you goin' ta Da'ron party tanight?"

"Girl, me and dat ho Porsche jus' got back!!! You damn near already miss' it," Shantel explained.

Dalanna smacked her lips in contempt. "Fo' real! I just' 'bout got ready!"

Shantel laughed lightheartedly. "My nigga you hella late!!! Ain't even worth goin' now. Era' bady goin' home. Jus' some drunk ass motha fuckas. Ha! An' da ugliest one was all up on dat ho Porsche!!!"

Dalanna laughed hard. "Ain't nothin' change in da X?!?!"

Shantel giggled furiously. "Okay?!?! So, yeah. I mean, ain't none of 'em still der even cute, well, most of 'em anyway..." her trailing voice betraying something on her mind.

"Except yo' new man right?" Dalanna teased, her intuitions razor sharp.

"Bitch please!" Shantel shot back. *Sheeit'!! Like I'm a' get down like dat. 'My man' afta one night, Sheeit!!!* "Girl you trippin'. My man? Hell no!!! He might be my boo' though!"

Dalanna smiled wide, the suspense building, tension mounting, huddling expectantly over the phone. "So quit stallin' foo'!!! Who is he?!"

Shantel shrank back, enjoying the little game of cat and mouse that had begun. "Don't worry 'bout it! Why you wanna know all a dis shit any damn way?!?!" *Sheeit, she prob'ly wanna know so she cou' come up an' try to take somebady man. I mean, like, my girl coo' as fuck. But she scandalous. All a these females is 'round here!!!*

"I'm just askin' damn! Don't be so scary! I ain't gonna do nothin'!" Dalanna pleaded as innocently as she could. But the crack in her voice betrayed dubious sincerity. She wasn't a very good liar, especially when the stakes were high.

"Yeah-yeah, I bet!!! Wha' you neeeeed ta do is go get yo' own damn man an' get up off 'a mines!" Shantel marveled. *Yup, das right bitch. Ain't 'bout to be messin' wit' my man!* The feeling of having Darrell to herself was exhilarating.

Dalanna scoffed, her pride hurt but feigning disinterest. "Sheeit don't worry 'bout me, I got mines linin' up! An' I ain't mean like linin' up, I mean LININ' up!!! Feel me?!" Just then her bedroom door swung open.

"Girl you need ta get back in dat bathroom an' line up that part in yo' hair!"

Shantel on the other end began laughing hysterically. "Ha ha, damn girl, yo' mamma cold!!!"

Dalanna snapped her head hard to the left, chin grazing past her chest, her left eyebrow arched, right eyebrow low, lips pursed, eyes blazing. Thoroughly enraged.

"Mama!" she gasped, pushing the phone and her friend's muffled laughter into her bosom. "I'm on da phone!"

Her mother took a couple of marching steps in and smiled tauntingly. "Who dat is, my girl Shantel?! WHAS' UP MY LADY!!"

Shantel laughed on the other end. "WHA'S UP GIRL!!"

Dalanna scowled. "Mamma goooo away!! Why you up in my room like dis? Can't you knock and don't choo gotta be somewhere right 'bout now anyway?"

"Girl don't be gettin' smart wit' me!" her mother roared, nearly rattling the clasps off the bedroom window. "You best remember who you' talkin' to or you might jus' be fit ta get a whoopin' that might help yo' ass 'member nex' time!"

Dalanna trembled fearfully, saying nothing, knowing that one wrong move could mean she was sure to get it right that minute.

Her mother looked her up and down. "See now das da problem with you lil' bitches!!! Ain't got no respect fo' yo damn selves or those who raised ya! Ya ought to be grateful for wha' you have, a mamma who wanna schoo' you on men an' how to take care a yo'self, but you too hard headed to see dat aintcha?!?!"

Dalanna frowned at her hands, wanting but not daring to say anything. Shantel on the other end of the phone was wishing there was some way she could just hang up.

At least now, Dalanna's mother seemed to have worn herself out, muttering a last lingering couple of obscenities before making her exit, slamming the door. The room seemed to grow colder.

"Hey?" Shantel piped up meekly, "You still there?"

Dalanna blinked hard, having forgotten she was still on the phone. A loud silence was her only answer. She was scared that, if she spoke, she would cry. She hated to cry, hated to be so vulnerable, so open, so defenseless, so weak.

She looked at her image reflected in the window. *My part really outta place?* Looking left, looking right. Brushing a loose strand of hair off her brow, hand sweeping across her forehead left and right again. She put her ear to the phone.

"Damn yo' mamma trippin' hard! She be mean as hell sometimes!" Shantel observed.

Dalanna breathed hard through her nose. "I swear to god I hate dat bitch!" she croaked, the phone in her hand beginning to quiver in her grip, knuckles whitening. "She com's 'round like my best friend one minute and then my jailer da next, cussin' me an' shit!"

"For real though girl, leas' she try sometime'," Shantel consoled. Thinking briefly of her own mother, longing, yearning. *'Leas' her momma care enough ta scream and holla. But, yeah, she fucked up though!!!*

"Girl, I swear to G.O.D. I wish she jus' bounce up outta here! Like fa' good an' don't neva' come back! It's like I ain't even got no motha any damn way."

"Yeah, me neither," Shantel related, "I don't know what I'd do without all a y'all. You and all o' the rest o' my girls."

The thought made Dalanna smile. *I don't know either.* She laid her weary head back against the pillow. Feeling dreamily comfortable, she let her thoughts become lost somewhere in the ceiling above.

"I don't know neither," Dalanna finally said out loud, a slight smile spreading reluctantly over her lips as she gazed lazily out the window, still wishing to be elsewhere, although some of the earlier intensity had diminished.

"I do know you still bes' ta find yo' own man though!" Shantel teased, barely above a whisper. Dalanna smacked her lips, catching herself before she laughed. *Sheeit girl, you bes' keep yo man away. 'Cuz if he fine, somebady might jus' steal him!!*

"Bitch, you got nerve!" Dalanna exclaimed, feigning outrage but feeling better. The idea that she wasn't utterly alone helped her out of the abyss that the last encounter with her mother had left her in.

"Okay, girl, go on to sleep an' I see you tamorrow," Shantel suggested, her eyes already half closed.

"Awright then," Dalanna agreed, clicking off her phone and tossing it effortlessly across her bedside. But then the aloneness returned. Dalanna quickly began to feel it in her bones, in the pit of her stomach. The night began to feel hollow, lonely, empty. But now she was too tired and after changing into her night shirt and clicking off the light, she drifted off to sleep rather quickly.

Shawn

Seconds on the clock ticked away, one by one. The suspense was astounding, tense, blaring. A hand in the air broke its path.

"I think that empowering disadvantaged communities and the people within is about more than affirmative action or the basic antidiscrimination stuff you see posted on the bathroom walls in your everyday corner McDonald's. Helping people to grow conscious of class and race in their influence on power imbalances and fundamental inequalities requires an understanding and application of knowledge imparted to oppressed people. But the knowledge and consciousness must not only be imparted to these oppressed people, but they must be conveyed in terms and conditions that they can relate to. Otherwise, such attempts may be futile given that knowledge imparted in discourse from mainstream oppressive regimes might more likely be received as distant and untrustworthy. Reality communicated to the people by and for the people is then more likely to raise one's consciousness." Shawn finally breathed, eager for signs of approval but fearfully expecting otherwise. You could hear a pin drop in the process.

His classmates stared off into nowhere. Shawn was unsure, but he almost did not want to know what they were thinking. Maybe there was some admiration in the residue left over from his having held the floor for the past several minutes. The silence continued, a silence just long enough to think.

"Well said," replied the instructor from the front of the class, smiling slightly, nodding her head. An elderly Asian woman with short hair, thin spectacles, and a calm, thoughtful presence eyed Shawn approvingly, seeming to appreciate his effort if not completely amused by his certainty. "Someone seems to have been doing his research."

Shawn beamed, taking her approving words as an invitation to say more, opening his mouth, rising to the occasion. But it was not to be.

"Alright everyone, have a good evening," the instructor announced with a friendly, dismissive wave. Shuffling papers, zipping backpacks, excited chatter following instantaneously. This was a first-year graduate class, overflowing with energy, bleary eyes, hope, and unabashed liberalism. The instructor began to pack up her things slowly, deliberately. Adjusting her rimmed glasses slightly as she draped her bag over her shoulder, she sensed that she was not out of the woods, noting Shawn lingering nearby.

"Professor?" Shawn piped up.

The instructor straightened and turned around to face the voice at her back. "Yes, Shawn?" she answered without looking at him.

"Well, I, uh, um," Shawn stammered. "I'm starting my internship tomorrow at the school where my girls' group will be meeting in the afternoon. I was hoping for some advice."

"Oh? What more do you need to know than how to impart consciousness by and for the oppressed people?" she teased good-naturedly. Shawn smiled weakly and with some slight embarrassment.

Okay, maybe I got a little preachy. "Yeah, I know I carry on sometimes, it's just that I read...," he started to demure. His explanatory efforts were dimissed by his professor's delicate wave of a hand. Wise and reassuring.

"I'm only teasing," she informed. "But you have studied long and hard and know all of this material. I'm sure that your group will be lucky to have you."

Shawn smiled grimly, hoping she was right, though he had second thoughts.

"Thanks Professor, but I've read our materials cover to cover I don't know how many times," Shawn insisted, his every word growing slightly more frantic than the last. "And this stuff all sounds great. But it doesn't say anything about how to take all this 'I Have A Dream' stuff and make it work for my girls."

She smiled again, amused. "*Your* girls?" She was almost enjoying this slight bantering with him. *A smart one,* she privately reflected. *They all come in so insecure and doubtful in the beginning of the year, so much more competent by the end, doubting themselves along the way. They don't really need to be so insecure.* She knew, as he didn't, that therapists who had more experience were no more likely to produce better therapeutic outcomes than inexperienced therapists. It was an idea premised on some results of a study explained in a 2005 book by Leon, Martinovich, Lutz, and Lyons. She understood that this grave uncertainty, this period of marked confusion and doubt and inner chaos, was necessary for him to grow. She knew—he didn't—that all would be okay.

"Well, I, uh, I meant..." Shawn fumbled, searching for the right words.

"No, I know what you meant," she replied in a motherly fashion, soothing, reassuring. "And I think that the way you speak of them shows how much you care. And it's obvious that you are prepared to go the distance in learning all that you can. You have the brains and the heart; you're just nervous because you don't have the experience. That will come with time. Just be yourself, work with your supervisor, and you will be fine."

Shawn nodded, resigned. Although he yearned to ask more questions, there were no more answers to be had at this juncture. "Thanks Professor, I'll let you know how it goes."

"I wouldn't have it any other way," she replied, closing the door on her way out, leaving Shawn alone in the classroom. Breathing heavily in and out, clasping his hands over his cheeks and running them down his shirt, he stared intently at an ink spot on the floor. The quiet of the classroom was dark and eerie compared to the former flurry of activity. But in a way, it was comforting. *The group starts tomorrow. My co-facilitator Terri will be there. I still don't know about her. She's so quiet all the time. I don't know what's up with that. Damn I'm hungry. That girl in the front of our class is cuuuute!! Never mind. I have to figure this out. Okay, tomorrow. I'll go get them from their class and...* It was all imagination from there. Dreams of his being front and center, inspiring them to greatness, their hanging on his every word, a remake of *Dangerous Minds* or another such portrayal of the resurrection of inner-city youths at the hands of a great white hope. And Shawn was hopeful. It was this hope that he carried with him out of the classroom, down the street, and all the way to his apartment. He began replaying the scene he had imagined, the scene of the group, his listening intently, drawing them to deep insights. The togetherness, the inspiration—all of that was sure to happen. This and other comforting scenarios helped him fall asleep peacefully that night.

The Group

BEEP! BEEP! BEEP! The sound of his alarm nearly catapulted Shawn out of bed. Clearing out the cobwebs, wiping the sleep from his eyes, autopiloting through a shower and a cup of coffee full of sugar, and moving out the door and onto the bus. *Today is the day! I'm going to meet with the girls in the group. It's going to be great!* Picturing inspiring words and hearing inspiring music coming out of nowhere in the background, the girls' heads nodding, minds and hearts healing, sharing. It all looked so perfect in his mind.

The bus began to pick up speed past tightly clipped lawns, commuting white faces, smiling school kids. As it stopped, he looked down on teenagers walking quickly to school, listening to headphones, with bouncing book bags. There were some little kids piling into a minivan as their mom and dad smiled and waved them off. Shawn considered what was in store for him. *The X in all its glory. Would be nice if everyone had it like they have it here,* he reflected grimly. He was walking into anything but a scene of harmony and hope.

The bus barreled through a tunnel. Flashing yellow lights overhead, the wailing of the tracks flying by at breakneck speed. His commute went from one side of town to the other. *From Disneyland to da ghetto,* as he had heard the kids say. Smiling at the thought, loving their humor and sense of irony, he thought of himself as a sort of poet, always an ear open for small strands of beauty in the world.

This reminded him of the girls. *Beautiful,* he had thought more than once. And not merely in a physical sense. This feeling, this draw was of a different sort. An admiration, an appreciation. *They are sooooo cool!!* The thought made Shawn smile. He had a certain love for them already. It was neither an attraction nor a curiosity, but a deepening appreciation and increasing interest. He wanted to know everything about them. Excited, eager to help, hopeful. Glancing at his watch. *Less than a half hour to go!*

Now passing through the long tunnel, coming out of the other side, chain-link fences with barbed wire atop, the sky somehow darker, empty streets littered with trash. Shawn barely took notice. Still thinking of them. *Rona, Dalanna, Porsche, Gina, Shantel, Venus.* The names even had a ring to them.

All of a sudden, he had reached *The X,* the nearly hour and a half trip having flown by like minutes. He shook himself slightly, came back to the real world. *Toto, we're not in Kansas anymore.* Black faces at his sides, not a face like his to be found. As he passed the bus driver, their eyes met. "Thanks," Shawn offered, but the driver, a middle-aged female, merely nodded "MMMM-HHMMM."

Stepping down onto the sidewalk, Shawn noted the neighborhood stores and people hanging about them. The gas station on his right had only four pumps and expensive gas but advertised cheap beer and cigarettes. He noted other aspects of the area that clashed with the images of the town he had just left less than an hour ago: bars on several of the windows; an old woman pushing a shopping cart full of junk; withered lawns and dry foliage; streets with potholes and giant crevices split open as though there had just been hundred earthquakes. Feeling a certain sadness hanging in the air, Shawn now wore the same flat expression as the bus driver.

Looking right and left, he stepped out into the street in semi-hurried fashion, trying to walk quickly without looking like he was trying to hurry. He strode past graffiti-laden bus stops, fast food wrappers and other garbage in the gutters, and tried not to notice the chipped and peeling paint on every grey- or salmon-colored stucco or wood building. Passing it all in long strides, he etched the scenery into his memory, snapshots of a moment's glance. Upon reaching the crest of the hill, he could see the school below. Kids in twos and threes were exiting the back seats of cars, some with rap music blaring. He watched them slinging backpacks over their shoulders, dragging their feet, looking at the ground. *Looks like judgment day.* No hugs and smiles. Grim, slow, solemn. Shawn could feel it.

Once he got to the sidewalk in front of the school, he thought he could see them better so he tried to search their faces. He caught only glimpses of their faces, all of them hollow; the rest had their faces buried between slumped shoulders, burrowed into their jackets. *It's like going to a funeral.* This thought made Shawn uncomfortable, so he let his mind wander elsewhere. *What is it about this place?* he wondered, as he made his way through the rusted chain-link fence. It reminded him of something. Then he remembered.

Several years ago, his mother had worked in the same district in a school with very similar circumstances. A substitute teacher, she too had tried to make sense of it all after working in place where the kids who needed the most were herded together and provided the least. A depressing reality. Maybe that's why their faces were long. His mother had started off the same—wanting to be helpful, hopeful, but feeling the despair in the air that first day. Her instincts served her well. She'd told Shawn of the horrors over and over again. There had been, upon her arrival, no lesson plans, no roll sheet, no chalk! The kids had played basketball all semester; no English teacher lasted more than a few days. They had no books, no pencils, no paper. So Shawn's mother had tried to teach them how to write without paper or pencils. She was getting somewhere with a few kids, but then "some knucklehead" threw a shoe, smashing a light bulb into a thousand pieces, which was followed by another kid jumping up and urinating in a garbage can, squealing with laughter. "That's it. Everybody out!" she'd ordered. They had quickly happily complied." It was now unsafe for anyone to stay in the portable classroom. She had nowhere else to put them, so she'd just watched them romping and skipping off to the basketball court while she had headed for the office to give back the key. "But, Mrs. Reynolds, the children need you." "They don't need me. They need someone, but it's not me. Here," she said, handing the vice principal the key, heading out the door toward her car. She heard the chain-link fence rattling strangely at her back. "MRS. REYN-OLDS WHERE ARE YOU GOING ?!?!" yelled a high voice. *Anywhere but here,* she wished she could say. She'd just waved the kid off and driven away.

When she'd heard that he was considering working in the same area, Shawn's mother had gently tried to persuade him to work elsewhere. *Maybe you could get an internship at the college where I teach? Maybe the guidance center?* Shawn had scoffed at the thought. *Those fuzzy boot girls, lazy ass kids who make excuses for not doing their work. The world's been handed to them and all they want to do is get drunk and play video games. Forget that!*

He wanted to go into the ghetto, and so into the ghetto he went. His mother knew it was useless to try to reason with him, so all she could do was resign herself, have faith in him, and stand beside him every step of the way. Shawn was glad she understood.

BRRRRIIINNNNGGGGG!!!! blared the school bell from every direction at once, jolting Shawn back to reality. He began making his way through a familiar set of rusty brown metal doors, closing them behind him, grateful for the rush of warm air inside.

"Good morning," said a familiar female voice.

"Hi Terri," Shawn replied, making his way past the boilers, unused desks, and tables piled in a corner and janitorial odds and ends in various nooks and crannies throughout their makeshift office.

Shawn dropped his bag on the floor, taking a seat at his desk. He eyed the clock overhead. "It's just about that time isn't it?" In her late thirties, Terri dressed well and usually wore two-inch heels and business suits. She had a certain calm demeanor, as if everything was fine and always would be.

"I'll go get the girls and be back in a minute," Shawn announced.

Terri barely seemed to hear him as she methodically unpacked her notebooks and sorted papers on the table before her. "I'll be here," she answered, rising and beginning to set up chairs in a circle. He strode across the lengthy blacktop, noting its crooked basketball hoops, a vacant swing blowing to and fro with the cool morning breeze. The peacefulness was good, gave him final moments to think. *Gina, Rona, Shantel, Venus, Dalanna, and Porsche. What have I gotten myself into?* The social worker in him couldn't help but answer.

Every teacher in this school put them on my list. Drugs, cussing, fighting, screwed up parents, crappy neighborhoods. And the way guys treat them. God it's terrible! The cat calls flying from the cars as they drove by and caught sight of this or that group of girls going to or from school. Unbelievable. Shaking his head at the thought. *But that's where I come in. At least with me, they can have a decent relationship with a male, a guy who won't beat them up or try to have sex with them. It must be something positive for them.* The thought of it made him smile, now passing rows of green benches, a group of eighth-grade boys laughing and poking at each other took no notice of Shawn. *I should say something to them, tell them to go to class or something. Well, err, I don't know…*

"HEEEEYYY!!!! ALL A' Y'ALL!!! GOOOOOO *TO CLAAAYAAAS!!!*"
ordered a dark-skinned, overweight security guard from the far end of the
school yard, bellowing through a cupped hand pressed to his mouth.

Shawn was relieved to be rescued from having to take the eighth-graders
on; they were not the type to go without a fight. *Good, it's his job anyway. I
have my own job to do.* He was glad that he had an excuse for not taking on
a group of eighth-grade boys who might be a little rough around the edges.
Not willing to admit it, he assumed that the boys would respond better to the
security guard who was African American.

And after what seemed like no time and forever all at once, Shawn arrived
at the door of bungalow 14. He gingerly stepped in. A multitude of heads
snapped up, eyeing the encroaching stranger. Feeling their eyes on him, he
stepped to the front of the class. Towering above the masses of kids huddled
over their desks, he felt almost frightened and small. An outsider. Alone. He
was right. Grateful to see a familiar face, he nodded to Mrs. Trenton. She did
not skip a beat, turning her body to face talkers who were quickly silenced,
finding the eyes of would-be class disrupters, quickly thwarting their every
attempt and without a word. *Amazing.* She looked back at Shawn. *It will be
okay,* she said without saying. *You will be and so will I.* Her unspoken words
were reassuring; they helped put Shawn at ease. Something about Mrs. Trenton reminded him of his mother, now that he thought about it. Her strong mind
and perspicacity. She stood in a neat black dress, with ornately styled hair and
fashionable and yet humble jewelry that made her look professional, yet with
an elegance that was not common, he guessed, for an inner-city classroom.

"Good morning, Mr. Reynolds," she invited, turning her attention his way
and yet never losing track of the classroom before her. You could feel it just by
walking in. She exuded this order, this grounding, this sense of having everything under control. He could learn from her. And Mrs. Trenton liked him.
Liked the passion and dedication he had shown while working with the kids.

"You can go ahead and take the girls. First, did you want to introduce
yourself to the class?" Shawn obliged. A surge of courage came through.

"Good morning ladies and gentleman!" he started out eagerly, the young
faces before him looking taken aback. His intensity seemed to silence the
hustle and bustle that had commenced after the initial introduction. No more
paper rustling, just hushed whispers now.

"My name is Mr. Reynolds and I am the new school counselor. I'll be
here on Tuesdays and Thursdays, so if you need anything, help with your
homework, to talk about anything, or whatever else, swing by anytime you
like." He stood there for a second longer, a long second, secretly hoping for
some sign of acknowledgment, something. He got nothing, only painstaking

quiet. This somewhat doused Shawn's spirits. *Guess I won't be winning them over overnight.*

"Okay people, back to work!" Mrs. Trenton ordered. And Shawn was grateful for her rescue, breaking the awkward silence.

"Gina, Rona, Shantel, Venus, Dalanna, Porsche?!?! Go with Mr. Reynolds," Mrs. Trenton continued once her classroom began to fall back into order. Eyes down into open textbooks, an occasional hushed whisper, pencils scribbling in notebooks.

Six forms were beginning to rise reluctantly, begrudgingly, from the rows and rows of bowed heads. Backpacks tossed lazily over shoulders, feet shuffling across the floor, not exactly up in arms. *Okay, don't take it personally. What do you expect?!?! They're not going to sing and dance because they're going to counseling.* Although his mind spoke to him reassuringly, it still hurt, hurt to think that, no, maybe they didn't like the group, maybe they didn't even like him. He started trying to see it another way, but it still hurt a little. Turning glumly, Shawn began to follow the girls out the door.

"White boy!" resounded an anonymous proclamation from over his shoulder.

Shawn whirled back around sharply. "WHO SAID THAT?!?!" he bellowed. A tense silence answered. Not a paper rustled, not a whisper. *Calm down; they're just kids. I gotta be the bigger man.*

"So let me tell you something then!" he continued, at a slightly lower voice, less demanding, but not inviting debate in the least. "I haven't come in here disrespecting anyone! For that I need the same in return! That's not up for debate because when you disrespect me, you disrespect you and poorly represent yourselves. We all deserve respect."

Again, you could hear pins drop. Mouths slightly open. Shawn saw that his work had been done. The girls were making their way awkwardly out the door. Shawn was soon at their heels after closing the classroom door quietly.

"OOOOHHHH you mean," came a muffled whisper from his crowd of onlookers. But now Shawn had a moment to get a grip on what just happened. *Did that really just happen?* Walking in the soft morning breeze, he said nothing out loud but was dying to exclaim, "Whew. That's over!"

He noticed that the girls had already moved on from the incident. Chattering, nodding, smiling, making little hand gestures to emphasize their finer points, they had a way of always making Shawn laugh.

"Rememba' dat lady?!?! Wha's her name again?"

"Da one was up in Mrs. Trenton class da otha day?"

"YEAAAHHH!!!"

"Sheeit I hate dat bitch!"

"OOOHHHH you in trouuuu-ble!" several voices giddily caw-cawed all at once. Three of their heads had turned to Shawn in anticipation. *Make your move,* they said without saying. *Well, I don't know. They shouldn't cuss because they will get in trouble. But, maybe they already worked it out. I mean, they already told whoever it was that cussing gets you in trouble. Maybe nothing more needs to be said and it'll set up this dynamic that isn't gonna make them wanna talk.*

"No, no trouble. Well, that isn't really what I do," Shawn informed, "But I think that even if I don't send you to the office for saying something you're not supposed to, you might start thinking, 'If I can get away with it once, then I can do it all the time.' But if you do that, you could get in trouble here…what do you guys think?"

"Mr. Reynolds said we can cuss!"

"I'm hungry!"

"You see dat new boy?!?!?! OOOOHHHHH!!!! He hecka cute!!!

Real girls get down on the floor, on the floor get down, blared a phone from inside a pocket. "Who dis? Hah!!! Whassup girl I just at school!!! Yeah, yeah…"

"Feel me? He ain't even cute, he hecka ugly!!!"

"Ha-ha, fo' real!!"

Shawn smiled to himself. *Maybe next time.* And in the meantime, they had reached their destination. He opened the door for them and they scurried inside, backpacks thudding to the ground, chairs squeaking across the floor as they were turned either toward or away from others, Porsche, Venus, Shantel, and Dalanna all huddling together, Rona and Gina islands to themselves, each beginning to fidget.

"Hello," Terri greeted.

"Hi," came a muffled response. Shawn beaming inwardly. *I got more of a hello!!! They like me better!!!* Meanwhile, the rest of the world carried on.

"Ooooooh!!! I'm tired a' dat foo' Mr. Stevens!!! He be pissin' me off!"

"I don't like him neither!"

"Giiiiirl if dis man don't stop tryin' ta get at me on ma' way to schoo'?!?! Feel me?!?! I'm gonna get my daddy to whoop his ass!!!"

Terri and Shawn looked at each other. *Let's see where this goes?*

"So, you married?" Porsche said eagerly through the chatter, her eyes demanding Shawn's.

He about fainted. "Err, a, well, no," Shawn answered, fumbling, stumbling. Terri was unsuccessfully fighting back a smile.

"You got a girlfriend?" Dalanna followed up, leaning forward in her chair, smiling. All of their faces were now turned toward Shawn, looking on in earnest.

"No, what a…" Shawn began to answer, moving to change the subject. But they had anticipated his next move and were not yet done with him.

"You be goin' on dates on da weekend?" pursued Porsche.

Shawn's mind began to wander frantically; nowhere to run but it kept running, its stumbles and stammers too quick to get control over. Somehow his mouth just seemed to find words. "No I work at a group home on the weekends, a boys' group home across town."

"How old?" Shantel goaded.

"Older than you guys, by maybe two or four years," Shawn answered, relieved at the changeover, now amused, warming to the subject.

"Oooohhh we should take a fieldtrip!"

"Yeah!"

"It be educational!"

Shawn laughed hysterically. Terri was watching intently, as if playing chess and planning her next moves.

"What about you guys? Do you have boyfriends?" Shawn asked, sitting up a bit straighter in his chair. *Okay, enough about me, we're going to talk about all of you now.*

Rona's eyes fell to the floor between her feet. Shawn filed the observation away for later. *Rona does not have a boyfriend.*

Venus was beginning to wind one of her long braids around a long red fingernail as her eyes bounced up from the ceiling to the left and right of her. She was warming to the conversation. "I got six…no seven," she boasted. Three or four heads instantly snapped to attention.

"You a ho!!!!" Dalanna proclaimed. Porsche laughed gaily. A few faces looked away as if to say, *oh no she didn't.* Venus smacked her lips insolently, twirled a long braid around a delicate finger, trying to look like her feelings had not been hurt.

"'Da girls in my house have hella boys," Gina offered. No one seemed to hear her. Shawn took notice and was sure she noticed it too. He wanted to somehow acknowledge her, but the group wouldn't slow down.

"OOOHHHH, GGGIIIRRRLLL. I saw dat man you was talking to the otha day!" Dalanna squealed at Venus, sitting up in her chair excitedly, clapping her hands and smiling wide.

Venus waved her off, feigning bashful. "Who? Aw yeah. Ain't nothin'. Das jus' one of 'em. You know, my Monday man!" All the girls laughed. Shawn sat and watched in earnest, captivated.

"Venus, how do you make time for all of them?" Terri inquired, the calm of her voice seeming to lower the volume of the energy. Venus shook her head and shrugged her shoulders as if to say, "I don't know either."

"I don't even have time to do my homework and my chores, even on da weekends," Gina complained resentfully.

"You go out with yo girl on da weekends?" Dalanna probed, as her eyes found Shawn's. Terri smiled ever so slightly, amused at the girls' game of cat and mouse. *Nope, they're not done with him.* She almost wanted to laugh out loud, but she wanted to see how he would respond.

After the first onslaught, Shawn was more prepared and rebounded quickly. "On the weekends, I'm mostly at that group home I told you guys about," he answered calmly.

"Do you guys know anyone that lives in a group home?" Terri quickly followed up, her eyes peering around the room, already knowing, inviting them in.

"Yeah," came a volley of responses.

"My cousins do, OOOOHHHH, they hella bad!" Rona declared, shaking her head in dismay, beginning to pick something out of her fingernails. The girls looked on in interest. There was little fidgeting, eyes forward.

"What do you mean? They're bad?" Terri probed.

"Well, LEMME TELL YA!!!" Rona began, with a wave of her hand, adding to the suspense. Shawn was amused. He loved their little mannerisms. "Dey some rippers!!! And some boppers!!!" All the girls laughed hysterically. Shawn thought to himself, puzzled. *What does that mean? Well, if they're laughing that hard, it is isn't nice, whatever it means.*

"MMM-HMM yeah," Rona continued. "Dey always in truuublleee!!!!" The girls all laughed again, Shawn along with them. Terri fought back giggles too. "Dey always yellin' and cussin'. Ol' dirty ass hoes!! Fo' real y'all!!!" Rona smacked her lips loudly, letting everyone know that she was done, instantly beginning to fidget, looking to the floor, practically kicking herself for what she said for fear that she had made herself look bad.

"Thanks for sharing that Rona," Terri offered. "Why do you think they act like that?" Terri asked, noting an uncomfortable shift or two in chairs. A little tension was rising.

"My mamma neva eva' eva' let me go ova' der!" Rona replied sullenly.

"Why not?" Shawn asked, folding his hands in his lap.

"They always fightin' and cussin' and my mamma don't want me around all a dat," Rona conceded, albeit reluctantly. "Sheeit, it be hella fun ova' der!!!"

"So then she is really trying to show you that she cares about you even if that doesn't always mean telling you what you want to hear," Shawn concluded.

"Yeah," Rona admitted in resignation, slumping back into her chair. Gina, who looked as if she had totally left the room, was staring off through the window. Porsche was feverishly pushing buttons on a phone in her lap. Silence ensued until Gina could bear it no longer.

"My foster sisters all like dat too."

"Yeah," Shantel added. "See das why my daddy be tellin' me to stay close to home. Feel me? Like, he say I ain't from out here and all. 'Cuz we from da country. So, it's like, I don't talk like different. I talk, like, um, wha' choo call dat?"

"GHEEEEEETO!!!" Three voices answered simultaneously and in rhythm. Shawn laughed, amazed at their quickness.

Porsche, Shantel, and Venus became more and more lost in muffled whispers. Venus, producing a cell phone, drew the attention of the others.

"Mmm-hmm, he hecka cute!" Venus whispered mischievously. Shantel and Porsche gazed on excitedly, huddling over the phone as if in prayer.

Shawn sensed that the group was eroding. *Maybe we have gone far enough today.* The bell rang overhead.

"All right everybody, we'll see you next week," Shawn announced. Backpacks jumped off the floor, barely audible goodbyes were followed by chortled laughter, the door closed behind them all too abruptly. Shawn could barely believe they were gone. *Not as bad as I expected. Maybe I did okay. Yeah, it went okay. Maybe it just went. Hmm, yeah. But damn!!! Am I married!?!? Girlfriend?! And I thought it was they who would be getting taken to school!*

Assessment

In this first meeting of the group, the girls engaged in provocative sexual behavior, including asking me about my personal life. To break silences or otherwise deal with uncomfortable feelings in the group, they would often discuss boys who they found attractive. This can be explained both developmentally and in terms of a more critical feminist focus on the influences of gender-based trauma and power dynamics.

How the Girls Relational Development Was Influenced by Being Objectified

The girls were adolescents and therefore at the age when children become more interested in exploring relations with the opposite sex. When the girls asked me about my personal life, they may have simply been having some fun with me.

The girls' flirtatious energies may also have been strongly influenced by a male-dominated society that encouraged them to behave this way. In *The X,* women tended to be objectified by men and encouraged to respond to this objectification in certain ways by other women. As was seen in the girls' stories, women gained status with their female peers by competently navigating relationships with the opposite sex. The girls who tended to be the least involved with and least interested in the opposite sex were often shunned by their female peers.

Thus the girls' objectification was perpetuated by men and reinforced by other women who were influenced by the male-dominated society. An example of this phenomena was seen in the group. Rona and Gina were the only members who did not seem particularly interested in the opposite sex, and they tended to be ignored by the other four members.

The other four members were friends outside of the group, so it could be expected that they would naturally form an alliance. It should be noted and considered that the members who talked the most about the opposite sex, Shantel, Porshe, Venus, and Dalanna, formed the group within the group.

Did Turning the Tables Really Help Them?

In a way, women in *The X* took their power back by dating multiple men, using men to gain material possessions, and otherwise doing to men what men had been doing to women throughout time (that is, manipulating them). The girls experienced men as being notoriously unfaithful, dishonest, and controlling. It was their position that what is good for the gander is good for the goose.

In a way, this parallels the acting out behaviors in Hughes's (2006) explanation of abnormal development as posited in his attachment theory. Children who are raised by loving, nurturing, and physically and emotionally available parents develop a secure sense of autonomy and independence. When their parents are abusive, children may initially be sad, hopeless, and experience other negative feelings, as did these girls when they were first lied to or otherwise hurt by men.

As abused children grow older, they may develop tendencies to act out in ways that intentionally elicit negative responses (Hughes, 2006). This reinforces their belief that they can only depend on themselves.

Acting out does not help abused children build a sense of security and stability. The pattern of preemptively striking out reinforces their core negative sense of shame that creates a sense of failure and a feeling of incompetence in their relationships.

The girls had experienced trauma at the hands of their perpetrators (men), so they had found a way to strike back. Their ways of striking back, including having multiple relational partners and behaving in hypersexualized ways, did not lead them to feel empowered and autonomous in their abilities to engage in relationships. Rather, their behavior suggested that they were overcompensating because they were so eager for the approval of their female peers. This behavior was necessary because it was socioculturally appropriate for the girls to appear competent with the opposite sex. Seeking approval from peers is typical of teenagers, and it is consistent with emotional insecurity rather than security.

The girls tended to have similar experiences with the opposite sex. These experiences tended to excite them, but they also affected the girls' self-esteem. The girls also lacked father figures and so may have been searching for this connection through the men they encountered (who often only wanted sex).

Sadly, the girls may have learned that sexual energy was the only way they could hope to connect with men, me included. Furthermore, sexual behavior was emotionally safe. If the girls behaved in sexual ways with men and men responded in kind, there was no risk of intimacy. True intimacy with men was unknown and terrifying to them. Getting close to a man in a nonabusive, nonsexual way was unheard of in the girls' experiences. For this very reason, their work with me in the group was so important. They had the opportunity for a nonexploitative, nonsexual, and emotionally available and connected relationship with a man, possibly for the first time in their lives. I was a man who would neither respond to their sexual overtures nor shame them for their behavior. Ultimately, by neither encouraging nor discouraging their sexual behavior, I was boundary setting. I validated their experience and gave them the clear message that "it's not going to happen." Furthermore, I thought that, in some way, chastising the girls for being inappropriate might have led the girls to stop coming to the group.

This theory of the girls' sexual overtures having deeper, emotional undercurrents is supported by their evident, repeated strong efforts to connect with me rather than with Terri. The girls might have been trying to have some innocent fun and break the ice in strange and unfamiliar settings, a situation that I apparently invited by being a more active presence in the room. But the explanation for the girls' behavior was deeper and more subtle, and will be revealed in upcoming sessions.

FIVE

Week 8

Porsche, Shantel, and Dalanna

"I'm not gonna tell you again to take dat trash out!" thundered a voice through the hallway, nearly sending the pictures tumbling from the walls, pulling Porsche back to reality from daydreams of muscle-bound boys and block parties.

"Awright already! You ain't gotta be yellin' and shit!" Porsche yelled back through her closed bedroom door. Turning her head reluctantly away from the window and the dreams she watched in her mind, Porsche swung her long legs around the bedside and hopped down onto her heels. Irritably swinging her door open with a resounding thud as it bounced off the wall, she waited for a brief second for it to bounce back and caught it on the back swing, slamming it triumphantly behind her. This routine of hers had been honed over years of practice. She even knew the door's rhythm, knew how much force was necessary to throw it open so it would bounce back to her but not leave an imprint on the wall and thus earn a balling out from her aging aunt.

"And stop slammin' my god damn door! Lil' Bitch! An' another thang..." came the scolding Porsche knew she had coming to her. This game had grown somewhat enjoyable in its predictability. Her aunt continued on, but Porsche just blocked her out.

"Sorry," she answered, feigning apology. Briskly marching down the hall-way and picking up the trash bag on her way past the kitchen, she whizzed by her aunt perched in front of "The Jefferson's," which was blaring from the television, meandered around a great bloated body lounging on the floor, careful not to look at his bad skin and uncombed mop of hair as he lolled amongst his fast-food wrappers and soda cans. The hair mop likewise ignored her. Porsche also became aware that her mother was nowhere in sight. She smiled insolently to herself, her twin ponytails swaying back and forth as if pulled to and fro by her haughty indignation.

"...Sorry my ass! Lil' bitch I told you..." her aunt's tirade continued. Porsche could feel the anger rising, her face heating up, blood rushing. *You the bitch! Fuck, always gotta be on my case!! An' I ain't even do nothin'.*

"Tell momma I went to the sto'," Porsche called over her shoulder, doubling back for a moment to catch a fleeting glance of herself in the mirror by the door. *Cute as hell!* Swinging the front door open, she began to unlatch the black steel bars on the outside of the doorway. *Sheeit, kind of like I'm bustin' out of jail too.* Smiling to herself at the thought and catching the door on its rebound, she pushed it closed with her right hand while popping in the earpiece of her iPod with her left.

"Hold on a god damn minute, you..." her aunt began at the sound of the front door slamming shut. WHHHAAAMMMM!!! The slamming door now at Porsche's back muffled her aunt's bellowing. *"Things will never change, that's just the way it is..."* Tupac resounded in her ears. Porsche grinned to herself at the irony. *Amen!*

She stole an almost reluctant glance over her shoulder, sucking her teeth loudly and remembering her aunt's hideous countenance. *Damn she hella nasty! Ol' fat heffer!!* Smiling at her little private joke, bouncing down the front porch, she could still hear curses behind the two closed doors, but they were growing dimmer as the right earpiece of Porsche's iPod grew closer to its destination. But her dream of salvation was destined to be deferred.

"OOOHHH-WHHEEEE, wha's yo' name woman?" slobbered a hungry voice from a stumbling figure two houses down. Smiling a devil's grin of dark yellow teeth minus the front two, a man was sauntering Porsche's way, drunk, wearing jeans with holes, an army coat with a hundred stains, a wild Afro that looked as if it had never been washed or combed. Porsche scoffed at his disgusting appearance. *Uuuuuhhh mutha fucka! Hell nah'!!*

"Get yo' ass away from me befo' my daddy come out here an' kick yo' ass!" she hollered back disparagingly, shaking her head in revulsion. The stumbling, bumbling presence was now several steps behind her; this day was starting out pretty badly.

Sheeit, I wish I did have a daddy that'd take care a dat mutha fucka! The thought came a little close to home. She knew very little of her father.

He had disappeared upon hearing of her mother's pregnancy, nowhere to be found, never seen again. She had learned what little she knew from her aunt. *He wasn't no damn good!!! A bum!!!! An' yo' ass a be nex' if ya don't quit yo' selfish ways!!!* she used to say. *Bastard* this, *no good* that. And it hurt. Porsche hated her for talking that way. She refused to believe. *Sheeit, my daddy ain't no bum. Prob'ly he left 'cuz a you!!! Sheeit. Auntie you a bitch!! I leave too. Bet my daddy come back someday an' get me up outta here!!! He prob'ly handsome, got some cash on him, take me shoppin'.* The daydream of it was always comforting. The hoping and wishing sometimes could make all the difference. Maybe her daddy would come back, someday. She was often angry that he didn't, but was ready to defend him to the death if one day he did. *"Some things will never change, Never be the same..."* Tupac continued. Porsche found solace in his words. *Amen.* She barely recognized the crowd of young ladies she was now approaching—girls lounging, laughing, enjoying their day in front of a liquor store.

"What's up girl? Wha'choo doin'?" rang out a familiar voice. "Sheeit, Shantel, I'm jus' happy to be outta that fuckin' house!" Porsche scoffed, frowning off into the twilight.

Shantel turned in to face her more directly. "Yeah, me an' my sistas just kickin' it," she answered, motioning to the crowd around her. No response, no one looking her way. They were all lost in something elsewhere, talking amongst themselves, laughing, drinking, smoking, hair twisting, exchanging information on Apple Bottom jeans and where to get those bright orange and yellow hifee (richly and brightly contrasted) jackets. They were lounging comfortably and yet with a touch of boredom against the salmon-colored stucco walls of the liquor store.

"Yo' auntie talkin' shit again?" Shantel asked concernedly. *Fo' real, my girl always be havin' dat bitch talkin' shit. Fuckin' with her without fail!* Looking into Porsche's face as she asked her question, she figured out the answer for herself.

A bright green Monte Carlo with large gold rims suddenly interrupted. Creeping up along the sidewalk, its driver leering out the window, it caused a group of young women to snap to attention. Shantel and Porsche watched in earnest.

"I swear I wish my auntie was dead! And if she call me a bitch one mo' time, my nigga I swear!!!..." Porsche finished, her voice trailing off into an ominous ending.

"But hold up though. Don't eee-ven be tryin' to play da innocent," Shantel retorted knowingly, running a soft hand through long braids, warming to the occasion. "You be doin' toooooo' much, jus' ta piss her off too!"

Porsche grinned in concession. "Yeah…" staring off into the horizon, watching a police helicopter, or "ghetto bird" as they called it, chop-chop-chop through the clouds. A searchlight surveyed the streets, careening left and right. *Oooh, somebody done got into some shit!*

The excitement gradually began to fade. Porsche's attention returned to the horizon, beginning to grow orange and blue and yellow in twilight. *The X* was so beautiful at night. It always helped her think. And with her mind suddenly in the clear, Porsche remembered when things were different. They hadn't always been this way. Her aunt once seemed to care for her. Pushing her on the swings, quilting with her on the porch in the summer, fixing her hair. The thought made her want to cry. She felt so alone. Only her anger kept her whole.

"Dat bitch make me wanna, like, ooooohhh! She always be yellin', callin' me names…My nigga I swear to god!! I'm gonna whoop her ass one a' deez days! Feel me?!?!"

"Anyways," Shantel responded, having heard this idle threat many times before. *Sheeit she ain't 'bout 'a do nothin'! Her auntie whoop her ass!! She hella big. And she cold too. My girl need her family ta love her, not be callin' her names an' shit.*

But Shantel said no more on the subject because nothing more needed to be said. "Wha' you wanna do?" she probed absentmindedly, just taking notice that her sisters and the men in the Monte Carlo had gotten a little cozier. Her oldest sister was leaning in the window, her tightly wound braids pulled back in radical twists and turns. She was seductively working on a Tootsie Pop, rolling it around in her mouth. She was ready for work in her skintight black blouse cut low, hip-high Daisy Duke shorts, smiling, cajoling. Shantel eyed her knowingly. *Ooohhh, my sista spittin' some game on 'em. Wha's about ta be goin' on up in her?!* The thrill of what might be next was at once terrifying and exhilarating. She was wondering if they would be hopping in for a ride through the night, having been on rides like that before. Who knew where they would end up? Her other sisters were beginning to creep closer, millimeter by millimeter.

"Giiiiirrrllll, let's step an' see what's happ'nin'!" Shantel's second oldest sister invited from behind the eldest. Ducking around her so that she was in plain view of the Monte Carlo's two passengers and the driver, she heard the driver grunt approvingly as he nodded at her second-eldest sister. The eldest was scowling at being passed up in favor of her younger sibling.

"C'mon my niggas!!!" her sister exclaimed, beaming, showing her high cheek bones. "Y'all wanna kick it o' what?!?!"

"Hell yeah y'all!" a male voice from inside the Monte Carlo invited. "We got some weed, some drank, and so, you know, we gonna take care ya. C'mon ova' and get in."

Shantel and Porsche exchanged nervous, giddy smiles. Excited, afraid, and uncertain but in that first-date kind of way, where it was a dreamy, pleasant kind of exhilaration. They started toward the car.

"Whooooa! Hold up a second," protested the driver. "Y'all look a lil' young fo' grown folk bidness." Shantel's sisters laughed scornfully at their youngest.

"For real girl," her second-eldest agreed, with a lick of her full lips and a look over her youngest sister from head to toe. "Don't choo gotta do some homework o' some shit?" They all laughed, piling in the car while Shantel remained awkwardly on the curb. *Sheeit, das fucked up. Man, I can't wait 'till I'm grown. Can't do shit when you a child!*

"Yeah, y'all just go do wha' you do," advised Shantel's eldest with a dismissive hand and a snap of her neck to the left and right. Her long braids bounced as she slid herself delicately over the cracking, black leather seats of the Monte Carlo.

Porsche scowled indignantly. "Das cold as fuck." *Sheeit, dey think dey all dat. But dey ain't shit. Ride all busted up and ghetto. Sheeit, ain't nothin'. Matta fact, they ugly any damn way!!!*

A closing door, followed by a jingling bell, broke the momentary silence. From inside the corner liquor store emerged a man, frail more from experience than age. He had salt and pepper hair, a neat mustache, light, patchy skin, and he walked gingerly, peering out into the street through squinting eyes, dragging a broom behind him. Eyeing the Monte Carlo and its entourage suspiciously, he was looking toward Shantel and Porsche with grandfatherly concern.

"It's too late for girls like you to be out in here in deez streets!" he scolded with a wag of a stubby finger. "You go home to your parents and families." The rest of the crowd had now piled into the Monte Carlo and were lighting up this and that. Shantel smacked her lips insolently.

Porsche snorted. *As if dat shit dat jus' happen ain't enough! Now I gotta hear dis shit. Mutha fuckas need ta mind dey business!!* "Why ain't you up in der moppin' up that floor o' some shit?!?! You ain't my daddy!!" Porsche sassed back.

Shantel laughed nervously, but felt a little guilty. *Damn, my girl doin' tooooo much!!! I ain't neva gonna say all a that to a old man.*

The old man stepped closer. "You need to have some respect!" he remonstrated in outrage. "And some brains to see I'm tellin' y'all da truth! Leave all dat alone before it kills the whole lot a ya. Trust me lil' girls. You don't wanna buy whateva mutha fuckas like that sellin'. You hear?"

"Sheeit buy deez nuts, old ass nigga!!!" answered an uninvited male voice from inside the backseat of the Monte Carlo. All of the passengers started giggling and clapping their hands as the Monte Carlo's radio began to blare and the car pulled sharply off down the street.

Porsche and Shantel fought back laughter of their own, suddenly more aware that the old man was still standing there, very aware of them. He had gotten over the passengers' insults in the way that elderly do, age bringing them a sense of self that was not so easily undermined. Porsche and Shantel were a different story.

"Yeah, you right," Porsche replied mockingly, rolling her head at the neck and looking off down the distant main boulevard at Shantel's back, tugging her sleeve slightly in that direction. "C'mon girl. Time ta bounce!! Let's go see what dat ho Dalanna doin'."

"Young sisters respect yo' selves!" encouraged the old store owner.

Shantel smacked her lips and looked off into the night. The sun was almost all the way down and shadowy figures were heard whispering, were seen pointing, running back and forth across the streets, holding up their sagging pants. The night was growing livelier as each star appeared overhead. The girls could feel it. Taking a leisurely walk up the block, they walked past overturned garbage cans, heard a police car blaring past, saw a fight in a nearby alley. *The X* always came alive at night.

A brown paper bag blew across the cracked granite street, up and over the rumble of a Camaro engine mixed with blaring rap music. The girls were heading further down the block. A bottle shattered into pieces across the street as another police siren wailed off into the distance.

And as they rounded the next corner and made their way up the sidewalk toward the projects where Dalanna lived, the neighborhood became more alive. They heard what sounded like a thousand voices at once, each trying to shout over the other. Boom boxes blaring. A large crowd of onlookers in the courtyard before them. A woman the size of a vending machine pointing a jagged finger threateningly at another woman, equally volatile in her wide-hipped stance, fingers snapping high over her head. Necks rolling around in wide circles. A third woman was beginning to take off her shoe. Shantel and Porsche continued their walk, watching what would probably be a fight. They didn't look for too long, knowing that being caught staring could easily bring them right into the thick of it. Staring in *The X* was a call sign for a fight. Walking further through the courtyard, their minds were suddenly clear, free. Watching. Waiting. Men rolled dice alongside the wall as others around them laughed, yelled, cursed. Someone threw up on the lawn. More laughter, hands clapping.

"God damn! They be doin' tooooo much 'round here!" Porsche observed, shaking her head and beginning to imitate the old shopkeeper. "Fa' sho' be lotta livin' around here for some shit like: *dem streets go' kill ya! Do ya hear me talkin' to ya?!?!'"* Shantel burst out laughing, almost doubling over.

"Wit' his preaching ass! You feel me?!?!" Shantel agreed. She could almost sympathize with his best of intentions, knowing he meant no harm. But still she marveled at how ignorant old people could be, how ignorant they were as to what was going on out here! *Still singin' dat old shit… they ever gonna learn what time it is?!*

Dalanna's door seemed to appear out of nowhere, and Porsche was rapping on its steel screen with her palm.

"HELLO????" she hollered, pressing her face to the screen, attempting to infiltrate the barred door guard with the closed door just inside it.

"Damn girl, why you gots ta holler?" Shantel questioned in annoyance. *She loud! No wonder her auntie be pissed off all da damn time!* Shantel would never say this aloud. She knew full well that her girl was not the innocent she claimed to be.

Just then the door swung open. Dalanna's curious eyes were peering around the hinges, a disapproving eyebrow high on her forehead, her brow creased into a frown.

"Which one a y'all out hear yellin' on ma' stoop?!?!" Dalanna demanded snapping her fingers left and right.

"Who you think?!" Shantel volunteered.

"Mmmm-hhhmm," Dalanna agreed. "Keep it up an you a see my Puerto Rican!!!"

Porsche and Shantel started laughing. "Yo' Puerto Rican?!?!" Shantel inquired with an I-don't-believe-you smile.

"Yeah!" Dalanna insisted. "See my hair? How straight it be?!?! Das dat Puerto Rican up in my blood!!"

"Sheeit das dat hot comb on yo' head!!!" Porsche corrected, Shantel falling over herself, clapping her hands and laughing triumphantly.

Dalanna scowled off into the floor. "Whateva!! Y'all just don't know what y'all talkin' about! Feel me? I am Puerto Rican!!"

"Sheeit, my nigga, you black as hell!!!" Shantel chimed in. She and Porsche were now laughing hard again, slapping hands. "Talkin' 'bout *I'm a Puerto Rican.* Sheeit nigga please!!!"

Porsche was smiling in agreement, ready to take their joke further, but then suddenly she noticed the cold, the wind picking up, and she began shivering, wrapping her arms around her torso for warmth.

"Annnnny-ways, c'mon girl let us is in awready! Sheeit! It's cold as a motha fucka out hea!!" Porsche demanded. Sliding her way past Dalanna and making her way into the living room with Dalanna and Shantel in her shadow, Porsche closed the black steel door gate behind her.

The television blared for an audience of no one. Dishes were stacked high in the nearby kitchen sink. Shantel noted a small child looking up in wonder, as if seeing another human being for the first time. From the outside in, the place may have looked abandoned.

The girls began to make their way through the house—Porsche and Shantel in no particular rush, Dalanna impatiently hustling them along.

"C'mon y'all!" Dalanna beckoned, as if trying to sneak past a sleeping giant.

"Whassup my ladies!" came an excited yelping.

"Mama, please!" Dalanna cried in exasperation. The giant had been awoken.

"Hi," answered Porsche and Shantel politely, slightly taken aback. Not in a bad way, but caught a little off guard there in the hallway. Silence prevailed.

"Wha's hap'nin'?! What it do?!" Porsche questioned.

Confirming Dalanna's worst fears, her mother rose to the occasion. "I jus' be chillin'. Ya know like y'all. Got me a man, well, a man a two comin' on through da house." Shantel smiled shyly. *Damn! My girl mamma be stayin' busy fo' real though!!!* But there was something endearing about it. *Sheeit, betta den my momma though. Ain't got no love fo' me.* She saw Dalanna's jaw drop, trying to shepherd her mother away. Shantel began shaking her head, only making Dalanna more frantic, more exasperated. But Shantel shook her head for other reasons. *My girl ain't even knowin' how good she got it. Sheeit it be tight if my mama like dat.* Porsche idly began to play with her hair in a nearby vanity mirror.

"Mama, we gotta go now!" Dalanna piped up, grabbing her friends by the arms and yanking them towards her bedroom. As Porsche was pulled along, she couldn't help but to cluck in dismay. *Oooh if I talk to my auntie like dat... True, her mama doin' a lil' too much, but my girl gonna get whooped if she don' back it on up.*

"Damn girl wha's wrong wi'choo?" Dalanna's mother retorted, bouncing at the hip in her cut-off Daisy Duke shorts. "Somebody been without a man a lil' too long!"

Dalanna nearly jumped out of her skin, too shocked to be angry. Porsche and Shantel *ooohh'd* and giggled as Dalanna quivered in rage, frozen in disbelief. She stood staring at her mother's sassy posture. Her mother remained, looking her daughter up and down with a daring, contemptuous arch in her back.

"MAMA YOU GOT SOME NERVE, I..." Dalanna hollered with a hand held high over head and a stern finger pointing down at her mother's lack of shame.

"NOW HOLD ON A GOD DAMN MINUTE!" Dalanna's mother roared. "YOU BES'A THINK TWICE BEFO' RAISIN' YO' VOICE TO ME IN MY GOD DAMN HOUSE! DON'T DISRESPECT ME AGAIN!"

Shantel and Porsche nervously fumbled, looking away, wishing there was somewhere else to go. Dalanna was outraged. "DISRESPECT? DISRE-SPECT? IS DAT WHA'CHOO SAID?" Shantel and Porsche were cautiously edging their way back, knowing all hell was soon to bust loose. "WHA'S UP WI'CHOO COMIN' 'ROUND ACTIN' LIKE YOU OUR AGE? 'Wha's up girl' dis an' 'wha's crackin' dat. MAYBE YOU GET SOME RESPECT WHEN YOU RESPECT YO' SELF!" A silence after thunder. Dalanna's mother's eyes were narrowing as she took a menacing step forward.

WHHHAAAAAAMMMMM! Dalanna's thin frame was slammed into the wall. RIP!!! BHHAAAAMMMM! The collar of her shirt was ripped by her mother's lightening fast hand, then came a deafening crack of a fist pounding against her face.

Cringing in agony, Shantel ducked into Porsche's shoulder, pulling hard on her sleeve, making her way for the door while pulling her friend along in her shadow. "OOOHHH girl, we out!" Shantel commanded.

With a few long, unbridled steps, they flew through the living room to the door, the television still blaring, the child on the floor wailing, lost, alone, frightened. Heart racing, breathing in hard, rapid gulps, Porsche lunged for the brass doorknob while Dalanna's mother blasted away in the background. Shantel and Porsche could hear the merciless thuds of fist and foot hitting flesh. Dalanna was screaming, begging for her mother to stop. The baby was crying even harder still. Tears were streaming down his little cheeks.

Shantel stopped at the door just before she escaped. Her eyes locked on the baby's. The baby seemed to be pleading with her, "Take me with you." Shantel almost did just that. *Can't jus' leave you!! Das fucked up. I ought to take you home with me. Me and Darrell raise you. You be my child.*

WHAM!!! BHAM!!! resounded the opening and slamming of a bedroom door.

"AND DON'T EVEN THINK 'BOUT COMIN' OUT FO' DA REST A' DA NIGHT! SHEEIT LIL' BITCH!! DAS A RAP. AN' NEX' TIME…" her mother raged on.

"GIRL C'MON WE OUT!!!!" Porsche pleaded, pulling Shantel hard by the sleeve, dragging her out the last stretch of hallway and back out onto the porch, closing the door frantically behind them.

Both breathed deep sighs of relief as they hurriedly made their way down the cracked gray slab of porch outside. Huddling close together for the semblance of safety it afforded them, they were both still able to hear muffled yells and bellows from inside.

The resuming chaos of *The X* was almost comforting, drowning the fallout from what had just happened. Still, images of their girl lying helpless inside lingered on.

The X was going full blast. Dice slapping up against a nearby graffiti-laden wall. Small children skipping over a patch of blacktop. A group of young women smoking, laughing. An old woman in a rocking chair. A homeless man pushing a shopping cart, growling something unintelligible at a passing garbage can. These were their streets. At least they knew what they would do. Dalanna and her mother were not so predictable. Shantel and Porsche walked back across that courtyard, solemn, brooding, resentful. "Man her mamma don't got no right to be whoopin' her like dat," Shantel whimpered, her slight and beautiful face frowning hard in sadness.

Porsche readily agreed, nodding her head hard and smacking her lips. "Feel me!?!?! I done heard dat shit down da hall. I mean, feel me? She ain't just slap her up an' shit. But, feel me? Her mama done whooped her ass like a mutha fucka!"

Shantel said nothing, beginning to feel a sense of sorrow, futility. *Man, maybe there was somethin' I shoulda done? Like, instead a' just walkin' out, leavin' my girl all laid up like dat.*

"See I ain't one ta put hands on my mama," Porsche proclaimed. "But if da bitch come at me foul like dat?! . . . Sheeit I'd be all over her ass!"

Shantel looked away, disagreeing but not really wanting to argue. *I don't know. My mama slap me like once o' twice, an' it ain't no thang. But I ain't neva hit her back. But den what 'bout Dalanna gettin' her ass whooped an' shit? I mean, she just supposed to be lyin' der an' ain't doin' nothin'?!*

Porsche was not the type to go looking for a fight, having learned along the way that she could fight just as hard with her sharp tongue and quick mind. She did not want to be known for "going ghetto" as they would say. But she wasn't going to get "punked out" either. At the end of the day, she could go toe to toe with the best of them. More often than not, when Porsche came out swinging, she came out on top. Remembering her lessons from church, never forgetting, "An eye for an eye, a tooth for a tooth." Words to live by.

"Hold up!" A hushed voice broke through the darkness from across the courtyard, as if the person it belonged to was trying hard not to be seen. A hobbling frame was making its way over the grassy plain and past the playground, spitting obstinately on the sidewalk, face hidden in the shadows. A helicopter was still fluttering overhead, spotlight searching the ground from left to right, passing over the approaching stranger in the courtyard before veering off.

"Damn girl!" Shantel exclaimed. *Das my girl Dalanna? Fo' real?!* Normally so vivacious, Dalanna was barely recognizable. Her face was lowered as she came limping along, slumped at the shoulders. A shadow of her former self. Shantel and Porsche waited in grim solidarity, waiting, watching, agonizing, wanting to shut their eyes.

Finally, Dalanna made it to their side. "I ain't neva goin' back der!" she declared, quivering in rage, her voice shaking, hollow. Shantel gasped as she got a good look at her girl.

Dalanna had an ugly gash across her neck, a swollen lump of what was left of her right eye. Gingerly limping, trying not to put too much weight on her left side, she was fighting back tears, biting hard into her inner cheek, choking back the taste of blood and her desire for vengeance. The physical pain from biting her mouth was growing, but Dalanna preferred it to her invisible scars. The deeper, scalding emotional pain of what had just happened to her was much more gut-wrenching. Although she tried hard to bury it deep inside her, her girls felt it with her, heard the tears she wouldn't cry, dearly wanted to cry with her. But none of them would give in to their tears. Shantel and Porsche wished there was something they could do to make it all better, but they knew there was nothing. Only the solitary comfort of marching at her side was in order. To Dalanna, nothing could be more comforting in this darkest of hours. Togetherness was everything.

So they walked, distancing themselves from the ugly scene, slowly making their way through the remainder of the courtyard that was long and wide as a football field, across the deadened grass and blackened concrete. As they strode along, each searched for words. The silence was long and harrowing. Shantel wished she had something soothing, something relieving, to say. Finding nothing and deeply angered at this nothing, they watched the rapidly darkening horizon, the sky growing from oranges and yellows to blues and purple. Awe-inspiring, but solemn and grim. Shantel noted Dalanna's backpack over her shoulder, stuffed to the brim.

"Damn girl yo' mama fucked up!" Porsche announced as they continued to make their way back up the block. Unlike earlier, they marched in short, choppy steps that seemed to drag with the weight of the world. A white Astro van cruised by packed with men whistling, cat calling, blaring rap music. Two boys were leering out the windows. But the girls' minds were elsewhere.

"Where you gonna go?" Shantel inquired softly, again noticing Dalanna's backpack, almost not wanting to know her answer. *Maybe she could stay at my place. Yeah? Maybe? Nah, my mama kill me!!! Maybe, like, um, fuck...* Shivering slightly in the night air, she pulled her puffy white jacket tighter around her shoulders. It was going to be a cold night. The thought of Dalanna alone in the world made it colder.

"Don't matter," Dalanna murmured softly. The rumbling of an engine in the distance was growing closer; a purple Cadillac with thin-spoked gold rims and white-wall tires was soon passing idly by. It lurched abruptly, pulled up alongside the girls, its tail end still darting out into the street as the driver had put it in park. Three quick blasts from the horn.

"Whas' up y'all? What's happ'nin'?" the driver invited, leaning heavily over the passenger seat to get a better look. Shantel was the first to look up, startled, scared, waiting in grim anticipation.

Another lecherous beep of the horn, the hulking form from inside leaning over further still in starving determination. He smiled widely, pinching his scruffy mustache, spewing foul breath. They noted his dark, rich-colored patchwork complexion. Porsche looked away. *Damn!!! He a ugly ass nigga!!*

Shantel hugged her torso, stared off into the distance. *C'mon jus' leave us alone!!!*

They began exchanging furtive glances, wishing he would just get lost.

"Nothin', wha' choo doin?!?!" Dalanna answered. The other girls' jaws dropped as Dalanna sidestepped around them in a half circle, discretely brushing her hair over the left side of her face while pulling the collar of her coat around her neck.

Her girls seeing right away what she was up to were fighting furiously to deny it. *She couldn't be serious!!! Couldn't be!!!*

The driver peered up at Dalanna, now leaning slightly into the interior of the Cadillac. She was huddling over just close enough to be visible but was still far enough away to make an attempt to hide her wounds from tonight's war, wounds that were now purple and hideous.

"Oohh its cold! Just scrubbed and fell on da street like a motha fucka too!" Dalanna supplied before he had a chance to speak up. She was hoping her flirtatious giggle and leaning over just enough to expose her breasts would keep his attention elsewhere. At first it did. Stealing a long look down her shirt, his eyes finally returned to her face.

"Damn shorty!" The driver was frowning as he peered over a little closer. Then suddenly he snapped his head back violently as if it pained him to look. "You must have fallen somethin' terrible to go out like dat! How 'bout choo step in da 'Lac and we a' see what we could do 'bout makin' you feel betta?!'"

Porsche smacked her lips hard. "Oooohh nu-uh," she exclaimed, tugging at Dalanna's arm. "C'mon now, we out. THANK YOU SIR!!!"

Shantel eagerly took a step away. *Ooohh fo' real get da fuck away from us!!! Hella old!! Tryin' ta pick up on lil' kids like us!! Man, das fucked up. Just go, sheeit.*

But Dalanna yanked her arm sharply back, giving Porsche that hard "go away" look, arching her back so that her rear said hello.

"Mmmm-hmmmm, whoooo-weeeee!!! Now das what I'm talkin' about," the driver croaked approvingly.

Once Dalanna had given him just enough of a look to whet the appetite, she spun back around to face him. "Yeah, I'm feelin' dat!" she agreed. She swallowed hard, bracing herself for what she was soon to be up against. She was trying to smile, as if to tell herself that everything was all right. They all looked at one another, searching.

"Guess I got somewhere ta go," she decreed.

Porsche and Shantel gasped, panicked, had to do something. They felt flustered.

Before they knew it, the Cadillac's passenger side door was swinging open. Dalanna had slung her backpack into the back and closed the door behind her.

She shrank back into the seat as if to become invisible. The driver, smiling in cracked-mouth glee, triumphantly thrust his arm around her shoulder, hand just above her breast, far too close for comfort. The Cadillac pulled off down the street, the rumble of the engine cranking up to a roar. Dalanna and the driver began to make small talk. He tried to be gentle and sweet, but his groping hands betrayed his real intentions.

And as the Cadillac began to find its way to away from it all, Dalanna became suddenly aware. Her smile slackened as she looked out the window and into the rearview mirror. Now that her girls were growing further from sight, she was regretting what was about to happen.

She watched out the passenger side window, breathing a heavy fog into it, almost as if to camouflage her friends' eyes trying to burn sense into her head. She wanted to cry, but wouldn't, maybe couldn't. After that night, she never cried again.

Rona

Staring hard, Rona was enthralled, eyes glued forward as if she were hypnotized. Not two feet in front of her nose, Shakira was working on her latest video. Bouncing hips, rolling washboard abs, beautifully woven braids slapping across her face as she twisted and twirled like the ballerina of hip-hop. The male dancers in the background seemed to vie to get closer. Her milk chocolate skin, hour-glass figure, and blinding white teeth made Rona turn green with envy. She watched, riveted, scowling. *She hecka cute. What I do ta deserve dis?* Shakira danced in Apple Bottom jeans and a skintight black belly shirt. *Sheeit I could neva wear somethin' like dat.* Visualizing herself in that outfit now, remembering what happened one day when she wore a more form-fitting shirt to school. A boy in her English class had pinched the side of her overflowing stomach roll, making a joke about Rona having a "muffin top." *Neva could wear somethin' like dat!*

"Baby you wanna slice of pie?" invited an endearing female voice from inside the kitchen.

"Mama I need ta go on a diet," Rona announced.

"Says who?!?!" her mother replied nearly in outrage. It was the first time she had heard her daughter say such a thing. She began wondering, in a mother's way of already knowing, if something else was going on. Not a petite woman herself, Rona's mother prided herself on standing tall, saw herself as a black, strong, proud, full-figured, *and* beautiful woman. Dutifully busy in the kitchen, cutting herself a piece of pie and halfway reaching for a second plate, she closed the refrigerator door and peered around the kitchen cabinets into the living room where her young daughter lay in wait.

"Child, where you come up with dat idea? Diet!" she inquired scornfully. "I'm tired a' hearin' all this looooose weight shit goin' 'round. Fo' who?!?! Fo' what? Le'mme tell you somethin'. You can be big an' beautiful at the same time. Hear me?" Rona nodded as her mother continued. "Jus' mo' ta love," she finished, shaking her pillowy sides for emphasis. Rona smiled good-naturedly, eyeing her mother in her arching heels, long, flowing black dress pants, a silk sweater, and stylish gold bracelets with a matching necklace. Her shoulder length hair was freshly straightened, makeup immaculate.

"So who sayin' all dat 'bout loooose weight anyway?" her mother inquired skeptically, a stern hand squared on her left hip, the other leveling a pie-drenched knife at her daughter in front of the television.

"Says who? Says me!" blustered Tyrone, suddenly appearing out of nowhere. He weaved sluggishly down the hall and into the kitchen, his mid-length Afro wild and unruly, his shirt and jeans stained red and brown as if he had spent the afternoon rolling around in the yard. Without looking up at either Rona or her mother, he ducked his head deep into the refrigerator, swinging its door right into Rona's mother, just hard enough to hurt a little, and pretended not to notice. "Damn lazy bitches!! Eat too much and ya talk too much! Time beez a comin' to start takin' care of yo man an' ya damn self!"

Rona snapped her head to the left in an arching circle, left eyebrow arched. She smacked her lips hard in revulsion. "First of all, you don't need to be hittin' my mama with the door cuz you ought 'a be lookin' where you goin'!" Rona growled in anger, pointing a pudgy finger at his sorry sight huddled halfway into the refrigerator like a raccoon in a garbage can. "An' matta fact," she continued, voice rising to the elementary stages of a roar, smacking her lips loudly for emphasis, "speakin' of lookin', look at you!!! With yo' know nothin' ass! No job, no muscle, no comb for yo' damn hair. Talkin' about take care a somebody, sheeit! Who you takin' care of?!?!" Yeah, it felt good to say that. But as soon as it came out, a wave of terror began to set in. *Damn, what I jus' done?!?!*

BOOM!!!! The refrigerator door slammed with vigor, the ominous sound of heavy feet stomped closer, just close enough to let it be known that one wrong word could mean serious repercussions.

"I DON'T NEEEEED NO LECTURE FROM NO BITCHES UP IN HEA' TALKIN' 'BOUT HOW I RUN SHIT UP IN MY HOUSE!" Tyrone thundered. The religious statuettes along the counter and framed family photos along the walls rattled. Rona's ears were ringing as she retreated to the living room, trembling.

A long, terrifying silence. Tyrone standing in the hallway between the kitchen and living room. With pale red eyes from countless nights of liquor and rage, fist clenched, he sensed Rona's fear and scoffed righteously.

"Yeah," he proclaimed gleefully, "das what I thought. But you' gettin' a lesson dis time. Young punks bes' have some discipline."

Watching him take a step further into the living room, his eyes glazed over, Rona's mother saw two minutes into the future in a split second.

"Hey-hey, no, hold on a..." her mother protested, taking a long, determined step between her boyfriend and her daughter. Her outstretched arm lavishly draped in gold bracelets and rings stretched all the way out like a barricade. Rona instantly felt her fear beginning to dissipate.

But Tyrone was relentless. Scowling menacingly, he grabbed Rona's mother by the neck of her blouse and flung her into the counter, her head bouncing hard off the overhanging wooden kitchen cabinet. The pots and pans hanging underneath rattled violently, clanking and clattering against one another, some falling to the floor. Her eyes wide with terror, arms up and bent at the elbows so as to deflect further onslaught, she cried out. "No, no, please!" she wailed. Tyrone was rearing back to gather strength for another blow, eyes dead and determined. Now Rona's own rage overpowered her.

"NUH UH!" she screamed, "Get off my mama!" Tearing off into the kitchen, leaping to her mother's defense, all nails and teeth, she began scratching, pounding on him with fists like hammers. At first, this caught Tyrone off guard; he glanced to and fro, lost and confused. Then realizing where the onslaught was coming from, he countered, snarling like a beast. Raising a dark, muscular arm, he clenched Rona's throat, squeezing the life out of her. She gasped and gulped for air, tried to fend him off, tried to peel away his fingers. But he was far stronger and his drunken rage knew no bounds. Rona was beginning to get dizzy, was sinking to the ground, writhing in agony. But then the death grip around her throat relented. Suddenly, she could breathe again. Gasping, crawling, back to her feet, she was running, terrified.

Inside her room, she sobbed beneath the covers. She stayed this way for a long while, the throbbing around her throat gradually slowing down. After a while, her mind cleared. How long had she been under those covers?

The squeaking of her door sent shock waves through her body. Cowering in fear, hugging her pillow tightly over her ears, hearing her heartbeat thump in her head. *Jus' leave me and mama alone. PLEASE!!!*

"Baby c'mon," uttered a soft, female voice through the darkness. A gentle form nuzzled up alongside Rona's crouched body under a thick layer of pillows and sheets and blankets. She felt the soft, soothing motherly fingers across her back, assuaging her fears. Was she safe again?

Gradually Rona unearthed herself from the covers. Seeing that her mother had cleaned herself up, had on a change of clothes, was making her best effort to smile although her eyes were red and darkened, she felt helpless.

"How 'bout we get you over ta yo' daddy's house where you can cool out fo' da night?" her mother suggested. Rona nodded in solemn agreement, wiping the weariness from her face. Sitting upright for what felt like the first time in her life, her whole body was aching. Sweeping the covers from her body, she stopped cautiously. *Where he at now?*

Her mother sensed her fear. Taking her instinctively by the hand, she guided her past the snoring figure deep in slumber. Rona breathed a sigh of relief. *Good, he sleepin'.* But both stepped gingerly, petrified of what would happen should he awake.

His snores were deep and long. He was asleep. *Prob'ly drunk*, Rona concluded. And so mother and daughter had their opportunity to escape from their home. Shuffling out of the bedroom and down the hallway, stopping momentarily to flick off the still blaring television in the bedroom, Mother and daughter went hand in hand out the front door, latching it noiselessly behind them. Clinging closely to her mother's side, Rona was relieved to return to the world outside. The cold night air felt liberating. For a moment, they basked in it, breathed in deeply, safe outside.

They made their way down past the front lawn and to the car in the driveway, a battered blue Ford Taurus with rotting tires. Good enough to take them away. Anything to escape that horror of a man. Rona looked forward to her father's house, which felt like paradise on earth. She imagined his strong hands, big smile. Surely he would have something to say about this. *Maybe he even come back an' kick dat foo's ass!!!*

Rona and her mother got in the car alertly, looking around, aware that they were vulnerable. Their neighborhood was known for carjackings and muggings. Two women in the middle of the night were the easiest of targets.

Folding her arms tightly around her torso and staring hard through the windshield, past the chainlink gate that led into the backyard, Rona stared off into nothing. "I'm gonna kill dat mutha fucka?!?!" she proclaimed, left leg beginning to tap up and down furiously. "Momma we need ta bounce!!! I know you ain't gonna stay with him?!"

Her mother said nothing as she started up the engine, heard its creaking and jolting to life as if it were painful to shift into reverse. Her brow creased into a deep frown, lips pursed. Silence prevailed.

Rona smacked her lips despairingly, leaning back in resignation. A sudden rumbling engine of a passing Cadillac and blaring rap music diverted her attention. There was a familiar face in the passenger seat. *Dalanna!* But something was wrong; it was written all over her face, which had that long, empty, sorrowful look of someone who was trying to turn invisible out of shame. *What happen at her eye? Who dat she with?* Rona almost didn't want to know.

As they drove on in silence, Rona collected her thoughts. *Dat motha fucka! Hit my mama! Den he try ta choke me out!?!?! I'm a tell my daddy an' he gonna fuck him up.* She smiled cruelly at the thought. Vengeance would be good. *Yeah!!! I'm gonna tell my daddy!!! My daddy . . .* She began remembering when she was little, the Sundays in church, the family dinners, laughing, complaining about work, sweet potato pie. *Why daddy gotta leave anyway?!?!* She often wondered this. Her father had packed his bags and left one night. She and her mother had returned home early from a mother–daughter night of dinner and a terrible movie. They found Rona's father on the couch, scrambling to his feet and pulling a blanket around his naked body while a strange woman likewise sought to cover herself. Rona had been ordered to her room. She heard screaming, hollering, the snap-snapping of suitcases, bitter cries and accusations, curses, the slamming of the front door. This time, it was for good; her father was never coming home again.

"Baby I know you still mad and so am I, but I just . . . He's under lot's a pressure an' . . ." her mother started to explain, fighting for her words, trying to sound like she believed what she was saying, like there was a reason other than how much she loved Tyrone.

Rona's eyes leapt from their sockets as she retorted in perplexed exasperation. "Mama please! He don't even do shit!!! And besides that?" Smacking her lips for emphasis. "He don't need to be puttin' his hands on you, an' me neither!"

Her mother breathed heavily through her nose, pursed her lips hard, and frowned as if she were searching for a way to reinforce her position. He just had a bad night and was a little stressed out; but the words wouldn't come, no matter how hard she searched. Nervously looking into the rearview mirror, she settled on keeping herself busy with driving, buying herself more time.

Finally she tried again. "I know sugar, but try to undastand," she pleaded, straightening herself high in her seat, raising her voice, as if trying to prepare herself for what she was about to say. "I's hard out der fo' men deez days. Tryin' ta find a job, raisin' children at da same time."

Rona snorted in disbelief, shook her head in disdain. "I know you' not talkin' about him!" she replied with a wave of her outstretched hand in a half circle. "He ain't been lookin' fa' no job?!?! And who' kids he takin' care of??? He a bum!"

Rona's mother tried unsuccessfully to fight off a smile. "Girl! Don't talk like dat!"

"He is!" Rona insisted. "Like them foo's standin' out front the liquor store." She hunched over at the shoulders, closed one eye, loosely shook her outstretched hands. *"Was' yo' name lil' gurl, you gosh'um change?"*

Her mother howled hysterically, unable to contain herself. "Ooooh nu-uh, girl, you ain't right!" Her daughter could be really funny. Still, she had to make her point.

"But for real," her mother continued, regaining her composure. "I need you to try ta undastand what's up wit' all a' this. He's a lil' drunk an' I'm sure he didn't mean it. I'll talk to him when I get home, an' by da time you come back tomorrow afta schoo', it a be all good again."

Rona shifted her attention to the house up ahead. *Damn! That was hella fast!*

There it was, the little white house with the freshly shingled brown roof surrounded by a freshly clipped lawn. Her father's black Mercedes gleamed in the moonlight. Paradise in the ghetto.

"Goodnight baby," her mother murmured softly, staring deeply off into the night.

"I love you mama," Rona answered with a thick exhale, placing a comforting arm around her mother's warm shoulder, her outstretched hand finding its place in the small of her back. Letting go of their embrace almost reluctantly, it was as though they had both taken a moment to be thankful not just for each other, but for the fact that they had survived.

Rona unlatched the car door, closed it, and waved goodbye to her mother. The Taurus pulled off down the street, and Rona felt a sudden wave of calm.

She made her way to the front door, past the well-manicured lawn, onto the porch with the swinging chair, remembering how she and her father used to swing together in one just like it in their backyard, back when they were all together. One of her most bittersweet memories was falling asleep in her father's arms. The thought made Rona smile as she rapped on the front door with its iron clasp carved into a lion's head.

The door swung open, almost abruptly, as if company were not expected.

"Um, hi daddy," Rona muttered. He was holding a towel around his waist. He must have just come from a spa; he smelled like oil and lotion. There was a slight trickle of sweat along his brow and well-muscled neck and shoulders; his usually perfectly ridging hair waves seemed a bit frizzy and unruly, as if he had just come back from a long run.

"He-Hey now," he replied tentatively, patting Rona on the head like a dog. Rona shifted nervously on the porch. A door from inside the house squeaked open as a trail of light flowed down the hallway. A half-naked woman appeared just inside, a matching towel around her body. She started to tap her long fingernails on the bedroom doorway and then cleared her throat just loud enough to be noticeable.

Rona leaned slightly around her father to get a better look. The woman in the doorway was a blond-haired white lady, young, thin-framed, attractive, obviously perturbed. Rona's father looked back, then returned his attention almost reluctantly to Rona, ushering her in but to the far right as if trying to conceal her from his upstairs guest of honor. He closed the door quietly behind them.

"What's happ'nin' baby?" he inquired concernedly, if a bit loudly.

"You wouldn't believe it daddy! Me and momma was in the kitchen when..." Rona rushed to explain, barely able to get the words out fast enough. So eager to tell. *Yeah!! Watch!!! I'm gonna tell daddy an' then he gonna fuck dat mutha fucka up!!!*

"Oh, no, hunny, I wasn't talking to you," her father interjected, staring frantically off down the hallway into the light. He seemed impatient. The woman also seemed impatient as she shifted her weight, tilted her head, and widened her gaze.

"Listen, glad to see you. You know it's late. How 'bout you get some shut eye and tell me about it in the morning, okay?" her father stammered. "It's late. You get some sleep and we'll talk tomorrow." He patted her on the shoulder and made his way back to the bedroom, clutching the towel tightly around his waist.

Rona watched him make a bee-line back to the bedroom and noted the voice of Marvin Gaye blaring from the stereo. The living room was left almost totally dark.

"Goodnight daddy," she murmured softly.

Venus

Cars whizzed by on the long stretch of two-lane road. The street lights over-head cast down an eerie yellow glow. A bus was rolling to a stop, its engine idling, spewing forth the odor of gasoline. It left behind a withered old woman in a grey overcoat and black bonnet who decided to stand behind a green bench that advertised the ease of "adopting a foster kid," as if kids had become pets.

Venus took it all in quickly. She was waiting impatiently, waiting too long for a pretty teenage girl used to boys and men of all ages and types racing to her side, ready to wait hand and foot on her every need. She stood tapping her foot in its $200 shoe. Soon there came a group of boys in gold jewelry, sports jerseys, and baggy jeans making their way across the street. Venus smiled to herself in satisfaction. *Sheeit, dey ain't even cute. Oh well, fuck it. He should have been on time any damn way!!*

After having gone through a lot of trouble to get to where she was, Venus was determined to make the most of her night. She had lied to her parents about being at Shantel's studying. She was already out a half an hour past curfew, and they had surely called Shantel's house by now. She was certain to get it later. *Mama's gonna be pissed! Well, sheeit don't matter now do it? I'm gonna be punished any damn way. Might as well go on an' have a ho' night firs' thang!!!* Noticing the not-so-cute boys getting ever closer, now mere yards away, she looked down the street in the other direction. *Sheeit, where Jerome ass at anyway? Niggas always be late an' shit. He lucky he fine as fuck. An' he betta have some money, take me shoppin' o' somethin'!!!*

"What's happ'nin' lil' ma?" purred a male voice through the darkness, attempting a deep pitch but the crack in it betraying a recent journey through puberty. He smiled widely, exposing gold teeth with *Playa* written across the front. Wearing a baggy Dallas Mavericks basketball jersey and sagging pants, he was one of three guys equally decked out in gangster baggies. All of them eyed Venus up and down, feet to her face, lingering in particular places.

Venus smiled back innocently. "Whassup…" She made as if to walk toward them but turned at the last minute in the opposite direction, having spied the SUV coming up behind her. "Jerome!!" she called. She smiled wide, enjoying the little joke she had had at the expense of the three. *Ha-ha!!! Sheeit, ugly ass niggaz thought I was tryin' to holla at 'em!?!?! Crazy!!! Sheeit, nigga please!!!*

The crowd that had been pursuing her went scowling off into the distance, muttering bitterly amongst themselves. Venus was really enjoying herself now, smirking quietly. *Nah-nah hold up y'all, I ain't done with y'all yet. Don't start trippin'.* She arched her back sturdily so that she could bend slightly over and gaze into the passenger side mirror.

"DAMN!!!" One of the boys on the corner exclaimed. "Dat right der like two midgets up in a gym bag!!" and they all laughed uproariously.

Venus feigned outrage. "Sheeit, nuh-uh boy please!!!" she spouted, still smiling just enough to let them know she kind of liked it.

She could feel Jerome's eyes burning through the side of her head, his irritable scowl. Now she was no longer just enjoying herself, but really enjoying herself. She smacked her lips in satisfaction. *Sheeit, serve dat nigga right fa' makin' me wait all damn night!!!* She took a long look into her hand mirror, gazing approvingly at her freshly cropped braids, pulling them back over her right shoulder, then her midriff black blouse, smiling triumphantly. *Man, I just be too damn cute fa' all a' these mutha fuckas out here. They ain't even deservin' me tanight!!* Finally, she opened the passenger side door to Jerome's black Cadillac Escalade. Climbing up into the seat and closing the door behind her, she was already beginning to miss the little show she had put on there on the street corner that she had turned into a stage. *Mens in da X jus' be too damn easy ta fuck wit'.*

But Jerome was in no mood for fun and games. "Who was dey?" he growled.

Venus dismissed him with arched eyebrows and a quick answer. "Nobody. Just some foo's tryin' to mack on me prob'ly." All the same, she enjoyed feeling their eyes still on her, knowing without even looking that the boys on the corner were still waiting, still looking. She loved that feeling of being so wanted, so desired.

"Bes' be nobody," Jerome mustered with a cool insistence. "Ain't nobody else out der fa' you girl. I'm yo' friend, yo' father, an' yo' confidant. All you need baby!"

Venus tried hard not to laugh, sinking back into her seat, aloof, weary. *Mmm-hmm, friend, father, an' confidant huh? Dis nigga soun' like a 50 Cent lyric, sheeit.* Not that she didn't appreciate the effort. Continuing to calculate her next moves, she watched her man without watching him, wondering, fearing, expecting. Becoming more and more adept at moving her pawns on the chess board, she had learned the game well from her sisters of the night, the game of girls and boys and how to play it.

She realized that boys, men, or something in between will tell you anything to get what they want and they'll do whatever they think it takes to get there. *Monkeys want dey bananas,* the girls used to chortle amongst themselves. The trick for them was to make the boys think they're going there and yet to give up nothing. Well, not unless he's really cute. Then, maybe. But not until you hit payday first. But you have to play your cards right. Can't get lost in the feeling. Can't get caught up in waiting for something good to happen, because it wasn't going to. Not in *The X.* They even used to brag about it.

X Men, as they called themselves, were notorious and even proud of their cheating, their lying, their many girlfriends at once, stealing from women, pimping young girls to older tricks, the list went on. They were notorious and relentless. As Venus had learned from her sisters of the night, the women who ran and hustled and drank and fought in the streets right alongside the men, men were manageable: *Be true to the game, and the game will be true to you.* It confused her to hear them say that one day and then hear others say, *Don't hate the player, hate the game.* It didn't make sense. *They sayin', I'm 'posed ta be true to da game den I'm 'posed ta hate da game?!?! That's some contra-dictin' ass shit!!!* Prudently holding her tongue, she silently promised herself that she would let Mrs. Trenton, her English teacher, know she had used one of their vocabulary words, albeit only in her mind. And it felt right!!!

And, after a while, so did the game. The game, an all-encompassing world of drugs and guns, boys and girls, hustles, drinking, fighting, gang warfare, ran the streets and would for eternity.

As Jerome pulled the Escalade off the curb and began to speed down the block with the stereo blaring, Venus took a moment to reflect. *Da game, da game. . .* smiling. . .*sheeit sound like a rap!!!* Venus remembered her favorite rapper Too Short once saying, "*get while the getting is good.*" That fit Jerome. Not yet 20, he was what was considered to be fully loaded with an impressive ride, fine clothes, gold teeth, and no formal job experience at all. He had never had a steady girlfriend either. Jerome was cute and even a little sweet at times, but a dog just like the rest, Venus figured. He had hit on two of her closest friends just the last week. She knew this because she and her girls told each other everything. But he didn't know that she knew. She would not bother to bring it up. He would only lie.

Knowing such things sometimes made her sad, sometimes lonely, but not hopeless. She dreamed that just once a boy would call her just to talk, tell her he missed her, even tell her he loved her. "I just wanna hold you, baby," he'd say. Maybe they would even go off and get married like on the soaps. Those pretty dresses and smiling little girls throwing flowers. The thought of it sounded wonderful, and the feeling sometimes took her breath away.

Then she woke herself up. Her girls had taught her well. Oh yes, the boys would say all those pretty words, smile big, buy you something nice, promise you the world. For years, women believed it, wanted to believe it. They always told themselves it would be different this time. They were waiting around, heartbroken, broke, played for the fool time and time again.

Once your man had a night with you, you'd be pregnant and he'd be up the block laughing with his boys about how you better go down to the welfare office and sign up to make the Cal Works public assistance program the father.

The Escalade was now speeding down the boulevard. Jerome was glaring and glowering at passing cars and drivers to his left and right, showing Venus who was boss, or at least trying hard to convince her. Venus pretended not to notice, but the authority of it excited her.

She had also learned to play it cool. *Keep your cards close to your chest,* her girls had taught her. *Let 'em know you like 'em, but not too much. They'll only use it against you.* Venus knew the rules of the game well; she learned them, honed them, mastered them, practiced them.

"So you all I need huh?" Venus probed over the blare of 2Pac's latest jam. She stole a quick look Jerome's way, nonchalantly, just long enough to size him up, to get a good look, returning quickly to looking out the window. *Oooooohhh he hecka cute!!*

"Das right girl, all you need!" Jerome adamantly proclaimed as he pulled the Escalade sharply around a corner. "Money, power, an' the fame. Seein' is believin' ain't it?" With that, he proudly produced a thick wad of bills wrapped in a rubber band from the inside of his pants pocket. Venus' eyes widened; she could barely believe it. She'd never seen such a wad of money outside of the videos on BET. Jerome, noticing her notice, beamed triumphantly and snorted, then resumed his glares and stares out the window, scoffing insolently at his ideas about women and their fairly scandalous overtures for men and their money.

"So you got it like that?" Venus inquired, betraying admiration. Jerome smirked, enjoying himself.

"Yeah-yeah twenty-fo'—seven." His soliloquy continued, "Thangs hard out here nowadays, feel me? Black folks out here bleedin' to death while da man gettin' mo' rich by da minute!!!"

Venus took a second longing look at the thick wad of cash Jerome placed lovingly back into his pocket, as a father would tuck in his beloved infant child. *Seems like da man ain't da only one gettin' rich.*

"Uh huh, so how you coming up?!?!" Venus piped up, curiously, eagerly.

Jerome was reclining further into his seat, tipping his White Sox baseball cap back, pulling the wooden steering wheel hard to the right, taking the Escalade down a dim alley off the main boulevard, a dangling gold watch jingling on his wrist.

"I'm a man of bidness," Jerome boasted. "Provide a service to da people, work a lil' harder than nine to five, an' my product is pas' competition. Not only dat but my customers get they shit befo' I get mine. I slang a lil' escape from all a' dis shit da man puttin' on black folks out here. Look at 'em! Feel me?" Gazing broodingly over the crowds on the corners all with dirty torn clothes, matted hair, sunken faces, and hunched postures, he was shaking his head in sympathy as he remarked, "Fo' real girl. You know my man upstairs G.O.D. know dey need it."

Venus took a good look for herself as they passed by dark alleys and vacant lots crowded to overflowing with women in tight skirts and belly shirts flagging down male passengers, men sleeping on the sidewalk with half empty liquor bottles in hand, young hoods in front of boarded up buildings, standing tall in beanies and hooded sweatshirts, guarding the street corners as if they were gold mines. And then there were the crack heads. Shivering and huddled forms, red eyes, hollow faces, torn clothes, zombies lost to the night. Venus looked long enough to make her shudder and then averted her eyes.

Jerome slammed on the brakes all of a sudden, almost plowing over a crowd that had just begun to skulk through the street, a green light for traffic and an oncoming SUV notwithstanding.

"MOVE MUTHA FUCKA!!!" Jerome bellowed out the window, beeping his horn angrily and swerving around the couple in the street who barely noticed that, just seconds ago, they had almost gotten killed. "Stupid ass niggaz!!! Fuckin' crack heads!!! Jus' gonna walk on through da god damn street like, oh well, fuck it. Ain't got nothin' to lose. Sheeit jus' a fuckin' crack head any damn way. Feel me?" He scowled and shook his head resentfully at others just like them on passing street corners. Back and forth across the street, mindless, aimless, shoulders bent forward, some standing on the corner, rocking from side to side on the balls of their feet. Venus smacked her lips in agreement but was a bit taken aback at the outburst. *Sheeit, my nigga here need to come to group an' get him some anga' management!!! I'm a bring him to see dat white boy dat be talkin' to us.* She smiled to herself but then came another feeling, just for a moment, of sympathy for these lost souls, wondering who among them was somebody's mother, had a mother, a sister. *Where dey families at?* The thought made her sad and even a little guilty.

The Escalade pulled to a sharp stop just outside of an abandoned lot and boarded up liquor store. Blinking hard in the dark of the night, Jerome took another good, long look left, right, and over his shoulder through the back window, making sure the coast was clear. Venus watched in earnest. *Maybe he gonna kiss me o' somethin'?* She felt a little scared and confused, but a little hopeful too.

But Jerome had other things on his mind. After determining that he was not being watched, he put the car into park and opened his door, licking his lips again, swinging his near leg down onto the sidewalk.

"I gotta go take care of some bidness, baby. I be back," he assured her over his shoulder as he closed the door behind him and made his way hurriedly toward a crowd of five or six lounging on the far street corner. Talking, gesturing, drinking, shaking, spitting in the gutter.

"Mmmm, hhhmm," Venus conceded, breathing deeply, and slumping back into her chair in resignation. *Well, they gotta do what they gotta.* Looking on in anticipation, she was curious and even a little excited to see what would happen next.

Momentarily taking a good look at her almost new air-brushed high-top basketball shoes, she began longing for a new pair. *They all messed up! Jerome need ta take me shopping.*

Glancing out the window in earnest, she started counting seconds on the clock. *Sheeit how much longer dis gonna take?* But Jerome was engaged in his business, hunched over at the shoulders, hand to hand exchanges with another boy, peering left and right to make sure that he was operating free of detection. Jerome directed his attention to another in the little crowd on the corner, exposing the two or three others he had been in transaction with. Venus casually sized them up. *Jus' a bunch a' heads, fiends an' all.* Then her heart suddenly leaped into her throat; one of them had familiarly dark skin, boxed natural hair with a hair pick in it, scrubby mustache, a long solid black t-shirt, and unmistakably dead brown eyes. *Ooooh shit!!! That's my brotha Percy?!?! What da fuck he doin' out der wit' dem heads?!?!* A question that begged an answer. *No, no, hell na'!!! My brotha can't be no crack head. Fo' real, hell na'!!! He prob'ly jus' kickin' it out der. Dey his friends o' some shit. Maybe he hustlin' too. Fo' real though. My brotha ain't no head.* She was so frightened, so ready to have a heart attack or faint. She wanted to cry, to run from the Escalade and pull her brother from the corner's clutches, to guard him with her life. Watching him slap hands with Jerome, each pair of hands immediately going from slapping hands into pockets, Venus did not want to believe it was true, wishing, hoping, longing for anything but. But she remembered what her brother had once told her when she was caught stealing at a liquor store and had to call her mother and tell her the bad news. *Reality's a bitch.* Watching her brother with Jerome, wanting nothing more than to forget this reality, wipe it away. *Nah, can't be. My brotha ain't no crack head. Fo' real? Can't be.* But this truth was one she could not escape. Those were crack heads on the corner. Jerome, her man, was their dealer. And Percy, her brother, was one of them. Suddenly, a loud squealing of tires tore through the night, thumping footsteps, and walkie-talkie static blaring in every direction. A flurry of activity seeming to come from everywhere at once.

"HANDS UP! TURN AROUND!" Boomed a deep and forceful command, coming from a man nearby. "DON'T YOU MOVE MOTHER FUCKER OR I SWEAR TO GOD YOU'RE DEAD!" Hearing the rhythmic sounding of clinking and clattering, handcuffs, and the hammer of guns being cocked back, everyone knew they were ready to shoot.

Venus had seen such scenes too many times not to know, and each time it scared her nearly to death. Her normally deep earthen skin tone had gone pale.

Hearing her heart pound in her head she was scared even to breathe as she watched Jerome's hands yanked behind his back by a burly police officer with sunglasses and dark, spiky hair. Then he was planting Jerome's face into the brick wall before him, muffling his wailing protests of innocence and lawsuits. A pistol pressed deep into the inside of his cheek, practically in his mouth. Venus could only watch, suffering in silence, terrified that this was the end, expecting to see the flash of gunfire and Jerome's head fly apart.

While Venus nearly lost her mind, Jerome remained alive. Venus felt her tears coming in rushing sobs. *P-please, jus' leave him alone!! Don't shoot him!!! He ain't even do nothin'.*

The officer roughly helped Jerome interlock fingers high over his head, grinning smugly, enjoying his work. Once he was subdued, the officer began digging through Jerome's pockets, which soon produced a large bag full of smaller bags containing an off-white powder. Waving it triumphantly in the air he shouted, "Surprise surprise? What is this? Fucking Walgreens? Hope you ain't busy for the next few years. Fuckin' piece a shit!!!"

Venus crying harder. *No, no!!! My man can't go ta jail. C'mon. Let him go. He ain't know no betta. I shouldn't ask fo' nothin' from him. All a' dat shoppin' an' shit. I ain't even need all a dat. Dis' my fault!*

A volley of curses from Jerome as he was dragged by the clasp between his handcuffed wrists to the squad car. A sinister laugh from one of the other police officers on the scene. Growling, snarling, more handcuffs click-clicking. Swears of innocence. Yelps for lawyers and cries of racism.

Venus now sobbing uncontrollably. Her face in her hands. Closing her eyes, never wanting to open them again. Wishing beyond wishing that this was a dream she would wake up from. Find herself in her bed. Awakening to her lovely ring tones. It would be Jerome. Not in prison but trying to talk her into creeping out her bedroom window for another wild night in *The X.* And a wild night in *The X* it was. But not the wild night she dreamed of. This was a wild night of reality. *Reality is a bitch.* Again, for the second time that very night, she was learning how deep those words went.

Opening her eyes to see flashlights and guns out of holsters, black men in the back of police cars, white police officers, proud of their catches of the day. Laughing amongst themselves. Jerome banging his head slightly against the rear window of his seat in the back of a police car. Closing her eyes again. *Dis can't be. Can't be. How cou' dis happen?!?!*

Eyes opening again. But now Jerome wasn't alone. A familiar face in the back of the car alongside him. An Afro with a pick, scrubby mustache, baby fat in the cutest of places. *Nah-nah. Dey got my brother!!! No!! No!!* But it was true. It was Percy there in the back of the police car. Head back against the head rest, staring up into the ceiling, eyes closed, lost within himself.

Venus was in there with him. Right there in the car. Lost, terrified, with her brother so captive and helpless. She could only succumb to fate, resign herself to invisibility. Able to bear it no longer. Wishing this night of all nights would just come to an end. The passenger side door suddenly flinging open, nearly coming off the hinges. Venus roughly yanked by the break in her wrist, nearly pulling her shoulder from its socket. Almost too fast for her to realize what was happening.

"Just along for a nice little ride through the night huh?" a man demanded sarcastically. "C'mon bitch you know the drill! Hands over your head!" The police officer bellowed, clasping her hands firmly behind her, slamming the door behind her, and pushing her up against its cold metal.

Venus began to panic, her face flushing. *C'mon!! no, please, I can't go ta jail. Fo' real?!?! I ain't even do nothin'!!!* She stammered out her best effort at an explanation or protest. The police officer roughly planted her face against the tinted window of the Escalade, her cheek pressing thickly against the glass.

"Save it!" The officer barked. Beginning to search her body with his hands, up her legs and over her waistline. Hands lingering a second longer, squeezing a little firmer than he had to. Feeling his fingers grip her body, Venus squeezed her eyes shut tightly, biting her lip, feeling her skin crawl. She braced herself as a woman does on a crowded subway when a man brushes past just slowly enough to betray his true intentions, though not long enough to provoke retaliation.

"Mmm, hmmmm," the officer hummed approvingly, hands glazing delicately past the underside of her breasts, smiling. That's when Venus's sorrow and anguish turned blindly to rage. Blind and powerful. Wishing her hands were free so she could grasp the officer around the throat and kill him, right there in that abandoned lot at a crime scene in the middle of the night. Wanting to cry, pull the hair out of her head, scream, disappear, and throw a punch all in that same moment.

"Bet these gangsters out here just love you don't they?" the police officer hissed in her ear. His breath was hot with tobacco odor, his silvery smirk just visible out of the corner of her eye. *Just let me go. I wanna go home. Let me out. Let my brotha out too!!! Let us go home.*

"Harris, what we got over there?" beckoned another officer from the far side of the street. Venus's captor was looking up from between her ear and neck, slightly irritated at the interruption.

"Just a babe in the woods, you know," Harris answered over his shoulder, snickering. "She's got nothin'. Ain't nothin'."

Fuck you!!! You ain't know shit about me!!! Bitch ass racis' ass cops!!! Don't know shit!! Heavy steps were coming closer one by one, stopping in front of the hood of the unmarked car, fumbling absentmindedly through her belongings that had been tossed unceremoniously atop the hood of the Escalade.

"Well, not so fast there," Harris's comrade corrected. "We got a Brady bunch kinda thing going on here. She's the little sister of the homeboy in the car." He motioned to a nearby police car.

Venus looked over her shoulder, saw her brother in the back, and wished she hadn't looked. His eyes were there, waiting for hers. How long had he been there watching? Not long, she hoped.

"Is that right?" Harris chortled, nodding over his shoulder in the direction of his nearby patrol car. "I caught her posted up in ol' boy's Escalade."

Venus's eyes grew wide. *Jerome! What happen to him?!?!* She found him with her eyes. In the back of a police car, just like her brother. But unlike her brother, Jerome held his head high, erect in his seat, shoulders broad, chest out, as if he were president. Venus couldn't help but admire that.

Damn, he ain't got no fear. Well, sheeit, if he do, he don't be showin' nothin'. This was why Venus liked him. She watched intently, dumbfounded, awestruck, even turned on. Watching his eyes dart to and fro in that casual but cool gangster way of seeing only what was necessary. So strong, so sure of himself, even while awaiting doom in the back of a police car. The thrill almost made her forget where she was. The arresting officer's gleeful chortles snapped her back to grim reality.

"It'll be a family reunion at the joint..." one of them joked. Both laughed in waves, making Venus angry as she recalled his hands on her body. *Bitch ass, crooked ass cops!!! Fuckin' child molesters!!!*

As the officers laughed on, Venus found her anger giving way to terror and sorrow. *Damn, mama gonna be hella mad. I cou' see dat look on her face. Shakin' her head an' shit. An' daddy too. An' Percy. Percy!!! My brotha!!! What dey gonna do wit' him?!?! Damn, dey need ta jus' let him go.* Feeling tears coming. *An' let me go to. Jus' don't do nothin'. Jus' don't hurt me no mo'. Leave me alone. An' my brotha too!!!*

The officers' laughter abruptly subsided. Harris's partner was glaring menacingly down at Venus's cowering, huddled form. "If I ever see you down here again," he swore, pointing over his shoulder with a jagged thumb. "See your brother on his way to the bootie house?"

Venus nodded with puppy dog eyes.

Harris chortled. "Bein' some big mama's girlfriend all night long," He took an ominous step closer. Now he was close enough for Venus to take in the foul stench of cigarette smoke as she closed her eyes in agony. *Sooner her den yo' ass.* Waves of terror and a thunderous rage rushed through her body. A long second of silence.

"You hear me!?!!" The first officer demanded.

"Uh huh," Venus replied meekly, her hands beginning to fall to her sides, taking a slight step backwards. *Please let me go, please, jus' let me up outta here. Jus' wanna go home an' get up in ma' bed. Please, god, lemme go home!!!*

"All right then, get out of here," Harris growled.

Venus wrapped her arms tightly around her waist and took off with long strides into the darkness, head bowing low, heart racing, relieved, exhilarated. She was grateful to be free but somehow knew that she would carry this night with her everywhere she went.

The police radios began to grow dimmer in the distance, but she was still feeling the police officer's eyes burning through her, glaring after her. The blackened night sky suddenly turned calm and the air was almost silent. The searchlights of the squad cars grew dimmer in the distance.

Jus' gotta get away. Jus' a lil' further. Venus could feel that it would not be long until she was home safe. Safe in her bed. Safe from . . . well . . . the list went on.

She was coming home long after curfew, sure to be chewed out by her parents, grounded forever, but that was the least of her worries. *Sheeit better then Juvy Hall*! She knew her brother would say nothing about what happened to her. *My Brotha!!! Percy . . . wha' gonna happen to him?!?!*

She hated herself for her selfishness. *Celebratin' while he goin' ta jail!* She was remembering some of the frightful tales she had heard through the grapevine. Some of the men in her neighborhood traded war stories about stabbings with shaven pens and prison gangs. *It be mo' safe in deez streets dodgin' bullets!!!* That's what they used to say.

Venus could only hope those stories weren't true. *Prob'ly just tryin' ta make they selves sound big so dey cou' impress da females. Maybe dey even let him go. Po-lice might jus' wanna talk a lil' shit, talk all a' dat stay out 'da streets shit . . . An', like, let 'em go too. An' Jerome too.* Seeing the police take the cuffs off her brother and her man, it looked possible in her mind. She began to smile as she walked. *It might a happen.*

Then she remembered. His hands on her body. Still feeling his hand on her breast, a scar left behind. Closing her eyes tight now, just like she had in that moment. Feeling tears welling, clutching her body tighter still as she walked through the moonlight, she heard a bicycle squeaking off into the distance, scanned the dilapidated houses she passed, feeling lonely and deserted. *Dat mutha fucka! Puttin' his hands up on me an' shit!! I'm gonna sue his ass!!! Watch, when Percy come out, I'm gonna tell eva'body up on my block an' have dat foo' fucked up. Don't give a fuck if he da po-lice.*

She felt another surge of rage as she made her way deeper into the night. She recalled the officer towering over her, laughing a torturer's laugh, enjoying his authority. *And I just sat der. Ain't even do shit. I shoulda said somethin'. Done somethin'.* She was wondering what she could have done, should have done. She walked past sleeping houses, past owls hooting in the trees, past *hey lil' ma* as she rounded a corner, past an abandoned lot with an ugly old wino lurking in the shadows.

"Fuck you! Leave me alone!" Venus bellowed with an anger that was blind and powerful. This shocked her a little, even scared her a little. But she actually kind of enjoyed it as well.

The wino retreated into the darkness from which he had appeared. Venus was again alone in her thoughts. A police car blared past at breakneck speed, sending Venus's heart leaping into her throat, feeling overwhelming terror. She was so relieved when it passed. *Thank god it ain't him again!*

The deadness returned. Crickets chirping on nearby lawns. A bottle breaking in the distance, chortled male laughter. Another police siren. Silence again.

The night wind was beginning to pick up, whistling eerily, making her shudder as she passed familiar multiple story apartment buildings with solid black screen doors and broken toys out front. She pulled her hooded blouse closer around her shoulders. She knew her efforts were in vain. No amount of clothing would make her warm again that night. No shower would again make her clean. The world she knew would be changed forever. *Jus' gotta get home…get home…Sheeit, mama gonna kill me. Please don't let dem be up. I'm gonna be dead!!! Well, hell, ain't gonna be as bad as Percy; he in jail!! He fo' real be dead. Maybe dey ain't give me dat much punishment.*

She wondered how it would be. She pictured long rows of cells, crazed maniacs, huge and twisted from violence and pumping iron in institutions, wild looks in their eyes, ready to fight and kill, and worse. She quickly changed her mind. *Dey might even let 'em go. He ain't even really do nothin' anyway. Maybe he only mess around wit' dat shit from time to time, and maybe he buyin' rock for somebady else.* Venus almost wished she could believe it.

She recalled those zombies in that street-turned-graveyard, aimless, meandering up and down the block, in and out of the shadows. Hunched over, redeyed, sunken cheeks, skinny, sick, half dead, making Venus shudder in her bones. They were without a home, without spirit, faceless, shards of human beings. They always scared Venus.

But now they were no longer *them.* One of them was her brother. Not just some bum, some dope fiend. Venus used to wonder who among those lost souls had a mother and a father, who used to swing on the swings when they were little. Now she knew. Maybe they all did. Percy definitely did. He had a mother and a father, used to play the trumpet and football, used to play basketball with Venus in Sunset Park until the wee hours of the night, always just barely letting her win. The thought made her want to cry.

She exited the main boulevard, now more than halfway home, surprised at the time she was making. She took a longer look at a hunched form pushing a shopping cart, then at a wino in an alley sucking hungrily on a bottle in a bag.

She barely used to see them as alive, but now she couldn't help but to wonder. Watching the wino closely, slowing her pace, trying to take a good look, but he was hidden in the bleak shadows, muffled in a dark corner, his hair wild and tangled, an overturned shopping cart next to him, crumpled paper and empty bottles all around. *Maybe he somebady brotha top. He been at jail? He got a family? Do they visit him up in jail if he go there?* She saw a family of raccoons burrowing through overturned trash cans and recycling bins; she took a long look at a smaller one that had its head in the air staring at her with sharp, dark eyes. *Damn, that one kinda look like Jerome. When he get out, I'm gonna tell him.* A low-flying airplane screamed by and off into the distance, its bright red light blinking good-bye. Venus watched it go, taking her eyes off the road in front of her, stumbling over something that squirmed a little at her feet.

"Oh, my bad, excuse me," she muttered apologetically, nearly tripping over a twisted form slumped against a stop sign. The twisted form had its mouth open, snoring in long and gurgling wheezes. Half asleep, half dead. Venus side-stepped and hurried past, clutching her body tightly with criss-crossed arms.

Venus continued on, wondering what it all meant in the grand scheme of things. *Damn, everybody on dat shit!?!?! Das da problem 'round here. Everybody sellin' dat shit o' smokin'. Prob'ly why thangs so fucked up 'round here.* Thinking of Jerome, wondering how it all came together. Frowning in the night, she was wishing her mind would go to rest and leave her alone. But it never did. *Sheeit, maybe das why dey do dat shit, give dey mind some ease.*

Stepping down off the curb, into the street, passing a familiar faded apartment project, busted out street lights, the basketball hoop with the chain-link net, she now saw things that were comforting. *Almost home.* She wanted nothing more than to find her bedroom window slightly open, the lights in the house off, her parents evidently long in slumber. Then she could crawl in her window, burrow under the covers, and drift off into serenity. She could then wake, go to school, and afterward go shopping, looking for boys. That thought made her unsteady. Thinking about boys used to energize her, but now she wasn't altogether sure. She felt a certain uneasiness about them, even a revulsion at the thought of their touch, their energy. She did not quite understand it or what it meant. It was a bad feeling, a feeling that made her long for the sanctity of her nice, warm bed. She would wake to breakfast, forget all that had happened. It would just be another night. No one would ever have to know.

She gazed sorrowfully down at her feet as she walked, at once jolted by the harsh streak across the toe of her left sneaker. Frowning harshly, she stopped in the middle of the street. Bending down at the waist, she spit on her right thumb, rubbed her blemished shoe with it. But the mark was indelible. Venus scowled disapprovingly, smacking her lips loudly in the dark. *Damn I ain't gettin' no kind of break for nothin'!* Standing back upright, she resumed her walk, upset about her shoes. Running a delicate hand through long braids, she felt them tickle against her neck as she pushed them back.

Venus's hand abruptly caught on a dangling root. Yanking her head slightly to the left from the force, she stopped again. *Shit, I gotta get my hair done too. Shoes an' hair? Prob'ly $300.* It was far beyond her $5 a week. Then she smiled knowingly to herself. *I got ways. It jus' a smile an' some lil' ass shorts away!* This thought used to make her feel triumphant, but now it died quickly. Suddenly, it wasn't so funny anymore. The world Venus had known had become so grave and joyless. Shoes and hair braids and boys just didn't seem to do it anymore. Something had happened to her. Something was missing. In the darkest corner of her soul, where the harshest of truths held onto her heart, Venus knew it was never coming back. The life she had known had been changed forever.

Finally she saw her familiar lawn and garden, the bars on the windows, statues lining the walkway up to the front door. She was home. *And da car ain't even here! I cou' get in and dey ain't gonna know when I came home!* Such a relief! Maybe this meant that her fantasies of drifting to sleep and waking up to a new life would come true. She noted that her window was still open. If her parents had gone in her room and found she wasn't there, her window would be closed and latched shut. *Daddy always yellin' 'bout how I fit ta get us robbed an' shit.* She stole a glance at the empty driveway as she tiptoed over the pavement. She crept up to her window and gingerly hoisted it upward, wincing as it screeched like nails on a chalkboard. *Maybe dey go down to da po-lice station ta get Percy.* The thought made Venus's spirits wilt. She was too worn out to grieve or condemn herself for not doing more to help her brother. All she could think about was crawling into her bed and drifting off into eternity. As she crept through her window and latched it behind her, she sighed in relief.

Her head bounced off the pillow as she flopped down lifelessly on her bed. Soon she was drifting off to sleep, although she still had thoughts of her brother. *Hope he got a pillow tonight, one jus' like dis one.*

Gina

Gina practically hypnotized herself by staring at the ceiling overhead, peering into the little white flecks of paint inching out in bits and pieces. Her breath came slow and heavy, her body lifeless, enjoying the peace, knowing that it wouldn't last.

"HEEEY! GET OUT 'DA BATHROOM!"

"SHUT THE FUCK UP BITCH! BE OUT IN A MINUTE!"

"I DON'T KNOW WHAT DAT HO THINK SHE'S DOIN'. DON'T HAVE NO HAIR TA DO NUTTHIN' TO ANY DAMN WAY!"

"WATCH I'M A PUNCH YOU IN YO' FACE, BITCH!"

Gina sighed deeply, shaking her head, wishing to be anywhere but here. She listened to her foster sisters arguing; the calm, peace, and quiet could not last long. She rubbed her temples tenderly; the shouting and cursing was already beginning to wear on her. Her room suddenly felt like a prison, her fellow prisoners in neighboring cells, rowdy on all sides, hollering, shouting, taunting, ready to riot.

God I hate it here! I wish my REAL sista Tarra a' come pick me up. O' mama!...mama. The thought came on too quickly to ward off. A surge of sadness overcame her. Then that sadness quickly turned to anger and bitterness. *Sheeit, I ought 'a known betta.* Knowing her mother was probably off getting high somewhere, sleeping in the street, practically dead, she hoped and prayed her mother would be okay. Maybe she would even come for her some day. *Maybe she a' stop fuckin' wit' dat shit, maybe she cou'find a job, maybe...maybe...*

"I'm a flirt, when I walk into the club I'm a flirt..." The familiar ring tone from inside her pocket broke her train of thought. She snatched up her cell phone and clicked it on.

"Hello?" she answered without a glance to the screen to see who was calling.

"Gina! You ain't gonna believe what he did!" howled a shrill voice on the other line.

"Loretta stop yellin'!" Gina barked back in outrage. She breathed in deeply with closed eyes, mustering the caretaker within her, bringing it down a notch. "I know you pissed off 'cause of ya dad and all, but you don't need ta be callin' ova' here yellin' an' all."

"I'm sorry," Loretta conceded meekly, but then rising quickly to her former level of intensity, began where she had left off. "But I can't take dis shit no mo'!"

Gina winced. *Sheeit, girl, neitha' can I!!* "So what he do to you?" Gina asked through a sigh wrought with irritation. Loretta took no notice.

"Well, I was comin' down the stairs, just miiii-ndin' my own business when he come stumblin' in the front do', drunk an' pissed off 'bout who knows what, then…" BOOM, BOOM! The thunderous knock on Gina's bedroom door made her jump up from her seat.

"GIIIIII-NA!!! I need to talk to you!" wailed a demanding voice.

Gina shook her head wearily. Breathing deeply, she regained her composure and wondered how she was needed now. Someone else needed mothering. *So what else is new?* She had lost track of Loretta who continued talking into Gina's shoulder where the phone lay dormant. Gina looked thoughtfully at the phone, her brow knitting. *Hmmm, if I left da phone on my bed an' wa'dn't even there, how long it be befo' she even know I'm gone?*

"Loretta, I gotta go, girl. I call you later," Gina murmured. Loretta began to sputter protests.

"Giiii-na!!!!" importuned the voice in the hallway outside, hands pounding on the door. Gina rolled her eyes impatiently. *Ooohh lord, deez girls all crazy.* "Loretta chill!!! I call you later. Don't trip, you a' be okay."

She put down her phone and began to rub her sore temples, grateful for her moment of silence, knowing it wouldn't last long.

BOOM!!! BOOM!!!

"GIIIIINNNNNAAAA!!! YOU HEAR ME?

Sheeit, I gotta get up outta here. Her feet took her to the bedroom door and she swung it open. "WHAT?!?!" She barked in exasperation. A young, dark-skinned girl of about Gina's age, in a sun dress and long braids, stared back at her, looking perplexed.

"Damn girl wha's wrong wit' you?!?!" the girl inquired.

Gina felt instantly guilty. *I mean, I know dey jus' my foster sistas. But still, dey need me.* "I'm sorry, it's nothin', my bad," she conceded. "I…"

"I don't know what to do," the girl interrupted.

So how I'm 'posed to? Gina wondered, but prudently held her tongue.

"See there's dis foo' I been fuckin' with that I met through Jarine. He's her ex. He used to go out with Taronda, das Jarine' cousin. He say dey not doin' nothin' no mo' but he still talkin' to Jarine an' talkin' 'bout it's coo' 'cause she his ex' cousin. But I don't think I's coo'. What you think?"

Gina was dumbfounded. *Damn, dis girl honestly think I'm 'posed to keep all a' dat shit straight? Too much drama!* Gina would ask her foster sister to repeat the story if she thought it would do any good. But her head was already hurting. And besides, maybe the who's who of it wasn't important.

"You like him?" Gina inquired, thoughtfully shifting in her seat to get a better look at her foster sister. Her foster sister subtly shifted away, blinking her long eyelashes twice, her eyes momentarily finding Gina's and then gazing off, deep in thought. Gina was now hanging on her every word, waiting expectantly for what she would say next, but she already somehow knew the answer.

"Yeah, I wish I didn't though," her foster sister admitted with a sigh. "But das da problem with deez foo's out hea! Like, how he gonna call me baby?!?! He tell me aaaall a' that kind a' shit an' den be talkin' to somebady he used ta fuck wit. You know?!?!"

"Shonda, I wouldn't even bother," Gina scoffed. *Sheeit, das jus' how boys is.*

Shonda smirked. "I know you wouldn't 'cause you neva do!" she accused, leaving questions in the air with a felicitous grin.

Gina shifted protectively, averting her eyes. "I don't know wha' choo talkin' 'bout," Gina pouted.

Shonda almost rejoiced. "Yes you do, stop lyin'!" Shonda corrected, grin widening to a full smile, rejoicing in her discovery. "You don't *baaaaather* wit' no boys. You just be pullin' dat old Brandy, *sittin' up in my room* shit. When you gonna get a man?!?!"

Gina dismissed her with a wave of her hand, shaking her head, trying to play it cool, as if it didn't matter. But the thought made her a little sad. *Yeah, a boy do sound kind a' nice...* "Girl please! When I fine' a man, I have a man, thank you!" Gina proclaimed, her voice growing shriller with each passing word. *Why should I make time for deez nappy headed boys out here! Nothin' but a bunch a' broke, scraggly hustlas an' playas any damn way!*

But somewhere deep inside she hoped that a special someone lay out there in wait. Somewhere out there, waiting and hoping for her as hard as she hoped for him. Someone strong and take charge, yet funny, and with a softer, gentle side that only she'd know about. She'd have the goods on him, know his top secret information, and he'd want to know hers too. Maybe she'd even share it with him.

The thought of such intimacy scared her a little, but it made her smile in that kind of dreamy way. Looking up and around with fluttering insides at her grand poster of R. Kelly perched majestically above her bed, his brightly glistening bald head, dark sunglasses, alluring diamonds and gold, glistening muscles near to exploding from the boundaries of his skintight black tank top. Gina knew who she was waiting for.

It took Shonda all but a moment to see. "Oh hell no!" she exclaimed vehemently. "G, you trippin' hard. That man jus' a liiiittle out a yo' league. Like he gonna exit da stage on triple platinum an' shit to come fuck wit' you!"

Gina snorted indignantly. *He jus' might!*

"Sheeit girl you know that's right though!" Gina insisted. "Dat boy all dat!!! But where da boys like dat out here? We need boys got some money an' some brains. You know? Like, coo' and kine' hearted, feel me?" She looked hard at Shonda, as if for some sign of understanding.

Shonda laughed hard from her belly. "Girl please! You need ta wake up and get back to da real shit. Feel me?" Gina said nothing. Shonda chuckled in pity. "Fo' real girl. Boys ain't rollin' like dat around here. Dey some sorry ass motha fuckas, no doubt." She noted Gina looking down at her feet. "But you jus' gotta keep yo' eyes open. Hell, some of 'em cute ain't dey?"

Again Gina lay silent, her most sincere of pleas falling on deaf ears.

Shonda clicked her tongue, narrowed her eyes, and smiled mischievously. "Or you chasin' some lady love type shit?"

"Hell no! I don't roll like dat!" Gina pouted, throwing a small pillow at Shonda.

"Ha, my nigga, you lyin!!" Shonda bounced up from Gina's bed and began strutting for the door. She grabbed the doorknob and flung the door open. She started marching through the hallway, parading triumphantly with heavy steps over the hardwood floor. "OOOHHHHH, I'm gonna drop it like it hot!" she taunted Gina over her shoulder. She swung open one of the bedroom doors where a cacophony of teenage girls' voices giggled and gabbled. "HEY Y'ALL GUESS WHAT? GINA IN HERE TALKIN' 'BOUT WA'IN' 'A GET DOWN ON SOME GIRL-GIRL…" WHHAMMM!!!!

Gina slammed the unclosed door. *Hate this place!*

"OOOOOOO"

"HAHAHAHA!!!"

"DAMN GINA!!!"

"I hate you!!!" Gina growled through her now closed door, standing for a while a few inches from it, breathing hard.

The phone suddenly rang on the nearby bedstand. Normally she would be rushing to answer it, but now she was blinded by rage. *Hate dis place! Why dey gotta act like dat?!?!* The phone rang again. *Dat the third ring? Maybe the fourth?* Sighing deeply to herself. *Somebady could miss a' important call!*

"Gina! Phone!" yelled a voice from the bottom of the stairs, only now Gina was about ready to explode. *NOW WHAT?!?!* Yanking the phone from its holster to her ear, she pressed the on button with such force that it nearly caved in.

"What is it?" she barked into the receiver.

"Damn girl what's wrong wit' you?" came a concerned voice.

"I'm sorry Tarra," she answered, blushing, slumping back onto her bed, her rear bouncing slightly back up from her weight against the bed springs. Her anger gradually subsided. Tarra always seemed to have that effect on her. "How's work?"

"You didn't answer my question," Tarra insisted. "Don't even try to get off the hook by playin' mama wit' me."

"Fo' real I hate it here!" Gina complained. "Deez girls be doin' just a liiiii'l too much! Dey always be talkin' so much shit. Talkin' about I be likin' girls!" Snorting resentfully. "Sheeit don't know what dey talkin' 'bout. Always talkin' loud and actin' crazy. Know what dey need ta do?"

"No," Tarra conceded. "But you doin' da same thang right now you mad at them for!" It caught Gina off guard and she had to stop and think about it. Nodding resignedly she conceded. *Yeah, she got me.*

"I know and I don't mean at be yellin' at you 'cause it' not yo' fault," Gina apologized. "But das exactly my point! Dey turn me into them! I'm not like deez otha girls! All loud an' outta dey minds. I want to go home!" A long silence prevailed and Gina felt sad to her bones. In the deepest corner of her heart, she wondered if she would ever go home, ever be home.

"Can we go to da movies or something?" Gina begged.

Tarra exhaled deeply. "Yeah, I think we both cou' use a break," she agreed.

"And we got it comin' too!" Gina added, sending a resentful glare toward the far bedrooms. Her foster sisters' giggles and gossip had now subsided. "When you gonna come get me?"

"In a minute. Let Kendra know wha's up okay?" Tarra inquired. Gina bounded off the bed onto her heels, whirling in an excited half circle. *OOOOOHHH da new Denzel movie jus' came out too!!!*

"Okay cool," Gina responded, hopping up and down on both feet with a big smile, already beginning to rifle through her closet for an outfit. *Hmmm, now, I'm in mo' of a puff coat o' hoody mood tonight?*

"And forget dem girls!" Tarra insisted assuredly, "Jus worry 'bout what you is doin'. Feel me? Let dem trip on each otha while we go trip on Denzel!"

Gina snapped her fingers and shrugged her shoulders up and down, her trademark victory dance. Uttering a quick "sounds good" before hanging up, she threw on her puff coat and bolted from her bedroom.

"KEN-DRA!!!..." Gina hollered, nearly tripping and tumbling down before grasping the rickety wooden banister to arrest her fall. She landed unceremoniously on her rear and instantly began looking around in embarrassed curiosity. She was relieved to find a lack of an audience. *Okay coo', leas' nobody saw dat.*

"Scrub!" exclaimed a shrill teenage voice from somewhere above. Muffled laughter followed.

"Bitch shut up!" Gina howled over her shoulder as she dusted herself off and made her way grumpily down the rest of the stairs. *Sheeit, dey always got somethin' ta say. An matta fact I'm 'bout tired of it.* "Fat ho!" she added just before making her way into the kitchen, pleased at having the last word.

"Fat what?" retorted a rich voice marked with grave disapproval. Gina was startled to see Kendra standing there before her, catching her, a scornful eyebrow high on her forehead.

Gina swallowed hard, bowing shameful eyes to the floor.

"Sorry Kendra," she said, but she was still smiling brightly in gleeful contempt. *Yeah, I won dat one!!!*

"You know I don't allow cussin' an' yellin' in my house, don't you?" Kendra continued. Gina had to fight back outraged laughter. *Well, sheeit. Ain't gonna be much talkin' up in hea!!!*

"I know, an' I 'pologize," Gina repeated. She was trying to sound sincere, but was growing quickly irritated. *Already said I'm sorry, didn't I? I mean, Jesus, what more she want? An' besides? I'm 'posed at jus' let dem say whateva dey want ta me? Hell nah. You trippin'.*

But she strategically held her tongue, knowing that going to the movies on school nights was against Kendra's rules. This was not the time for bantering. "Kendra?" she began sweetly.

Kendra returned her attention to the pots on the stove, stiffening up her spine to a firm bristle, sensing that an "I want something" was coming. "Yes?" she responded suspiciously.

"Well, my homework is all done," Gina began to plead. "And since Tarra can take me to dinner afterwards, is it okay if I go to da movies? She already on da way." Her mind already was reveling in the possibilities, how to make it all possible. *Well, if I get home by ten, well…maybe 10:30, Denzel's 'til 10. Ooooooohhhh he hecka cute too!!! If I'm home at 10:30? I cou' do my homework, go to bed, and that's a rap!*

Kendra clicked her tongue in dismay. "Looks like you already answered fo' me befo' you even got off da phone, didn't you now?"

Gina chewed the inside of her lip and began to fidget nervously, avoiding Kendra's scornful eyes. *Sheeit, she ain't gonna let me go.*

"HEY GET YO' ASS OFF ME!!!"

"SHEEITTT!!! WHA' CHOO GO'NNA DO 'BOUT IT!"

"OOOOOOHHHHHHHHH!!!!!!!"

Kendra and Gina both fairly strained at the neck in unison, traded perceptive glances, eyes meeting for just a couple of seconds, sharing in motherly weariness. Kendra set the utensils down on the counter and made her way purposefully toward the nearby ruckus. Stopping suddenly, she glanced reluctantly back at Gina, breathing deeply as if thinking hard, and then bowed her head in silent concession.

"All right, go ahead. But next time, ASK FIRST! You hear?" Kendra demanded over her shoulder.

"YOU BETTA STAY OUT MY FACE O' I'M A PUNCH YOU IN IT!!!"

"BITCH YOU AIN'T FIT TA DO SHIT. HA-HA!!

"OOOO!!!" interjected two or three others.

Gina hopped up and down in gleeful victory, opening her mouth to pledge that, yes, next time she would ask first, but before she could speak, Kendra had vanished.

"HEEEYYYY!!" Kendra roared with such force that its fallout could have sent the glass dinner pieces inside the cabinet clanking against one another. Gina winced. "WHO DOIN' ALL O' DAT GOD DAMN YELLIN' UP IN MY HOUSE?!?" Gina backed up uncomfortably. *Uh-oh. She gone heck a ghetto! Dey might even get whooped.*

A knock resounded at the door, so soft and gentle, at least for this home, that it could only be one person. Gina beamed happily and swung the door open expectantly.

"Hey, Tarra!" Gina greeted, drawing her coat tighter around her shoulders as a gust of evening air reminded her what time it was. Tarra smiled in return, looking refreshing to Gina's weary eyes. Her older sister's very presence was soothing. Her elegantly straightened hair was all brushed back, looking stylish in its permed curves and waves. Her faded blue jeans and ribbed deep blue blouse fit well, just enough to be attractive, but not skintight and ghetto like most other women's clothes in the neighborhood. Tarra wore just enough makeup to look ready to meet the kind of man Gina would want her to meet.

"Hey girl," Tarra greeted. "You don't look too eager to raise up outta here. Wha's been going on around..."

"NOW I'M NOT GONNA TELL Y'ALL AGAIN THAT..." boomed Kendra through the walls as both Gina and Tarra simultaneously recoiled from the blast of the wave.

"OOOOHHHHH, neva mind," Tarra said, pulling Gina out the door, both of them oddly tiptoeing quickly down the concrete steps of the front porch.

"AN' I'M A TELL Y'ALL GHETTO ASS LIL' GIRLS ANOTHA THANG AN'..."

"Um, yeah. Jus' a second," Tarra said, hurrying to open the car door. *I hope dis place is good fa' her,* she thought in dismay.

"Coo'," Gina responded, breathing in deeply through the nose, grateful for the fresh air and the freedom it implied. "I'm tellin' you! Dis house is crrrrrazy!"

"That right?" Tarra inquired with a curious smile as she clicked open the door for her sister to enter. Gina admired the smell of the almost new Honda Accord.

"I ain't lyin'!" Gina insisted, sensing her sister wasn't taking her too seriously, staring at the house and her foster family. "You see how dey yell an' cuss at each otha? I can't get no sleep, do no homework, nothin'!"

Tarra cocked an eyebrow as she turned the key and warmed the engine.

"I heard you ain't been doin' no homework anyway," Tarra corrected, returning her gaze to the road before her as she put the car into gear and pulled off into the street.

"Says who?" Gina demanded. *Damn snitches! Bunch a' heffers!!! Always up in my bidness and don't do shit no how. Watch, I'm a snitch right back soon as dey do some foul shit!!!*

"'Who says' don't matter!" Tarra insisted matter-of-factly. "I say ain't nobody goin' to da movies o' shoppin' if she don't start gettin' it done an' don't nobody betta tell me she ain't doin' what she gotta do fo' whateva reason!"

Gina smacked her lips in acknowledgment. *Shit, ain't my fault, if dey wa'dn't so loud all da time, I cou' get hell of it done.* She momentarily considered letting the issue die as they picked up speed on their way to Denzel Washington's new action thriller.

"I can't do nothin' with all dat hollerin' an' screamin'!" Gina pouted. *No mo' shoes an' puff coats? No mo' Denzel? She gotta be kiddin'!* "I swear at God those bitches…"

"Uhh-uhh, you need ta watch yo' mouth lil' girl," Tarra commanded, just slightly louder than normal, but Gina heard her louder than any of Kendra's most blood curdling screams and bellows. Tarra quickly looked over at her now-sulking little sister, shook her head in stark disapproval, then quickly returned her attention to the road ahead. "Since when you talk like dat anyway?"

Gina sat mute.

"You prob'ly be mad at me fo' sayin' dis, but fo' all a' yo' rantin' and ravin 'bout dem bitches be doin' too much,'" Tarra continued, playfully mimicking her sister—and Gina couldn't help but laugh hysterically—"Gina, you sound just like 'em!"

Gina stopped laughing and wished she had something to say in protest, but she smiled, knowing she had been defeated. *Ain't dat a bitch!* was what she wanted to say, but she would be sure to face Tarra's wrath if she did.

Tarra noted her silence with satisfaction and drove on, leaving her sister alone with her thoughts. The movie theater appeared in front of them much sooner than expected. Sister exchanged excited giggle with sister, Denzel in all his glory just moments away.

Gina snapped off her seat belt, unlocked her door, and bounded from the inside of the car, eager to make her way forward. *Mm-hmm, Denzel fit to be lookin' hecka cute. I'm gonna get me some nachos an' popcorn, an', an', an'. . .*

While Tarra closed her own door and clicked on the car alarm, Gina swallowed hard, deciding to pipe up about something that had long been on her mind. "Tarra?" she began hesitantly, "Where, um, where you find a boyfriend? I mean, a good one?" Gina inquired along their way to the entrance.

"Sheeit, lil' mama, you got one right here fo' ya!" intruded a low male voice from a Jeep Cherokee on their right. As it pulled alongside, two of the men, blowing smoke and sipping from beer bottles, tried out a couple of pickup lines. When they received no notice, they drove off, one of them hollering back, "Damn babies."

"Well, you don't find a good one in da movie parking lot," Tarra answered, just loud enough for their solicitors to hear. Scoffs and hoots followed.

Gina laughed in a silvery giggle, ducking into her sister's bosom as she did so.

"Naw, but like, fo' real?!" Gina persisted.

Tarra sighed to herself, glancing over at her sister curiously.

"Since when you all, like, gotta have a man?" Tarra probed as they reached the far end of the parking lot and began to make their way to the ticket booth.

"Naw, it ain't like dat," Gina assured. "But, I'm sayin', it's just dat everybady at schoo' all hugged up with this dude or dat dude, an' about to call that one or dis one. . . Feel me?"

Tarra nodded, thinking back to her own junior high school scene from years ago. Considering the possibilities, she inquired, "So you got somebody on yo' mind?"

Silence ensued for a full minute as they approached the line at the box office. Gina was totally unprepared to respond.

Tarra paid for the tickets and smiled knowingly. "I mean, 'sides R. Kelly?"

"No!" Gina giggled, hopping playfully on both feet. "Ain't nobady else." She took her ticket from Gina. "'Sides, all dem boys hella ugly and nappy."

"So, don't worry 'bout it!" Tarra assured. "When Mr. Right comes along, you'll know. Can't tell ya how, but I know ya will." She glanced back, looking pointedly down at her sister as they made their way through the glass double doors into the theatre. "Those girls you talkin' 'bout don' know nuthin'. BE-LIEVE me. You might not see the whole thang, but they just latching on to any man wit' a dolla' bill o' a pickup line. Like dem foo's in the parkin' lot." She was motioning over her shoulder with a look of revulsion. Gina looked over at the cars. "Wha'? You wanna go catch you one? Some knuckle head ass nigga talkin' alla same lines ta era' female walkin' past? Women all da same, too. No one any different."

Gina smacked her lips. "Neva!" she proclaimed, violently shaking her head left and right. She had been spending many a night longing for a boy to hold her hand and call her pretty and lay with her all night. But men like those fools in the car scared her. *Hey baby, whassup ma,* the same gibbering she heard in the halls at school or out cracked windows pulling alongside her on her way home. Such conversation, if you could even call it that, made her skin crawl. She wondered sorrowfully if that was as good as it got.

Tarra watched her closely as they made their way through the theatre full of smiling little kids running full speed ahead into the arcade on the right, which was dark and stuffy-looking with high-pitched beeps and whistles coming from everywhere at once. The red carpet at their feet felt soft and inviting. The smell of buttered popcorn was ever-alluring. A happy young Latino couple sat kissing with eyes closed and mouths open, lost in passion. An angry old attendant was waving his fist at them to take their business elsewhere. Each ducked into the other, giggling, huddling, and skipping away. Tarra watched Gina as she watched them, noticing the quietly longing look on her face.

"Girl, trus' me," Tarra continued. "It ain't 'bout how many you cou' get or who got who. Let 'em have all that, 'cause foo's like them out in da parkin' lot be da only ones girls like dat gonna end up wit'. You young an' you don't gotta rush fo' nobody. Just be patient and keep yo' eyes open, a boy a come yo' way when he s'posed to."

Gina smiled flatly. *Sounds like a fortune cookie.* She smiled at the thought as they handed their tickets to the usher, nice smile, little dimples, white teeth, big eyes, thin lips, thin but shapely build, shirt tucked into freshly pressed pants. *Cute!!!* Gina thought to herself as she ducked into the theater, too shy to look up. Tarra noticed, smiling to herself.

"Tarra, what you mean 's'posed to'?" Gina inquired.

"What I mean s'posed to?!'" Tarra repeated haughtily. "A boy come along when you tell him to, das when he s'posed to," Tarra professed. Gina smiled at the thought and how it made her feel better. "Now let's go holla at our boy like we s'posed to!"

Gina laughed as she happily found a seat not too near the front. Amidst the noise and smells, shouts and excited giggling, Gina reflected on her profound admiration for her sister. *Damn, Tarra like Lil' Kim, Rosa Parks, an' every otha real lady all in one. I hope I be like her someday.*

To Gina, her sister was all that was good in the world. Tarra was always there, always benevolent. Always made her feel better when she was down. Always able to make her laugh. Always having the answers that no one else did. Tarra brought her more than relief; she provided strength and solace. She helped Gina decide who she wanted to be, and she showed Gina who she wanted to be. Sister showed sister what it meant to be graceful and how to maintain some dignity.

They found good seats and settled in for a night of thrills, adventure, and some female-to-male admiration. Denzel traveled through time as a cop facing intergalactic criminal mayhem, fighting off the burliest of foes with his usual exuberance. Locking up the bad guys, snapping clever repartee along the way, pulling the audience from hysterical laughter to points where they were hanging on every poetic speech somewhere between contemplation and awe.

As they exited the movie, happy and spent, Gina was ready to ask the big question that she had been sitting on long in her mind. Hoping, wishing, dying to hear her say yes, as if anything but yes would be impossible to bear.

"Tarra, I' been thinking 'bout what you said earlier," Gina began. "And I agree about bein' as bad as da rest a dem when I start doin' too much."

Tarra smiled slightly, appreciating her sister's insight yet sensing this was going somewhere in particular. "Oh?" she inquired in a tone reeking of *get to the point.*

"Yeah, 'cause I don't wanna be like dat," Gina continued persuasively. "I think dem girls a bad influence an' da mo' I'm 'round dem, the mo' I get like them. But den, like, when I'm aroun' you, you ain't hearin' me hollerin' an' cussin' an' all a' dat. Feel me? Like, when was da last time you seen me like dat out they house?"

"Earlier in da car," Tarra observed as they made their way for the exit, past the concession stands and video arcades.

Gina breathed deeply, fighting back her frustration. "But, feel me?" Gina persisted. "Das my point! I jus' came up out' the house an' look what happen!" Tarra said nothing as they made their way back out into the parking lot, a look of deep thought creasing her brow as she began considering the possibilities.

Gina sensed she was gaining ground. "But then all a dat don't be happ'nin' as much when I'm with you. So I's thinkin'..." she resumed hesitantly, bracing herself mightily, "maybe it be better if I jus' stay wit' you." Tarra slowed their pace, smiling slightly, thinking.

"Awww baby I knew you couldn't stay away..." slurred an excited male voice from inside a jeep several yards to the right. Its owner was under the impression that the sisters were stopping for his convenience. They both rolled their eyes. Returning to a fairly brisk pace, taking several long strides to her Honda Accord at the far end of the parking lot, Tarra got out her keys. She heard male scoffs and grumbles in the background. Gina walked behind in suspense, waiting intently for her answer.

Tarra turned off the car alarm and opened her door, stopping abruptly and leaning over the roof of the car, breathing out heavily, and gazing off into the stars. "Gina, you my girl an' I love you," she began hesitantly. Gina's spirits began to crumble as she sensed she was getting the answer she dreaded the most. "But…" Gina started to reply. Tarra stopped her with a delicate wave of her hand. "Hold on baby. Lemme think fo' a minute."

As silence ensued, to Gina, a minute began to feel like forever and then some. *Damn, what she thinkin'?! C'mon. Pleeeeease say yes! I can't be up in der no longa'.*

Tarra breathed heavily in defeat, opening her car door slowly as if leading a caravan to a funeral. "I don't know," she sighed wearily. "Let's talk about it later, okay?"

Gina's face fell in disappointment. "Okay," Gina reluctantly agreed. "But fo' real! I think dis would help me a lot. I cou' help you out wit' da chores an' cookin' so you won't have to do all dat when you be home from work an' tired an' all."

Tarra smiled, acknowledging this was tempting but that this would be the least of her worries.

"Oh, I ain't worried 'bout dat," Tarra replied, knowing better than to fall for her sister's seductive charm. "I heard all 'bout choo doin' all a dat fo' Kendra an' I know you like to be helpful. And das a good thang."

Gina brightened.

"But den that's why you don't get no homework done an' you pull Cs in yo' grades, right?" Tarra asked pointedly. "Basically, 'cause you takin' care a everybody else's shit instead a yo' own."

Gina found herself growing mighty angry without exactly knowing why, sitting down in her car seat in a humph.

Gina was searching fast for a retort. "If I didn't take care a them, nobody would!" she insisted. "Das why I wanna be wit' you. Cause den I wouldn't have to be everybody mama an' I cou' take care of ma' own respons'bilities!!!"

Tarra smiled whimsically, springing the engine to life and putting the Accord into gear with an acknowledging shake of her head. Her little sister could be convincing when she wanted to be. "You thought 'bout dis seriously?"

Only been thinkin' about it fa'ever!!! "Uh huh!" Gina answered readily, her eyes brightening, clasping her hands together. So close she could almost taste it! *Pleeeeease say yes!!!*

"Now hold up!" Tarra cautioned, "I didn't say yes." The Accord was now pulling out of the parking lot, but Tarra's mind was tearing down the road as if on the freeway in many directions at once. Several questions popped into her head at once. She knew that it would probably be better for Gina to be away from those girls and their big mouths and bad tempers. She had also noted that her sister had indeed upped the attitude progressively more over time since moving in with Kendra. But, practically speaking, how could it be possible? Tarra already had two jobs, stacks of bills, errands to run. Where did a teenager fit into that? This was her kid sister, the one who wanted to be with her all the time and needed constant oversight and direction to make sure she was okay, especially where her schoolwork was concerned. As Tarra considered these possibilities, Gina gazed upon her heavily with pleading eyes, yearning, begging.

"I need time ta think 'bout dis," Tarra finally answered. "When I know wha's happ'nin', I'll let ya know. But jus' give me some room fa' now, okay?"

Gina nodded, conceding if a bit begrudgingly. She was momentarily pleased that she seemed to be gaining ground but didn't want to let the issue go when she might be on a roll. Still, she knew better than to push too hard. "Thanks Tarra, I love you." The Accord pulled up to a traffic light, stopped just before the crosswalk where an old woman pushed a shopping cart full of empty cans and bottles. *Wish she jus' say yes, but I's coo' do. Sound mo' like yes den no.* Smiling brighter, shaking her big sister playfully by the shoulder with both hands, she remained hopeful.

Tarra knew that Gina knew that it was a strong maybe, but she wasn't ready to decide for sure. Not just yet.

The light turned green and the Accord sped off, passed by a purple Chevy Impala carrying four young black men, all decked out in gangster baggies and gold jewelry, with rap music blaring and bass thudding from the trunk. Gina and Tarra were removed from the world outside. They were listening to what they were thinking rather than chatting as usual. Normally, they would be trading excited words back and forth about boys, men, school, work, love, hate, boys, men. They had shared everything together. Kind words, laughs, ice cream. They had shared each other's warmth in alleys when their mother would disappear to buy crack. They shared wound-bandaging duties when either was beaten for spilling food. Shared in cries of *don't take her away from me* when they were sent to separate foster homes by family court. Now they shared a ponderous silence. Gina gazed up and saw Kendra's two-story house approaching, bordered by its immaculate lawn with little statuettes out front and sporting fresh paint and a welcome mat. It looked so inviting from the outside. *Just like Hansel an' Gretel when dey went to da witch.* She smiled at her little joke and reminded herself to tell her foster sisters when she got home. But her smile died quickly. This was home for now, but she couldn't imagine calling this place her home. *If she jus' say yes.* "Aw-right now," Tarra began as she pulled the car into park. "Don't be askin' me 'bout dis era' five minutes neitha, okay?"

Gina nodded. She had lost a lot, suffered a lot. Hope was dangerous. Tarra looked over at her in concern, sensing that something was suddenly wrong, but she decided to let it be. She had her own problems to worry about, mainly, how she was going to take care of herself and her little sister. The thought was overwhelming, but she had just made up her mind that she would try. She still didn't know all the details, but she was beginning to sort them out in her head. She could cut off the cable television, eat out once a week instead of twice, walk to work instead of drive, convert the living room into a bedroom. Yes, it was beginning to sound possible. But for now, she kept it to herself, not wanting to get Gina's hopes up.

"I won't bother you 'bout it," Gina pledged as she unlatched the car door and stepped out onto the sidewalk with one leg, stopping short and glancing back endearingly. "Thanks fo' da movie." She gazed a little longer at her sister behind the wheel. *Wish she a' take me home wit' her an' neva bring me back.* The thought made Gina want to cry and she might have, but she had long ago promised herself she wouldn't. She swore she had run out of tears.

"Anytime baby, we gonna get togetha again soon," Tarra promised. Affectionately stroking a loose strand of hair back over her Gina's ear, she pulled Gina toward her and they hugged goodbye and exchanged hushed "I love yous."

Gina stepped onto the sidewalk and closed the door behind her. The Accord pulled off the driveway with a farewell beep of the horn. Gina waved, imagining the car suddenly turning around to take her away again. Gina dragged herself back up the porch.

A dark part of herself was still fighting off her hopes, trying to keep herself safe from the disappointment that tainted her whole life. She was learning fast not to wait around for something good to happen. But the little girl in her crossed her fingers and wanted to skip again. She was somewhere between a daydream and the real world; she was trying hard to be realistic, but in the way that people try to think themselves out of falling in love. *Bein' wit' Tarra all da time! Late night popcorn wit' Tabasco sauce an' Blockbuster nights... Denzel! Shoppin'! Christmas shoppin'!* Now unable to help it, she was skipping. Christmas... Christmas was months away. *If 'it' happened dis time, dis a be the bes' Christmas. Da way it s'posed to be. Like, how it do fo' white people. All happy and perfect an' era' thang.*

Even as she reached for the front door handle, returning to the world she knew and hated, her mind was still twisting and turning. *A tree an' presents, dinner, family. Family . . .* the word seemed to echo. *My family. Cou' have a family again.* As Gina released the doorknob, her hand fell lifelessly to her side. She tried to come back to the real world, breathing in heavily, looking down at her feet, smiling to herself. *My fingers crossed! I ain't even notice doin' dat.* She almost laughed at herself as she unlatched her fingers in one hand and opened the door with the other.

"Gina? Is dat you?" called a voice from inside the kitchen as soon as the door opened. "Can you help me with the dishes?" Gina hurried off to oblige, knowing playtime had been fun but it was time to get back to work. *Hello woulda been nice. So much fa' homework.* But maybe it wouldn't be long now. Maybe it was just a matter of time before she was gone. No more dishes and screaming teenagers or battles over brushes and who said what. It was always such a joy to be with Tarra. Always so refreshing, so relieving. Wishing upon wishing that the next time it would last forever. Smiling to herself at the thought, she crossed her fingers one last time.

Shawn

Tomorrow was the day. The big day. Thursday. The day of reckoning. The day of the group. Shawn wasn't sure if he wanted to celebrate or call in sick, maybe they weren't mutually exclusive. Anyway, thank God for his group work course being on Wednesday, the day before today. He would at least have a chance to pick up some tricks of the trade before being taken to the limit. It sure felt like being taken to the limit with what awaited him, a rise to 10,000 feet above sea level in a *Top Gun* movie or something. Always moving, always changing. One minute on top, but all of that could change in a split second. Like a fighter pilot being overpowered by an enemy in pursuit. Shawn knew this feeling well. Considering it as he made his way across campus to class, passing protesters in the quad, blond girls in shorts, Shawn momentarily took notice. *Low self-esteem shorts must be in style*, he thought, smiling at his little joke. He observed some break dancers busting moves on the grass over blaring music. The line at the nearby coffee stand extended practically around the corner, each waiting person looking more impatient than the next.

When the group was moving in a good way, when the girls listened and were engaged, he was ecstatic. On top of the world. *I can do this!* His heart sang as he watched variants of inspirational movies like *Lean on Me* in his mind, visualizing the girls hanging on his every word, getting well by the second, with inspiring music blaring from somewhere overhead, just like in those movies. His daydreams carried him and accompanied him across town on the bus, into *The X*. He was ready to charge into the group before him, determined to make a difference.

But this was not always the case. When things got a little out of order, when many voices started to talk at once, or an issue came up that he didn't have the answers for, it was hands across America. *WHAT DO I DO?!?!* He wanted to yell. And Terri just sat there, with her hands folded, calm as could be. *Damn her!!!* he would think jealously.

Class interrupted his silent reflections. He swung open the door to room 114 and walked past the front row where everyone seemed to know each other and took his seat toward the back.

"...and my guys were talking to each other, back and forth as if I wasn't even there. And I just sat back. I wanted to get their attention and so I..." carried on one of Shawn's more experienced peers. The rest of the class, closer to Shawn's age than the more experienced man who was talking, sat in silent awe, gripping the edges of their desks, hanging on his every word. *Must be nice,* Shawn thought enviously. He coveted being the center of attention. His eyes wandered unintentionally and settled on a pretty African American girl three rows down. *HECKA CUTE!!! What's her name? I gotta find out.*

The classroom door was swinging open, a wise-looking gray-haired elderly man in a sweater vest and freshly ironed pants was making his way in. Definitely the professor.

As he made his way to the head of the class, slowly and deliberately, not needing to move fast for anyone, the commotion of the classroom almost reluctantly gave way to excited whispers and rustling papers and backpacks thudding to the floor.

The elderly man's kind, purposeful voice commenced just a second or two before the class came to attention.

"Alright everybody," the professor began, kind and deliberate, silencing the last of the more talkative in the audience without having to lift a finger. "As you will see on page 224, the authors note the stages of group process, engagement, conflict..." he began.

Shawn listened and commiserated. *I hate being interrupted, too, especially in the middle of something so stimulating, intellectually of course!* He had resumed thinking of the African American girl in the front row. He stole another glance, saw her looking at him, smiling, and looking away. *She was looking at me!*

"...and termination." the instructor continued unabated. "So how do you know when you have successfully engaged with your group?" Shawn quickly shifted his attention, beginning to thumb through the pages in the book, impatience increasing with each turning page. *It doesn't say anything about getting hit on!*

Shawn composed himself and put his hand up, answering before being called on. "Depends on how you define engagement," he answered. "Like, last week? My girls' group started up and within two seconds they asked me if I was married and…" Shawn's classmates laughed as he sat there flustered. He had not intended this to be funny.

"So what could that mean?" the professor asked somewhere between amusingly and pointedly. Shawn's apt mind flew over possibilities. He looked at the rest of the class. Girls his age in the back row were whispering, a man in his thirties with wispy gray hair and a dark sweater rested his head back against the nearby wall, the African American girl in the front row—*hecka cute!*—was attentive.

"I'm wondering if it was defensive, like keeping the attention off of them by putting it on me," Shawn replied, waiting expectantly for approval.

His professor nodded in consideration, stepping right foot over left, his finely pressed khakis making a kind of swishing sound as he changed positions. "What else?" he probed to the rest of the class.

"Maybe that's how they are trying to connect with you. Maybe it's the only way that they know how to connect with guys," answered the older, more experienced man who had held the student audience captive earlier. Many heads nodded thoughtfully.

"Could also be true," the professor agreed.

But Shawn found himself getting frustrated. *Okay? So which is it?* Woulda, coulda, shouldas were not exactly the answers he was looking for. He was wondering if there was more to it. He started to tap his pencil rhythmically against his desk, tapped and then looked up at his professor with eager, approval-seeking eyes. "Maybe that's the kind of attention they get from men, so they expect it?"

His thoughts coalesced. *I hadn't thought of it like that. Wow, that sucks! They must have been uncomfortable in that group, probably expecting that since I'm a guy…*

Shawn was lost deep in his mind; the discussion, raised hands, laughter, and cell phone ring tones were all practically muted.

Backpacks zipped, chairs scraped, and feet stamped across the floor while the professor began erasing words in chalk from the blackboard. *Time to go already?* Shawn shook his head in disbelief and glanced at his watch. *Less than 12 hours to go.*

Breathing in heavily, he gathered his things and made his way back outside and into the darkness. Through the courtyard, past campus houses that all looked like each other, neatly clipped lawns, a few beer cans in gutters out front. Loud music, crowds of twos and threes. Laughs, yells, pledges of love, promises of partying like a rock star. Shawn was oblivious. He barely felt his feet gliding over the concrete as he proceeded to his apartment. This world around him was so small and insignificant. He glanced again at his watch. *Less than 11 and a half hours to go.*

The Group

BEEP! BEEP! BEEP! Shawn's alarm clock resounded. It seemed like only a minute had passed after resigning himself to *I'll never get any sleep tonight!* He rubbed his eyes, showered, made coffee, pulled a striped blazer over his shoulders, fixed his hair, glanced at his watch. *6:40am!!! The bus leaves in 10 minutes!!!* He sprinted down to his bus stop and just made it. *Someone up there likes me.* He wiped a drop of his sweat from his brow, dropped his book bag at his feet, heaved a sigh of relief. He was a genuine exercise enthusiast at most times, just not at seven in the morning. He settled into a seat near the front of the bus; as he caught his breath, the lack of sleep caught up to him. His eyelids became heavy, shoulders slumped. Soon he was out like a light.

"*I hate that bitch!!!*"

"*OOOOHHH. Me too, she do too much!!!*"

A rude awakening. Displeased at the sudden interruption, four-letter words came to Shawn's mind. He looked around, still half asleep. High school kids were piling onto the bus in twos and threes, full of energy, full of chatter. Normally, Shawn liked their intensity. Most of the time he even shared it with them, but not before eight in the morning. *Probably for the best though,* he admitted to himself, shaking off the last bit of grumpy. The view out the window told him he had been asleep for over an hour. The 7-11 on the corner and high school students now crowding the interior of the bus told him his destination was not far away. He sat up sleepily and dug in his book bag. He spent the last 10 minutes of his ride reading a few pages of a book he had so greatly enjoyed, *8 Ball Chicks,* by Gini Sykes. It was a story about teenage girls trapped in violence and gang life.

> *Once we see them as individuals, we might become more determined to find the time, money, and people to help them. If we want to save them, we must be willing to pay the cost of education and prevention and intervention programs for kids who are hard to reach. But first we have to listen.*

He rushed to finish the last few words as his stop rapidly approached. *Yes, we have to listen.* Finally, he closed his book and headed toward the exit, nodding politely at the bus driver. She gave him the same peculiar look she had the week before. Unlike last week, Shawn paid it no mind.

But first we have to listen. The words gave him courage. He walked along the street, passed a woman in a stark black coat guiding a little girl carefully down off a curb and into the crosswalk. The little girl skipped as she counted her steps. Shawn smiled. The little girl and, he guessed, her mother looked like they belonged together.

As he rounded the corner, past "cash for your home" signs, he noted the boarded up windows, then a strip club. He shook his head disapprovingly. *That place, so near a school?! They ought to move it somewhere else!!!* He almost laughed out loud. Being around eighth graders was starting to wear off on his thinking processes. *Just move it somewhere else; definitely the kind of thing they would say.*

Continuing further on his way, he met the gaze of a construction worker with an orange safety helmet and matching lunch pail and an elderly woman pushing a shopping cart. Both gave him that second look that seemed to ask the question, *"Are you lost?"* Shawn was beginning to get used to this reaction; the familiarity of it made him less uncomfortable than the week before. It just made sense. After all, there were no other white people for miles who were not teaching in a classroom or driving a police car. These thoughts carried him further into the morning, through his final stretch. Finally, he was walking through the parking lot where kids piled out of cars, mothers waved goodbye, and rap music blared from stereos. Shawn watched and smiled. *I love this place.*

Terri walked up alongside him, startling him a little as she seemed to have come out of nowhere. A flat smile. A flat hello. Shawn's the same in return. How are you, ok, and you, ok. Shawn felt slightly irritated. *This feels like a bank teller–customer conversation.* Walking side by side across the yard, past basketball players, they saw two taller girls chasing a smaller boy, pairs of hands yanking backpacks off shoulders from behind. Lots of hands were on other people's bodies. Shawn almost wanted to laugh. *Hands-off week. What would happen if they had a hands-off week?*

"It's almost nine," Terri informed him as they reached their halfway point. Dead center in the middle of the school yard, halfway between the cafeteria and playground, the counseling office was now half a football field away.

"I'll go get the girls," Shawn announced, already beginning to veer off toward the bungalows on the right.

"I'll go get the room ready," Terri replied, making her way left, never breaking stride. Shawn watched her depart. He could almost hear Taps playing *"all is well, safely rest,"* following in her presence. At the core, he was secretly a little jealous; he had always been a little high strung; he had to admit that her seemingly unbreakable sense of calm must have its advantages.

As he made his way further through the playground, past swings and overflowing garbage cans, a loud bell began blaring from every direction at once. The schoolyard's bustle of activity gradually melted away, doors began opening and closing. The bellows of nearby security guards shepherding the flock soon rang out. "HEEEEEEEYYYYYY!!!!" one of them yelled, his voice deep and raspy. "GOOOOO TO CLLAAAAYAAASS!!!!"

Shawn fought back laughter. Reaching the end of the bungalows, he made his way up the ramp, past the barred window door, the red door with the chipping paint just steps away.

He pulled the door open gently. The light from the sky lit up the floor, sprayed over the desks, caused curious heads to turn. Eyes begin to watch as Shawn entered. The disruption, though, was far less than the week before. Mrs. Trenton nodded at him, somehow still watching the class simultaneously. Was there nothing she couldn't see?

"Good morning, Mr. Reynolds," she greeted. "Can I speak to you for a minute?" she said, ushering him to the door. Shawn was at once nervous, excited, and a little scared. A couple of voices murmured, a desk squeaked, muffled laughter emanated from the far corner of the room. "Keep your hands to yourself!!! Mitchell sit down!!!" Mrs. Trenton demanded without having to look in that direction to see where the disruption was coming from. A body plunked down begrudgingly in a chair and the murmuring subsided. Shawn almost laughed, shaking his head, smiling admiringly. *She sure knows her stuff.* Something else about her now reminded Shawn of his mother. It was the softness of her care mixed with a determination, a stiffness of her spine, purpose, a certainty as to what needed to happen and what she had to do to make it so. This purpose appeared in her eyes as they found Shawn's again.

"I thought you should know. The kids are all saying that Dalanna ran away from home," Mrs. Trenton reported with grave concern. "I just thought you should know."

"Wow, do we know why?" Shawn inquired, frowning as he bit his lip in search of the possibilities. Mrs. Trenton shook her head adamantly, sorrowfully, a deep frown on her face.

"Okay. Thanks, Mrs. Trenton. This is helpful to know. Maybe I can dig into it a bit," he promised.

She smiled as if to say she hoped that it would help but that her experience caused her to worry. Then she was back, snapping the girls to attention. "Dalanna, Gina, Venus, Shantel, Porsche, Rona. Let's go!!! Go with Mr. Reynolds."

Heads bowed in slumber or buried in books began to rise up from jagged rows of desks, periodically scribbled with obscenities. Jackets slinging over shoulders, backpacks dragged on the ground. It was a bit apathetic but by far the most functional classroom on campus. Shawn noted this as he and the girls behind him made their way out onto the blacktop, closing the door behind them with a solitary thud.

In neighboring bungalows, heads hung out windows, forms sauntered in and out of classrooms, lounged against the tetherball pole. Kids were opening doors and shouting or throwing things inside, slamming the doors behind, running away in chaotic laughter. Shawn and the girls were making their way further down the row of bungalows.

A girl was chatting inattentively on her cell phone, ignoring the pleading from an elderly male teacher for her to get off the phone and return to her desk inside. As Shawn and the girls made their way past, he staring on disapprovingly. *Unbelievable!*

"HHHEEEEEEEEEEEEYYYYY..." came an urgent declaration from a security guard across the yard. His steps toward the bungalows were methodical; there was a limp in his left leg, halfway pimp and halfway old age. "GOOOOOOOOO TO CLAAAYAAAS!!" A head or two drifted back in the windows, the girl on her cell phone looked up irritably, then ducked into the crevice of the door and wall as if to continue her conversation invisibly. Shawn and the girls were now almost past the last of the bungalows. A little head with a big smile popped out of a door, neck and body invisible. He looked like one of those heads that pop out of the amusement park games that you have to hit with the hammer before it pops back inside.

"Whassup Mr. Reynolds!!!" The little boy piped excitedly. Shawn opened his mouth to answer.

"JOHNSON!!!!!" thundered a deep male voice from past the cracked opening of the door. Johnson's eyes widened and his smiling face plummeted to agony; he jumped back suddenly, as if stung by a hornet. A heavy-set African American man with wild, natural hair protruding from either side of his baseball cap marched to the door. Lumbering with heavy steps, his windbreaker jacket seeming to flow over his shoulders, his coach's whistle bouncing on his chest.

His heavy glare through thin-rimmed spectacles was practically burning a hole through the side of Johnson's head. Johnson slumped back inside, skulking over to his desk. His keeper, whistle and all, peered out from the open door. Nodding in greeting to Shawn, unobtrusively scanning the nearby school yard, over and through heads protruding from classroom windows to a makeshift jukebox of older boys, two or three sputtering into their hands and another putting together his best effort at rap lyrics.

"HEEEEEY YOU KIDS!!!!" he screamed in outrage, "GET BACK IN der!!!" By his first word, they had scattered like pin balls. By his third word, the formerly lively schoolyard was a ghost town. Shawn fought back laughter, knowing that he had another story to tell his mother in the car ride from school at the end of the day. The door slammed behind the P.E. teacher. Superfluous noise began to build.

"Heeyyyy foo!!!!"

"OOOOOOOOOOOOOOOHHHHHHHHHHHHH!!!"

"QUIET!!!!" the P.E. teacher bellowed again, followed by stony silence. This time, Shawn couldn't help himself and he burst out laughing. The girls glanced up, scowling at the just departing classroom scene.

"Damn that foo' always talkin' shit!!!" one of the girls remarked contemptuously.

"YEAH!" the others agreed.

Shawn gazed over curiously, searching for words. "Is-is that the best way you can say that?" he asked. The girls looked at him perplexed, looked at each other the same way, saying nothing. Shawn smiled to himself. *Maybe this is the therapy—the silence.*

After a longer silence, they reached the counseling office. Shawn held the door for the girls as they dragged their feet inside, walking in single file. Backpacks cast to the ground, rears plunking into seats. Porsche and Shantel sitting next to each other. Venus taking her seat on the right of Shantel. All three moving inward, a group within the group. Shawn picked up his chair, motioned Venus to the right of him and sat in between them. *They need to break this up. Wonder what this will do? Well, only one way to find out.* A couple of them were watching him, waiting for his next move.

Terri was frowning at the hideous-looking black eye that Dalanna tried to hide by lowering her face into her jacket. Terri said hello, and a few of them offered hellos in return. Shawn noticed Terri noticing something. *She always has that watchful eye. What is she seeing?* He followed her eyes to Dalanna's left. *Oh yeah! She ran away. We've gotta figure this out!*

"Girls, excuse me and Ms. Terri for a minute," Shawn exclaimed, hurriedly making his way up from his seat, motioning Terri to follow. She obliged. The girls began to chatter amongst themselves.

"What's up?" Terri inquired, her eyes soft, hands folded across her lap and her fingers interlaced as if she was sitting down. Shawn, leaning toward her, began speaking in hushed whispers.

"Just wanted you to know that Mrs. Trenton said that word has been getting around that Dalanna ran away from home, but nobody's sure why," he reported. Terri's head began nodding in concern. She didn't say anything; she appeared to be deliberating.

Shawn grew impatient. "What do you think we should do?" he inquired, quietly frantic. He hated to admit it, but he hoped beyond hope that she had the answer he didn't. *C'mon, we gotta do something.*

Terri breathed in heavily, looking back to the girls one by one. "Let's see if they bring it up," she proclaimed, returning to her seat without waiting for an agreement.

Shawn nodded to himself. *Okay then.*

Meanwhile, the girls had already gotten underway.

"OOOHHH he do too much!!!"

"Fo' real!"

"The way he be yellin' an' shit!!!"

"OOOOHHH!!!"

"I mean stuff like…"

"How does it affect you guys when people yell at you?" Terri probed.

Good question, Shawn admitted. *I'll have to remember that one.*

"Make me sad," replied Venus.

"Sheeit, I holla back!!!" Porsche pronounced, "Ain't nobody gonna talk ta me like dat. I don't care who dey is!!!" Gina and Venus both seemed blown back into their seats.

"Damn girl, I ain't even done yet! Hold up!" Venus exclaimed in outrage.

Porsche frowned, holding her hand up high and making a wide pointing gesture. "Yeah, but you was jus' talkin'!" Some other mouths opened to comment. Shawn began to feel more and more out of control as if tumbling down the rabbit hole in Wonderland.

"Okay," Terri intervened, silencing the dissenters in the audience. "So how does everyone want to handle this?"

"Well, I think we all should have a turn, an' everybody else be quiet 'til it's they turn," Venus suggested.

"YEAH!" exclaimed several voices at once, heads nodding affirmatively.

"Okay, so is that what you guys want to do then?" Terri inquired. "We'll each take a turn and then go around in a circle?" The girls all nodded, exchanging contented smiles.

"OKAY I'S MY TURN!!!" Porsche announced, again. She sat up further in her seat.

"So let's see," she began, smacking her lips loudly. "Me and my girls was out kickin' it, you know?" Heads nodding, Gina leaning forward attentively, Venus frantically pressing buttons on a cell phone just beyond the confines of her pocket. "An' der was dis old man who was tryin' to preach an' shit? Ha! Talkin' about 'respect yo' self lil' girls.'" The girls all began laughing at her impression; Shawn was fighting back laughter of his own. "And I fit ta go get my hair an' my nails done, my auntie gonna kick me down some scratch an' we fit ta go shoppin'. Gonna go down to da mall an' der 'bout ta be some cute ass boys. Like dat boy at Foot Locker?!?!?"

"OOOOHHH YEAH!!!"

"HE HECKA CUTE!!!"

"Yeah! But you bes' ta back off do," Porsche cautioned. "'Cuz giiiirll das my man!!! Feel me?"

Rona stared down at the floor, obviously elsewhere. Shantel and Dalanna looked dubious.

"OKAY I'S MY TURN!!!" Venus proclaimed. "Yes, mm-hmm, I done met up wit' some hecka' cute boys y'all. 'There's dis boy Jerome I been messin' wit'. Oh, yeah. He got a six pack."

"OOOOHHH I like dat!!!"

A couple of heads nodded hard in agreement.

"So anyway," Venus continued. "Yeah he hecka cute. Den da otha' day? I was up on da bus, you know, da twenty fo'."

"Uh," Shantel grimaced. "Der some ugly ass boys up on dat bus an' dey always tryin' ta holla."

"Fo' real!" Dalanna agreed mightily.

"So I was der an' dis oooolllllld ass man came up tryin' ta mack. He hella old. But den der was worse shit too. My boyfriend in jail."

Shawn was confused, and even a little dismissive. *Boyfriend. Which one? You've talked about at least a few different men so far.*

"My brotha in jail now too," Venus continued, face falling to the floor, hands folding in her lap. "Ain't even knowin' when he fit ta be let out. Then my momma' an' my daddy, whooo-wee dey gonna be trippin' y'all." Pausing for a breath. "Okay, das it."

"Okay now I'm gonna go! It's ma' turn!!!" Dalanna announced.

"Well, just one second," Terri asserted gently. "I want to check in with Rona. Rona, how are you doing?"

But Rona remained motionless. Staring hard at the floor, tense, sullen, saddened, lost. Saying nothing in return, frowning off into the distance. Venus fast growing lost in a long braid she had been twisting around a jagged fingernail. Shantel looked on with an almost motherly concern. Porsche smacked her lips loudly.

"Rona? What's been going on?" Shawn encouraged, leaning slightly forward, watching her closely, and feeling ever so protective.

"Let me tell y'all," Rona finally began. As she paused, the ensuing suspense was terrible. "My week was bootsy as hell!!!"

The girls all laughed triumphantly.

"Let me tell y'all," Rona continued. "They doin' a lil' too much up in my house. My mama man was off da hook. Tryin' to be all loud and shit! With his no job, no showa' ass!!!" Giggles followed, Shawn fighting back his own. "I ain't about to let dat motha fucka talk ta me like dat. Be all yellin an' shit."

"That must be hard for you," Shawn said in barely more than a whisper.

Rona looked up at him dauntingly. "Ain't even da half!" She nearly yelled, smacking her lips again and thinking hard amidst the prevailing silence, "He was out of pocket last night. Gone crazy! Look at my face! Dat motha fucka try ta choke me an' den he slap me hella hard. Watch! I'm gonna get my daddy ta bomb on him like a motha fucka!" Shawn was feeling the onset of panic, knowing there was something that needed to be done but not sure what, scrambling, wondering what to say.

"He did that to you?" Gina piped up like a mother tending to an infant child who had fallen from a swing. The other girls were on the edges of their seats.

"He came at my momma too! Pushed her an' he whooped her hella bad!" Rona exploded, meeting Shawn's eyes fiercely.

"Rona, we're going to do something about this," Shawn interrupted, sensing that she was beginning to come apart just as his protective feelings were growing stronger. Rona looked up, for a second hopeful and then suspicious. Turning away, she darted her eyes to a faint spot on the wall and breathed hard.

"That's right," Terri agreed. "Rona it's not okay for anyone to hit you, and that goes for all of you."

"Y'all jus' don't get it," Porsche muttered just loud enough for the group to here.

Shantel and Dalanna concurred by shaking their head and arching their eyebrows.

"All black people whoop der kids!" Porsche concluded.

"I don't care who does it or for what reason," Shawn insisted. "It's not okay for anyone to hit you guys. Especially men! And especially people close to you. If we, the adults around you, don't keep you safe, who's going to?" He was searching the girls' faces for a sign of understanding. Each was looking the other way and a dreadful silence continued for 15 or 20 seconds.

"Nobody will!" Dalanna declared. "Fo' real y'all! Das how black people be livin'. My mama too. See? Look wha' she did ta my eye an' up here too!" Dalanna pulled down her collar, exposing a wicked looking gash on the side of her neck. Shawn looked away, his face flushed in embarrassment. *Don't want anyone to think I was looking down a girl's shirt.*

"Yo mama mean," Shantel murmured, leaning forward to look closer at Dalanna's scar. Gina frowned hard in concern. Venus looked mightily uncomfortable and made herself busy by pushing buttons on her cell phone.

"Dalanna, we're going to do something about that too," Shawn told her, watching her closely. She was looking at him intently, as if she wanted to believe him.

"Ain't gonna change nothin'," Porsche muttered. Each of the girls looked away, dejected, resigned.

"Maybe it will," Shawn ventured, though silently wishing that he was as sure as he sounded. "Maybe everything can't change overnight. But when we started, I told you guys that Ms. Terri and I were going to help you guys. That wouldn't mean anything if you told us what you told us, and we just sat back and did nothing. We're going to do everything we can. And that means not going home as if all of this is okay. I need to be able to go home at the end of the day saying 'I did what I could.' But that means we also need to tell somebody outside of this group so we can make sure that something gets done."

Rona looked up, wide-eyed, jaw dropping. "They gonna put me in a foster home?" She demanded fearfully, almost dreading the answer. Gina shivered inwardly.

"O' a group home!?!" Shantel piped up, feeling the need to jump in and inform. "My cousins had problems wit' they family an' they up in group homes." An ominous weight fell on the others, as if Judgment Day itself lay just around the corner.

"Probably not," Terri assured. Shawn was grateful that she had taken over. "Most of the time, someone just comes out to talk to you about what happened and then wants to talk to whoever hurt you. Then they work with you guys to figure out what can be done so that the hitting stops."

"But dat be messed up," Porsche insisted. "'Cuz den dat foo' gonna be hella mad an' gonna whoop you hella bad."

"But you guys already did get whooped hella bad," Shawn replied. He wanted to say more, felt like there was more to be said but nothing came. And the girls all looked the same. Dalanna looked ready to escape. Rona looked a little worn out. Venus had resumed sending text messages. Porsche shifted back and forth in her seat, fidgeting, as if pulled by the harshness of all of the elements of the world, all at once, unsure of where to go.

A quietness permeated the room, and somehow Shawn knew that it was a quietness that needed to be left alone. He looked around, noticing that the eight chairs in a circle seemed closer to each other. Each head huddled closer into the circle. Solemn faces, folded hands, deep breaths, peace, comfort. By this time, they had been a group for some weeks. But this was the first time that it felt like they were all truly together.

Assessment

The girls had experienced significant losses and traumas in their lives, but it was around these experiences they shared in common that they were beginning to connect with each other. They had abusive parents, were objectified and violated by men, and tended to lack the social supports and strong attachment relationships that would help them work through their times of distress. The result was that they had to live in a world where they could be threatened or attacked at any time, and they had to develop strategies for survival that they could readily call upon. This included their tendencies to stay out late, to behave aggressively, and to be sharp tongued and adept at talking their way out of troublesome situations. They also associated with at-risk peer groups and pursued multiple opposite-gender relationships at once. A certain degree of these behaviors could be considered developmentally normal for adolescents. However, the girls tended to engage in these behaviors to a significant degree.

One of my primary motives for telling these stories is to reveal the normalcy of their lives in this situation; any one of their stories is experienced in common by young African American women in *The X*. Sexual harassment, drug abuse, and child abuse are harsh and abnormal; but for the girls in this story, these experiences were harsh and common.

Cultural factors were particularly noteworthy in group this week. The girls seemed to agree that "all black people beat their kids," which almost seemed to justify the abuse they survived. Part of this relates to their sense of loyalty. Herman (1996) noted that children need to be able to look to their parents or protectors as benign, even if the parents are abusive. If the children see the parents as bad, they will feel utter despair, which is intolerable. Thus, to survive, abused children will often defend the abusive parents and sacrifice themselves to protect the abusers' position. Although Herman did not say as much, I wonder if this theory may be transferable into cultural communities. In essence, I wonder if the girls' statement that "all black people beat their kids and you don't get it" was their way of protecting the necessarily benign position of their cultural community, as if it were a surrogate parent. Thus their assertion that "all black people beat their kids and you [the white facilitators] don't get it" may have been their way of surviving and avoiding the utter despair noted by Herman.

Rates of childhood abuse were high in *The X*, but it was important for the girls to hear from adults that the abuse was not okay and that, despite sociocultural trends, they deserved to feel safe and to be protected. Given mandated reporting laws, reports were made to Child Protective Services on Rona and Dalanna's behalf. It would have been good for the girls to explore the larger sociocultural issues they introduced, but that exploration would be better undertaken with a therapist (or co-therapists) who were also African American.

Group therapy was a particularly powerful medium, because it helped to bridge the cultural gap between the co-facilitators and the girls. More specifically, *The X* was over 95 percent African American, and Terri and I were the only clinical resources available. This ultimately meant that if the kids were to be treated individually, they would have to be treated by white therapists. This is not meant to say that cross-cultural therapy cannot work. Rather, it adds credence to the group model; it may have been more difficult for the white co-facilitators to relate to the girls in an individual therapy setting than for the girls to relate to each other in the group setting.

In addition, group therapy offered them a viable treatment option for healing from their traumatic experiences. Herman (1996) noted that, once trust and safety begin to be re-established, group therapy can help survivors reconnect to the world, which is an integral step in the healing process. This was definitely the case for the girls in the group.

For the girls, full recovery would be difficult given that they continued to suffer the daily traumas of being harassed, violated, and threatened. Nevertheless, in the group, the girls could begin to talk things out, get support from peers, and recover in incremental steps. In addition, if the girls had good experiences in the group, they might be more willing to seek out additional clinical experiences down the road. Even though the group was unlikely to serve as a corrective factor for the immense totality of their suffering, it did provide them with an hour a week of sanctity, spirit, and connection.

SIX

Week 12

Rona

"SIT DOWN!"

BOOOMM!!!

"FUCK!"

Laughter.

Mr. Justice's English class was again in shambles. Rona couldn't help but laugh along with everyone, but soon her mind reverted to her darkest fear. She was worried beyond worry over the talk she had the previous day with her principal, Mr. Johnson. *Failing all of your classes. Won't be able to graduate,* he had told her sternly. And Rona had worked up a sweat.

Held back? Seventh grade again?!?! Aw hell nah'!!! The prospect of it was harrowing, humiliating. Some of Rona's peers had been held back. The boy yelling in colorful metaphors just moments ago had been held back twice. Towering above his fellow classmates, a Goliath in a valley of Davids. The butt of all the jokes. *Stupid, lazy,* and worst of all, as people in *The X* would always say, *N.C.N.* or *no count niggas.* They could disappear from the world, the ghetto they knew, and it wouldn't make a bit of difference. No one would even miss them. *No count,* Rona thought grimly to herself. The worst of the worst, unreachable, the lowest of the low, and they knew it as well as everyone else did. Many of their parents were addicted to alcohol and crack and did

117

not care or did not notice or just yelled as they were held back year after year until they finally dropped out of school and went in and out of juvenile hall and group homes. Drunk in front of liquor stores, slurring feigned attempts at English, leering at little girls on the street. On the fast track to prison. Thoroughly disgusting. Being held back was something Rona just could not deal with. How could things be any worse?

Just then, the classroom door swung open and a white woman in a business suit and high heels strode up to the head of the class as if walking through walls. Smiling a Bank of America teller smile at the dark eyes that met hers, she was greeted only with suspicious stares.

Something was up. All of the kids knew it. When white people showed up unannounced, something was always up. They wouldn't even sit next to the kids on the bus, look them in the eyes, or walk past them without nervous fidgeting, let alone make the trip, as the kids called it, *from Disneyland to Death Row,* unless something was up.

"Ray-Ray yo' lawya here!"

"Shut up motha' fucka', das yo mama!"

"OOOHHHH!!!!"

"HAAAA HE ROASTED ON YO' ASS!!!"

"Fuck you!"

"HEY HEY HEY!!!" yelled Mr. Justice, more begging them to stop than ordering.

The commotion subsided temporarily, but the hum in the air remained. Hushed whispers were exchanged between Mr. Justice and the woman; she motioned to Rona, attempting to be discrete but fooling no one. Now the kids definitely knew something was up. Their heads began turning simultaneously and their eyes located Rona. Rona was trembling inwardly. *'Da fuck I do now?!*

And then she put the pieces of the puzzle together. *Tyrone, group... 'we're going to do something about this,'* Mr. Reynolds had said. And Rona knew. Even before she knew, she knew.

"Hello, Rona?" the white woman asked, suddenly at Rona's desk, smiling and leaning over. "Can I talk to you outside for a minute?" Rona shivered involuntarily, wishing there was some way to say no. But her feet worked where her words failed. *Clip-clop-clip-clop* went the white woman's heels across the classroom floor. Rona rose and followed her, closing the door behind her as she and Ray-Ray's lawyer made their way just outside. Rona felt as if she were on trial, awaiting her fate, the pale gray sky above her confirming her sense that this was judgment day.

"Whassup?" Rona probed suspiciously, her eyes bouncing from nothing in particular to the grim reaper in wait. "Who you?"

"Rona, I work with Child Protective Services," the woman informed. "I came here to talk to you about a report I received about something that happened at your house. Did your mother's boyfriend, Tyrone, ever hit you?"

Rona had to swallow hard to prevent choking. *What I'm s'posed to say?* She was somewhere between sorrow and panic. *What I done?* She hesitated, knowing that the words that were to come out of her mouth were to have dire consequences.

"Rona, I'm not here to cause your family problems," the woman assured, leaning over slightly. "I heard that something happened to you, and I'm here to try to make things right. No matter what happened, no matter what it all means, it's not okay for anyone to hit you. Never. Not your father, not your mother, no one."

That's when Rona remembered. *Mama*!!! Her mother's head being smashed against the kitchen cabinets, her eyes wide in fear. Rona's own fear overtaken by hatred, hatred that was bald and limitless and powerful. *Dat mutha fucka! Nobady hit my mama!!!* Glaring in bloodlust. Hungry for revenge. The rest of the interview took care of itself.

The rest of the day was a blur. A fight on the yard. Two police cars showing up. Police officers marching down the hall. Shouts and whispers and uproars in the classrooms. A dice game out on the yard. A helicopter overhead. The latest schoolyard gossip of who likes who and who said what about someone else. Usually this was all exhilarating, but not now.

Rona could no longer hear or see. She was lost in her thoughts, with her mind racing. *What gonna happen?* Trying to retrace her steps. *What I tell dat white lady?* As much as she tried, she couldn't quite remember all of it, but she recalled enough to figure out that she had said plenty. A twisting in her gut told her something was wrong, really wrong, and something dreadful was about to happen.

They gonna put me in a group home? Or a foster home? Fuck! I shouldn't a' said nothin'!!! People always be sayin' don't trus' dem white folks. Sheeit them motha' fuckas' quick ta snatch you out yo' house an' home. I shouldn't have said nothin'. And when she stepped onto the bus at the end of the day, Rona almost wished she didn't have the money for the fare. That way, she might have had to walk, delaying the inevitable. She had a dreadful feeling that there would be hell to pay for both her and her mother.

'We're going to investigate further,' that's what the white woman said. Rona didn't understand quite what that meant, but it sounded horrendous. It meant they weren't done yet. Rona thought and thought about it, remembering one of her grandmother's gospel sermons. *When white folks get up in black people's mix, most a' da time it mean somebody ain't gonna be 'round no mo'. Somebody goin' to prison, fosta home... white folks come up in black people's*

shit, an' somebody goin' away. They don't come up in yo' house wit'out takin' somethin' o' somebody with 'em.

Yeah, but Tyrone gonna be in trouble! Rona smiled at the thought. It actually cheered her up a bit. She began picturing the darkest of her fantasies: Tyrone behind bars and fed bread and water, thin, starving, a black eye or two. *Maybe get booty played by some big ass nigga!!!* Rona laughed out loud. She grinned the rest of the way home, until she heard the sound of crying and despairing sobs from just inside the door. *What da fuck he done now?! I'm gonna get my daddy ta fuck him up with da quickness.* Thrusting her key into the lock in the front door with one hand, swinging the door open wildly with the other. Ready to take on the world. Knowing he had nearly killed her the last time, but she didn't care. Didn't care what happened to her. Her fury knew no bounds. And its wrath would be felt in all its scarlet hatred.

But the house was full of little emptinesses. The closet near the front door was wide open; one half full of women's dresses and business suits, and the other side empty. Clothes hangers dangled lifelessly. Stereo, gone. Television and radio, gone. There was a gaping hole where Tyrone's comfy armchair usually resided. *Dat where his lazy ass always sit an' be listenin' ta corny ass music an' watchin' TV. Why it ain't der no mo'?*

Rona finally got it. At once shocked and then thrilled. *Gone! He, like, fo' real gone!* Rona couldn't believe it, wouldn't believe it. She looked around the room and knew it was true. No other way that Tyrone's most treasured possessions would be gone. Barely able to believe this most wonderful of truths!!! *At last! He out fo' good! 'Bout time!* Rona was so happy she couldn't help but to hug herself tightly and spin around like a little girl. Couldn't wait to share in the good news with her mother.

How they would celebrate! They would turn on the radio and drop it like it's hot, mother and daughter style, like they did on Rona's last birthday. The most good of good times.

BOOM!!! The slam of a door resounded at the far end of the house. Then came a shuffling of feet down the hallway, crude and sluggish. Rona cringed in expectation. Shrinking further back into her skin with each approaching footstep, having long ago learned what the sound of those footsteps meant, that someone in particular was coming.

"Oh, shhhooo' I fine'ly see ya' deciiiide ta grace us wit'choo' presence…" slurred a sarcastic male voice. Rona snapped her head to the left, scowling furtively, her eyes finding Tyrone's. His eyes were red and weary as if he hadn't slept. He stopped halfway into the living room and started looking Rona up and down with a look of bitter disgust. Then he turned halfway back the way he had come so that he could just barely growl over his shoulder.

"See bitch?!?!" he hollered, "I told'ja...Yo' damn child do whateva' da fuck she waw'na do!!! Come home late, callin' the CPS, don't know what da damn world comin' to!"

Rona felt the anger building. *He just call ma'mama a bitch?* Taking a long step forward so that she could just peer down the hall in outrage, she waited for her mother's next move. *I know my mama ain't 'bout ta go out like dat!!*

But silence prevailed until it was broken by the soft sound of crying in the distance. Her mother was solemnly mourning at the kitchen table, staring through the carpet at her feet, her face long, and her hands folded sorrowfully in her lap.

Tyrone was relentless. "Don't got nothin' ta say for yo' self?" he demanded. "Yeah, das right. I wouldn't neither!!!" Staring down at Rona's mother in gleeful contempt like the owner of an abused dog, he was enjoying her suffering. He stood for a good minute or two, barely able to keep his balance. His stained white shirt sagged over atrophied muscles. Something oozed from the corner of his mouth.

Rona smacked her lips in revulsion; he was so thoroughly disgusting. *How cou' mama' even like dat man!! Damn he ugly.* "She ain't gotta say nothin' ta you!" Rona screamed, unable to sit idly by any longer. Her cheek was slightly quivering and her fists were clenched.

Tyrone chuckled scornfully as he took a menacing step forward, his jet black Timberland boots sending haunting vibrations through the floor. He was just an arm's reach from Rona.

"Child Po'tective Service ain't get here fast 'nough this time!" Tyrone growled, his oppressive right arm flexing and rising to attack position. Rona felt a powerful grip on her bicep, sudden and total. It flung her stunned form backward. But it wasn't Tyrone this time.

"TAKE ONE MO' STEP AN' I'M CALLIN' YO' PARO' OFFICA'!!!" Rona's mother boomed, her neck wagging mightily from side to side, her left eyebrow cocking high on her forehead. Rona had never heard such finality in her mother's voice.

Her mother's protective arm shielded her daughter. Tyrone looked caught off guard as he wobbled there, holding his breath, perplexed, angry. *He's dat bully at schoo' who pick on you 'til you punch him in da mouth, and he run screamin' fo' his mama.* The fear, the uncertainty. Rona could almost feel sorry for him.

"Mmmm-hmmm," Rona's mother continued, "But you ain't doin' dis no mo.' Hear me? Get the rest o' yo' shit an' get out my house!!"

Tyrone scowled, kicking the carpet and shaking his head like a little kid made to clean his room. Grabbing a box full of electrical cords from behind him, he stumbled toward the door.

"Maaaan, fine. Y'all wawn't me gawn'?!" He said, hazardously turning around to leer, "Den good, cuz I'm walkin' on outta hea' fo' eva'. Go on an' say dat shit now, cuz ya' know ya' be back bitch!!! You with yo' fat ass, ain't no man gonna want ya'. Why you think lil' Kentucky Fried's father out there with dem white bitches?!"

"GET OUT!!" Rona's mother screamed. But Tyrone was already halfway out the door, boxes under his arm. He tried to slam the door behind him, but it bounced back open. Rona's mother marched up behind him and slammed it firmly, latched it, and looked at it.

Rona couldn't have been happier to see him go. *See ya an' I wouldn't wanna be ya! Sheeit!!! 'Bout time.* She wanted to yell out loud, take her mother's hands and have a little victory dance. But Rona could tell that her mother did not share in her ecstasy. No celebration, no dancing, no smiles.

"Mama? You awright?" Rona piped up, confused, afraid. But her mother said nothing. She just stood there looking more alone than she ever had. She was fighting back tears, stealing her way to the living room window. She was following Tyrone's every footstep around the corner until he was out of sight. She sighed and stayed at the window, slightly shaking.

"Mama?" Rona wondered out loud. Suddenly frightened, panicked. *He gawn!?!?! Why she all sad an' shit?!?! C'mon mama!!! Say somethin'!!!*

But still, her mother said nothing, making the silence between them all the more dreadful.

Finally, her mother looked up and steadied herself. The sudden loneliness, the tears on her cheeks would have to be put aside for now. She wiped her tears away gracefully with the back of her hand and looked halfway over her shoulder to her daughter behind her. Her mouth began to open, and Rona awaited her words. Her mother always had this way of knowing just what to say. Only this time, there were no words.

Rona could only watch, wonder, wait, worry. Biting her lip hard, her face creased into a frown, sullen and confused. She watched her mother watch the empty street, remembering what just happened, remembering that night, that terrible night. Her mother shoved from the refrigerator, Tyrone's hand strangling the life from Rona's neck. Group. *We're going to help you.* Child Protective Services. The front door slamming. Tyrone gone. Rona always figured it would be the happiest day of her life. She used to daydream that one day she would come home from school and he would be gone. No goodbye. No explanation. Vanished. Leaving just her and her mama. And everything would be fine.

Only now she wasn't so sure. There in the living room, watching her mother watch the night go by. So beautiful in most respects—wavy gold earrings, beautifully straightened hair shining brighter than any Vidal Sassoon commercial. Her flowing black dress, elegantly deep purple nails, smelling of sweet perfume, and yet with the saddest of sadnesses wearing heavy on her face.

What I done? Rona worried.

Shantel, Porsche, and Dalanna

Shantel closed the door behind her, dropping her backpack to the ground, stealing a quick glance into the mirror hanging just beside her front door, whisking a strand of bright green braid out of her eyes and back through her long extensions.

"Mama my track slipped!!! We need ta go to da shop!" She hollered through the house. *Damn! I just got dis shit put in too!*

"Girl who you yellin' at like dat?" retorted a deep, and yet quietly outraged, male voice from around the corner. A stern face with deep chocolate complexion, salt and pepper hair, a collared shirt fresh with starch. Shantel shifted her eyes left, smiling halfway apologetically.

"Sorry daddy," she replied sweetly. Her father gave her the once over look, taking her in with not quite approval. Her tight-fitting jeans, shirt open halfway down her chest.

"And what's dat outfit all about?" he demanded, clicking his tongue in dismay. He began wiping imaginary loose strands of his mustache to their respective sides with a thumb and index finger.

"What? Dis?" Shantel inquired, feigning obliviousness.

Her father cleared his throat. "No, not that," he motioned at her outfit, wagging a stubby finger. "That. That's what I'm talkin' 'bout," making the same motion all over again.

Shantel insolently smacked her lips.

"Go on upstairs an' put somethin' else on. And throw dat shit out. What kind a' way is dat to carry yo' self???"

"C'mon daddy?!?" she whined. Looking up and left as if thinking hard, her father watched her closely in the silence, frowning, knowing she was up to something. She always was up to something when she got quiet like that.

"Okay," she initially agreed, "I could go to da mall an' buy some new shit…"

"Watch yo' damn mouth!" her father ordered. "Don't you got nothin' upstairs you cou' go put on?"

Shantel shrugged her shoulders. "Ain't got nothin' clean daddy."

Her father snorted. "Mmmm-hmm."

"Maybe I could go to da mall an' pick somethin' out?" Shantel encouraged. *Ooooohhh c'mon daddy, jus' go on an' break me off. You know you gonna do it. Always tryin' ta act like you fit ta say no. Just go on an' do it, hell.*

Her father breathed heavily through his nose, muttering something that sounded resentful. Jamming his hand into his back pocket, returning with his wallet, pulling a few bills out, he handed over a few 20s.

"So where you gonna get dis outfit at anyway?" he asked suspiciously.

"I know daddy," Shantel readily supplied, nodding affirmatively. "I can't be going up to the mall up on South Side?" Her puppy dog eyes were looking anywhere but at her father. Had he been paying attention, he would have known right away that she was saying what she was supposed to say and had no intention of following through. But after handing over the money, he had quickly diverted his attention to elsewhere. Did he have his keys? Grabbing his jacket from the nearby coat rack, he commenced smoothing his hair over in the mirror.

"All right, baby I gots ta go ta work," he informed, feverishly glancing to his watch, pulling his heavy tan Parka around his shoulders. "Cold as hell out der too…okay. I'll be back late tonight. You be in by eight o'clock." Shantel sucked her teeth.

"An' don't tell ya' momma I gave you money, awright?" he inquired.

Shantel beamed, throwing her arms around his shoulders, kissing him mightily on the cheek. "I won't," she promised. "An' I love ya' daddy. And I prob'ly be home even earlier. I gots lots a' homework!"

"Good girl," he affirmed, kissing her lightly on the forehead before making his way for the door. "Okay then. Bye baby." Shantel watched him make his way down the porch and to the car, excitedly punching digits on the phone.

"Hello?"

BOOM, BA-BOOM, BA-BA-BOOM

THUD!

QUIT SLAMMIN' MY GOD DAMN DOOR!!!

"Daaaamn girl, what da fuck goin' on over there?" Shantel asked into her phone's receiver, almost not wanting to know, taken aback by the sudden raucous activity evident on the other end.

"Sheeit you know how it is 'round here," Dalanna answered on the other end. "My mama got some people ova', dey doin' dey thang."

Shantel sighed to herself. *Damn, guess I ain't even appreciate da quiet around here. I mean, it get boring as hell. But, damn, dey be doin' ova' der at Dalanna' house.*

"Hey I'm 'bout ta be ova' der," Shantel informed. "Hold up, I'm gonna call you back on my cell." Hanging up before Dalanna could answer and whisking her cell phone from her pocket in a quick motion, she was already beginning to make her way out the front door. Opening it just a crack, latching it behind her, and making her way down the street as she began to dial Dalanna's number.

Dalanna laughed half-heartedly. "Mmm-hmm. So wha's goin' on ova' der?!?!"

"Girl you know how it is 'round here," Shantel answered, both laughing playfully but with an underlying touch of sadness. "Jus' some more fools gettin' rolled on by da po-lice."

There were three boys with their hands on the fence letting a police man and woman go through their pockets. Shantel also noticed a group of onlookers across the street.

"Sheeit, ain't no thang," Dalanna clucked, feigning sympathy, smacking her lips. "Jus' anotha' day up in da X, feel me?"

"Mmm-hmm," Shantel agreed. She rounded a corner and stepped high over a split-concrete sidewalk, either side of the cavity arched high as if it were a buried volcano. The sky was turning to twilight, the sidewalks in front of the liquor stores were beginning to fill up, helicopters could be heard chop-chopping in the distance. The night was beginning to come alive.

"Ooooooh girl, da ghetto birds out tanight!!!" Shantel cooed.

"Sheeit, ain't even eight o'clock yet," Dalanna agreed.

Shantel ducked off the main road, past fences of black steel bars and signs advertising "keep out" and warning that there was a neighborhood watch program in effect. She made her way through a gate that hung lifelessly on one hinge and strode into a courtyard filled with drinkers and gamblers and smokers throwing her glaring looks followed by uproarious laughter as she passed by. Dalanna's dingy apartment was not far away.

"Boo!!" someone said from behind a tree. Shantel jumped at least two feet in the air.

"Boo? Whatchoo mean boo?!" Shantel snapped, more scared than angry.

Dalanna laughed gaily, hanging up and putting away the cell phone that had just been at her ear. "I'm just playin'," Dalanna explained. "Whassup?" she asked, pausing just half a second for an answer. Shantel opened her mouth to respond, but Dalanna overrode her. "Okay, let's go get dat ho Porsche an' roll ova' ta Brandy' house." Shantel smacked her lips and turned around to walk the way she had come as Dalanna followed.

"Girl, wha' choo doin' out here anyway?" Shantel inquired, "Ain't you gotta tell yo' mama' where you goin'? She gonna whoop you , you jus' watch…"

Dalanna just scowled and shook her head. The two girls proceeded through town rapidly, their footsteps keeping in time with one another. They gracefully meandered past graffiti-laden walls, a Baptist church, a light-skinned woman with short shorts and long hair pushing two strollers simultaneously, a man in a bus driver's uniform smiling and nodding as he passed in the opposite direction.

Dalanna ran an off-white press-on nail over the part in her bangs, collecting her thoughts. "Sheeit, I ain't been home," she proclaimed. *An I ain't goin' neitha'!!! Tired of all a' her shit. Bitch!!! Always talkin' shit.* She was watching their last argument in her mind, growing angrier and angrier by the second.

"All dis time?!?!" Shantel worried out loud. *Damn! I mean, her momma' fucked her up an' all, but...* "Where you stayin' at?"

Dalanna looked off into the sunset, jamming her hands into her pockets. "Don't matta," she retorted.

Shantel bit her lip, considered the possibilities. *Dat motha' fucka' in da Cadillac.* Not asking because she wasn't sure she wanted to know. Everything she wanted to ask or say to Dalanna was too weak.

"HEEEEEEEYYYY!"

SLAM!

"WHAT?"

"BITCH COME BACK HERE!"

"I WILL LATA!"

"I SAID..."

BOOM!!!

A door a few houses down slammed like thunder. Porsche double-timed down the steps, her flip-flop sandals making slapping sounds on the soles of her feet. "Damn! She always talkin' shit!" she muttered on her way down to the stoop, her long braids waving good-bye behind her. A Tootsie Pop dangled from her wide-lipped mouth. Once on the sidewalk, she saw Dalanna in white, low-top K-Swiss sneakers, white shorts, and a matching gray and white tank top. Her well-dressed friend had impeccable timing. "Oh, whassup y'all?!?!" she exclaimed.

"Yo' auntie on one again, huh?" Dalanna asked flatly, she and Shantel never breaking stride. Porsche rushed to Dalanna's side, matching her pace to theirs.

"Sheeit," Porsche muttered, just the way her auntie would when the checks from foster care came in late. "Ain't no thang. That's how it always do."

But Shantel, ever tender-hearted, couldn't help but wonder. "Don't dat shit bother you none?"

The thought made Porsche sad. *Hurt like hell sometimes.* "Hell nah!" she insisted, "Got me wantin' ta whoop dat heffer's ass every once in a while. Maybe twice in a while. NIIIIII-GAAAA!"

All of the girls laughed.

"Mmmm," Shantel continued, looking off into the twilight, trying to imagine the world that Porsche knew. "I ain't no punk, but if my mama talk ta me like dat? Sheeit, I prob'ly be cryin'."

Porsche thought for a second. *Jus' 'cuz you don't see no tears don't mean I ain't cryin'.* "Well, if *you* live up in my house? *You* be cryin' a lotta tears den. Feel me?" No one answered. The girls rounded a corner and proceeded onto the main boulevard where crowds loitered in front of liquor stores and abandoned cars cluttered the sides of the road.

"But yeah," Porsche conceded. "I be trippin' off it sometimes. You know, like, not fo' long. Is what it is 'round here. Like all a' this shit." She was pointing out to the street, her arm tracing a half circle, circumscribing the world they knew. A police car came tearing down the middle of the road. Prostitutes in mini dresses walked up and down the sidewalks. The men across the street exchanged baggies for crumpled bills.

Porsche let her point sink in for a second longer. "And," smacking her lips loudly, "matta fact" she said slowly, nodding her head at the women, "same shit wit' my auntie, same shit as up in der.'" She pointed now to the far corner where a fight was just beginning to break out, with loud shouts and pushes back and forth. The girls watched intently as they walked on, past a barking Rottweiler chained at the neck, past a pretty young Mexican girl with dark eyes and long hair, a baby in her arms. Dingy blue apartments now on all sides, snarling pit bulls in front yards, old tennis shoes hanging from power lines, dirty water flowing through the gutter.

It was suddenly becoming too much, too hopeless to look at anymore.

"Y'all wanna go smoke somethin'?" Shantel offered, smiling coyly at the thought.

Porsche and Dalanna fairly sprained their necks in snapping to attention.

"YEAH!"

"HELL YEAH!"

"Gettin' stank-a-dank-dank!"

"Gettin' high as a motha' fucka'!"

"NIGGA!!!" they all chorused simultaneously, slapping hands triumphantly. Cooing amongst themselves about how high they would get, how much smoke they would take into their lungs, how good it would taste, how there could never be an experience like it.

A gigantic man, at least 6 feet 5 inches tall, with dark skin and long braids protruding out from under a beanie hat lumbered past, pulling up his sagging pants half-heartedly, grunting his approval at the backsides he watched as he walked looking over his shoulder. Shantel trembled inwardly, smiled flatly, subtly picking up her pace. *Ooooohhh leave me alone!!! Ugly ass nigga bes' keep on walkin'.*

"So you got some?" Porsche demanded.

Shantel kicked a rock as they continued on. "Nah," she admitted. *Damn. We fit ta get some dank wit' da quickness.* Pulling her front braids over to the left side of her face with a delicate hand, she thought and then snapped her fingers excitedly, her eyes wide. "OOOOHHHH but check dis out!!! Feel me? We cou' prob'ly get da hookup from my sistas."

Porsche snorted. "Dem hoes ain't about ta do shit for us!" she said, smacking her lips loudly, simultaneously side stepping a homeless man who watched her with red eyes and a toothless smile.

"Fo' real, the otha' day talkin' about 'grown folks bidness'," Dalanna agreed. "They some X-grown hoes!"

Porsche and Dalanna laughed and slapped hands.

"Ol' heffers!" Shantel exclaimed, "Don't be talkin' 'bout my sistas' like dat!"

Porsche smacked her lips. "Awright y'all, kill dat noise. Where we s'posed ta get some weed?" They all thought to themselves, momentarily distracted by a television flying out of a second-story window, the glass shattering into a thousand pieces on the sidewalk. They stared up at the apartment balcony, hoping for some more drama, more entertainment, but the argument within the apartment was muffled by walls and a just-closed sliding glass door.

So much drama in da X! Dalanna thought to herself. "Hey y'all," she thought out loud. "Brandy prob'ly got da hookup!"

"YEAH!"

"HELL YEAH!"

"And she jus' up da block!" Dalanna concluded.

It was true; they had already walked to the far side of *The X*, past the elementary school and the liquor store. The moon was beginning to creep up over a thick layer of smog from the distant chemical factories.

"Fo' sho'!" Porsche agreed. "She probably puffin' up right now jus' like she always do. C'mon y'all. Let's roll on ova' der."

The girls giddily picked up the pace. They walked five blocks until they reached a courtyard with a basketball hoop and sandbox for the little kids. Brandy's second-story apartment was just ahead.

CLANG!!! A chain-link basketball net danced after a ball rammed through it, followed by a chorus of triumphant hoots and hollers. As the girls passed the court on their left, they slowed to watch. They were not particularly interested in basketball, but the sweaty muscles on display made them fans any day of the week. The streetlight over the court gave those six-pack abs and broad shoulders a particularly golden hue.

Dalanna smiled dreamily. *Ooooohh I hope Brandy got some boys up ova' der!!!*

Shantel stole a quick second look at the basketball players before losing herself in the twilight, the sky now beginning to turn darker rainbow colors. Majestic in its own beautiful way.

Porsche smacked her lips loudly. *I need ta go shoppin', need some new kicks and gotta get my hair done. My mama bes' ha' some money. I ask her when I get home.*

As the girls passed the court, they had to walk along the grass to get to the back rows of apartment projects. The shouts and thuds of flesh hitting flesh grew quieter in the distance. Three young boys were sitting on a nearby stoop, chattering among themselves, glaring, guarding the stoop as if it were made out of gold.

"Hey now, lil' mama," cooed one of them as he bounded down the steps, taking a running leap directly into the girls' path, stopping them short. "You eva' been to McDonald's?" He asked Shantel, running a smooth hand back over his long braids. Shantel took a better look. He wore a long white t-shirt, practically a W shirt, baggy black jeans, and brand new Timberland boots. He had dark skin, bulbous eyes, and a kind of a smooth-talker smile. *Kinda cute.* Shantel arched her eyes brows in consideration.

"Nah, so' you ain't gotta go," he continued, staring at Shantel's half revealed breasts and slapping a closed fist into his other open palm, "Got all da milkshakes you need right der!"

Shantel snorted insolently. *Awww, here he go!* Resuming her walk toward Brandy's at the same time as her girls, each inherently knowing the exact moment when it was time to go.

"Hey now!!! Hold on now…" Shantel's admirer began to protest.

"Don't trip, I got some shit ta do," she commanded over her shoulder, and then she added "I be back." He smiled and waved a peace sign before bounding back over the grass to his eagerly onlooking friends. Their heads were in a huddle, plotting, scheming, lustful.

"Fo' real I hook you up!" Shantel's pursuer continued, sucking his teeth briefly for emphasis as the girls moved away. "I give you 'least two kids, you be da mama, welfare be da daddy!" His friends almost doubled over laughing, the light reflecting off gold teeth, hands slapping hands, resting elbows on bent over shoulders.

"Uh-uh!" the girls all exclaimed at once.

"Some ho ass niggas out here!"

"Say dat shit!"

The girls finally arrived at the far end of the courtyard. They went through the broken open security gate into the apartment's lobby and up the elevator, its walls inlaid with graffiti of black and silver—*The X's* trademark colors. They took the elevator to the second floor and marched down the hallway, past long rows of closed doors, each with blaring rap music, several voices talking at once, uproarious laughter, shouting, and what sounded like a hundred babies crying.

Porsche shook her head wearily. *Damn it's crazy 'round here!!!!*

KNOCK, *KNOCK*, resounded Dalanna's knuckles against Brandy's door.

Porsche looked on in excitement, chomping at the bit for the door to open. *I'm gonna be fuuuuucked up, watch!!*

Her girls waited with her in equal impatience, hearing the sounds of blaring television static interspersed with the thud of a distorted stereo and a baby's cries.

No one answered. Shantel sighed, knocking again. "BRAAA-NDY?!"

The thudding of approaching footsteps could be heard from inside. Finally, the lock began to turn and the black metal door guard swung open with such force that it banged into the black bars of the adjacent living room window, making a gong sound that had the girl's ears ringing.

"WHO DIS KNOCKIN' ON MY MA' FUCKIN' DO'!?!?!" wheezed a raspy, unfriendly voice from the dark confines within. A head peered out from beyond the doorway, exposing a crack-mouthed woman with patchwork skin, tired-red eyes, and hollow cheeks. Catching sight of the girls, losing her sleepless glower, she made an unintelligible, drunk-sounding effort at a laugh.

"Damn, Brandy!!" Porsche exclaimed, "Whassup wit' you?!?!"

"Oh shit my bad y'all," she chortled, smiling widely and breathing foul breath. Dalanna hid her automatic wince by pretending to wipe her nose. The woman took no notice, staring off into oblivion at no one in particular.

"Thought yous da' po-lice or somethin'!" Brandy continued, "C'mon now, bring yo' asses on in'." She ushered the girls in, straightening her bra strap underneath a dirty black tank top and peering to and fro out past the porch, making sure that she wasn't being watched. The girls stepped off the welcome mat, stained reddish-brown with barbecue sauce, and into the living room, swinging the door guard closed behind them with a bang. The smell nearly doubled them over, a mix of baby feces and what might have been peanut butter. They took hesitant steps forward, wrinkling their noses as they went deeper into what remained of the living room.

"Dang! Shit ain't right up in here!" Dalanna muttered.

"Wha' cha' say?" Brandy leered, as she stepped over a wailing infant on the floor, its diaper sagging down around the knees.

Porsche's jaw dropped. *That's where dat comin' from. Scandalous!*

"Who me?" Dalanna inquired innocently, "Oh nothin'. Jus' me an' mama's county check ain't right up in here!"

Porsche and Shantel stepped over garbage littering the carpet and plunked down on a plastic-covered green and yellow couch in front of the static-hissing television. Brandy made a feeble effort to clean up, moving fast food wrappers and empty matchbooks from one side of the coffee table to the other, accidentally sending an almost empty bottle of Old English tumbling down on the carpet.

Shantel shook her head discretely. *Daddy gonna fuck me up if he came home to a place like dis. Need ta call da po-lice or somethin'.*

"God damn house!" Brandy muttered, "Know wha' choo mean 'bout dem checks too. Mines for all these lil' fuckas still ain't shown up. Y'all wanna smoke somethin'?"

"YEAH!!!" answered all three girls at once.

"Some hungry ass mouths ta feed ain't 'cha," Brandy clucked. Lumbering with bruised legs atop dirty feet over to her stash lying in wait, she winced as a sharp squeal erupted from beneath her.

"Move ya lil' motha fucka!!!" Brandy screamed down at a sobbing infant, roughly pulling him aside by the arm, nearly yanking his shoulder from his socket, making his cry turn into an agonizing wail. "Damn ungrateful bastards! Don't none of they daddies help wit nothin'. An' I whoop dey assess era day. All da time! An'dey still don't shut the fuck up!!!"

Shantel and Porsche fidgeted awkwardly.

Dalanna's eyes met the big brown orbs belonging to a little girl sitting quietly at her feet, mouth open, her little fingers opening and closing. Dalanna noted the large bags beneath her eyes from sleepless nights, chubby cheeks, soft-looking skin.

"She bee-uu-tiful," Dalanna announced, smiling, her eyes lost in the baby's and the baby's lost in hers. They lived in their own world for eternal seconds. Looking. Staring. Dalanna picked the baby up and sat her in her lap. Their eyes never wavered. For just a second, Dalanna knew what it must be like to be a mother.

"Always droppin' stanky loads all ova' da house. Eat like fuckin' Oprah, fuckin' a, whas' her name, ah..." Brandy continued to rail. Two boys of about kindergarten age were beginning to fuss and squirm on the floor in front of the television.

But the world beyond Dalanna and this little girl had gone away. Just Dalanna and this little girl. *Just me and you. Yo' own mama don't even ra'memba' yo' name. Das' why shit so fucked up 'round here. Be different if you was mine.*

"Le'mme tell y'all," Dalanna informed her girls, catching sight of Brandy rolling up a thick marijuana joint and lowering her voice. "I'm gonna be a momma someday. Feel me? And a good mama. Not like dis here. How many she got anyway?"

"One, two, three, four? Four!" Shantel counted.

"Naw only three of 'em." Porsche corrected.

"Wha', my kids?" Brandy inquired, delicately placing the joint lengthwise in her mouth, all the way in, and twisting it back out.

Dalanna watched her. *Damn, she mo' nice to dat joint den her child!*

Brandy smiled approvingly at her creation, sparking a lighter and drawing it back and forth over the length of the joint, twisting the joint in her hand so as to dry it under the flame. "Naw, I got five. Two of 'em in da closet. Lil' niggas on tam' out cuz dey do too much."

All of the girls' eyes about sprang from their heads; the girls were struggling to maintain their composure as they stared at one another, mouths open.

The closet? Dalanna worried in silence, looking to her new little friend, still hugging her tightly in her arms. *No wonder you be lookin' so sad. I'd neva' put you up in der.* As she held the baby closer to her breast, the baby curled her little head into Dalanna's neck. Dalanna winced from the pain of her mother's last beating, but she didn't care. She loved this little girl. And so she just didn't care. Didn't mind the pain even as it was beginning to throb.

But the baby was somehow cold, far away. She came close, but she didn't warm to Dalanna's touch. Her hollow eyes gazed through the paint-flecked walls. Her little fingers could barely grip Dalanna's blouse no matter how hard she tried; she was too weak and tired. She began to squirm. Dalanna took this in at a moment's glance. *She 'sleep even when she ain't sleepin'. I should be yo' mama.*

"Look like you about ta, like, adopt a foster child," Porsche teased. "Like it say on dem benches at da bus stops: make a difference in da life of a lil' nigga." The girls giggled amongst themselves, struggling to stay quiet enough for Brandy not to hear, speaking in hushed whispers.

"What y'all laughin' about ova' der?" Brandy called over her shoulder, holding her arm out, joint in hand so as to admire it from a distance, like the work of a fine craftsman. "Don't matta dough. Y'all about ta be gigglin' like a motha' fucka' once y'all hit dis chronic!"

"Das what I'm talkin' 'bout!" Porsche goaded. Shantel looked on excitedly, not so patiently waiting.

The flame hit the end of the joint, crackling and spitting, and Brandy took a long hit and inhaled deeply into the pit of her stomach and finally exhaled a billowing cloud of black smoke. Her eyes began watering.

"Here," Brandy croaked, handing the joint to Dalanna, "I traaaade ya." She motioned to Dalanna for the baby. Dalanna hesitated momentarily.

Brandy sucked her teeth impatiently. "Wha'choo don't speak English?" she teased, "Like dem damn Mexicans? Le'mme break it down fo' ya. Hit dis' weed and gimme dat lil' motha fucka. He need ta go ta bed."

"She!" Dalanna corrected, with just a touch of annoyance, looking back to her little bundle of joy, not wanting to let go, wishing to keep the contact for just a minute more.

"Well 'cuse da fuck outta me," Brandy snapped back. "Seem like somebody gotta attitude. Guess dat mean you fucked dat one up didn't ya?" Her arm retreated from its previous position, offering the joint to Shantel instead, her free hand waving aloofly at her children, scattered on the living room floor. They were almost lifeless, lined up one after another after another. "When you got one a' deez ta worry 'bout, den come holla at me. Feel me?"

Dalanna considered this. *If I had one of deez . . . a child. My child . . . das it! Das what I need. Why I'm here! Ta be a mama. Better than deez otha' mommas up in da X. Like Brandy an' my mama too. Das da problem around here. Don't nobody know how ta raise dey kids. But I'm a be different.*

"Giiiiirrrl, whassup wit' you?" Shantel purred, red-eyed and smiling. "Sittin' there lookin' dusted an' disgusted!" Porsche and Brandy laughed, tumbling into one another. Brandy fell halfway off the couch due to the slippery plastic covering and marijuana's impact on her balance and coordination.

"An' she ain't even had no chronic!"

They laughed hysterically again, almost to the point of tears, clapping their hands, holding their stomachs in, blowing clouds of marijuana smoke through the air.

But Dalanna was on a thrill of a different kind. Brandy was right. Dalanna was truly lost, having found a sense of purpose in the world. Looking down at this little girl who looked up at her, she finally knew why she was here, why she was alive. Smiling at the remembrance of the little girl in her arms, she mused. *Some day.* She shook her head with softening eyes in that dreamy, lost-in-love kind of way. *She love me an' I love her. Don't nothin' else matta.*

The girls carried on, pledging love and devotion to each other, how they would always have each other's back and the like. To Dalanna, love had never sounded so sweet. Hope never so precious. *Dis lil' angel, smilin' at me.* Dalanna smiled again. *Dat a' be yo name. Angel.*

The thought of that little girl and her smiling face, her dimpled cheeks and bulbous eyes, pulled Dalanna suddenly back into the real world. She came back almost reluctantly upon hearing a child's cry muffled by the barrier of closed doors.

Dalanna looked around frantically, eagerly. *Where my lil' girl at?*

"Wha' choo lookin' fo'?" Brandy croaked, wheezing out remnants of marijuana smoke, eyes red and swollen. "Wha'? Yo' lil' friend? Told ya. She on time out." Brandy motioned over her shoulder to the closet where the cries were now becoming pitiful, wailing sobs.

The girls' laughter quickly subsided, and they began exchanging looks that betrayed shock and horror. They had just begun to notice a faint scratching against the door and a pitiful whimper from within. This only infuriated Brandy further, swinging her legs up and then to the floor with a mighty heave as if dragging herself upright.

"God damn, era' time I try to have me some peace an' quiet," she muttered angrily, making her way for the closet and thudding her fist hard on the hollow wood. "HEY!!!" she hollered, "SHUT DA FUCK UP IN DER! DAMN DEVIL CHILDS! LIL' MOTHA FUCKAS NEED TA BE STILL!!!" The girls sat stone-faced and solemn.

High-pitched wailing began to emanate from within the closet. Hollow and despairing child-cries, as if they were being bitten with a thousand sharp teeth. They were there inside, huddled, frightened, and alone in the dark.

Brandy smacked her lips loudly and cracked her knuckles. Dalanna's eyes grew wide, sensing trouble lay just ahead. *Nah, nah, c'mon, leave 'em alone!!!* she wanted to yell and scream and plead. The thought of her little girl frightened in the closet with her brothers and sisters nagged at her. *C'mon please. Dey awready had enough, leave 'em alone.*

"Awright now, there about ta be some ass whoopin' goin' on," Brandy informed the girls, shaking her head in frustration. The children's shrill cries continued, now even louder still, as if they could sense danger lying just ahead. The girls sat on the edges of their seats, terrified, awkward, panic stricken. Palms down, eyes red and wide, mouths open, too scared to speak or to move. In those seconds that never seemed to end, the girls were the babies in the closet.

"Y'all gotta get da fuck out right about now. Gotta handle some bidness, an' da' type of bidness that y'all lil' ma' fuckin' kids prob'ly don't need ta be seein'."

The girls fairly flung themselves toward the door.

Porsche was the first one out the door. *Damn dat bitch crazy!*

Dalanna followed, wishing she could dive back in and go get her little girl. *Man, she don't deserve dem kids!*

Shantel was bringing up the rear, shaking her head, though her mind was elsewhere. *Sheeit I'm outta dis bitch. Need ta go down ta da sto' an' go pick me up some chips an' a soda an' some pop tarts.*

Closing the door quietly behind them, as if not wanting to disturb the raucous hollering inside, the girls then quickly made their way off Brandy's stoop and back out into the courtyard, Porsche nearly doubling over on her way, bouncing off Dalanna and sending her careening into Shantel.

"Oooh, my baaaad my!" Porsche croaked, laughing loudly with her eyes closed, leaning on Dalanna's shoulder.

Dalanna scowled irritably and pushed her lightly away.

"Damn!!! Can't y'all niggas be still?!?!" Shantel blustered in a raspy, deep voice, imitating Brandy, spilling into Dalanna's other side, unceremoniously making Dalanna a teenager-high-on-marijuana sandwich.

"Get up off me!!!" Dalanna barked, roughly pushing out with her palms and sending each of her friends off onto a patch of dead, brown grass side of the courtyard. Shantel hugged her stomach with crisscrossed arms, getting up, tumbling right foot over left over right, stopping herself just feet from a crowd of young men.

"Oooohhh whassup lil' mamma. See? You jus' can't stay 'way could ja?" invited a familiar male voice. His peers looked on in earnest with all the excitement of a pack of wild monkeys, gibbering and fidgeting amongst themselves.

"Oooooh whassup my nigga?" Shantel slurred, smiling widely, her eyes nearly closed, pulling her long braids away from her face.

"Get cho ass outta here nigga!" Dalanna exclaimed, pushing him back with a forbiddingly outstretched hand, yanking Shantel back to her far right side, sending her back into Porsche pinball style. Both laughed hysterically, doubling over one another.

"Damn bitch! Why you gots ta dick block? Don't hate da playa, hate da game!" Shantel's admirer hollered, putting his open palms high into the air and shrugging at the shoulders, raising his arms from the long white t-shirt that was torn at the inseam, exposing toned biceps.

"Fuck you!" Dalanna called over her shoulder, bounding over to her friends now weaving down the sidewalk, coming closer to falling over with each passing step. *Damn! Seem like Brandy kids ain't da only ones needin' a mama!*

"Whassup girl?" Shantel chortled to Dalanna with a wide grin, draping a lazy arm over Dalanna's shoulder.

Dalanna revolted, spun around and threw Shantel's arm from her shoulder.

Shantel pulled her jeans up with her left hand and scoffed. "Well, fuck you too then, nigga!" She and Porsche giggled and slapped hands.

"Fo' real, don't hate da playa, hate da game!" Porsche continued, shrugging her shoulders and stretching out her palms in imitation of Shantel's just-passing admirer. Shantel had to hug Porsche to keep from tumbling over into the street as they slowly made their way down the block. Two steps right, one step forward, two steps left, occasionally even one fumbling step backwards.

"Can y'all shut da fuck up awready?! Let's talk some real shit!" Dalanna insisted, smoothing the part in her hair firmly to the left.

"Some real shit!" Shantel repeated, "Fo' reeeeal! Like, let's go holla at dem boys back up ova' der! Feel me?"

"Fuck dem scrubs!" Porsche retorted, "I'm fo' some Mickey D's. Feel me?!?!"

"Whattup' bitch!" She and Shantel exchanged high fives again, fiercely rattling off the half of the menu they each planned to order.

"Mmmm-hhmmm," Dalanna humphed, waving her hand in a wide circle as if to say *I give up. Dis why everybody smoke da chronic! Ta be stupid! Man, I ain't neva' gonna touch dat shit!*

Porsche was just describing how she would insist on hot fries, fresh from the deep fryer, how much salt they would have, and whether she would have a large or extra-large chocolate shake, when she and Shantel noticed Dalanna surging ahead, her long legs carrying her several yards down the street in a matter of seconds.

"Hey, hold up!" Porsche called out, jogging to catch up with Dalanna. "Oh shit I bes' not run 'cuz deez jeans tight!" she observed out loud, looking over her shoulder to her backside. "C'mon foo'!" she called over her shoulder to Shantel.

"I'm comin'!" Shantel assured, heaving herself forward. "So's the split up yo' ass, girl."

Porsche scoffed and waved a middle finger in the air. "Bitch shut up!"

"Y'all done now?" Dalanna barked, growing more exasperated by the minute. *Fuckin' heffers! Swear I ain't neva' smokin' dat shit!*

"Awright. Damn!" Porsche conceded, stealing a quick look into the passenger side window of a lowrider truck on the side of the road, smoothing over her thinly painted eyebrows and replenishing her lipstick as if to summon herself back into reality.

"Damn, you ugly anyway," Dalanna teased. But Porsche just scowled and smacked her lips loudly. "Naw, I'm jus' playin'. But fo' real though, y'all. What we gonna do 'bout all a dat?"

"What?" both Porsche and Shantel inquired, clueless and confused.

"Lawd have mercy on y'all souls for bein' so ignorant!" Dalanna prayed exaggeratedly, imitating her mother in looking to the sky and holding out her hands with her palms up. "Brandy an' dem kids! Who da fuck you think?" *My lil' girl still up in der. Up in da closet, wit' Brandy whoopin' her. Shit ain't right.*

"Girl what da fuck we s'posed to do?" Porsche responded almost apathetically. A silence settled on them as they made their way through the last stretch of courtyard, past the now empty basketball courts, walls nearly fully covered with graffiti, deadened grassy fields, and tipped over trash cans.

Shantel didn't know what to think. *Fo' real though, ain't right up in der. But...shit...I'm hungry as fuck...What we s'posed ta do? I mean...das how shit go up in here, up in da X. But...*

"Man I'm a call da po'lice!" Dalanna proclaimed, beginning to pick up the pace. "Dey could take dem kids an' put 'em up in fosta homes an' shit!"

Porsche scoffed and waved off Dalanna with a defiant hand. "Man, you don't know wha' da fuck you talkin' 'bout! Fosta homes hella weak! Takin' black kids an' puttin' up town wit' white folks. Den they be endin' up actin' white an' shit. Like, 'hello sir, how are you today?' C'mon my nigga please!!! Das how I stay wit' ma auntie."

"You a foster kid?" Shantel inquired surprisingly. Porsche flexed her eyebrows and licked her lips to indicate yes, not wanting to talk about it.

Shantel shook her head wearily, wishing she knew which way was up or which way to McDonald's. "I don't know y'all. Fosta' homes ain't even right. I heard dey jus' put you up in der fo' da checks. Feel me?" The girls nodded and grunted as Shantel continued. "My otha' girls was bad up in they fosta home an' they sent 'em to a group home."

"Yeah," Dalanna agreed reluctantly, smacking her lips. "But den what 'bout dem babies up in der? Fosta homes be fucked up, but...I mean...c'mon y'all. THEY WAS UP IN DA CLOSET?!?! Hear what I'm sayin'?"

The girls all nodded solemnly, remembering, silent, somber.

A slow-moving car pulled up alongside them as they walked and one of the passengers leaned out and hollered, "Sheeit baby I know I'm feelin' dat!" The purple Monte Carlo with wide-spoked gold rims kept pace with them. "C'mon baby why'nt choo swing on through an' come holla."

The girls continued walking, slowly and with an all-too-visible hesitation.

"Man, hold up," the passenger bellowed to his driver who screeched the Monte Carlo to a halt. Before the car even stopped, the passenger had bounded out onto the curb, his heavy black boots thudding against the concrete, his shiny bald head glimmering in the moonlight. "Da fuck wrong wit' you bitches!?!?!" The man snarled, stepping menacingly out into the sidewalk with his thick eyebrows creased into a frown, his heavy gold chain swinging to and fro atop an oversized black t-shirt and baggy black jean shorts. "Jus' tryin' to be a nice guy an' shit. An' what? Y'all think you too ma' FUCKIN' good fo' niggas out hea?!"

The girls halted, stood quite still, fearful, confused, frozen. He was big and muscular and at least twice the girls' age.

Porsche's mind moved quickly. "Naw, sheeit ain't like dat," she answered, draping a soft hand over his forearm. "Jus' my daddy stay up the way, an', you know how dat go. Jus' ain't tryin' to have him be out here trippin' an' all. Whas' yo' name?"

"Mar-quis!" the man answered, a wide smile showing his mood was changing. "Da X" was written across his teeth, front and center in black. "Wash'yo name girl?"

"My name Loretta," Porsche offered, smiling, and at the same time leaning back ever so slightly, shifting her weight to her back foot. She was prepared for a quick getaway, leaning away enough for another woman, but not a man, to notice.

"Is 'zat right?" Marquis continued, his companions in the Monte Carlo looking on in interest, the driver beginning to pull the car's steering-wheel lever into park.

Shantel jammed her hands in her pockets uncomfortably. *I wanna go home.* But somehow she sensed that she was not free to leave.

Dalanna scanned left and right, wanting out, measuring escape routes. "Girl c'mon get his numba an' let's go, daddy gonna whoop dat ass."

"Damn I can't get no communi-cay-do?!?!" Porsche pouted, "Damn! das my sista right there," she informed Marquis. "Aw, well, fuck it. Nigga, was' yo numba? Give you mines, but we ain't got no phone turned awn."

Marquis looked her up and down, "Yeah, awright," he conceded skeptically. But then, with odd little smile he added, "Girl c'mere fo' a minute. I wanna whisper a lil' somethin' to ya." He moved in for a kiss, hand to the back of Porsche's neck, getting in a quick, sloppy one before Porsche was able to yank her head back.

Dalanna shuddered. *I know that shit wa'dn't right.* She was eyeing her girlfriend quickly, feeling her discomfort even before she saw it. The fake smile, the slight trembling.

Shantel's breathing became labored. *Wha' dey gonna do ta us? C'mon, we gotta go.* She wanted to tear off with her eyes closed and never look back, scream at the top of her lungs for her father. But the men in the car were far stronger and faster, and there was nowhere to go.

"Take it easy, baby. Ma' daddy jus' ova' der!" Porsche insisted, making an inviting gesture with her open right hand. "C'mon we gots ta bounce. Lemme get yo' numba an' I call you tamorrow!" Her girls watched in suspense, waiting in an anticipating second of silence, hoping beyond hope.

Marquis sucked his teeth loudly, running a hand over his bald head as if pondering possibilities. The girls watched him closely, half ready to run, waiting for his next move.

A police car cruised by, slowing down briefly as it passed the Monte Carlo, the officer in the passenger side leaning out the window to get a good look. They were not ready to pull over and investigate three young girls and a crowd of adult men on a street corner in a dangerous neighborhood, but they were taking a good, long look. Marquis noticed them notice, looked off to the horizon, breathed heavily in a defeated sigh, and licked his lips in resignation.

Reaching coyly into his front pocket, finding a pen and a pad of paper, he began scribbling something down and handed it to Porsche with an ear-to-ear golden-toothed smile. The officer in the passenger side of the police cruiser shook his head in disgust and motioned to the driver, who sped off down the street. Marquis and the girls each took a long second to watch them go. For what may have been the first time in the girls' lives, they wished that the police would come back. But it was a well-known fact in *The X*: the police were only around when they were not wanted.

Marquis continued, "No doubt, hit me up baby! I got it fo' ya like dat! I get you anythang you need. Marquis got it all for ya!" He was getting back into the passenger side of the Monte Carlo, picking up the bottom of his shorts and blowing a kiss in the girls' direction before closing the door behind him. Finally he was gone.

Shantel was relieved. *Dis foo' got some nerve! Anything we need. Nigga please!!! Aw, well, fuck it. 'Lease we gettin' outta here alive! Ain't no tellin' what a' mutha fucka like dat a do.*

Dalanna shook her head, watching the car cruise down the street. *Damn, dat fool sho' was a rough neck and he prob'ly da type to be slappin' females up and all…Still, he was kinda cute.* Men like this held a curious attraction for her. Popping a stick of gum into her mouth and blowing a big bubble, she began mulling over the possibilities. *But, sheeit, he ain't even look at me! Must be blind or somethin'!* She glanced into a nearby car window. *Yeah, my hair kinda fucked up. But still, sheeit, I still hella mo' cute den Porsche. Any damn day a' da week. Sheeit!*

Dalanna scoffed in disbelief. "So yeah girl, feel me? 'Ay'thang you need, Maaar-quis gotch'choo,'" she mimicked, draping a teasing hand over Porsche's shoulder.

Porsche laughed uproariously, "Mutha fucka thought he all dat! Feel me? Sheeit! I ought ta' call da po-lice 'cuz he a' adult. Can't be gettin' up on younger females like dat."

"Sheeit the po-lice pro'bly worse!" Shantel interjected, "Y'all heard about dat shit that happened ta Venus? She wuz rollin' through deez streets and…"

"Wit' one a her many men an' shit too!" Porsche interrupted.

"Mmmm-hmmm," Dalanna agreed.

"Dis fuckin' white boy cop had his hand all up in her shirt an' shit! Dey need po-lice fo' da po-lice up in da X."

"Oh yeah!" agreed Porsche and Dalanna at the same time.

They were getting closer to home. Dalanna remembered what they had been talking about before. "OH YEAH Y'ALL! What we gonna do 'bout Brandy kids? I mean, we thinkin' about callin' da po-lice on dem niggas, I mean, damn. They was jus' some lil' kids. Feel me!?"

A long silence prevailed. Deep thoughts, hard questions, and no answers.

"But…I mean, feel me? Like, wha' we gonna do 'bout it?" Shantel wondered out loud, pulling her long braids back from her face and over her left shoulder as if to clear her mind for answers to come. "I mean, we could tell dem counselors about dis shit. Dey prob'ly do somethin'."

Dalanna snorted. "Hell nah, y'all," she insisted, sucking her teeth for emphasis. "Look wha' dey did to ma' shit! My mama gonna be hella mad if da CPS come up to ma' house! Den I'm fo' real gonna get whooped! Feel me? So wha' choo think gonna happen if dey up in Brandy' house? Dat bitch crazy. She a' lock dem babies in da closet fo' no reason. Wha' choo think she do ta us?"

"Yup," Porsche agreed.

Shantel hesitated, but her heart spoke to her in a way that couldn't be ignored, not even if she really wanted to. "Yeah," she answered, hesitantly, her voice slightly quivering. Porsche was the leader of their group, always the one to have the final say, and her girls usually followed. But Shantel could hold on no longer. "Yeah, das real," she conceded. "But dey right too. Feel me? I mean, wha' Mr. Reynolds an' dem talkin' 'bout. I mean, dem jus' lil' babies! Ain't coo' fo' dem ta be gettin' whooped like dat. Ain't even do shit." She was looking hard from one of her girls to the other. Neither said anything. Their thoughts were racing, chaotic. *Should do it, shouldn't do it, be worse if, no, yes.*

Even in the thick of it all, Shantel knew she was in the right. She was confused, but she was convinced it was something she had to do, something they all had to do. "I mean, feel me…like you was sayin' girl," she continued, nodding her head in Dalanna's direction, making her long beaded braids click and clack off one another, a bright green one shifting from the left side of her face to the right.

Crickets could now be heard in the nearby bushes, a police helicopter circled over head, its bright searchlight pouring over the street not 10 feet away. The girls didn't bother looking up. Just another day in *The X* as far as they were concerned. That meant it was getting late.

Dalanna remembered that little girl, Brandy's beautiful little girl. *Should be my lil' girl,* she wished sadly. She was thinking of the girl's hollow little face, locked away in that closet and for god knows how long. Tired, cold, afraid, hungry. A life so young, a life so devoid of love. Dalanna knew what they had to do. "Girl you right," she conceded.

"Yeah," Porsche begrudgingly conceded, suddenly recalling more of her life before foster care than she was comfortable remembering. "Awright, fuck it. Oh, shit y'all, der go my mama' house!" She was grateful it was time to go in. It had been a long night. So much had happened. For a moment, all three of the girls shared a longing for climbing through their bedroom windows, drifting off to sleep, and awakening to another boring day of school with their teachers half preaching "I have a dream" rhetoric and half of them screaming at the tops of their lungs.

"Damn y'all!!! We home already?" Shantel declared, looking across the street from her far left to the right where her bedroom window almost called out to her, inviting her to the safety of her heavy down pillow and black comforter. *All dis drama kill' my high 'long time ago anyway. I'm tired as a mutha fucka!*

"I know, huh?" Porsche exclaimed, "Time fly when shit jumpin' off in da X!" Dalanna humphed in agreement.

"Awright den," Shantel said in good bye, making her way across the street.

"Fa' sho'," Porsche concluded.

This left Dalanna standing in silence, watching Porsche and Shantel make their way home, veering off diagonally, in opposite directions from one another. Porsche looked halfway over her shoulder, as if pretending to watch something in the distance. She stuck out her head, moved forward and back and taking a lurching step in Dalanna's direction hollered, "Wha'? Y'all think you too ma' FUCKIN' good fa' niggas out hea'? Too good ta say goodnight? Want me come whisper d' shit to ya'?" She heard the girls giggling as they waved her off.

Dalanna smiled dreamily and shook her head, giggling furiously. *Damn. Don't know what I do wit'out my girls.*

Venus

Darkness. Darkness even when there was light. That was all she knew. At one time, life made so much sense. Not all of it, not in *The X*. But at least the important parts did. Men, look cute, go to school, hang out. *But now thangs' different. Percy up in jail. I coulda done somethin' too,* she told herself. Venus lay there on her bed, hands behind her head, somewhere between asleep and awake.

"Baby!" called a frantic and yet forceful bellow from the bottom of the stairs.

"Whassup?!?!" Venus answered, letting her head fall apathetically to the side of her pillow, her newly dyed bright red braids falling slackly off the edge of the bed.

"Girl don't answer me 'what!' Dis yo' motha' talkin' ta you! And you know 'what.' We goin' ta see Percy up in county. C'mon girl, we gonna be late."

Venus sighed heavily to herself, giving in to the weight of her heaviest of burdens. She began remembering what she did not want to remember. Percy in the back of the police car, his head bowed low for long minutes and then their eyes meeting. *My brotha fuckin' wit' crack,* she pondered sorrowfully. *Can't be, my brotha can't be no ma' fuckin' crack head. Dat fuckin' cop, all up on me an' shit. I'm a tell Percy when he get out an' he gonna whoop his ass hella bad! Watch!*

"C'mon girl let's go!" insisted a deep, impatient male voice from the foot of the stairs. Venus sighed to herself in defeat, knowing it was time to get up. She pried her stocky legs from the foot of her bed and swung them over the side and onto the floor, slipped her red-painted toe nails into flip-flop shoes and threw a zip-up black hooded sweatshirt around her shoulders, pulling the hood up over her face as if to hide her guilt behind woolen camouflage. She closed her bedroom door behind her, descended down the stairs with methodical steps, one after another with as long a pause as possible between them without angering her parents further. As she got closer to the foot of the stairs, her feet began to feel heavier and heavier.

"Mama, I don't wanna go!" Venus protested, unable to look her mother in the eye.

"We not havin' dis conversation," her father stated matter-of-factly, running a weary hand through his salt and pepper hair and straightening his thin-rimmed glasses before giving his wife a knowing look and making his way for the front door. Venus scoffed loudly, leaning back insolently against the wall, facing away from her mother, jamming her hands into her sweatshirt pockets.

"You heard yo' fatha," her mother reinforced, her voice raising slightly. Venus's keen instincts picked up on the implications immediately. "Either get yo' ass in da car o' you gonna be walkin' to da jail. Sheeit, yo' fat ass prob'ly need da exercise."

Venus's instincts never fully braced her for the impact of her mother's harsh words. They stung in many ways, leaving Venus to wallow for a moment, only to pick herself up and move dutifully out the door for fear of further reprisal. For her mother, her moment's hesitation was intolerable.

"About time, ain't it?!?!" her mother resounded as Venus shuffle-stepped past her, out the door, biting her lip hard for what composure it offered her. Looking at the ground at her feet, she felt a rage building inside her. *God damn! Why she always gotta be on me like dat? Why I even gotta do this? . . . Bitch.*

Venus found her way into the back seat of the car, pulling her hood low over her eyes and peeking grimly out the passenger side window, noting the littered sidewalks, brick walls that used to be red and had almost rotted to brown, a playground with broken equipment. Life in *The X* had never seemed more desolate; the rain had chased away the usual flurry of activity. For Venus, the same was true on the inside. Her usual world, the hustle and bustle, so lively, so active, was gone, replaced by this grim and solemn one. *Fuckin' hate dis place, own mama don't even love me! Call me fat! Maybe i's dis hoody, all baggy an' shit. 'Bout time fa' me ta go 'n get some new outfits any damn way.*

The rest of the long drive through the projects grew brighter; the rain gradually dying until it stopped completely, the sun just beginning to peek out. The streets seemed to come alive all at once as they neared the city. They eventually ran up against some gridlock due to slow-driving lowriders, blaring rap music, hydraulics bouncing alternatively up and down on front and back wheels. There were unobservant pedestrians walking in the street rather than the sidewalk, occasionally scowling at Venus's passing car intruding on their walkway, the city streets.

The family car turned around a sharp bend, headed out of *The X*, gradually entering the world outside. For Venus, who rarely left her own neighborhood, this world was quite a contrast. Cleaner streets, an old woman waving to a passing police car. Venus almost wanted to laugh at the sight, smiling to herself as she watched out the window. *A whole otha' world ain't even five miles away.* Eyeing a group of blond-haired white girls walking down the street in short shorts and tank tops, she noted the passing men smiling politely and waving. No rushing for kisses. No scared looks and intrusive hands. Venus shook her head in amazement. *Like Disneyland o' some shit.*

"See girl?" her mother interrupted her thoughts. *Here she go with all a' her preachin' shit.* Just when Venus's momentary reflections were starting to comfort her in a sad sort of way. "Dis where you need be headed! Do better den ya' momma an' ya' poppa'? Hear me?"

Venus nodded her head upward, blinking her eyes hard in affirmation. Yes, she heard her mother who continued with her point. "This what ya need ta be doin' with ya life. Movin' up in da world!!! Ain't dat right?" she inquired of her husband, half looking his way. He wearily nodded his head, not so much in strong agreement, but because, like Venus, he felt there was no other option but to agree. Her mother continued, taking a hard look at her daughter, twisting her body around to look at her straight on.

"Ya need to be workin,' savin'. Develop some in-teg-ri-ty. Hear me?" her mother finished.

Venus nodded her head as Percy did in her nightmares, when he was sentenced to prison. At least she could wake up from that dream. *Damn, shit's awready fucked up. Now I gotta hear dis shit? Please be done!*

The prevailing silence told her that, yes, her mother finally was done. Gratefully, Venus slumped back in her seat, pulling her hood tighter around her face, peering out of the car window. She watched the passing street scene, the coffee shops with businessmen reading newspapers, happy couples holding hands, stores that seemed to be doing lots of business. Venus snorted to herself. *Ain't one black person out here neitha. Damn, what is like ta be white?!?! Shit be easy as hell.*

As the traffic light turned green, she and her family made their way forward, picking up speed, past a police station and a courthouse, a welfare office with a line around the corner. Venus looked at the many black faces she saw, sorrowful, impatient. Mothers and babies, weaves wrapped up in scarves. Men in hoodies smoking, talking, pacing back and forth.

"Visitation?" barked an interrogating voice. Venus sat up to see a white security guard at the gate, glaring into the rolled down driver's window. Venus's mother nodded, looking eager to move on. They drove past police car and after police car and grave-looking older white men bustling past in pressed suits. Venus assumed they were attorneys or something. Then the scene became more foreboding. Guard towers atop chain-link fences with razor-sharp barbed wire outcroppings. Thick-looking steel doors. Little windows that didn't look like they let much light in.

"Which one Percy's?" Venus thought out loud without really meaning to. As she looked over the world of incarceration before her, her eyes met those of another. Broad shoulders, blond hair, dark motorcycle glasses. When he took off his glasses, Venus froze, held in a viselike anger that was followed by fear, tension, and despair. The officer smirked and drove on. Venus remembered that smirk, cold and lecherous.

"Motha' fucka'!" Venus grumbled.

"Girl you need to watch yo' mouth!" her mother barked into the seat, snapping her head sharply to the right. She nodded despairingly to her husband. "Das da problem wit' deez kids nowadays. Ain't got no damn respect! Think dey can jus' say whateva da fuck dey want. Like dey grown o' somethin'!! Ain't dat right?" Her husband breathed in heavily, nodded in resignation. He looked at his wife and at his daughter. They looked remarkably similar.

"Kids nowadays! All fucked up with dey fuck da po-lice shit!" her mother continued, "Ain't got no respect. An' anotha thang. Dey…"

But Venus heard nothing more. She was recalling his eyes on the side of her head as she felt his hand on her breast. *Dat punk ass motha' fucka'! I'm gonna get Percy to blast dat foo' when he get out of jail! Wait 'til I tell him what dat foo' was doin'!!*

"Awright y'all let's go on now," her father proclaimed as he opened his car door. And Venus awoke. She blinked, still half dazed, remaining for another long moment in the car.

"Girl c'mon now!!!" commanded her mother impatiently.

Venus shook herself back to consciousness, peered this way and that. Her oppressor of the previous night was gone. *Was he even der? Ain't here no mo'. Know I saw dat foo'. But maybe I was jus' trippin'. I had to, he was just…* Meanwhile, her body moved itself even while her mind was elsewhere. Opening her door, swinging her legs down onto the pavement at her feet, she began to follow her family, jamming her hands in her pockets. *Damn, wish I ain't have to go.*

Walking through the parking lot, they saw police officers pass to and fro, some guiding prisoners in handcuffs, some talking amongst themselves with prisoners in the back of nearby cars. All of the prisoners were young, African American men. Venus snorted insolently. *So what else new?* she wondered dismally. It was the same sorry sight as they made their way into the jail visiting area. Young, mostly African American mothers holding screaming babies, old women rocking back and forth on waiting area benches, praying, whispering among themselves. In one room, she watched African American men in orange jumpsuits talking on phones behind thick, dirty windows. They were hollow-faced with uncombed hair. Their faces showed sadness and rage at the same time, feelings Venus knew well.

A heavy-set white woman with a set of tiered chins gruffly pointed Venus and her family to window 13 without looking up from what she had been writing. Venus's mother led the procession, past mothers and young girls, babies being changed, unhappy girlfriends.

A loud buzzing resounded from behind the guard's station. A thick metal door clanked open, exposing two burly sheriff's deputies and their captive. On the left was a huge white man with glaring eyes, well-clipped goatee, and short, slicked-back hair, peering left and right, as if eager for something to get out of control. On the right was an older officer, skinnier, a bit smaller than the prisoner but far more at ease. His eyes took in only what was necessary, not looking for trouble but still ready to spring into action at the first sight of it. Each lead the prisoner to window 13 by an arm and plunked him down in front of a family that barely recognized him.

"Percy!" Venus exclaimed. A hideous scar stretched from his left ear to his jaw line. He sat wide-eyed, his usually well-groomed hair wild and unruly. He was gaunt, unshaven. Venus had to fight back tears. *He been gone only a few days!* He looked like a different person. It was her brother before her, but not the brother that she had grown to know and love.

Long moments passed as the family on both sides of the glass stared at one another, stares that told stories and shared a world. So much was said by saying nothing. Venus's mother was fighting back tears and her father was breathing heavily through his nostrils, keeping himself preoccupied by cleaning his thin spectacles. Venus looked long into her brother's face, pleading through her eyes. There was so much she wanted to ask, so much she wanted to say, but the words wouldn't come.

Father and son spoke first. "Hey now," Venus's father murmured into the telephone receiver, nodding his head in greeting. Percy said nothing, just continued looking anywhere but toward his little sister. She finally looked away, began to run her index finger in lazy circles over the glass between them.

"Ma'am, please back up from the glass!" barked an officer in passing as he made his rounds up and down the walkway, hand on his club, firm jaws clamping down on chewing gum. Another sat nearby, his arms crossed against his chest. He too was chewing gum. To Venus, it looked like this one was hoping for an incident, ready to strike at the slightest provocation, his eyes wide, eyebrows arched, looking directly at her.

Venus snapped back to attention, hands folding into her lap. Percy and his father exchanged brief questions and answers about the case, how neither had gotten a return call from the public defender. Percy was swearing to God that he hadn't done anything, but his father grew angrier with each of Percy's excuses and responses. He began cursing his son for "playing himself."

"Percy," his mother intruded, snatching the phone from her husband's grip, "Hear me? Dis yo' motha talkin' ta you."

Percy's eyes reluctantly met hers, stealing a momentary "here we go again" glance up and to the right, as if bracing himself for a dressing down that he knew was sure to come.

"Boy, I don't care if you in jail, I come across dat glass an' handle somethin' somethin', hear me?!" his mother threatened menacingly. "Don't you be rollin' yo' eyes at me!"

Percy nodded, head halfway down then looking up at her with tired eyes, as if he wanted to be anywhere else.

"You need to get some help!" his mother admonished.

Percy scoffed, his eyebrows arching upward as he shrugged his shoulders and held up his right palm as if to ask a passing pedestrian for a quarter. "Help? Wha' choo talkin' 'bout. Don't need no help. Fo' what?"

"For yo' problem smokin' crack! Das what!" his mother growled, inching her face to within inches away from the glass.

"Momma, I put it on ma' life! I ain't no crack head!" Percy protested, licking his lips and looking to each of his family members for support. Finally his eyes met Venus's.

Venus gave him a knowing look as she thought, *Give up. You know it useless talkin' back to mama.*

"Boy you need ta go ta one a' dem programs!" their mother continued. "Or what you gonna do? Sit up hea' in jail?!"

Percy opened his mouth as if he knew what he was going to say before his mother had finished. Somehow she knew that he knew. "Boy, stop listenin' to what you thinkin' an' listen ta what I'm sayin'! C'mon now, I mean...look at yo' face!" she insisted, pulling a makeup mirror from her pocket and slamming it hard against the glass. "Jus' look!"

"Ma'am please back away from the glass!" the same guard bellowed from the far end of the corridor.

"DIS WHA' CHOO WAW'NT FO' YO' LIFE!?! DIS IT?! LOOK AT CHO SELF!" their mother screamed, slapping her free hand against the glass. Loud thuds of heavy boots echoed over the tiled floor.

"Awright let's go," the officer ordered, pulling Venus's mother by the back of her forearms, lifting her out of her seat. Once the guard released her, her husband got up, came over, and put a soothing hand in the small of her back, trying to calm her as best as he could. But then she started up again.

"DIS WHO YOU GONNA TURN OUT TA BE?!?!" she raged blindly. The officer came back over and escorted her sternly from the window once more, a firmer grip on her bicep, yanking her away as she screamed over her shoulder, leading her toward the door. Venus and her dad got up to go too.

A loud buzzer sounded overhead just as Venus was almost out the door. "Alright bro, time to go," announced another officer from the other side of the glass. Venus couldn't help but to poke her head back in, suddenly terrified that she would never see her brother again. But there he was, still there at the visiting booth, head tilted upward, staring off into space, lost and hollow, just as he had been in the back of the police car. Only this time, Venus was right there with him.

Gina

Alone in my thoughts
Alone in the world
Alone, all alone
All alone
This girl
All that she knew
All that she saw
Mom on the pipe
Dad broke her jaw
Alone in the corner
All on my own
When will it end?
Forever Alone

Gina read over this scribble in her diary, followed the lines with her fingers, smiling sadly to herself. *Real talk though,* she noted to herself. Writing in her diary was her sole escape from the world around her. *Mama an' daddy gone who know' where. My sista be around when she wanna be.* She smiled sadly to herself.

She reached for the phone, speed-dialed a number, waited anxiously, her heart beat quickening from ring to ring. *She gotta be der! We bes' go do somethin'!!*

"Whassup girl?" answered a soft, reassuring voice on the other end.

"Tarra, when you gonna come get me?" Gina pleaded, huddling over the phone without knowing exactly why. A sigh on the other end.

"C'mon now, you know I got double shifts tanight," Tarra answered. "Why don't you go kick it with one of dem girls ova' there? Dey prob'ly wanna do somethin' anyway."

Gina scowled. "Sheeit, girl. Dey ghetto!!!"

"C'mon now. Dey not so bad," Tarra reassured.

Not so bad??! Now I know you trippin'. Gina opened her mouth, preparing to set the record straight, but her bedroom door suddenly flung open, swinging away her next words with a blasting draft.

"Yo, G!" boomed a demanding female voice from just inside the door, almost before it opened. "Where da glue at? My track slipped out! And da red one too!" The girl in the doorway held out a long red braided extension, a frantic and exasperated look on her face. She leaned heavily on a hip barely covered in skintight shorts, straightened the strap of her black tank top with her free hand. Her deep brown eyes bore down on Gina as if waiting any seconds longer would bring the apocalypse. Without looking up, Gina raised her right arm at the shoulder, extending her elbow outward and pointing in a take-it-and-go fashion. "See what I mean?" she murmured into the phone, knowing Tarra had heard.

Tarra laughed in concession. "Awright, awright, you got me."

The girl with the missing extension found the glue with a satisfied smirk and began to make her way for the door.

"An' knock when you come in ma' room!" Gina demanded.

"Bitch need some hair club fo' women!" hollered another young female voice from the far end of the hallway, followed by laughter and clapping hands.

"Bitch shut up! You best watch yo' mouth, fuckin' heffer!" retorted the girl with the extension as she stomped out to answer her challenge.

"HEY!" bellowed a strong, deep female voice from the bottom of the stairs, "WHAT I TELL Y'ALL 'BOUT ALL A DAT CUSSIN' IN MY MUTHA FUCKIN' HOUSE!?"

Gina sighed heavily in despair, dropped the phone momentarily onto the bed, swung her legs over the side, and latched the door closed in exasperation. Leaning her back against it for a second, her eyes rolled back in her head. *Oooohhhh!!! Can't take much more a' this... Sheeit, deez girls crazy as hell! I gotta get up outta here.*

The thought of it gave her an idea, and she snatched up the phone purposefully from her bed, pressing it to her ear.

"You see what I'm sayin'?" she pleaded, "Tarra, I ain't lyin'! I gotta get up outta here!" Looking longingly out the window, past the rows and rows of apartment complexes, the dice rollers in the alley, a police helicopter and its spotlight overhead sending them scattering in all directions.

Tarra sighed to herself. "Mmm-hmmm. Girl, I jus' got home an' I gotta get dressed an' go right back to work! I'm tellin' ya, enjoy bein' a child while ya can!"

Gina sat up. "No! No! You cou' talk when you gettin' ready!"

Tarra smacked her lips in resignation. "Mmm-hmmm, awright, awright," she conceded. "My man need ta wait any damn way!"

"Yo man?!?!" Gina squealed. "Fo' real? Who dat?!?!"

Tarra giggled. "Damn girl, you act like I can't pull a man no more o' somethin'! I been schoolin' these fools since befo' you was even at school."

Gina's head fell back against her pillow, kicking her legs playfully. *'Bout time she got a man! I was thinkin' I was 'bout ta have one befo' she did!* A second later, the thought caught up with her, making her a little sad, a little lonely. *Damn, I wish I had a boy.*

"Mmmm-hhmmm girl, das right," Tarra informed. "Big sis got a good one too! Let me tell ya somethin' somethin'!"

"Tell me!" Gina encouraged, leaning closer into the phone, huddled over in anticipation as if the suspense were killing her. On the other end of the line, her sister chuckled gaily.

"Awright then," Tarra agreed. "He cute, tall, dark-skinned, got some waves, dress nice, kinda like Will Smith. Like dem pretty boys down south, feel me?"

"Awright!" Gina confirmed.

"An' he handsome too. You know. Buff, thick, kind a' like Tyrese, but den he got a goatee. It be nice too!"

Gina clapped her hands and bounced slightly on her bed. *Ooohh sis, man soun' hecka' cute!!* "Fo' real? It like dat?"

"Oh, it like dat," Tarra assured. "Matta fact, here he come now..." Gina felt the silence through the phone and down into her finger tips. "Huh. It look like he ain't alone."

Oh shit! I'm already knowin'. Gina sat up on her bed, her legs crossed. The tension was ominous.

"I'm a call you back," Tarra informed, a muffled static following. But the phone had not clicked off. There was no way that Gina was going to miss this. Huddling over the phone in anticipation, momentarily considering that eavesdropping was a little nosey, she couldn't bear not knowing what would happen next.

She heard tires squealing to a stop and then the thud of a car door slamming. "Whassup playa!" Gina heard her sister announce on the other end, followed by the sound of heavily approaching footsteps on pavement.

"Oh–oh, you, you ain't, um, like...," protested a male voice.

"Da-da-da-don't even start motha' fucka!" Tarra interrupted. "I..."

"OH HELL NA!" yelled another female voice, "WHO DA FUCK IS THIS?!?!"

Gina's jaw dropped. *Ooooohhh. It on now!!!*

"DIS HIS LADY!!! WHO DA FUCK IS YOU?!?!"

"NA-NA HOLD UP Y'ALL, AIN'T EVEN LIKE DIS."

"AIN'T LIKE WHAT?!?!"

"BITCH YOU NEED TO TAKE YO' HAND OUT."

As the voices grew louder and louder, angrier and angrier, Gina's eyes widened. She instinctively drew the phone away from her ear. The battle on the other end continued.

"I DONE TOLD'JA TOO MANY TIMES."

"YOU AIN'T TELLIN' ME SHIT !"

"BITCH, I'M A WHOOP YO' ASS DAS WHAT I'M TELLIN' YOU!!!"

"OOOOOOHHHHHH!!!!"

Hands clapping, muffled whispers, a showdown in full uproar. This last interchange came from down the hall, a rising tide of shrill female voices. Gina could only shake her head and stare up at the ceiling. *Good lord.* Now there were two battles going on around her, one on the other end of the phone in her hand and one just two bedroom doors down, leaving Gina in the middle. *Dis fucked up. I gotta get up outta here. All deez people crazy.*

"DA'S MY MAN!!!" from the phone.

"BITCH YOU BEST BACK UP 'FO' YOU . . . ," from the bedroom just down the hall. The phone, which sat resting in Gina's wilting grip, suddenly vibrated. *Who else calling now?* She had zero inclination to answer. The vibrating stopped.

"HEY SHUT UP Y'ALL! SOMEBODY ON DA PHONE!!" bellowed a women's voice shouted from downstairs. *Damn, why Kendra always gotta yell?! All a dem too.*

"GINAAAAAAA!" Kendra roared over the girls in the bedroom, immediately hushing them to a whisper. "DAT GIRL ON DA PHONE FA' YOU!! SOUND LIKE SHE HAVIN' DAT TIME O' DA MONTH O' SOMETHIN'."

The girls in the far room laughed and clapped their hands in rousing amusement. They returned to talking all at once. The phone in Gina's hand began to beep in earnest. Almost reluctantly, she hung up on Tarra. *She need me now, but she up in some shit too. I call her later . . . Loretta . . . lord have mercy.* Gina sat up on her bed for a moment, staring hard at the floor. She spied her diary at her feet where it was still open to the poem she had just written. *Forever alone,* it said. Never had she read more fitting words.

Shawn

BEEP! BEEP! BEEP! Shawn rolled over in bed with his eyes still half closed, peered out the window through slits. *Still dark outside. Mmm, another 10 minutes would be enough.*

The sun was just beginning to rise into the pale blue morning sky. Shawn glanced to his blaring alarm clock. *5:00 a.m.*

Shower, shave, protein shake. *Group today.* Coffee, shirt, tennis shoes. Backpack over the shoulder. *Wow, last week was intense.* Out the door, down the elevator. *What's going to happen now?* Only three or four people on the bus, each looking like they agreed that 10 more minutes in bed would have been enough. Grabbing a nearby window seat, Shawn fell asleep almost instantly.

"HO'D UP BLOOD?!?!"

"DAMN FOO' WHA' 'CHO PROBLEM?!"

"FUCK YOU!"

These and other youthful rumblings awoke Shawn with a start. Rubbing his eyes sleepily, scowling into the haze around him, he gradually came back to reality. Watching kids pile onto the bus in threes and fours and sevens. *Got about 10 minutes 'til I'm there.* These were high school kids. Shawn could tell because they were all at least a head taller than the kids he was working with. In the beginning of the internship, he had found these rude awakenings annoying, but he now appreciated them; they kept him from sleeping past his stop. Shawn always enjoyed watching the older kids.

Plunking down into their seats, backpacks thudding to the ground, iPod earphones blaring loud enough for bus patrons to hear colorful metaphors. Some of the kids did not even bother with earphones, just played their music out loud as if their iPods were boom boxes. At least three songs blared simultaneously. *Sounds like television when you don't have a signal,* Shawn thought.

One young man with long braids and an oversized white and black shirt with a dollar sign had 50 Cent's latest hit single cranking at full blast, loud enough to draw an annoyed look from an elderly man sitting just across from him. Frowning over thin-rimmed spectacles, crinkling his brow, grimacing, his cracked, dry mouth pursed, he barked "HEY!" disapprovingly. The young man grooved along, undaunted, oblivious, hearing nothing or at least pretending not to. This only infuriated the old man further. Momentarily eyeing the young man's flowing braids as they bounced along in time with his music, he tried again.

"HEY!!!" he bellowed even louder still. "SHIT LOCKS!!! TURN DAT SHIT DOWN!!!" he ordered, poking at the young man with the butt of his cane.

The young man inwardly jumped, sat up, caught off guard by the sudden intrusion. He lowered his head and scowled menacingly, unhappy to have been interrupted, roughly pushing away the old man's cane. "Da fuck yo' problem old foo'."

The man looked the boy up and down as if sizing up a chicken for purchase at a farmer's market. "Dat damn shit too loud das what! Turn dat shit down! Stupid lil' motha fuckas makin' all dat god damn racket! This why deez punks need to get a beatin' from time to time, maybe mo' then that. Sheeitt!!!" the old man preached, shaking his head in dismay, looking over at the bus driver.

"SHEEIIT!!!! Beat deez nuts old ass nigga!!" the young man retorted, grabbing his crotch for emphasis as he stood up and made his way to the back of the bus, holding up his pants with one hand and making a rude gesture with the other. The other kids ooh'd and ah'd and smirked, raised their arms and pointed, watching in earnest.

"OOOOOO!"

"HE BAD!"

"That ain't right, to talk like dat to a old guy an' shit."

"Look like yo' mama!!!"

"Fuck you!!!"

"OOOOOO!"

Shawn very slightly smiled to himself. He took a mental note to tell this story to his mother. Gradually, his attention drifted elsewhere. Watching the street as it flashed by. Broken bottles. Two mean-looking dogs tied up in a front yard, snarling at each other. Boarded up windows. That was enough. He closed his eyes again, leaning his head back in the seat, aware that he was still sleepy. Suddenly, he snapped himself back up in his seat. *No, no time to sleep, almost here. I need to get ready.*

The bus lurched to a stop. Kids were piling off and spilling into the street, tearing across oncoming traffic. Backpacks bouncing, sneakered feet pitter-pattering across cracked concrete, horns blaring, fists shaking out windows.

"WATCH OUT!"

"HEY, HEY!"

"STUPID ASS MOTHA' FUCKAS!"

"NOT WHA' CHO MAMA SAID LAST NIGHT!"

"OOOOOOO!"

Shawn watched in wonder. He realized he was beginning to get the hang of it.

The Group

Crossing the street, he glanced at his watch. *Eighteen minutes to go.* Kids piling through the gates. Goodbye hugs, beeping horns, blaring rap music. The motherly looking woman there again on the porch just next to the school, her eyes already on Shawn. *Wonder how long she's been looking.* He waved, she nodded without smiling.

"Whassup, Mr. Reynolds!" piped an excited voice from below. He looked down and found a big smile on a familiar face. Shawn remembered the last time he had seen his little friend just outside of the P.E. class.

"Johnson!!" he teased, hoping he would get the joke as he tried to sound like the P.E. teacher. The boy smiled big, laughing with his head tipped back, getting it completely. What Shawn was doing suddenly caught up with him. *Mmm, it's probably not a good idea for me to make fun of the teachers, but, oh well, fuck it.*

"I know, huh?!?!" Johnson replied, making his way along Shawn's side like a puppy.

"What's going on?" Shawn inquired good-naturedly.

"Chillin'. I'm doin' good!!! Got a B up in English on my progress report," Johnson boasted.

"Johnson, you da man!" Shawn proclaimed, hailing him up and down with both hands as if giving obeisance to a god.

Johnson smiled, shrugging his shoulders immodestly. "Ain't no lie." Shawn laughed whole-heartedly.

As they continued through the yard, Shawn noticed that the crowds of youngsters were beginning to thin out. Most of the softer-spoken, studious types were piling out of the schoolyard and into classrooms, doors thudding behind them, leaving smaller groups of twos and threes, laughing loudly, grabbing one another, pushing. Shawn recognized at least half of those remaining as being kids he was working with or those who were on his list to be picked up for counseling. After considering whether he should bark at them to go to class, he decided that he probably should but was a little unsure how to do it. *Besides, my supervisor told me not to. The school needs to take care of discipline.*

Shawn suddenly noticed that Johnson was still by his side. "Can I go ta yo' class now?" Johnson asked. Shawn was flattered but remembered that he had group soon.

"No, I have a group and you have to go to first period," Shawn pronounced. Johnson rolled his eyes in exaggeration, groaning sadly. Shawn was again flattered. *He likes talking to me that much. He probably also doesn't want to go to his class.*

"No, no. C'mon you gotta go." Shawn smiled, reflecting on last week's turn of events. "And don't poke your head out of the door anymore. You're going to get in trouble."

I need to say that with a straight face.

But Johnson was already making his way in the opposite direction. "I ain't got no trouble. You got trouble?" Johnson inquired over his shoulder.

Shawn laughed. Almost reluctantly, he went left while Johnson went right. Shawn thought about what he knew from the case files. *Found eating out of a dumpster when he was seven, foster homes, hospitals. The kid deserved better. Lots better.*

"Good morning," greeted a familiar voice. Shawn shook himself back to reality. Long black dress, sweater, dangling earrings, heels clop-clopping against the floor, putting chairs into a circle.

Shawn's legs had taken him where he needed to go even while his mind was elsewhere. Dropping his bag and quickly scurrying in to help, he replied, "Hey, Terri."

"Do you wanna go get the...," Terri began.

"Oh yeah, the girls! Shit!!!" Shawn interrupted, going back for the door. Terri took notice as she looked up, smiling inwardly to herself. *He's good. Likes the kids. Lots of energy.*

In half a second, Shawn had already marched out the door, swinging it closed behind him, shivering from the wind outside. The sun was just peeking out, brilliantly dodging the clouds. Shawn was grateful for its warmth. It was like his mother's voice at the end of a long day, warm and bright as they sat in the coffee shop. She was always there, ready to hear his long, sad, or funny stories about what happened throughout the day.

Meanwhile, his day was just beginning. Crossing the schoolyard in long purposeful strides, he once again passed the swings blown by the breeze. Shawn quickened his pace, realizing he was close to being late. He swung open the rusty door to the portable.

"Good morning, Mr. Reynolds," called a pleasant, woman's voice.

"Hey, Mrs. Trenton," Shawn replied, her eyes settling on his for only for a second before she resumed her watchful surveillance of the room of children. "Jamar stay in your seat," Mrs. Trenton ordered firmly but politely in that voice that said "please" and "thank you" in the same breath.

"But I ain't even get up!" Jamar protested with his arms raised high like he was a clerk being held up in a convenience store.

"Thank you, Jamar," Mrs. Trenton replied, quickly switching her attention somewhere else, knowing that the trick with these unruly, attention-seeking boys was to contain them and move on.

"Okay, girls!" Mrs. Trenton announced.

Two heads popped up from desks in the far corners of the room.

"I ain't goin'."

"An' me neitha'."

"Girls, c'mon, time to go," Mrs. Trenton insisted. Shawn was perplexed, confused, afraid, hurt. His mind was beginning to race. *What's going on? Something I said?*

The girls continued in their silence.

"Okay, everyone. I'll tell you what," Shawn announced, the three heads rising though still none looked his way. Three other heads bowed into textbooks. "Let's do our thing for 15 minutes today. If you don't want to stay, you're free to leave. If you want to stay, that's fine too. Deal?"

No response. You could almost hear the clock ticking. But then the girls left their seats, slung their backpacks over their shoulders, and shuffled across the floor. Shawn and Mrs. Trenton exchanged quick glances. *Whew!* they both seemed to say. Mrs. Trenton smiled. *Well done,* she said.

Shawn was too relieved to notice. The previous silence was a little overwhelming, and it stayed with Shawn and the girls as they made their way out the door. They walked slowly and no one spoke. They did not look at Shawn. By the time they reached the counseling office at the far end of the yard, it had seemed like forever. Backpacks thudded to the floor, chairs scraped the hardwood, hands jammed into pockets. Two of them pulled their hoods to partially cover their faces. Lips smacking and gum popping were the only sounds as the girls stared down or out the window.

"I guess we're not very talkative today, are we?" Terri observed. Tick-tick. Scrape. The room fell dark as a cloud eclipsed the sun.

Shawn was searching for words but at the same time was momentarily impressed by the girls' unified silence. Shawn was dying to say something. He stole a glance at Terri, who also silent. *Maybe the silence is the therapy,* Shawn wondered. Nevertheless, he couldn't hold it in any longer.

"What's going on, you guys?" he probed in a voice that sounded wounded. His eyes peered over the room. Still silence. Suddenly, it was they who could bare it no longer.

"You bein' da po-lice, das what!" Rona accused, looking up at Shawn icily and then quickly returning to staring at nothing out the window.

Um, err, uh, Shawn stuttered in his mind, back peddling mightily.

"Rona, can you say more about that?" Terri probed.

Rona breathed in heavily and smacked her lips. The girls all watched her closely, leaning slightly away from her as if sneaking out their windows past sleeping parents.

"Yeah!" Rona answered, "Thang's fucked up at home 'bout now!"

"OOOOO!"

"She said…"

"No, no it's okay, go ahead," Shawn reassured his excited audience.

"Coo'!"

"Awright then!"

"Mr. Reynolds say we can cuss!"

"Hell yeah!!!"

"C'mon you guys," Terri encouraged. The chatter dropped down a bit.

"I ain't playin'!" Rona insisted, the whispers of her peers falling silent. "Da CPS done come out an' ask questions an' shit. Now my mama mad at me! Don't wanna talk o' nothin'!"

Shawn swallowed a lump in his throat, not quite able to get it down. *My worst fears come true. I knew it!*

"Dey did, huh?" Porsche inquired with a note of sympathy.

Rona smacked her lips in affirmation.

"See, y'all?" Porsche continue, eyeing Shawn and Terri. "No offense o' nothin', but y'all don't understand. Das how it is 'round here. Kids jus' get' dey ass whooped. An den like, when y'all do shit? It jus' make it worse."

"How do you think that affects you?" Terri probed.

Shawn looked on in earnest. *Good question. I wonder who will answer first.*

"I don't know," Porsche mumbled.

Shantel looked deep in thought.

Dalanna squirmed in her seat.

"Das why it's all messed up out here," Gina proclaimed. "After a while, you jus' wanna be like, fuck it. Oops!!! Um, I mean, um, excuse me, fa'get it."

"Fo' real," Dalanna agreed.

Venus stole a glance out the window.

The tension seemed to be growing.

"That's prob'ly why my brotha up in jail," Venus answered.

"He up in county?" Shantel probed.

Venus nodded, her braids bouncing off her shoulders.

"Oooohhh, my mama' boyfriend need to be up in there too, ol' nasty ass motha' fucka'!" Rona proclaimed.

"OOOOHHH!!!" they all chimed in.

Shawn fought back his laughter.

"So you guys think that all this stuff we are talking about has anything to do with this? And if it does, don't you think we should do something about it?" Shawn inquired, regaining his composure.

"Fo' what?" Porsche challenged, "Ain't nothin' gonna change. And you jus' make it worse callin' da CPS an' shit. Like callin' da po-lice. Das when somebody fo' real gonna get hurt!"

"Fo' real. So don't nobody gonna talk to you!" Rona agreed.

Venus stared off, hugging herself with crisscrossed arms.

Shantel picked at flecks of dirt on the press-on nail of her index finger. Gina looked up like she wanted to say something but wasn't sure if it was okay to.

"Nah, but das prob'ly true though y'all," Dalanna piped up, leaning slightly forward.

"I mean, like, dat lil' baby?! How you think he gonna turn out?"

The girls exchanged furtive glances, each seeming to ask the other for permission.

Porsche made the first move. Looking down to the floor as if she wanted to hold it all in but knowing she couldn't any longer, she ran a weary hand through freshly straightened hair. "Yeah, y'all," she began. "OK!! So is my turn!! I'm gonna tell da story!!! Firs' thang. It was fucked up wit' my auntie dis weekend. Ooooo...she hella ugly. An' I need ta jus' whoop her ass. But I got up out da house and was out kickin' it, you know."

The girls all looked on in earnest.

"So, anyway, it was over da weekend right? We was over at dis lady house dat live up da block."

"Ol' heffer!" Dalanna murmured, scowling and jamming her hands deep into the pockets of her gray hooded sweatshirt.

"An' a no-count bitch!" someone emphasized, followed by smirks.

Venus crossed her legs.

Shantel stole a glance at an incoming text message.

"Okay," Porsche said, "anyway, she was doin' toooo much up in there! She had dat lil' baby up in da closet. No lights on. Stankin' ass diapers on da floor. An' she drag that lil' boy by his arm across da floor. Might 'a broke his arm o' somethin'!"

"Yeeeaaah!!" Dalanna exclaimed.

Shawn and Terri looked on, stone-faced and solemn.

"Okay, we're going to need to tell somebody about this," Shawn proclaimed shakily. *Yes, this is the right thing to do. Well, yes...um, shit...I hope so.*

He looked to the girls for something like approval. A couple of pairs of eyes met his, looking almost hopeful.

"Alright you guys," Shawn continued. "We have to let someone know. I know this can be difficult, but we have to do this."

The girls smirked, exchanging knowing glances that said, "Yeah, that's the idea."

"It's good that you guys are telling us about all this," Terri encouraged, crossing her legs and folding her hands in her lap. She sounded a lot more secure than Shawn felt. *I wonder how she does that,* he briefly wondered to himself. *She always has this way of, I don't know, being okay, no matter what.*

A long silence ensued. Unlike others before, this one didn't feel awkward. Shawn watched the girls closely, wondering if the others would take "their turns" as they called it. But he somehow knew that everyone had had their turn, even if only a few had spoken.

Assessment

A Child Protective Services report was filed immediately after the group, and, soon after, a formal investigation took place. There was not enough information to prosecute Brandy or for the system to take other protective action. No further information about the investigation was known. Nevertheless, the girls coming forward and telling Terri and me about what had happened in Brandy's house (knowing that their disclosures would be reported) showed that trust was beginning to build.

Corey and Corey (2002) noted that, after the initial introductory stages, a group typically goes through a conflict stage. In this stage, the group members may challenge the facilitator. If the conflict is successfully worked through, the group will reach a deeper level of intimacy.

This theory of group behavior held true for what happened in the girls' group in this last week. In the previous week, the girls had challenged Terri and me when they had insisted that their being abused was okay because "all black people beat their kids." Given that Terri and I are white, this was a touchy subject for us to handle as the facilitators. We handled it effectively by not challenging the girls' understanding of their cultural reality but, instead, informing the group that we were mandated reporters. In addition, Terri and I asserted that we, as caring adults, had to do everything we could to protect the girls from harm. This may have helped the girls to feel that we could be trusted to take protective action on their behalf. Furthermore, secure attachment behavior is demonstrated when children come to trusted adults when there is a threat of some kind.

This is not meant to assert that the group was making the girls' attachment systems secure. The girls had survived extensive trauma and had displayed predominantly insecure traits, including Porsche's attempts to provoke her aunt into conflicts and Venus's tendency to emotionally detach at key moments of deeper group process. This suggests that the girls would need long-term therapy and more stable home environments to achieve learned security. Still, this last interchange could be considered secure attachment behavior.

This is also an example of one of the girls' cultural strengths—their ability to give and to be responsive emotionally in ways that they did not often experience from others. In 2009, the East Bay Community Recovery Project hosted an African American women's panel in which an African American female facilitator stated that African American women suffer the trauma of always giving (emotionally) and never getting back in return. It felt like the group members were often forced to survive in a world where the adults in their lives were not protective and were not responsive to their emotional needs. The girls found the strength and concern to be available for each other and to take protective action on behalf of Brandy's children, even when speaking up meant violating the sociocultural norms of staying out of other people's business and not involving the authorities.

SEVEN

Week 21

Porsche

BRRRRIIIIINNNGGG!!!

"Who da fuck is dat callin' on ma' phone?!?!"

"Why you don't get up an answer it den?!?!"

"'Cuz this my house an' I do what da fuck I wanna do, hear me?"

"I got it y'all!!!" Porsche interjected. *All a dat ova' da phone. Coulda answered it by now. Sheeit!!!*

"Go on then child, be useful for somethin'!" a cranky sounding elderly voice encouraged.

Porsche opened her lips, a million responses coming to mind, considering which was the sassiest, the most cutting and piercing.

BRRRINNNNNNNGGG!!!

Oh well, fuck it. She answered the phone. *Don't want 'em hangin' up. Might be my ladies!*

"What it do?" Porsche inquired into the phone, leaning lazily against the wall and crossing her legs at the ankles.

"What it do?!" barked the cantankerous voice, "What da fuck kind a way is dat to answer da phone?!"

"Damn! Why you always talkin' shit?!?!" Porsche muttered.

"Wha' choo say?!" rumbled a challenge followed by an ominous squeaking of couch springs.

Porsche had long ceased paying attention, twisting the phone cord apathetically around a delicate index finger.

"Damn girl. Dat yo' auntie?" inquired a concerned and yet weary voice on the other end of the phone.

Porsche sucked her teeth and leaned against the wall. "You know," she offered, just loud enough for her auntie to hear, "ain't nobody else go ghetto like dat around here!"

"Who you talkin' 'bout 'gone' ghetto?!" Her auntie interjected, the floor squeaking with each of her approaching footsteps.

"C'mon now, I'm on the phone," Porsche groaned as she bent over the nearby kitchen counter. "Can I get a lil' privacy? Jus' have a lil' conv-a-sation?!?!"

"I heard dat," agreed the voice on the other end of the phone.

"You know?!" Porsche continued, still embittered by her auntie's harsh words. "And see dat why..." Suddenly the phone went dead, a loud snapping sound in the background, loud enough to be heard, but no match for the attention span of a teenager deep in girl talk.

Porsche grimaced, looking to and fro for some rhyme or reason. "Hello? HELLO? What the..." Her eyes followed the phone cord to its lifeless end on the carpet.

"Yeah, what da fuck you doin' runnin' up ma' phone bill an' shit?" her aunt grumbled, scowling down at Porsche with beady eyes blinking behind thick glasses.

Porsche stomped her foot on the floor, whirled around, stomped away with clenched fists, "Oh I hate you!" she shrieked.

"Well I hate yo' ass too!" her aunt retorted, pointing a long, gnarly finger at her niece's fleeing figure, "And I hate how all a' y'all come up in here like ya pay da rent! Always on my phone, up in my food, ya need to go get a job o' somethin'! Damn free loader, jus' like ya mama!"

Porsche almost exploded. *Oh now you seriously fucked up!! You gonna talk 'bout my mama?!?! Oh hell no you didn't.*

"Man you got some nerve!" she called over her shoulder, snapping her head hard to the left in a half circle. She began waving her arms up and around with a loud snap of her fingers. "You wit' yo' welfare self! You...."

"GET YO' HAND OUTTA MY FACE BEFO' I CUT IT OFF!" her aunt roared, taking a few long-legged strides through the kitchen and getting just close enough to show that she meant business.

Porsche rose to the challenge.

"YOU AIN'T 'BOUT TA DO NOTHIN'! AND DON'T BE..."

"BITCH I SLAP DA TASTE OUT YO' MOUTH!!!" her aunt bellowed, making a mad dash through the kitchen, pushing Porsche hard into the refrigerator, jutting her chest out and standing up on the balls of her feet so that she could look down at her niece as if from a tower.

Porsche regained her balance and ducked deftly out of the way. "BITCH YOU BES' TA KEEP YO' HANDS OFF ME FO' REAL!" With a middle finger in the air, she made a mad dash for an exit. Through the hallway between the kitchen and living room with family pictures and Jesus Christ on the wall, she made long strides past the couch inlaid with plastic covering, the Cosby's blaring on the television. Flinging the front door open, slamming it behind her with all her might, she heard obscenities follow her as she was tearing away as fast as her legs could carry her, down the porch and out onto the sidewalk. She was only deterred momentarily by a stumbling, dirty man's slobbering attempt at hello and how are you.

"Hee, hee, hee," he chuckled, his wide smile exposing foul breath and missing teeth.

"Whoooo-weee. Wash yo' name, sweet thang?!?!"

Porsche eyed his disheveled visage, wrinkling her nose mightily, snapping her head high in the air contemptuously. The man's clothes were badly torn, and he wore only one shoe. The overpowering stench of malt liquor and feces almost caused Porsche to dry heave.

"Get yo' drunk ass away from me!" she barked. *Now I gotta get dis here shit too?! Fuck dis."* Just as she was beginning to make her second mad dash away, she ran headlong into a woman who was standing to the side of the man. She also smelled horribly, seemed equally out of it.

"Daayaam!" the woman growled, "Watch where you goin' girl!!"

Porsche was now enraged, ready to let the woman have it, having finally reached her boiling point. She began rearing back to gather her strength and was ready to blacken an eye, fatten a lip, bust a nose, maybe all three. As her clenched fist drew back, she zeroed in on the woman, taking aim. She stopped short just before letting her fist fly.

"Mama?!" A long second passed, giving Porsche long enough to get a good look. Her mother's eyes were almost closed, her hair twisted up in wild and gnarly tangles. The harsh smell of liquor told all.

Her mother looked up, woozy, trying to get back to reality. Staring hard through slits, smiling a wide, intoxicated smile, she recognized Porsche. "Ohhhh, whass'up my girl? You bein' a good girl, hee hee hee hee hee."

"Whhhoooo-wwweeee, she look like she could be a baaaad girl do! Mmm-hmm!" the surly man proclaimed, finding his way to the side of Porsche's mother. Her mother frowned at him and pushed him slightly away.

"Hey, dash not coo'!!!" her mother reproached, "dish ma lil' girl. My chil, hee hee hee." She smiled wide at Porsche, wobbling, reaching out to touch her face with outstretched hands.

Porsche ducked away, suddenly fighting back tears without knowing why. Taking a step back, she'd barely evaded her mother's touch. "Just…mama, I…" but the words died on her tongue. Her tears began to well up. She moved up tentatively and kissed her mother on the cheek. "Bye mama." She ran down the street, fast as she could go, running until her sides hurt. Finally she turned the corner and slowed down.

Rap music was audible in the distance. Dice clanking to the ground. Men arguing. Many voices at once. It could only get worse. Porsche normally felt exhilarated by all the commotion of *The X*. Always exciting, always lively, always entertaining. But not tonight. Tonight, she just wanted to be left alone. Pivoting hard on her left foot, she spun around and began marching determinedly back the way she had come. The arguing male voices suddenly stopped.

"DAMN BABY GIRL! Why don't cha' do dat again?!"

"Yeah, she done got a lil' twist in her don't she!"

"And all kind a' ass too!"

All three voices laughed uproariously.

"Shut up!" she roared over her shoulder, "you broke ass mutha fuckas!!!" Breathing hard as she continued on down the block, she frowned at snarling dogs and boarded up houses. A police car pulled over to the side of the road, its overhead lights glaring. Two white officers with guns drawn forced three young African American men down on their knees and made them interlock their fingers behind their heads. But Porsche was off in a world all to her own. Somewhere deep inside, she found the nerve to keep on going. She just kept walking until her key went into the lock and she opened the door to her aunt's house.

"Say now. Nice of ya to grace us with yo' mutha fuckin' presence!!!" snarled a disparaging female voice from the couch in the living room. Porsche swung the door closed forcefully and scowled back while eyeing her aunt slumped partially beneath a blanket covered in potato chip pieces. Porsche despised everything about her, her great bloated mass of chins, the old dress she wore every day, her uncombed hair.

"You shut up!" Porsche yelled back, slapping her palm insolently atop the door with a satisfying thud.

"HEY NOW!" her aunt protested, the creaking springs of the couch alerting Porsche that trouble might be on its way. "YOU BES'A KEEP YO' FILTHY HANDS OFF MY DO' LIKE DAT!!!"

But for once, Porsche was too mad to argue. Her blood was boiling. She had no idea what she was doing, but her legs took her out the back door to the patio. She stepped over broken toys and moved aside hanging laundry, went up the fire escape, and then up a flight of stairs, higher and higher until she reached the roof. She looked up to the sky, into the stars, then past the hills. She was just wishing there was a God and that he might hear her now. Hear her, and comfort her.

Wish I could just fly away. Then she smiled to herself, imagined that she could just spread her arms and away she would go. *No mo' a' dis shit. My auntie be gone, fuckin' bitch!! An' I take mama with me, too. Wouldn't be no liquor an' no crack. No more nasty ol' men, an' no po-lice neither.*

The thought made her smile, a dreamy kind of smile. Stretching her legs out, Porsche lay down flat on the gravel and stared right up into heaven. Watching the stars. Listening. Feeling the wind. *I wonda' what it be like if I ain't here...Like...I don't know. What it be like if I was neva' born?* A police siren screamed by at breakneck speed with ear-splitting volume. Normally, she would have been giddy with wonder. Not tonight. Tonight, she just wanted to be left alone.

Rona

Click. "George Jefferson, where oh where, George Jefferson the man with no hair." *Laughter.*

Click. "And da lawd shines down on me wit' the hope of his livin' water!!! An' let us hear him an' say..."

Click. "In other news, a man was gunned down in front of the Harvest Street housing projects on the east side of the city. Police spokesman reports that he was 18 and survived by his infant children and..."

Damn! Same old shit on up in here!!! Rona grumbled silently to herself.

Click. "It's all for you!" *Janet Jackson.* Rona gazed forward in a deep trance. Six-pack abs, high cheek bones, award-winning smile.

Damn, why I had ta be ugly?

"If you really want me, it's all for you!!!" Janet continued, twirling, flashing her smile, beauty in all its glory.

Rona watched in complete envy. For a moment, she closed her eyes, crossed her legs Indian-style, and drifted off far away. She pictured herself the way she wanted to be. Thin. Pretty. Smiling. New clothes. The boys would be watching, succumbing to her every movement. Idolizing. *If only shit was fo' real,* grumbled her inner critic.

But, maybe…like, I jus' gotta stop eatin' so damn much. She ran her hand over the remaining tangles in her hair. *Need ta get ma' hair done again, been like fo' months o' somethin'. Momma might be down. She mad now, but she be over it soon. I could lose some weight, get some braids.* Smiling at the thought. *I be pretty den!!! Hecka cute!! Get ma' hair up in long braids, an' make dis one in da middle green. OOOHH!! All cute an' shit!!!* Almost squealing out loud, she clamped her hands over her mouth in excitement, beaming.

Suddenly restless, bones aching, she clicked the television off, rocked back and forth to heave herself upright. She shuffle-stepped toward the door with mincing, awkward pitter-patter steps. She looked down at her feet along the way. Walking with her head low had long ago become a habit.

My feet ugly too!! Need ta go snatch some a' mama' nail polish. Do my toes up nice!! Slipping into flip-flop sandals. *Naw, need to do my toes befo' all a' dat. Uuuhh!! My feet hecka big an' black!!!* Sitting back down on the carpet, pulling on footie socks and Converse high-top basketball shoes, she noted they were worn thin, the laces frayed. *Need to go shoe shoppin', too.*

"Mama!!" Rona hollered, the vibration echoing through the house. No answer. Rona sighed in impatience. *I know she here. An' she heard me fa' sho'!!*

"MAMA!!!" she hollered again, louder this time. The bedroom door at the far end of the hallway swung abruptly open.

"Miss Rona," her mother answered flatly, an eyebrow arched high, betraying contempt and disproval. She was tapping her long red fingernails methodically against the door frame, looking at Rona. *Have you lost your mind?* she said without saying.

"I'm sorry, mama," Rona confessed, swallowing hard. *Damn, I hate it when she look at me like dat.* But the ferocity of her desire for new shoes helped her recover quickly. "Can we go shoppin'?"

Her mother looked wistfully away as she collected her thoughts. Rona watched her closely in anticipation, noting her short, wispy hair, stylishly parted off to the side, sleek and shiny, her flowing beige, red, and black dress, matching shoes, her ornately painted toenails and fingernails.

Finally, Rona could bear it no longer. "C'mon mama, please?!" Rona pleaded. "I do the dishes an' mop da floor tonight!"

Rona's mother dropped an imposing hand to her hip and cocked an eyebrow. "You s'posed to do that anyway, ain't ya?" she inquired wisely.

Rona looked up and around as if searching for words. *Damn, dat is my shit too. Fuck!!! Now I'm a' have ta do it.* "Well…um, maybe," she stammered.

Her mother shook her head, smiling in resignation, exhaling mightily. "Uh-huh, yeah, das right. Why you don't jus' maybe get in da car."

Rona clapped her hands and did a little victory dance. *Thought she 'gone say no fo' sho'!!!* "COO'!!!" She exclaimed triumphantly. "I'm a go get ma' Nike 'fit on. Be lookin' soopa cute."

Her mother pointed to the front door. "In the car befo' I change ma' mind," she ordered, trying to be firm but definitely amenable. She considered her own ideas for what lay in store for her. Shoes, a new dress, maybe a purse. Not to mention that six-foot something dark-skinned security guard with the muscles and tattoos!

Grabbing her black leather purse from the coffee table, she strode gracefully through the hallway, past the kitchen, the black sofa, the Malcolm X portrait on the wall. Rona almost caught up with her but ran back to flick off the living room light. *Sheeit, I shoulda done my hair o' somethin'. Der prob'ly be some boys up der too!*

Her mother was soon out the door, Rona in her shadow. Closing the front door, latching the steel protective gate behind it, she proceeded down the porch steps. Rona began to make a move to slide down the hand rail but an unmistakable look from her mother put an end to that idea. Down the cracked walkway between green and yellow grass on either side, they headed for the car.

"Nice out today, ain't it?" her mother observed.

Rona smacked her lips. "Yeah," she agreed. "'cuz ain't no people outside."

Her mother laughed as she unlocked the door of her battered blue Ford Taurus. "I know das right!" Once in her seatbelt, Rona quickly began to fumble with the radio. The engine struggled to come to life. Dr. Dre was playing as mother and daughter nodded their heads rhythmically in time. The car slowly began to slip out the driveway. Rona's mother placed an arm back across the passenger side head rest where her daughter sat beside her, looking behind her for the first time. Suddenly she slammed on the brakes, which sent both mother and daughter lurching forward.

"Whoa!! Hey now, uh, hee hee hee, whoooo-weee" came from outside near the back of the car. A stumbling figure was careening around their driveway, smiling a wide, crack-mouthed smile. He continued on down the street, arms flailing beneath a heavy-looking army jacket draped around his shoulders. Scowling faces of mother and daughter watched his slovenly departure, both heads shaking somewhere between pity and disgust.

"Crack head!" Rona muttered. "Lazy ass nigga!! Shoulda hit him an' nobody even miss him!!!"

Rona's mother frowned hard. "Girl, don't talk like dat. Lot a' deez black men need help. Ain't no jobs for 'em. Thangs hard out here. We gotta have the love of da lord in our hearts, love for all our brothas an' sistas. Hear me?"

Rona blinked hard and nodded. *Yeah? Well, I don't see da lord doin' nothin' right now 'though. Why he let dem jus' be all up in here an all?"*

The Taurus began to pick up speed, mother and daughter making headway down the main boulevard past rows and rows of houses, each one like the next, worn paint, garbage in some of the walkways, driveways with either flashy luxury cars or badly worn clunkers. Many of the homes had for sale signs pounded into withered lawns. Attractive, smiling Latino sales people smiled on signs that advertised foreclosures at rock bottom prices. On some of the signs, local artists had added blackened teeth and smoking cigars.

The car pulled to a stop at a traffic light. A shopping cart lady crossed the walkway, slow and determined, her cart piled high with junk of all kinds. She wore at least two coats and oversized slippers and a rain hat, although the sun was shining. Rona's mother sternly pointed her out to Rona.

"See right der?" she directed Rona's gaze to the stringy haired woman pushing the cans and other garbage down the road, making her way slowly across the street. "Could be somebody' mama, somebody sista. See what I'm sayin'?!"

Rona had to think about that. Not that much came to mind. Rona's eyes returned to the road ahead. Pretty Ricky's latest erotic jam was almost bursting through the speakers. Both of their heads were bobbing in time.

Soon they were passing through an arched entrance marked, *Short Hills Mall*. The Taurus meandered through rows and rows of cars in the parking lot. They saw moms pushing baby strollers and carrying big shopping bags. Energetic boys were hanging around out front, talking noisily.

Rona could barely contain herself. "Mama I'm a get dem new Jordans, COO'? And my hair did?! And den a new jersey, a red one wit' da'..."

Rona's mother steered the Taurus slowly through the parking lot with one arm, breathing in heavily as if to brace herself for the onslaught on her household finances soon to come. "Okay, okay," she reassured herself and her daughter, recognizing her own impulsive habits. Her eyes gazed over at the red Macy's sign, hungrily remembering the new ebony dresses she had seen in the fall catalogue. "Girl, we gonna look around a lil' bit. See wha's what. We gonna each have ourselves one outfit an' some shoes. Coo'?"

"Yeah!!! That's coo' mama. OOOH!!! Mmmm-hhmmmm. Let's do this!!" Watching Rona clapping her hands excitedly like a little girl, her mother was grateful that Rona was pretty easy to please.

Glancing over her hair and face in a nearby car window on their way in, Rona's mood was somewhat tempered. *Still ugly. But I'm a' be cuuuuutteee in dem new Jordans!!*

They passed a thin-framed, darker skinned African American man standing with a heavyset white woman with painted eyebrows, a puffy white coat, and heavy gold jewelry. "Damn my nigga! We gotta go on and do this!!" she blustered loudly to the man at her side as Rona and her mother made their way past. Rona and her mother glanced up at her as she spoke, looking for a second longer at him. Looking embarrassed, he ducked his head and looked into a nearby car window, busily fixing his hair and mustache, his back now turned to the passing females.

A group of boys huddled in the corner of the parking lot about 30 feet from the elevator. They were shooting dice, making lots of noise, carousing. Rona took a harder look. A pair of pretty brown eyes met hers. He was wearing an A-shirt tank top that showed off his firm biceps. "OOOOHHH now!!!" Called the voice belonging to the body, "You a thick one too!!!" and he looked up from his game with a wide smile.

For a moment, Rona shivered in wonder. *He talkin' ta me?!* "You got da front," observed the boy, snapping his neck hard to the right to get a look behind, "an' da back!! Whas' yo' name?!?! Maybe I jus' call ya 'big mama'?!" Rona's heart pounded in her chest as he made his way forward. *Oooohhh he 'bout ta talk ta me. He gonna holler!! An' ma' hair fucked up.* Brushing her hair back over her ears with nervous fingers, she was hoping that his eyes would meet hers.

As he stepped in Rona's path, he moved past her and stood beside her mother. Rona's heart sank and her head bowed low in crushed agony, feeling stupid.

Her mother smiled self-assuredly, trying hard to say go away, but the flattery was hard to deny. "Boy, please. How old are you?" she asked with arched eyebrows, trying to sound stern, continuing on her walk at a pace just leisurely enough for him to catch up but not so much that she couldn't deny it later. Rona marched along dutifully by her side, holding in her anger.

He shrugged his shoulders and responded nonchalantly. "My age bother you o' is it jus' s'posed to?"

Rona's mother laughed and waved a hand backward. "Boy get outta here," and she feigned an effort to slap him on the shoulder.

He cooed and began to drift back, subtly realizing he was losing his case. "Yeah, it's all good, baby," he promised, backing away and blowing her a kiss with one hand, holding up his pants with the other. "But I'm gonna holla at you on da way out. Maybe we cou' have a lil' condo' on da way out. I mean you know how it do?" and with that, he spun on his heels and was gone.

Rona's mother shook her head, laughing faintly, somewhat confused. "Dat boy said 'Condo'…"

Rona glared at her mother. "Con-va-sa-tion, mama!" she growled irritably without looking up. Her mother glanced down at her as they made their way past Foot Locker and Starbucks, past jewelry stands with African American teenage boys gathered hungrily around in baggy pants and oversized t-shirts, looking from the watches and chains in the case to the elderly Asian woman at the nearby check stand. A tall, handsome African American security guard was watching the boys, and Rona was watching him.

Rona's mother picked up the unspoken message: "Girl please, dat lil' boy ugly anyway. You way too cute fa' him."

"I ain't like dat boy!" Rona insisted.

Her mother smiled quietly, wondering if Macy's was around the corner. A young, light-skinned mother with brightly colored braids, pushing a crying baby in a stroller, passed on her left. An older African American maintenance man unobtrusively pushing a broom said, "Excuse me." Another security guard in a Smokey the Bear hat wrestled with a young Latino boy with greased back hair; he was adamant that the gloves in his pocket were gloves he had brought *into* the store. Dirty green and yellow tile floors, elevator music, droves of people.

"Whassup Rona," a young man's voice invited from somewhere inside a crowd of patrons just ahead. Rona strained to find the owner of the voice. It was someone familiar, the name just on the tip of her tongue. *Who dat is?* It was a wonderful sounding voice, soft and yet soothing, like her father's, but it wasn't her father's.

Crowds of mall-walkers were coming from the opposite direction. A sudden smile through the crowd and a wave let Rona know who it was. Pushing his glasses back firmly into place, a young man with dark skin and natural hair, dressed in a white sweater vest and baggy jeans now appeared. He was a little overweight, but he had attractive, deep-set dark eyes and full lips.

Rona's lip quivered into a smile, looking anxiously away before looking back, her eyes finding his again.

Her mother chuckled knowingly. "Oh, I hear somethin' somethin' callin' my name ova' there at Macy's. I see you later, girl." Turning on her heels, she strode off toward the north end of the mall, waving over her shoulder without waiting for a response from Rona.

Her eyes wandered back to the approaching young man, a giddy smile beginning to crease his lips as he ran a nervous hand over his hair. He walked sort of on the balls of his feet, trying to stand taller.

Rona smiled nervously. "Hi, Johnny!" Her voice sounded stilted and shaky. She sat down on a mall bench, crossing her legs a couple of times, hands flat on the bench.

Johnny nodded his head and bit his lip, still beaming, all teeth, all energy. "How you doin'?" he inquired, his eyes meeting hers. "Fine, whas' goin' on?"

Rona replied, looking down at her feet. She couldn't look in his eyes any longer. She bit her lip.

Johnny began to stammer, assuming she was losing interest. "Well, everything, yeah, it's all good, well, I mean, you know, it ain't all good, but good enough." He felt like his mind was all over the place weighing possibilities, unable to straighten out.

She kicked the ground with a worn basketball sneaker and then looked up halfway into his face, somewhere between the neck and chest. *He got a lil' muscle too!*

"So...," Johnny blustered, fumbling for what to say next. "How's school?"

Rona nodded her head and crossed her arms across her chest. "Coo'," she responded. *Damn he cute, jus' don't say nothin' stupid.* She then looked directly into his eyes for an awe-inspiring second. *Mmm-hmm, he dress nice, speak good, but my hair fucked up taday and he lookin' at my hair. Damn!!! I shoulda gone up into Macy's first, got my new fit an' put it on. I'd a' been hecka cute. Oooohh, he hecka cute!!!*

The awkward silence was fast growing louder. "Awright den," Johnny conceded, smiling and looking into Rona's eyes. "Maybe I see you around?"

Rona smiled, bowing her head. *Ooooooohhh I hope so!!!!*

And Johnny began his departure, seeing her smile, smiling back. Taking two long steps in the opposite direction, he spun sharply over his shoulder in here-goes-nothing fashion. "MAYBE I COME HOLLA AT CHOO AT SCHOO' ?!" he yelled, walking backwards, then turning around again before she could answer.

Rona smiled big, fighting hard to hold in her joy, looking down over the tiled floor of the mall. Looking up to watch him leave, she realized she didn't need to hold it back. Johnny was elated too, evident as he slammed an excited hand into the outstretched palm of his other hand and then turned to see her watching him.

Oooooh shit he like me too!!! "Yeah, okay," Rona agreed, trying to play it cool, but her heart wanted to sing and dance.

Johnny turned around and nodded his head victoriously upward. "Awright den, I catch up wit' cha!" and then he was gone. Rona watched him all the way. *And he got a nice butt too!*

Rona squealed once he was out of ear shot, hopping up and down in a half circle, hugging herself before bolting into Macy's, nearly sending an old woman careening into a mannequin along the way. The old woman glowered as she regained her balance. Wild blue hair, cracked mouth, withered skin atop a great bloated body, paper bags with handles strung over her arms as if she were Christmas shopping for the whole city, she shouted after Rona, "Watch where you goin' child!!"

Rona would have normally been sorry and apologized, but not now. Now, her mind was somewhere else.

"MAMA!?!?!" Rona bellowed, weaving around patrons and racks of bras and underwear. So much had happened, Rona didn't know where to begin. Eyes everywhere at once. *Mama!! Ooohhh!! I got some shit ta tell ya!!!* But her mother was nowhere to be found.

"MAMA?!?!" she called again with her hands cupped around her mouth like a megaphone.

Her mother's head poked up from behind a nearby bra rack as if it were a head popping out of a whack-a-mole game. Rona's yell was total and mighty, drawing annoyed looks from other shoppers.

"Child…calm yo' self!" Her mother insisted, moving up close to her with a frown creasing her brow. She pulled her daughter over to her. "Lawd in heaven, can't imagine what so important dat you gotta be hollerin' like da devil."

Rona jumped up and down giddily, her eyes wide with excitement. "Oooooooohhh mama!!!" she exploded, grabbing her mother firmly by the shoulders, hopping on both feet like a bunny, kissing her firmly on the cheek. "You gotta…"

Her mother grabbed Rona's hands in hers, giggling slightly and only half serious. "Child fo' real. Calm. Breathe."

But Rona paid her little mind. "Mama…I…He…Come talk to me…" She was fighting to catch her breath. "…Said I see you late…he, he…"

She finally stopped trying to keep herself together. "OOOOOOHHHH!!! He gone holla at me at school!" and mother and daughter laughed triumphantly together, hands clapping, heads tilting back.

Rona was practically drunk. "Ooooohhh, he sooo cute!!"

"Mmm-hmm," her mother encouraged, beaming in interest. "Caught you one didn't ya?! An' who was dat boy out front da sto'?!"

Rona smiled wide. Lurching in heavy footsteps out of the store, her mind lost, her mother smiling and shaking her head, rushing to catch up, each striding briskly in excitement.

"MMM-HHMMM," Rona answered gleefully. "He hecka cute."

"Awright now, child," her mother reassured. "Take it easy, slow ya roll a lil'. You don't wanna be too eager. An' you ain't exactly old enough ta be doin' a whole lot a' anythang anyway!" Rona nodded softly in begrudging agreement. Her mother watched her spirits dip a bit, shrugged her shoulders in oh-what-the-hell fashion. "Awright I tell ya. Now when he…"

While her mother made a concerted effort to provide some motherly advice, Rona drifted off into fantasy. Her mother advised her to take her time, play it cool, not allow anyone to do this and that, no touching, too young to date, but....

Rona didn't hear a word of it. She was floating through the mall, buoyed by romance. She envisioned parading through school with Johnny, hand in hand, all of the other girls green with envy. The boys stopping and staring, whispering amongst themselves. Sweet and soulful R and B music sounding from somewhere. Rona could see it all now. Even as she picked out a pair of shoes and got a Big Mac from McDonald's, she was entranced. *OOOOOHHH he gonna come holla! Das what he said!* She could see exactly how it would play out. She'd be on the yard at lunch, hanging out with a crowd of girls with braided extensions. All their voices going at once. Just another day, and then along would come Johnny. The crowds would melt away as her man approached, smiling, easy going, not a thought on his mind but being by her side. She would see it in his eyes as he took her hand in his, smiling, standing tall, leading her by the hand to the rest of their lives together. It would be so beautiful.

Her mother was taking notice, suspecting where her daughter's imaginings had led her, but she decided not to interrupt. She was a little worried, but she was pleased to see her daughter so happy. The sight of it made her happy too.

They walked on in blissful silence. Twilight formed around them; an azure sky with just a few stars canopied the parking lot. Rona's mother opened the battered doors of the Ford Taurus. The car started with Snoop Dog on the radio. Rona's smile was beginning to fade.

Damn, shoulda had my other 'fit on. And not be eatin' so much. She yanked the overhead visor down so that she could stare disapprovingly hard into the little mirror inside. Scowling, she scolded herself for being overweight. *Dem slices a' pie from da otha' night did me wrong. I even look mo' fat today.*

Her mother noticed the change in her daughter's demeanor as they passed the boarded up buildings and dark alleys, graffiti-decorated brick apartment buildings, and crowded corners. "Child, wha' choo lookin' at? Yo' pretty face?"

Rona half smiled, staring long out the window, wishing it were true. *I must a' put on some more weight. My cheeks all round an' shit. OOOOHHH he fine!! What should I wear come Monday ?*

Rona's mind continued its wayward path. *He loves me. He loves me not.* Past deadened lawns. An old woman in a rocking chair on the porch, staring off to the horizon. Stopping at a traffic light. A lowrider Impala was bouncing down the other side of the street. *He loves me not.* The traffic light changed and the Taurus picked up speed. *He loves me.* The car parked. The radio and engine died. *He loves me not.* Doors closing in rhythm. Choppy steps up the walkway to home. *He loves me.*

"Wash up befo' dinner," her mother ordered as they made their way inside, the front door closing behind. Into the bathroom, hot soapy water. *He loves me not.* The dinner table, prayers, clanking forks, napkins on laps, R. Kelly in the background. *He loves me.* Her mother talking. Taking big gulping bites that made Rona feel guilty.

"How's school? Eat your greens, girl," her mother encouraged.

Rona found a way to make it through dinner, leaving her plate half-full, professing she wasn't hungry. *He loves me not.* Her mother insisted she finish her food. Rona agreed but could feel herself getting fatter with every bite. She finally left the table with a lot on her mind. *He loves me.* Teeth brushing. Soapy water. A long look into the mirror. *Damn I'm ugly.* She stared hard in determination, taking a deep breath in, holding her stomach in for a moment. She smiled approvingly at her hidden waistline. Into bed. Covers pulled over. A motherly kiss, "Sleep well child, may da lawd bless ya an' keep ya while ya sleep." After five minutes of gazing up into the ceiling, dreaming, hoping, wishing, Rona drifted off to slumber. *He loves me.*

Shantel and Venus

Hundreds of thousands of voices all cheered at once. Men clapped their hands and called loudly through hands cupped around their mouths. Their wives and daughters cooed and giggled, Venus among them. Neck draped with diamonds and gold, new Michael Jordan basketball shoes, hair in long, fine braids. Her husband was running the length of the basketball court, ball between his legs, spinning, ducking, hesitating, faking. Up. Down. Left. Right. Poetry in motion. Venus and the other wives sitting courtside occasionally looked on, appreciated the sleekness of it all. The men were muscular, sweaty, and quick. Sneakers squeaked against the slick wooden floor. The crowd was loud and wild.

Venus's husband, star player and muscle boy extraordinaire, was front and center in the spotlight. A head fake to the left, to the right, down the middle, three quick dribbles inside the free-throw line. Up and high over his head with the ball in one hand. *SLAM!!!* Nearly prying the backboard from its cemented holster. The crowd cheered and hollered. The other courtside wives were green with envy. Venus could only sit back and smile in satisfaction. Just when it couldn't get any better, her man looked up to her. Their eyes met for long seconds. The uproarious cheers and yells were somehow quieted. The world outside became small and inconspicuous as her husband waved....

"WAKE UP VENUS!!" commanded a man's voice as a hand clapped down on the wooden desk beneath Venus's huddled form. She jolted upward, yanking her head from its flattened position against the desk. Blinking hard in the daylight, she was confused only for a second as she rubbed the sleep from her eyes with the heel of her palms.

Scowling, she avoided looking at her teacher. "What da' fucka?!?!" Venus muttered, sitting back into her chair and pulling her blue hooded sweatshirt around her face so that it was barely exposed. She glared through slits at the person who interrupted her most beautiful dream, his hunch-backed form, no hair, high-riding pants, and too-small black polo shirt. She heard the legs of his polyester pants slightly swishing against one another as he walked through rows of students at their desks, waking some up along the way, breaking up arguments that resumed as soon as he was out of ear shot.

Sitting next to Venus, Shantel smiled wide at her girl's rude awakening. "Yeah wakeup nigga!!!" she insisted, butting Venus with her right elbow.

Venus nudged back resentfully. "Get off me," she murmured, debating half-heartedly about whether she should go back to sleep. *Dream was nice too!!* She decided against it. *Ain't tired no mo' any damn way.*

BRRRIIINNGG!! A loud bell sounded overhead, followed by raucous stampeding feet, jackets slinging over shoulders, arms through sleeves, desks screeching against the floor. Muffled laughter, yelps, snickers, pairs of hands finding others bodies in rough-housing.

"HEY!!!" The old man shrieked at his departing classroom, "Hands off!!! C'mon, get to your next class, let's go." No one seemed to hear him.

Shantel watched him for a second to make sure the coast was clear, then popped a stick of gum into her mouth on her way out, offering Venus a piece along the way. For long moments, they chewed silently, dragging their feet across the schoolyard on their way to their final two classes of the day. English and Science. Not much to look forward to.

While they were passing through the schoolyard, a boy several heads smaller than Venus flew past her, backpack bouncing left and right, nearly smacking her in the chin. Girls their age with permed hair and tight jeans were lounging against the railings that lead into the bungalow classrooms. Chattering voices filled the air.

The girls bounded up the steps at the end of the yard and into the main office building. A full-figured woman in a business suit was holding a blaring walkie–talkie and barking "go to class." Most kids were dutifully obeying, hustling and bustling, but some were noticeably taking their time, lingering in front of lockers, taking half-hearted steps forward to attract minimal attention. They were not in any hurry to get where they knew they had to go, but they knew how to look like they were going where they had to go. Meanwhile, the hallway remained in uproar. Hands on the backpacks and bodies of anyone within arm's reach, pokes, pushes, hand slapping encouragement, and outcries were everywhere at once. Venus and Shantel paid it no mind.

Shantel breathed in heavily through her nose. *Maaaaaan, why we gotta go to schoo'?!? Don't learn shit. I ought a' jus' bounce up outta here... Matter fact, dat don't sound like a bad idea!*

As the bell blared overhead, the crowds began to drift away, dispersing behind closed classroom doors, the bustling hallway losing life by the second. Shantel looked up and down the hallway, nearly empty after a few moments. The coast was clear. "C'mon girl," she motioned to Venus, bucking left with her head as she took a sharp left turned toward the front door, assuming Venus would follow.

Venus hesitated for a second. *Sheeit, my momma gonna kill me. Las' time da schoo' called an' I was in trouble fa' like, hella long!!! An' dis time ?!... Aw, well, fuck it.*

Smiling wide in excitement, she consented. "Okay. Let's do dis!" she whispered as they hurried down the last stretch of hallway past row after row of closed classroom doors and blue-tinted lockers, through the iron-clad front doors, clanking them shut on their way out. Back out into the free world. Long shadows. A light breeze blowing a tetherball a few inches off its pole, bouncing it back against the pole with a clang of metal against metal. A pretty kind of hypnotizing sight. The girls each watched it for a brief second before resuming their purposeful march. That split-second hesitation was enough to catch someone's attention. The iron doors of the main school building screeched open and a slightly audible blare of walkie–talkie noise came from just inside.

"HEY HEY?!" called a deep and raspy male voice. "WHO DAT OVA' DER? GOOOOOOO TA CLAYAS!?" The girls bolted, slinging their backpacks off their shoulders into open palms.

"GO GET A REAL JOB!" Shantel called over her shoulder. "TOY COP ASS NIGGA!!"

"OOOOOHHH!!" Venus squealed with a hand over her mouth as the girls ducked down along the chain-link fence in the school yard. "Nuh-uh, Shantel you wrong for dat."

"HEY! I'm talkin' ta y'all!" bellowed the male voice with hands cupped around his mouth. Heaving at the chest from a few long strides out the door, staring after the girls with deep-set, saddened eyes, he recognized one of the girls. "Who dat? Shantel?"

The girls picked up their pace, darting through the fence and down the block, briefly looking over their shoulders, thrilled to see the security guard relinquishing the chase. Braids and beads bounced along their faces and down their backs as their hands brushed their long extensions backward. Basketball shoes pounded against cracked concrete. In no time, the school was in the distance. The girls kept up a half jog, glancing every now and then over their shoulders. Finally they slowed their pace and leaned over with their hands on their knees, gasping for breath. Their eyes connected and they smiled triumphantly, sweat pouring down their brows.

"Damn girl, whas' yo' problem?" Shantel exclaimed. "Why you gotta be sayin' my name an' shit? Now he know it was me. My mama' an' my daddy gonna be hella mad!!"

"Sheeit dey always mad at 'choo any damn way," Venus retorted with a loud smack of her lips. Shantel fought back a smile as they rounded the corner of the main boulevard.

The girls were beginning to walk leisurely up the block toward the corner, past lawns with sprinklers going, barred windows, trash in the streets, garbage water running in the gutters. They walked past boarded up apartments that looked abandoned and yet not quite empty.

The girls stopped at a traffic light. A black SUV with men whistling and cheering out the passenger side window passed going the opposite way. Shantel looked up momentarily and nodded just enough to avoid giving the impression that she was stuck up or afraid but not so much to convey a real interest in connecting with them, she hoped. *Damn, hope dey don't come back. Ol' nasty ass mutha fuckas. Tryin' ta get at some young ass females. Yeah, I gotta say whassup so dey don't come back an' be flashing on me. They pro'bly would too…Sheeit…I could see dem comin' back an' talkin' about—'what's up den? You too good o' somethin'?!?!?'* Thankfully, they continued on their way. Venus and Shantel each breathed a quiet sigh, as if they had just escaped something dreadful.

Shantel looked off into the distance, shading her bulbous brown eyes. Check-cashing stores and fruit and vegetable stands decked the streets. Tires screeched in the distance. The sun became brighter all of a sudden.

"Damn. My momma an' my daddy be comin' at me with hella shit. They do tooooo much!! Dey do be up in ma' shit all da damn time. But, feel me? Dat foo' gonna call ma' house. Watch, my daddy take my phone? Feel me?! I'm gonna be hella mad at you."

"I thought yo' daddy took yo' phone da otha' day," Venus inquired, eyeing a crowd of young men about a block and a half away. Dark skin, multicolored braids, gangster baggies, red bandanas just barely visibly dangling out of pockets. *OOOO, dey cute!!* She ran a delicate hand through her long braids and began pulling her low-cut tank top down to leave just a little to the imagination.

Shantel instantly took notice, following Venus' eyes. "Wha'?? You lookin' at dem boys up der?"

As they walked, they passed an elderly Asian man picking through toma-
toes on a nearby rack. A police car crept down the street and Venus trembled
momentarily, quickening her pace. They noted a homeless man coughing in
a nearby alley, a long, wheezing cough as if he was on death's door. The girls
watched him for a second as they gradually came nearer to the boys on the
corner. They both looked down as they walked, noting that the sidewalk was
gradually becoming more uprooted, the streets more desolate.

Many of the businesses were boarded up solid. Several of the apartment
windows were broken. Homeless people were walking through the middle of
the street as if disinterested in the possibility that they could be hit by passing
cars, perhaps by one of the tricked out rides that notoriously sped through the
streets of *The X.* The girls watched a red Cadillac New Yorker rumble past,
blaring rap music, golden spokes glistening in the sunlight. They watched it so
intently that they didn't realize where they were until they were there.

An excited body bounded into their path, a wide smile exposing heavily
inlaid gold teeth. "Ooooohhhh shit!! Whassup lil' mama?!" hummed a familiar
male voice. Big eyes, a stubbly teenage mustache, tall and slim figure, gold
chain, glistening dark skin. Shantel smiled.

"Whassup my nigga?!" she responded. *He was dat boy from the party.
Darrell. Oooh he lookin' goooood too!!* She took a deep breath. *Calm down,
don't be lookin' desperate an' shit.* "What's yo' name again?"

"My name?" he inquired with a smile, licking his teeth with a seductive
tongue, tapping his chest with long rhythmic fingers, "My name big poppa, lil'
mama." The girls laughed hard and the boy in front of them smoothly laughed
along with them. "Nah, my name Darrell. See I rememba' yo' name though!"
Shantel smiled as Darrell's three comrades eyed her and Venus. Venus took
satisfied notice. *Yeah, das right,* she celebrated quietly. *Yeah, y'all know ya
want me. Even if I ain't gonna give it to ya. Go on an' look.*

Shantel eyed Darrell in amused suspicion. "Nah. You ain't rememba' ma'
name," she challenged, laying a firm right hand on her hip, the long green
fingernails of her left hand beginning to tap her thigh.

The other two boys hung back, each beginning to take a subtle step forward, then a half step back. Forward and back again. They were watching
Darrell and Shantel, but their focus was clearly on Venus, who was standing
with her weight on one leg, head back, watching the conversation.

Venus was growing impatient. She could barely hear what they were saying, what with the noise of traffic and the murmuring of the other two standing
between her and Shantel. *C'mon now. Damn!! How long I'm 'posed to wait?
Y'all gonna talk ta me o' jus' stan' around admirin' da scenery?*

Meanwhile, Shantel and Darrell continued to toy with one another. He didn't remember her name, and she didn't seem to care much anyway. "So y'all wanna ride wid us?" Darrell offered excitedly, nodding his head up and left in the direction of a purple Cadillac with thin-spoked gold rims and a white leather top. His companions looked up in earnest, wide eyes betraying definite interest.

Venus shifted her focus to Shantel for agreement, maybe even approval. *Oooh shit, das dey car?!?! Sheeit, den dey got some money, an' dey cute too. Yeah! It's on now!*

They smiled and nodded at each other. *Mmm-hmm, we down*, each seemed to say without saying anything. "Coo'," they agreed out loud.

They began to make their way through the boys who had been standing between them and the Cadillac as Darrell's friends stepped to the side, opening up like a parting of the waters just enough to let the girls go by, to allow for some slight body contact, enough to feel a warm sensation, and then pass their hands on the girls' lower backs and hips as they moved toward the car.

"Excuse me ma' nigga," Shantel purred softly, pivoting on a graceful ankle so that her hips breezed over Darrell's waistline.

Venus took notice. *Oh, so ma' girl think she got it like dat?* Rising to the challenge, Venus followed in her footsteps, back arching high as she made her way through the boys, knowing where they were looking without even watching, feeling their eyes on her body. Amusing. *Ha-ha, yeah, y'all like dat?!? Das right.*

Slowly, but excitedly, the five of them made their way to the Cadillac. The car alarm was clicked off and the doors were opened, allowing Venus to bend down and climb in, but a presence suddenly blocked her way. Suddenly she was looking into glistening red eyes barely visible beneath a black beanie hat. She winced at the foul breath emanating from his wide smile. "Hold up baby, why don't cha' slide up front wit' me?" His hands passed lightly over her ribs and then her hips. Venus allowed them for just a second longer than she had to. She removed a Tootsie Pop from her pocket and popped it into her mouth, then nodded her head in agreement. *Mmm-hmm, dis mutha fucka high o' drunk o' somethin'!!! Know he ain't 'bout ta have him nothin' tonight. Breath stankin' an' shit.* A smile came to her lips.

"Yeah baby," her admirer observed, snickering, assuming that her smile was for him. "Yeah-yeah, let's do dis. Back a' da lack my niggas!!!"

Venus held back a scoff. *Back a' da lack?!?! We sittin' in the front a' the lack. Dis foo' trippin'.*

"So whas' yo' name anyway? Or should I jus' call ya sweet thang?" he inquired, springing the powerful engine to life, causing the interior to tremble.

She pulled the Tootsie Pop slowly out of her mouth. "My name Rochel," Venus answered flatly.

Shantel and Darrell were making hushed conversation in the back seat. Venus watched in the rearview mirror. *Gettin' cozy ain't y'all now?*

The driver pulled the Cadillac from the curb, letting it roll smoothly and slowly down the road. He stopped at a stop light and lit a black cigar.

"Rochel…" he thought out loud. "Is dat right? Pretty name fo' a pretty lady. My name's Face. So y'all smoke weed?"

"C'mon now you know deez hoes smoke weed, blaze dat shit up nigga," commanded the third wheel on Darrell's other side, obviously miffed at being the only boy in the car not receiving attention from the opposite sex. Shantel scowled at him and leaned around Darrell's cradling arm, which was now outstretched over her shoulder and over the black leather seats of the Cadillac's interior.

"Nah nah nah," she corrected, eyeing her accuser's brooding form, slumping sideways against the door at his right side. "I know you ain't tryin' ta call me no ho'."

"It's all good baby," Darrell intervened, huddling closer to her. "My man jus' mad at ya cuz' he ain't havin' himself no female." His scowling friend coughed into his hand insolently. Face chortled as he pulled the Cadillac around a steep banking corner, past boarded up houses and a housing project courtyard packed with onlookers, smoking marijuana, rolling dice. Activity seeming to bustle in every direction at once. A police siren was wailing in the distance.

Darrell leaned his head slightly in the direction of the high-pitched blaring. Satisfied that it was out of sight, he popped a marijuana joint into his mouth with his left hand as Face pulled into a vacant lot just off the road. Darrell lit the joint, inhaling deeply, twisting it periodically as he breathed in, eyes watering. Venus leaned back in her seat and watched out of the corner of her eye. Darrell obligingly passed it up to her in the front seat. Venus took it, drew the smoke in delicately, her throat burning. Surveying the scene around her to divert her mind from the burning in her chest, she noted a chain-link fence topped with barbed wire, and two Hispanic women with long crimped hair wearing skintight jeans and black t-shirts pushing matching strollers. A crowd of several homeless men stood across the street in front of a check-cashing place with bulletproof glass advertising "Cash for food stamps" in bold red letters. A long line of customers flowed from the front door.

Venus, exhaling a thick cloud of black smoke that seemed to bounce off the windshield and swirl in deep circles before settling into a cloud along the dashboard, passed the joint to Face who reached for the power window control and rolled up all four windows simultaneously.

"Yeah yeah!" he triumphed. "Roll 'em up! We 'bout ta hot box up in dis bitch!!!"

"Fo' real my..." the womanless boy began, but then he doubled over at the waist as began wheezing and coughing. He was beating his chest with a closed fist and then brought his fist up to his mouth trying to contain the smoke. Everyone laughed.

"Nonsmokin' ass mutha fucka!" Face chortled as he took several long exhales before passing the joint back.

Venus laughed ecstatically, the effects of the marijuana sending her into a tizzy. "Can't get no rotation neitha'! Look at dis shit. 'Posed to pass it to da left! We passing back, back 'n forth, like some old alien type shit!" They all laughed hysterically and doubled over each other, leaning against the doors. The joint was flowing merrily from hand to hand. Higher and higher they all climbed. Everything was funny. Shantel and Darrell began to make out in the backseat. Eyes closed, lost in passion.

A bone-rattling thud of bass and a squeal of tires suddenly interrupted. A black Monte Carlo, decked out with chrome and tinted windows, slid up beside them in the parking lot. Painted along the driver's side were four playing cards, all aces. Four scowling teenage boys glared at the passengers in the Cadillac. They all wore loose black clothing, gold chains, and backwards bandanas into which were jammed black pagers. Tupac's jam, "Hit 'Em Up," blared from the car. Venus and Shantel began quivering; the boys were a tad anxious, although pride demanded that fear stay on the inside. They motioned for Face to lower his window.

"Whassup, nigga?" the driver of the Monte Carlo interrogated, his glaring eyes just barely visible underneath a lowered bandana. "Where y'all from?"

Darrell began straightening in the backseat, clenching a fist. Womanless boy was likewise now sitting up, stiff at the spine. Face inconspicuously reached under the front seat and pulled out a shiny, nickel-plated nine-millimeter hand gun and placed it surreptitiously on his right thigh. Venus took notice of this instantly and began to tremble even more, the marijuana heightening her fear, her mind racing in panic, thoughts coming fast, incoherent. *Damn...I...I don't, I can't...I gotta get the fuck outta here!!"* Explosion was imminent.

"We from da *X,* nigga!!" Face barked back, tipping his chin up and sliding his hand from the steering wheel to his heart, crossing his fingers, middle over index. He raised the gun with his left hand and held it out horizontally so that the barrel faced the roof. The driver of the Monte Carlo eyed the nine millimeter suspiciously, sized up the boy holding it, and waited for his next move. Face held firm, watching, implacable.

The driver of the Monte Carlo leaned back into his seat. Darrell leaned out his window, beat his crisscrossed fingers against his chest. "Yeah yeah, da X, mutha fuckas! What y'all bitch ass niggas gotta say now?!"

Shantel was trembling, although she was also more than a little impressed. More than impressed even, downright wooed. *Damn, that's a real man for me. He jus' all up on 'em like dat! No nonsense type nigga!* She found herself moving closer to him across the leather seat. Darrell showed subtle acknowledgment but was inwardly elated. The hairs on his arms and neck rose as a deep, warm sensation rushed through his body, feeling Shantel's attraction.

"Yeah das right!!!" he resumed victoriously, "Y'all ain't about ta do nothin'!" Then to Shantel, "Betta let dem niggas know how we roll. Strapped all day mutha fuckas!"

The Monte Carlo started up and then rolled out onto the street, the driver taking one last look from Face to his gun and back to Face again. "We'll see ya," he proclaimed ominously. Tupac's raps blared again as the Monte Carlo lurched forward, the tires burning rubber, black exhaust smoke spewing back.

"Y'all niggas ain't 'bout ta see shit!!!"

"Bitch ass niggas!"

"We'll see deez nuts nigga!" chimed in Womanless.

Everyone howled with laughter.

The boys in the Cadillac began praising their strength and unity, warning that the boys in the Monte Carlo had better pray that they never saw them again.

Only Venus wasn't so sure. She was huddling, still trembling a little in the front seat. *Damn!! Dey coulda killed us right der!!! These boys took it like some soldiers, but damn!!! Das some fucked up shit. Oooohhh, where da weed at?!* She reached for the joint in the ashtray and grabbed the lighter Face offered her. Taking a couple deep puffs, the rest of her worries soon floated away and she began to laugh uproariously.

"Das right ma' niggas!!" Venus proclaimed, "Up in da X where da real gangsters at! Bes' ta let y'all know wha' time it is!!!"

Shantel was still somewhere between fainting and crying, breathing hard, her heart going a mile a minute. She began looking around frantically. She breathed in deep and gazed out the window. After a bit, she looked at Darrell who looked into her eyes and then at her soft, full lips. They began to kiss while laughter and hand slapping mingled with the music.

Bottles of malt liquor were opened as the tires peeled around corners. Too Short's latest jams were playing. They passed police frisking a group of Latino men alongside a pickup truck with its emergency lights flashing and made racially suggestive jokes about illegal immigration. Twilight, Popeye's Chicken, another joint. Kissing and touching in the back seat. More than that in the front. Womanless boy falling asleep with his mouth open, snoring loudly through his plugged-up nasal passages. Face throwing a chicken bone into the back seat, the chicken bone clanking off of an unguarded gold tooth. Uproarious laughter, a slew of four-letter words. Swearing that revenge would be sweet. The chicken bone flying back into the front seat, missing Face and sailing out the passenger side window, hitting a scantily dressed woman passing by on the nearby sidewalk. Jokes about a chicken bone hitting a chicken head. Fist shaking, more four-letter words, laughter to the point of tears and stomach pains. Bone Thugs-n-Harmony, the latest jam. Night fall, crickets chirping, police sirens, crowds appearing on corners. The night went by quickly.

The Cadillac pulled up slowly to a curb, the music growing quieter. The neighborhood was still except for a helicopter overhead. Shantel and Darrell were still lost in one another, kisses on the neck and the mouth, hands in many places at once. The windows had fogged up an hour ago. The others were all somewhere between dreaming and awake, their highs beginning to wear off. The late night was finally beginning to take its toll. Eyes half open, bodies slumped in their seats, almost asleep.

Face half-heartedly stopped the car. Leaning lazily over the leather headrest into the just barely visible back seat, he tried to rouse the passengers. "Yo," he murmured sleepily. Faint grumbles. Shantel and Darrell unmoving.

"YO!" he barked louder, practically throwing his arm into the backseat, slapping Darrell's shoulder to get his attention. Darrell and Shantel looked up dreamily.

Just, like, two minutes more 'a be nice, Shantel thought.

"Dis yo' crib girl. Ya gotta go," Darrell informed, trying to play it cool. He was telling her to go but still held her close.

She stayed still for a moment, basked in his warmth, smiled serenely, sad to see the night end. Gradually, she raised herself up. Although she was reluctant to say good-bye, she was looking forward to her own bedroom, her soft down comforter, more throw pillows than she could count, clean sheets. *Hope mama did the laundry taday. Sheets feel nice when she use dat fabric softener.* But still...

"You gonna call me?" she inquired more than a little fearfully, already knowing the answer.

Darrell removed his hand out from underneath her shirt and smiling a car salesman's smile, he said reassuringly, "Fa' show ma'," a crack in his voice creeping in. He cleared his throat in order to hide it.

Shantel smiled and eyed him one last time, giving him an excited farewell kiss despite feeling that something wasn't quite right. *Yeah, he prob'ly up on hella otha' ladies an' shit. But yeah, he do like me. He so fine!! He gonna call me!!! Gonna be pickin' me up at schoo' an' takin' me shoppin'!* Her mind continued to travel along these lines for a few seconds longer as she fairly floated out of the Cadillac onto the street, closing the door softly behind her. Her house was there on the left. She barely remembered the long drive from wherever they had gone to her side of *The X,* only recalled that it was as far as it was long and that the night had been some journey. As she took a couple of careful steps out onto the sidewalk, she glanced furtively over her shoulder, getting one last look at Darrell, wishing he was coming too. Maybe this was it; maybe she would never see him again. His smooth skin, dark eyes, full lips, the way his arms made her feel so safe when he put them around her and pulled her to him. *Even if he was jus' tryin' ta get wit' me, ooooh he felt hella good. I love sleepin' in his arms.* Her heart was beginning to race as she headed toward her bedroom window, the Cadillac rumbling off down the street, music resuming, though just above audible.

There it was, her long-awaited bedroom. Now she was returning to reality, beginning to fear possible discovery of her hushed sneaking in. *Hope ain't nobody seen me. Dat 'Lac an' da music was hella loud! Deez nosy ass people tell my momma if dey hear anything.* She looked left, right, and over her shoulder.

A car came rumbling up the street behind her, but it was not one she knew. The coast was clear. She stole her way across the grass, creeping on the balls of her feet, ducking slightly as if to melt into the shadows all around. Now she heard an engine rumbling behind her getting louder, screeching to a stop 10 feet away. Shantel instinctively turned her head so that she could almost see behind her, but not around far enough to not be in a position to run. In *The X,* this was a position that people knew well.

"Whassup lil' mama. Wash' yo' name?!?!" a male voice slurred out the window, its high pitch suggesting youth, the garbled words suggesting intoxication. Shantel rolled her eyes and pivoted sharply on her left foot. Normally she would have kept going, so close to home, but she wanted to shush her pursuer for fear that he would wake her parents.

"C'mon nigga, damn!! Shut da fuck up!!! You gonna..." she began in hushed whispers. She arched an eyebrow and snapped her neck to the right for emphasis. Her dangling earrings were swaying to and fro, her bright green braid whipping into her face. She pushed it back over her ear, giving her audience a full view, wanting him to see her scowl. *Niggaz ain't got no sense. Don't deez fools see I'm creepin' up to my house?!*

"Wait, wait, hold up," the driver of the car announced, leaning over into the passenger side to get a better look. Shantel now took a better look herself.

It was the black Monte Carlo with the spoked rims, the driver with the gold chains, bandana, and a beanie pulled low over his eyes.

Oh shit!!! Shantel's mind began to rattle.

The driver squinted through the darkness and then broke out into a quiet, sinister laugh. Each recognized the other. Fear. Revenge. Silence.

"Yeah, I got ya bitch!" the driver proclaimed, leaning to the side to look over at his companion in the front seat. Gazing pointedly at the numbered address on the mailbox to Shantel's right, he said "1-3-8. Yeah, yeah. We gonna get cha." Pointing his index finger out and bending his thumb into a gun aimed at Shantel, cocking his middle finger on an imaginary trigger. "Boom," his lips mimed ever so quietly.

Shantel froze, her heart pounding in her head, temples throbbing, mouth dry, eyes wide, nervously scanning to see if anyone else was watching.

The driver took notice and calculated. He laughed, as did his passengers. It was muffled laughter, soft, certain of the future. The black Monte Carlo pulled slowly down the road leaving Shantel still frozen, unable to think, let alone run to the safety of her home.

Dalanna

Walking. Walking. A dull throbbing pain that seemed to come from everywhere at once. Limping along. Eyes swollen shut. Barely able to stand. Meekly crying out for help. People on the street walking by as if they couldn't hear her cries through the night, her suffering in the darkness. The pain was excruciating, so bad that she could only wait to die.

What seemed like forever later, Dalanna opened her eyes, blinking. *Jus' a dream. Damn.* It was so real that being there in her bed under the covers was hard to believe. She sat there for a long second, still somewhere between asleep and awake. Still feeling it. The alone of it all. So alone. Sitting up wearily, swinging her legs off the edge of her bed. Heart pounding. A viselike grip in her chest. Breathing hard. *I gotta get outta here.*

Dalanna sighed and pushed herself forward. *I gotta go somewhere.* Slipping into loosely laced sneakers, tank top, baggy jeans, and overcoat, she donned her gold chain with the cross that always seemed to help her feel safe.

Straightening her hair, she applied lipstick and then slung her purse over her shoulder. Closing her bedroom door quietly behind her, she slipped through the dark hallway past her mother's bedroom. *I'm gonna go for a ride.* Thinking about it for a second longer, she slowed her steps down the hallway as an idea occurred to her. *Yeah, das right! Da 58 run all night.* The bus was only $1.50, and something about riding its long and windy path always helped her get herself together.

Now she could see it all. An hour ride through *The X*, past the mall, through the park, and back home again. Winding curves and main boulevards that seemed to go on endlessly. People getting on and off. Even at this hour, any hour, *The X* never slept. Teenagers would be blaring head phones and boom boxes. Drunks and homeless stragglers would be meandering through the streets. The bus driver would smile or peer down at her in a cautionary manner. Just depended on the night and who was driving. Dalanna could almost see the passing scene, even as she took one last look into the mirror before flicking off the light switch and closing the door quietly behind her. *Yeah, I'm gonna go people watch.* Mincing steps down the hallway, short and awkward, she was extra quiet, extra careful now, ever since her mother had hit her, since she had run away. Lonely. Alone, just like in her nightmare.

"Mama, I'm gonna go out," Dalanna announced timidly to her mother as she made her way cautiously into the living room. Her mother had been slightly smiling at Bernie Mac's latest comedy jam on the television. Legs crossed, shoes off, light-hearted, comfortable. Lazily picking at a bowl of pop-corn sprinkled with Tabasco sauce, her right hand on the remote control, she coughed harshly into her palm as if blasted by foul air, her eyes never moving from the television screen.

A long couple of seconds passed. Dalanna's eyes fell to the floor. "Awright den," she murmured sadly. *Guess dat mean go ahead.*

Pulling her coat tighter around her shoulders, she began to walk past the couch, perceiving a cold void between her and her mother although they were merely inches apart at one point. Dalanna deftly moved around the outside of the room so as not to obstruct her mother's line of sight. Looking fleetingly into the mirror on the wall on the side of the hallway, she combed her newly straightened bangs with her long fingernails. Shining fine like silk.

"Still look fucked up," her mother growled, not averting her eyes from the television. Dalanna began to burst at the seams, stopping insolently in her tracks, her left foot a long step in front of her right, a few feet from the door.

Her mother sensed that something was amiss, snapped her head hard to the right, arching an eyebrow and lifting her shoulders high. "Whassup den?! You got somethin' ta say?!?!" she challenged.

Dalanna took a heavy breath in through her nose. *Sheeit. I gots at least a hund'ed thangs ta say!!!* But her body moved enough for her to take a final lunging step for the door, snatching its brass handle, swinging it open, her eyes drifting unintentionally to the dinner table on her left. Her diary was lying in wait, a black pen clipped to the inside cover. Pause. *Yeah, I'm gonna need dat.*

She took another long step to the left, grabbed her diary, and made a bee-line for the front door.

"Yeah das wha' I thought!!! You ain't gotta say..." her mother continued in bitter triumph as Dalanna slammed the front door.

Dalanna quivered hard in a rage that was deep and powerful, covering profound despair underneath. Bolting down the steps, fighting back tears, her mind exploded. *I ain't even gots a motha'!! One day I'm gonna fuck her up hella bad. Bitch!!! If I had a gun right 'bout now?!?! Sheeit...I don't know who I do first, her o' me.*

Taking long and lonely steps down the stoop and up the sidewalk, she passed street lights, a bottle breaking in the distance, dice clattering against a nearby wall, a cat-calling whistle from across the street. But the world outside Dalanna had become distant and small.

I hate my mama!! She doin' a lil' too damn much right 'bout now!!! Yellin' an' shit!!! Talkin' like she gonna hit me again!!! Should call da CPS again. She ain't no real motha'. Bitch had it in fo' me since we done called 'em da last time. Should do it again! Ha' dat bitch up in jail where she belong!!

In a darkly majestic kind of way, these fantasies of revenge were almost comforting. They carried her further down the block as she passed a brick wall slathered with gang tags. From the other side of the street, she heard shattering glass then hoots and laughter; a group of boys had just broken a street lamp. She finally arrived at the bus stop marked by a bent pole. Dalanna plunked down in the center of a weathered bench, suddenly tired and worn out.

I should run away again. She don't want me any damn way. She don't care if I live o' die. Why da fuckin' schoo' have ta call da po-lice any damn way?! Das wha' I should do. Go pack some shit. Take a bus up town, get a Greyhound. Maybe go down South o' somethin'. Go hook up wit' Lil' Wayne, raise some babies. An' I be a real mutha too!!!

Smiling dreamily at the thought, she started to seriously consider. Could she actually do it? Run away for good? Leave *The X*? It was the only home she had ever known. The thought was a little scary, but it was also inviting. Out on her own. Cute boys, freedom, smiles, parties.

A familiar light blue Cadillac was creeping up along the curb. The driver leaned out the passenger side window. "Whassup lil' mama'. How you been doin'?" wheezed a male voice, the driver showing yellow teeth like fangs.

Dalanna was frozen in panic. She looked without looking. Zeroing in on a scrubby mustache, dark skin, bad complexion, those horrible-looking teeth. She remembered the warmth of his breath on her neck and in her ears, shuddered inwardly, her skin beginning to crawl. She tried not to look afraid, hugged herself tightly, nodded her head in greeting without looking at him.

She looked left and right uncomfortably, digging the ball of a nervous foot into the pavement as if she were a track runner taking the starting line.

"H-h, hi," she stammered, briefly remembering the night she had run away, been bruised and battered, the long walk to nowhere, this vulture swooping in for his morsel of flesh. She saw it all again, him taking her to the edge of town, his crummy apartment. It was a night she didn't want to remember.

"Hey now," he continued excitedly, smiling a pawn dealer's greeting. "How you been my pretty lil' thang?" He was leaning further still out the window, merely feet away. Dalanna stood up and took a subtle step backwards, wincing slightly, her big brown eyes widening, stealing a fearful glance up the block, relieved to see the bus approaching from not too far away. Knowing she needed to stall for just another minute longer, she was mentally treading in the silence until the bus arrived, counting seconds. She could hear the bus now.

The man in the Cadillac frowned haughtily. "Wha'? Some-in wrong?!?!" he demanded. "Fa'get who ya daddy was? I mean is?"

Dalanna half-smiled meekly, shrugging her shoulders. The bus was coming so she began to cautiously edge away, longing for it to arrive. Hopping quietly up and down as if she had to pee or was terribly cold, she replied, "Naw, I mean…I, um…It ain't gotta be like dat," she stammered, grateful to hear the bus lurch to a stop. She bolted away as if all the demons of hell were in hot pursuit, shouting over her shoulder, "Here go' my bus. I gotta bounce!" She charged up the steps and the bus swallowed her up.

"Hey!" barked a deep male voice. Dalanna could feel all eyes on her from behind. Her face went pale, frozen as she slowly turned around.

"It's a dollar fifty, baby," the bus driver reminded her.

Dalanna shook herself back to reality, bending slightly, looking out the window in fearful expectation. The Cadillac was nowhere to be found. Had she really just escaped?

"Baby girl, c'mon now. People waitin'," the driver repeated, leaning back in his seat and draping a lazy arm over the headrest behind him.

Dalanna nodded feverishly, suddenly remembering where she was, and made her way back up the aisle to the front, trying to hide her embarrassment as she passed rows and rows of passengers that glared at her. *Damn, dey prob'ly think I'm crazy!!*

Dalanna dropped a handful of coins through the pay slot and automatically made her way to the back, grateful to feel the bus lurch forward and bump along as she sat down. She took one more long look out the window, relieved to see that the Cadillac was nowhere in sight. She was beginning to feel safe again, at least for now.

She got up and moved to the back, to the "dark corner" as the kids called it, because that's where the black kids sat in droves. An old woman had once remarked to her that black people were now putting themselves in the back seats by right rather than by law. Now, she was glad just for the safety of the bus and to be left alone. All she wanted was to plunk down in her seat, watch people get on and off, write what was in her heart, and try to make it through the rest of the evening.

A woman in a seat just a few rows up rose and weaved her way over to the back of the bus where Dalanna was sitting and took a place just across from her. She was a dark-skinned woman with red and black hair, scantily dressed in red and black. Dalanna didn't look up. She had writing to do.

Thangs I'm knowin
Thangs I'm feelin
Ways I'm growin
The world be stealin
My dreams and my hopes
The moon and the stars
My tears and my laughs
My blood and my scars
Good and the bad
Up and the down

Stopping and thinking, she held her pen just above the paper. *Wha' rhyme wit' down? No, dat don't work. Sound?*

Reading it over again, she began looking for an opening.

Thangs I'm knowin
Thangs I'm feelin
Ways I'm growin
The world be stealin
My dreams and my hopes
The moon and the stars
My tears and my laughs
My blood and my scars
Good and the bad
Up and the down
the harsh of the world
the soft of the sound

Nodding approvingly as the bus careened around a sharp corner, she smiled a little. *Now I just gotta call it somethin'.* The bus lurched to a stop, letting some passengers get off while others got on. A boy Dalanna's age with long braids and blaring headphones bobbed his head in time to music as he took his seat. Several other young people sat on all sides, looking out the window, sizing each other up, all seeming to be aware of each other. Dalanna was simply sharing the space, not really there. *Mmmmmm ... No ... Well ... Fuck!!! I don't know, it ain't just a lil' somethin'. I'm talkin' about, like, everythang. Da whole world an' shit. All a' deez thangs out here. OOOOOHHH!!! Das it!!!*

Pen hit paper: "These Thangs" was written on the top of the page. Dalanna stared at it hard, began to twirl her pen, and read it again. She nodded in approval as she heard her own voice.

The bus bumped along and then stopped suddenly at a red light, the driver having planned to blaze through until the very last minute. The passengers all bounced forward and back, scowling and muttering obscenities. Dalanna's expression said it all, lips pursed, frowning, mouth open. *Mutha fuckin' bus drivers!!! Can't drive fa' shit!! 'Bout to cause a accident!!* She glared up toward the front of the bus as if to scorch a hole through the driver's stupid head. Her eyes inadvertently met those of the woman in front of her. The woman had been watching her closely and was now smiling slightly.

Dalanna began to grow uncomfortable and averted her gaze; she focused instead on the world outside the window. *Why she lookin' at me? I know she ain't tryin' to stare me down an' shit. Bitch gonna try ta talk some shit, I jus know it! I bust her lip in a big mu' fuckin' way she come at me!!"* Dalanna snorted through her nose, shifted exaggeratedly in her seat, doing her best to say "go away" without saying anything. But the woman stared and stared.

"Whas' up lil' mama?" she cooed, cocking her head to the side and nodding upward, crossing her legs and draping a flirtatious arm over the empty passenger seat at her left.

Dalanna was confused. "Hey," she replied with no enthusiasm. *Called me lil' mama, like she a boy o' somethin'. But she a girl! Girls don't be talkin' to girls, 'cuz dey like boys 'n ... oooooo ... no ... shit!!* The picture was becoming clearer.

"Wha's wrong baby?" the woman purred, beginning to dangle an open-toed shoe off one foot with a chipped and faded red toenail.

Ooooh she like otha' girls! And she hella old too. Dat nasty!

The woman watched Dalanna watching her, believing what she wanted to believe about the look on Dalanna's face. She followed Dalanna's eyes that were looking at the dangling shoe. "Oh, so you like dat, don't cha?" she assumed.

Dalanna's insides were rumbling. She was still unsure of exactly what was happening. "N-no," she answered affirmatively.

The woman giggled. "I's all good baby." She stared hard at Dalanna's hair and eyes and nodded her head. Watching, calculating.

Oooooohhh nah-uh, I gotsta go, I gotsta, I gotsta... Almost too suddenly to be real, Dalanna's fear and confusion turned to anger and outrage. She was just damn tired of everyone wanting something from her, everyone trying to get her to do something, taking advantage.

Snapping her head back, sniffing her spine, and scowling back at the woman, she got up from her seat and, with a fierce switch of her neck left and right, stretched out her arm, palm flat as if she were holding back traffic. "Oh hell nah. You trippin !!"

The woman was undaunted. "C'mon now girl," she continued, smiling slyly, brushing a long and tightly knit shoulder length reddish-black braid to the left.

"C'mon nothin'! Leave me alone!!!" Dalanna retorted loud enough for all to hear as she began to make her way eagerly to anywhere but here, youthful faces around her beginning to turn and look on in earnest. They were sensing the drama to come, eagerly alert. Dalanna's blood was beginning to boil. *Maaaannn, dis bitch betta' back up on dis shit!* "Oooohh, so you got a lil' attitude on ya don't cha?" the woman carried on, cocking an eyebrow and smiling excitedly, still not ready to give up the pursuit.

Finally, Dalanna had truly reached her limit. Dropping hard into a seat in the midst of several kids her age who had watched and waited, she waved a wide, dismissive hand in the woman's direction. "Uuu-uhhh bitch back up off me. Sheeit! Ol' nasty ass heffer tryin' to get up on a younga' female! Fuckin' lady faggot!!"

"OOOOOO!!"

Raucous laughter. Elbow jabbing.

"Hell yeah, get up on some lady-lady shit!"

"Yeah. Can I watch?!" a couple of the teenage boys began to encourage.

"Nah nah nah...*you* best hold up and watch yo' mutha fuckin' mouth, lil' girl!" The woman roared back, coming up the aisle, pointing a formidable finger down at Dalanna from high over her head. "You cute an' all, but you keep yo' damn mouth close before I get up in dat ass..."

Dalanna rolled her eyes and smacked her lips. "Yeah, yeah you prob'ly like to do dat don't cha?" she sassed, wagging a cat-out-of-the-bag finger at the older woman. She had caught the undivided attention of her spectators and now rose to the challenge. "Sheeit I ain't even tryin' to hear this bitch!!" she erupted, glancing to her peers on either side. "I'm jus' sit up here with y'all. Can't be all back der wit' no faggot female!"

Hoots and hollers galore.

"OOOOOOHHHH!!!!"

"DAAAAYAAAMM YOU TRYIN' TO GET AT DA BITCHES??"

"YOU A BITCH YO' SELF?!?!"

"DAS NASTY!!!!"

They were all looking at the woman and laughing at her, which wasn't helping her mood but was taking the pressure off of Dalanna.

"HOLD UP BITCH I KNOW FA' DAMN SHO' THAT CHOO AIN'T TALKIN' TA ME!!" The woman bellowed as she took off one of her shoes and waved it threateningly over her head. She took an ominous stride forward, daring Dalanna to carry on.

"Watch out y'all. She about ta use dat shoe like a dick!!!"

"OOOOHHHH!!!"

"AAHHH. SHE COMIN!"

Uproarious laughter and hand clapping.

The woman was now furious. "SHUT DA FUCK UP!! ALL A' YOU LIL' MUTHA FUCKAS!!! WHEN I DONE WIT' DAT BITCH I'M A WHOOP DA SHIT OUTTA' ALL A Y'ALL!!!"

The bus lurched to a stop. The group quieted down, temporarily. An elderly woman was making her way off, shaking her head, scowling disapprovingly over her shoulder. The bus driver took a moment to look in his rearview mirror, caught the eye of the one-shoed woman, and waited. She gradually complied and sat down. Seeing no real trouble, he resumed his route.

It wasn't long, though, before the scene continued to play itself out.

"FO' REAL IS A...A...WHA' CHOO CALL DAT???"

"WHA'?!?! DAT SHOE SHE 'BOUT TA WHOOP HER WIT'?!?!"

"I'S A DEE-LDO!!"

"YEAH NIGGA!!"

Laughter, high fives. Chaos. Holiday. When the bus rolled up to another stop and the door snapped open, Dalanna took the opportunity to escape although they were still a few blocks before her house. Creeping away into the shadows in quick strides, she proceeded with her head low as she ducked away, out into the night. No one seemed to notice amidst the yelling and laughter.

She walked right through "don't walk" signs, angered honks, and shaking fists from motorists screeching to a halt. She was wondering how much more she could take. The thought scared her a little, started her wondering if she might be going crazy. Maybe chaos was just going to follow her wherever she went. No peace. No quiet. The bus ride had not accomplished what she had hoped, and now she was just tired and ready for bed. She bounded up the front porch steps, passed her mother's slouching form, and found herself back in the confines of her bedroom. Putting down her diary, she dressed for bed and got under the covers. Before she fell asleep, she wondered what it would be like to never wake up.

Gina

Gina stared intently forward. Brooding, gazing, feeling like a hospital patient given too much medication.

Click…News

Click…Cartoons

Click…Chiseled abs, shiny bald head, leather clothes, dark sunglasses.

"Oh, yeah. R. Kelly!!!" Gina exclaimed out loud, leaning onto the edge of her seat, the couch cushion rising up in the back like a teeter-totter. The sound of keys and hurried footsteps just barely registered.

"Miss Gina???" inquired a subtly irritated voice from behind the couch. "We waitin' on you."

"DAMN GINA!!!" called a pair of teasing female voices from the next room over, imitating Martin Lawrence on his nighttime television show.

Gina scowled over her shoulder. "Shut up!!" she growled. "Hate all a' you!" She began bouncing back against the couch, crossing her arms sullenly, retreating into resentful brooding.

"Miss Gina, we gonna meet with yo' social worka' an' we awready late. Child, will you get in da car?" the voice from behind the couch pleaded, reinforced by an impatient tapping of fingernails against the wall just behind.

Gina breathed in heavily in resignation, as if hating to admit that she had to move. Prying her rear from its comfy spot on the couch, mourning as she clicked off the television, saying goodbye to R. Kelly, she sulkily and quietly got herself together. *Why I gotta go do all o' dis anyway? Dey neva' do shit dat I wanna do any damn way. Just axe a bunch o' stupid ass questions, sign this, how's schoo'? Some stupid shit. Coulda kept my ass at home. Sheeit.* She opened her mouth wide for a second, considered saying what she really felt, but at the last moment decided otherwise. *She ain't gonna listen anyway.* Smiling flatly, she replied, "Coming Kendra." Pulling her coat over her shoulders, she followed Kendra out the door, closing it with a vibrating thud. She trudged out and noted the gray skies and heavy clouds, pulled her jacket around her shoulders as they made their way down the block past four boys in basketball jerseys, sweat bands, and baggy jeans. They were maybe a year or two older than Gina. Heads held high, superior smirks, loud banter. One of them was chattering away on a cell phone, four-letter words flying. Some casual shoves and pushes, smirks, more four-letter words, off in their own world.

As Gina and Kendra passed by, one of the boys darted out alongside Gina, beginning to walk backwards in a kind of smooth shuffle step. "Damn lil' ma' wha's yo' name?!?!" he inquired hopefully, smiling wide.

Gina dared not stop with Kendra right there but turned slightly right and slowed her pace so as to get a better look. *He a lil' short, kind a scrawny, but still…* She was casually eyeing his black and red letterman jacket, matching baseball hat, caramel-colored skin, alluring cologne. It was a little more than he needed but less than the average teenage boy. So that was a plus. Soft, pretty brown eyes, big as they were feverish. *Mmm-hmm, kind a' cute though.* Gina smiled a little, not too much, but just enough to encourage him to continue if he was aware enough to get it.

Kendra sized the whole thing up in a moment and stepped between Gina and her boy-hopeful. Ushering Gina along with a knowing "mmm-hmm" and practically shoving her to the passenger side door of a sparkling white Lincoln Continental, she unlocked the door and opened it for her. "Come on."

Gina smacked her lips irritably. *Damn Kendra!! He cute too!! Why you always gotta mess my shit up?!* But, as the door closed behind her, she knew it was over. Slouching back into her seat, she extended her legs and slumped down so that her knees rose high.

Kendra got in after her, not seeming to notice Gina's pouting in the slightest. Tossing her purse into the backseat, closing the door, putting the key into the ignition, springing the Continental to life, she considered she had better say something.

"Now child," she began, turning down the gospel music on the radio. "I know why ya get so upset when we go see ya social worka'."

Gina fought back a scoff. *Fa' sho'?! Dis ought to be good.*

Kendra looked hard at Gina for a second before directing the Continental around back and out into the street.

"Yes, Jesus," Kendra sermoned. "You wanna be home don't cha? And not home fa' now, but home fa' good. In yo' own home, not somebody else's. Do I got that right?"

Gina gazed out the window, looking at the home she knew—little kids bouncing a ball on the sidewalk to her right, bigger kids throwing a bunch of toilet paper rolls over a house a few yards down. On the far corner, kids were standing tall, decked out in gangster baggies, hands in pockets, chins up, hard scowls. Further down the street, she saw a few boys her own age doubling over and laughing hysterically in front of a liquor store, gripping bottles covered in brown paper bags. Home.

Gina exhaled deeply in resignation. *Yeah, she right.* Glancing knowingly up at Kendra before turning her attention back to the road before them. *But she*

think I wanna be up in her house. An' dat ain't true! I wanna be with my sis.
The thought of it made Gina smile and close her eyes.

Kendra took notice, saw that Gina was off somewhere in a happy place, and decided to leave her undisturbed. As the traffic light turned green, the Continental picked up speed through the intersection. After a mile or so, Kendra thought she had better prepare Gina for the meeting.

"Girl, when we go up in der, speak up fa' yo'self," Kendra encouraged. "Black people always bein' told wha' ta do by white folks. But dey s'posed ta help you, s'posed ta listen ta you. They work fo' YOU. Hear me?" she queried, nodding her head sharply for emphasis. Gina grunted in concession as Kendra drove past the welfare department, bordered by a line of people stretching out the door and halfway down the block.

Kendra breathed in heavily and gripped the steering wheel tightly with both hands, bracing herself to say something she knew she had to but didn't want to. "Yo' sista gonna be there today, too." Gina smacked her lips mightily as she sunk more deeply into her seat, her quick mind beginning to scan possibilities. Taking notice of all of the luxury cars without gold rims, unmarked government sedans, and men in dark suits outside the government buildings. *Yeah, we almost at da county buildin'.* Stealing a look at Kendra before turning her attention forward, she began to grow a little uneasy without exactly knowing why. *Damn, she trippin' hard!!! Think I wanna stay wit' her! She crazy. Den she talkin' about da social worka' supposed ta help me. Help me wit what? Social worka' don't neva' do shit.* Chewing her lip and frowning resentfully. *Why dey can't just let me go stay with my sista? Oh, it be so nice too!! Havin' ice cream an' watchin' R. Kelly videos and staying up late talkin' 'bout our boys. Come home from schoo' an', an'...an'...* and so her daydreams carried her the rest of the way to their destination.

The big brick human services building appeared before them, with the towering white staircase winding upward. The Continental slid into the parking lot across the street. Around the building were social workers and unhappy kids, almost all of them black or Latino, and police officers were mounting the stairs in twos or threes or getting into vehicles or motorcycles. Gina took particular notice of one little boy standing on the steps staring down into nowhere, solemn and lonely. Gina watched him kicking a plastic cup, jamming his hands into his pockets, spitting hard onto the concrete at his feet. She knew exactly how he felt.

"Awright child," Kendra proclaimed, "Here we are." Gina rolled her eyes hard to the left, but her mood completely changed on finding a familiar gray Honda Accord just across from them. *Tarra!*

Kendra was still aware of Gina's reluctance. "Now child, I know you excited an' all, but jus' stay calm, an tell 'em wha' choo wawn't. Can't do no harm, can it?"

Gina nodded thoughtfully, eagerly, fearfully, hopefully. Closing her door behind her, she followed Kendra's hurried steps toward the entrance. They went past a young couple in a heated argument, trying to get reception on a cell phone; police officers walking too fast to be doing anything but heading off to take someone to jail; a white woman in a business suit leading a little boy with dark skin and tears in his eyes. But Gina saw none of it as she was focused only on what might happen.

Ain't even no point ta askin'. She jus' gonna say no. Don't neva' do nothin' I ask for. Hate comin' here! After trudging up the wide cement stairs after Kendra, she pushed through the large glass door into the lobby and noted rows and rows of unobservant clerks in glasses and cheap business suits. The large room was filled with black people sitting in metal chairs, talking with their hands, panic in the eyes, pleading, begging, negotiating, practically demanding. Kendra made her way to the information desk, exchanged words with a large African American woman behind it who directed her apathetically to elsewhere.

Gina took in this familiar scene in a moment's glance, dumped herself into the cold, hard metal of a chair in a waiting area. *Feel like jail up in here. Don't even know why we gotta do dis. Ain't shit gonna happen anyway! I ain't neva' gonna get up outta here.* A grandmotherly African American woman with thin spectacles and blue and gray natural hair ushered a cheerful looking teenage girl to the exit. Both were smiling slightly, well dressed, eyes forward and happy. What a stark contrast to the rest of the place, the tired looking adults next to sullen and deeply saddened kids. Gina humphed in recognition. *Dey is definitely kids an' dey fosta mommas. Ain't no real mommas!* She imagined barbecues and sweet lemonade, furniture polish, and fireplaces. She was green with envy. *Ain't my life, and not deez otha' unwanted bastards' neither. Sheeit. We all just da cut list, not gonna make no team.* She shook her head, smirked bitterly at this harshest of truths.

"Gi-na," a delicate female voice cooed. Gina slightly irritated at the interruption of her thoughts knew right away that it was a white lady who had an agenda for her. She always could tell by that sweet voice that never quite sounded sincere.

Looking up from her trance, testing her hypothesis, she saw fuzzy boots, a blond ponytail, a skirt that was too short to look professional, a bank teller's have-a-good-day smile. "Hi! How are you?"

Fucked up and so are you, Gina thought, but mustered a semisweet, "Fine, and how are you?" because she knew it was better to have white people in your corner in some circumstances.

Still, she just could not understand why these white ladies in the courthouse were always smiling. *What da hell! Like dey cheerleaders o' somethin'. I gotta come in here an' watch people talk about where I'm gonna be an' who I gonna live wit'. And dey smiling an' shit. Like, fuck you bitch! Wha' choo got ta smile about? Make me wanna bust yo' lip o' somethin'!*

"I'm great, thanks for asking," the woman answered, leading them through winding cubicles and rows and rows of poor and unhappy people, overwhelmingly African American and female. Their blond hostess was chattering away as Gina and Kendra made their way to a back room. *Hate comin' here. Dis bo' shit!! Feel like jail. Everybody sad an' cryin' an' pissed off an' shit. Might as well kept my ass at home up in da projects for all a dat. At least den I could call Tarra!!*

"Whassup girl?" rang out a familiar voice. Tarra was in the room, waiting for them.

Gina's eyes widened, mouth opened a little, surprised to see Tarra there already. She swallowed hard before opening her mouth and finding words. "Tarra. I saw yo' car out in da parkin' lot.

"How you doin'?" Tarra replied.

"Tarra. I wanna come stay wit' you."

"Well now honey that's a big decision," the social worker cautioned.

Gina had finally reached the limit of her patience and understanding. "I know dat!" she retorted irritably, "Don't all a' y'all think I know dat? I mean…" and she began calming herself, bracing herself. *Awright, calm down. Don't go ghetto on 'em. Even when dey got da shit comin'!* Seeing Kendra's falling face, she was starting to feel guilty. "I'm sorry, Kendra, I-I really do 'ppreciate you takin' me in an' all, you know? Like you was der fo' me when I didn't have no place ta go. And that was coo', but… you know? Like, I wanna be wit' my, my, like, no offense, but, my fo-real family."

The room stayed quiet. The girls looked at each other. The social worker looked at the girls, and Kendra looked at Gina.

"We talked about this," Tarra informed them, exchanging furtive glances with each person in the room. Her eyes met Gina's and rested there for a long second before moving on. "I mean, I think that Kendra knows a lot mo' about bein' a mom than I do. But, you feel me? I cou' learn. An' I make enough at my job to take care a' her. An' my man help us out, too." Looking back at Gina, staring hard in that loving, got-to-have-you way, she thought a second and added, "She need me, she need her family. I mean, Kendra, you her family too, but you know. She need to be wit' me."

Each pair of eyes was looking for Kendra's understanding. Kendra's eyes were focused on her folded hands. "I unda'stand," she finally conceded, breathing in deeply. She was sad at the thought of seeing Gina go but understood that she was doing the right thing. A hush settled over the room, hovered over the four women sitting there on metal folding chairs planning lives, whole futures of lives, in so little time. Ten minutes in that office would shape the rest of Gina's destiny.

"Well, if we are all in agreement, I will put in the paperwork this week," the social worker announced. Gina leaped to her feet and shrieked, hopping up and down gleefully, throwing her arms around Tarra, dancing with joy. The social worker smiled with her face cupped in one hand, deeply moved. Even Kendra was nodding in resigned approval. She wiped away a tear. She was fighting to stay strong for she had already begun to miss Gina terribly, even with her still two feet away.

Meanwhile, Gina could barely believe this was real. It was a dream she never wanted to wake up from. She started planning the rest of her life. *Okay now, I gotta get ma' bed broke down, my clothes in a bag, and dat take hella long!!! But we ain't got no truck ta move stuff in, but if we get one from somebody, den maybe we cou' move all of it tanight. OOOOHHH!!! Den we could stay up an' watch Glory! Grub on some popcorn wit' Tabasco!!! OOOOHHH an' I gotta tell Tarra about dat boy who tried to holler…An Kendra's hater ass fucked up my game!! He hecka' cute!! I might just have ta come back up dis way, even it up!*

She could hardly contain herself. All was finally set right. She and her sister, together again. No more of those girls and their off-the-hook drama. Loud, cantankerous. Gina herself so quiet, thoughtful, brooding, surrounded by complaints and pleadings everywhere at once. *Help me set the table. Gina, I need to talk to you. Gina, what do you think about this boy? Gina, the world ain't fair. Gina this. Gina that.* Kendra and her foster sisters alike. A never-ending tidal wave. Now it would all be in the past.

The thought made her smile. She began mentally packing her clothes away, almost stuffing them into boxes. She would soon be taking the big poster of R. Kelly off the wall. The girls in the far room would be going at it like they always did. Gina wouldn't pay them any mind; she would just shake her head and keep on packing. *Sheeit y'all cou' holla an' scream an' shit all y'all want. I ain't neva comin' back!!!* She had spent years wishing that Tarra would take her away for a few hours, save her from it all for a while, and now it was almost for real and forever. From now on, everything was going to be okay.

Shawn

Shawn was unsure of his decision. In his bedroom, staring deep into the sky, he tried to figure things out. *I hope I'm doing the right thing. I mean, I know we have to make reports when the kids get hurt, but still . . . it just doesn't feel right.* Since the last week, something had felt out of place. But for the time being, it was a mystery. He continued his long look out the window. The splattering rain pouring out of dark clouds offering little in the way of answers, though it did bring Shawn a calming kind of comfort. A vibration in his pocket pulled him out of his soul searching. Picking his cellular phone from his pocket, he noted the identity of the caller: *Mom.*

"Hey," he greeted.

"Hi," his mother answered, "I'm out front." It was a voice that didn't quite reach impatience but subtly implied not wanting to be kept waiting.

"Okay, I'll be right down," Shawn answered, hanging up the phone and pulling a corduroy jacket around his shoulders, momentarily fixing his hair in the mirror. Clicking off the TV and the light switch, with three long strides he was out the front door, locking it behind him. In the elevator, heading down to the lobby, he watched a couple of Asian college-aged women get on at the second floor, shorts and tank tops leaving little to the imagination. *Hecka cute!!!* The elevator reached the lobby and the women exited first, Shawn behind them enjoying the view. Shawn walked forward to his mother's red Toyota Camry, his head turning to the left at just the right angle to watch the girls go down the street. His mother leaned over to the passenger side to unlock the door, smiling knowingly to let him know that he had been caught.

"Whenever you are ready, son," she teased, a black overcoat pulled around her shoulders, sunglasses hiding her eyes. Shawn knew how her eyes would look. That all seeing, all knowing look. A mother's smile of dismay and love all at once. *Men!* she would say without saying.

"Hey now," Shawn greeted in return, hiking his blue jeans up slightly higher so they reached his waist, ducking into the Camry, and closing the door behind him. "Hi mama," he said, hugging his mother and nodding his head invitingly.

"Ready to go?" she inquired, pulling away from the curb and beginning to pick up speed down the street. They passed several manicured lawns, healthy looking trees, freshly painted green and white campus housing. College students were marching off with massive backpacks. Girls with fuzzy boots and muffin top midsections hanging out of shirts several sizes too small. Skater white guys crowding around each other in twos and threes. A few older, graduate students standing in line for coffee at the kiosk. Asians, whites, blacks. The racial rainbow. The local college was known for its diversity. Still, the groups were pretty homogenous. Whites with whites, blacks with blacks. He was thinking over how *The X* was only several miles away and yet there were hardly any black people living where he lived. It was the same for *The X*, where there were hardly any white people, practically none from what Shawn had seen. Why do they do that? Segregate themselves. Shawn just couldn't figure people out.

His mother was listening to him thinking and smiling slightly, leaving him be for a time. "How is your internship?" she inquired. The Camry began to surge forward as they hit the freeway onramp.

Shawn warmed to the topic. "It's okay," he answered, breathing heavily and eyeing the passing cars. The sun was just beginning to creep out from behind the great hills far off in the distance, and Shawn squinted slightly as his eyes met the glare. "The group is going good, I think. You know the girls' group I told you about? They have a lot going on. I've had to file like hella CPS reports."

His mother laughed. "Listen to you, 'like hella.' You're talking like the kids, you know that, right?"

Shawn laughed with this sudden realization. *Guess they have worn off on me a bit.* "Ma, I'm serious," Shawn insisted. "I mean, it seems like it just keeps coming and coming, one thing after another." His mother stole a furtive glance at her contemplative son before turning her attention quickly back to the road.

Shawn shook his head, frowning. "Dalanna ran away, Rona got smacked around by her stepdad, and..."

"Wow!!!" his mother interjected, outrage in her voice. "It's really good that they have someone to talk to. They have you."

Shawn found himself growing irritated without exactly knowing why. "Yeah, I know," he conceded. *I ought to be doing more, I mean, what good is that anyway?*

Shaking his head, he resumed. "I would have killed for someone to talk to when I was their age." Shawn didn't realize what he had said until seconds after he said it. He almost wished he could take it back.

His mother watched the road ahead. Each wanted to say something, to make everything okay, but neither was able to find the words. And so the silence said something instead.

To the right of Shawn, the landscape had changed from houses with green lawns and new shopping malls to factories spewing thick smoke, big rig trucks in massive rows, auto wrecking yards. The few houses around were broken wooden structures that had been painted several times.

"They do talk about a lot in there," Shawn continued. "I mean, so much happens every week that I can barely keep up. Venus talks about boys a lot.

And Dalanna always seems to want to say something, but then it's like she holds back and..." His mother, listening faithfully, somehow sensed that he was trying to get himself back on the ground rather than initiating a conversation. A mother's intuition. And so she drove and let him talk, sitting and listening. He carried on with all that had been happening, at times in a rapid, pressured fashion as if the intensity of it all was becoming overwhelming. At other times, he spoke quietly and in a hollow kind of voice, almost giving in to despair. The Camry went through the last round of industry and approached dilapidated apartments; police cars began to appear on the street. They passed crowds in front of liquor stores, who were talking loudly, aimlessly meandering in the street, walking across the busy intersection without regard for heavy traffic. His mother had to slow the car down several times, although there were no stop signs coming up. They each remarked about the situation at the same time and concurred that the people walking in the street was always a clear sign they were near downtown, just a couple of miles from his work.

The Group

The Camry crept up to the curb in the back parking lot of the school. Basketball players raced up and down the courts with chain-link nets. Girls were sitting on the swings and on the railings leading into the building. A security guard could be heard all over the yard hollering at a group of seven or so older boys, each having his hands on another's body, a colossal wrestling match in the making. Shawn absorbed it all instantly.

He and his mother observed for a moment, watching the life spilling over everywhere. "Did I ever tell you what it was like at Lincoln Parkway?" Shawn's mother inquired, shaking her head disdainfully, "God! It was a nightmare! They hadn't had a teacher for weeks. They had no books, and I had no roll book. There were kids of all different ages and levels. No chalk, no paper. One of them peed in the garbage can, another knucklehead broke a light bulb. I wasn't even there for half an hour total." She stopped her story to motion to the droves of kids everywhere on the schoolyard before her. She'd told the story before, but he didn't tell her so. "You got your work cut out for you, my boy."

Shawn smiled grimly, knowing it was true. His mother's story, he knew, didn't apply to all of these kids. Slinging his backpack over his shoulder, hugging her tightly goodbye, he wondered what he would ever do without his mother and then he wondered what some of these kids did without theirs. He knew quite well that some of them had to. Then he realized he knew quite well what some of these kids did without their mothers. Gina. Rona...

As he walked past the administration building, the tardy bell rang out as if from every direction at once. About half the kids remained on the swings outside or continued their conversations in groups of three or four. Swearing. Mild pushing. A girl with a head full of beads and braids was banging a tetherball against the head of a much smaller girl who was held by an accomplice, the victim's arms pinned behind her so that the girl with the braids could pummel her unabated. The shouting of a nearby security guard finally stopped it. As the guard turned around, a few others took the cue and scattered in all directions across the playground. Boys wearing basketball jerseys and shoulder length braids yanked each other along by the straps on their backpacks.

"GOOOOOOD AFTERNOON BOYS AN' GIRLS," a booming voice announced over the loud speakers positioned at three locations throughout the yard. "JUST WANNA REMIND EVERYONE OF OUR SCHOO' HOLIDAY. IT'S HANDS-OFF DAY. THAT'S RIGHT BOYS AN' GIRLS. HANDS-OFF DAY!" Shawn wanted badly to laugh out loud. He looked over at four boys now on top of one another in a dog pile and two more pushing a third from behind, yanking on the hood of his sweatshirt—*more like whoop dat ass day.* The thought made him giggle hard; he would have to remember to tell his mother.

As he got to the front of the building, the crowds were beginning to thin out, classroom doors were closing, and the raucousness was fading away. *About 10 minutes 'til I need to get my girls.* Hastening up the staircase, he neared the gates of the main building. The paint was chipped away, the light bulbs exposed, and the linoleum floor looked like it had been set there in the 60s. Outside, the sky seemed to sag, as the clouds became heavy and foreboding. A slight drizzle started. Shawn took it all in. Sometimes, the craziness of *The X* was funny. But then, it was not so funny when he really thought about it, especially in these times when it went from crazy to quiet. Only then did the real meaning of it all sink in. *God, it makes me feel like shit when I really think about it. And the kids are in it all the time! Wonder how they must feel?* This thought carried Shawn the rest of his way. He almost wished he could be alone just a little longer, take more time to process what he had been thinking, but then again, there was Terri, getting the room ready, and it was time to get down to business.

"Hey, Terri," he greeted.

She smiled flatly in return, arranging several chairs in the circle, taking out her notes. A dark sweater covered her body, and it seemed like she was still wearing that same draping skirt, the same buckled shoes—*like the wicked witch of the West.*

"Good morning."

"I'll go get my girls," Shawn proclaimed, dropping his bag and making his way for the door, pulling the collar of his coat tighter around his neck and rubbing his hands together, more to brace himself than for warmth. Terri looked up at him curiously for a moment and then smiled endearingly, dutifully returning to setting up the room. Meanwhile, Shawn yanked open the door and bustled back out into the world, back out into the drizzle. His feelings were mixed—sad and exhilarated, hopeful but anxious. *Here goes nothing.*

He arrived at Mrs. Trenton's classroom almost too quickly and opened the door quietly.

Inside, head after head was atop desk after desk, noses dutifully in textbooks, hands busy scribbling on notebook paper. He heard a couple of kids exchanging muffled whispers with one another and then saw them fall silent as Mrs. Trenton used her subtle and not-so-subtle ways of letting them know that she knew, arching an eyebrow, nodding her head.

Shawn stood halfway in the classroom in that slightly awkward moment before the girls would be called to go with him. He felt somewhat energized, wanting to see how things would go today, but he did not want to interrupt. He leaned back against the wall and folded his arms across his chest. *Well, it was hella more awkward in the beginning... hella...* he started, smiling in concession, hearing his mother's voice in his head, "You *sound* like them."

By the time Mrs. Trenton's eyes met Shawn's, his were waiting for hers. She smiled in greeting and returned her attention quickly to the kids before her. "Okay ladies," she announced. "Dalanna, Porsche, Rona, all of you."

"Go on to da' crazy class!" a male voice piped up from the back of the room. Laughter rippled through the classroom

"Uuu-uhhhh, I don't wanna go!" Porsche groaned.

"Feel me?!" Dalanna agreed, smacking her lips loudly. Venus ran a lazy hand through her long braids, pulling them back over her shoulder, muttering something that did not sound approving.

Shawn's spirits fell mightily. *Crazy class?* What had he done wrong? He must have missed something, said something, or implied something? He thought back. Nothing came to mind.

"C'mon now," Mrs. Trenton insisted, standing in front of two boys at their desks. They had been jabbing at each other with sharpened pencils but were now sullenly returning to their notebooks before them. "Let's go. It's time. Gina, Rona, all of you. Let's go."

The girls conceded with moans and grimaces. Then jackets were slinging over shoulders, rears prying up from wooden desks. A stout-looking boy with a wild Afro and a bright orange polo shirt crumbled up a piece of paper and smiled wryly at Venus who was just about to pass by his desk. He began raising his hand with the paper ball inside, taking aim.

"Xavier, throw it away," Mrs. Trenton ordered with the kind of quiet, firm but light dignity in her voice that expected that the boy would do as he was told. Sure enough, Xavier bowed his head low, scowled in defeat, and tossed the paper wad into the garbage by the door.

Shawn and the girls made for their exit. This time he was almost embarrassed, still unable to believe his ears. *Crazy class?!* Feet dragging, flat faces, theirs and his. Shawn held the door open for them and they walked out one by one, heads bowed low as if walking the plank. By this time, Shawn was almost reeling. They began to make their way across the schoolyard. Usually, this was a time for gearing up, idle chatter. The silence was deafening. The drizzle had stopped, but the dark clouds overhead remained. They crossed the yard, passed the bungalows and the empty playground. Not a word from any of the six girls at Shawn's back.

Shawn was dumbfounded, hurt, even a little scared. *What is this? Crazy group? Maybe it was those reports? Maybe we didn't let them talk long enough? That last question I asked was kinda stupid. I don't know. Shit!*

Swallowing a heavy lump in his throat, he ventured, "Hey, if you guys walked any faster, I'd have a tough time catching up with you." No response. No one looked up. More scraping of footsteps against concrete.

A tall boy with dark skin and clothes that sort of hung off of him passed idly by in stilted, awkward steps. He was eyeing the girls behind Shawn, snickering. One of the girls smacked her lips and another made a rude gesture.

"Dat fool look like one a dem kids in da Christian commercials!!! Feel me? Talking about 'save da lil' niggas out here!!!'" Porsche observed. Two or three of them laughed while the Christian child was still within earshot.

Shawn fought back relieved laughter; the kid in him was subdued by the adult. *I gotta stop encouraging them.* He wondered what his supervisor would say if she knew how much he enjoyed their humor. *Hard sometimes though. They can be a little mean to each other, but it is funny.* He was smiling to himself at the dichotomy of it. *Oh well, it is what it is.* He decided he wouldn't say anything. It wasn't that important, and, even if it was, the girls might really want to say nothing in the group if he started censoring them. Ultimately, Shawn was just relieved to hear their voices and did not want to interrupt what he hoped might be some momentum.

Shawn swung the door open, holding it for the girls, and they ducked in, feet dragging, backpacks thudding to the floor, resigned sighs, backsides plunking into chairs, leaning back, hands jamming into pockets, teeth sucking, lip smacking. Phones coming out of pockets, beep beeping. Rapid button pushing. Hushed whispers. Shawn was relieved to see them returning to life.

"Put the phones away," Terri ordered. It was said with that same kind of finality that Mrs. Trenton put into her voice, and it had the same result, unquestioning obedience. "Alright you guys. Where do we start?" Shawn queried, rubbing his hands together, peering into each of the girls' faces, one by one, from left to right. Each was gazing off, some down at the floor at their feet, others out the window, two with their heads to the side looking into their cell phones half hidden in pockets. Porsche smacked her lips. Venus twisted in her seat. Finally, Rona looked slightly up, her eyes meeting Shawn's, saying something to him by saying nothing. Shawn smiled slightly and nodded his head upward, silently telling her to go ahead.

"OOOOHHH y'all let me tell ya what happen' da otha' day!" Rona proclaimed, folding her hands excitedly in her lap and bouncing slightly up and down almost as if she had been hit with a current. Then she sat back, something having hit the reset button. She began anew, tentatively this time to let out her story. "Y'all gonna keep dis on da hush?!" she inquired, wide-eyed, hoping they could keep quiet so she could spill the beans. She looked around at each of her peers for acknowledgment.

"Do we all know that what is said in here is confidential and what that means?" Terri asked, looking for reassurance that everyone knew the rule. Heads nodded in acknowledgment.

"Awright den," Rona affirmed, breathing in heavily as if bracing herself for take-off. "I was up at da mall yestaday, right?!" she began, stopping momentarily to smack her lips. "Let me tell y'all!"

Shawn fought back laughter. "Mmm-hmm, yeah, I was out shoppin' wit' ma' mama right? Mindin' my own bidness, an' dis' boy come up hollerin' at me. 'What's yo' name?' an' 'what's yo numba' ? An' all a dat. OOOO. He fine!!" The girls all giggled furiously.

"Who was he?" Shantel inquired curiously.

"Yeah!" Porsche added.

Rona stared hard at the girls on all sides. "Fo' real tho', y'all." she insisted. "Y'all gonna keep quiet? You know what I' sayin'? Like, on da down low?" Murmured agreements were followed by suspenseful looks; breath was held in as the girls sat on the edge of their seats.

"Okay den," Rona conceded. "Johnny."

"*Big* Johnny?" Dalanna wailed.

Gina looked on in earnest.

"You like dat boy?" Shantel reiterated. Hearing such shock, Rona shrank back in her chair, pursing her lips, bowing her head, nodding half-heartedly. Silence prevailed for long seconds.

Shawn watched and waited curiously. *Wonder who'll break in and take it up?*

Venus looked down into her lap, as if sorting something out inside herself. "Awright, I go. See da otha' day, dis boy came up on me too, tryin' ta get wit' me. He ugly as…Anyway…He had some Adidas wit' four stripes instead a three!"

Everyone laughed uproariously.

"Mmm-hmm, yeah," Venus continued. "He kind a' old too. Not, like, hella old, ya know, but like…"

"Too old for *you*," Shawn finished.

"Yeah!" Venus agreed, "So he say like 'whassup baby' and all dis and…But den dis otha' boy, he call da otha' day. He know my brotha. An' he kinda cute, but den he my brotha's friend so dat ain't right."

"See den yo' brotha be all up in yo' bidness," Gina predicted.

Dalanna shifted around in her seat and glanced longingly out the window as if getting impatient. Shawn saw Terri noticing but deciding not to bite and followed her lead.

"Yeah, you feel me?!" Venus agreed whole-heartedly. "But den everybody know everybody up in here anyway. So, I don't know…"

Shawn considered possibilities. *It seems like she always has to have a guy around.* "Venus, it seems like you always have a guy around, you know?"

Venus nodded.

"Yeah, see ma' girl get-get-get around feel me?!" Porsche teased. Shantel giggled. Venus scowled.

Dalanna shifted in her chair again, this time more abruptly, as if she could no longer stand it. Smacking her lips loudly, she went forward. "Okay is' my turn!" She announced, running a determined hand through long braids, pulling them back over her right side.

Shawn looked on in wonder; Terri waited patiently. They were eager for what would happen next.

Dalanna waited for a second longer in the silence, just to ensure that she had everyone's attention. "So I was up on da' bus right?" she continued, "Checkin' out a couple a' boys an' all. You know. On da 58? Da one dat go all up an' through da X an' past da mall?"

Heads nodded, eyes widened, following her every word, suspense building. "Yeah, so anyway, I got hollered at by dis female!! Feel me? It was fucked up y'all!!" The girls all laughed hard. Shawn tried not to smile. *I shouldn't laugh at that.* He just shook his head slightly in weary wonder. *Okay, but how am I supposed to not find that funny?*

"Oooh na-uh," Shantel exclaimed disgustedly.

Venus shook her head mightily.

Gina made herself busy by picking at something under her fingernail.

"Dalanna, what were you afraid of?" Terri inquired.

Good question. I should have thought of that myself, Shawn realized, annoyed with his momentary lapse in awareness. He'd missed a beat there. He straightened up and vowed not to miss another.

Meanwhile, Dalanna looked away and shrugged resignedly.

"How would it be different if you were hit on by a guy?" Shawn probed.

Gina stopped picking at her finger and looked up at Dalanna, waiting for an answer. Venus began to comb her long fingernails through her hair, looking to Dalanna and then looking away. Dalanna stared hard into the wall between Shawn and Terri, as if trying to add it all up. Dumbfounded, uncertain of what to say, she ventured, "Well, like, see...I's a female!"

"Mmmm-mmm," Venus affirmed.

"Do any of you know anyone who is gay or lesbian?" Terri probed.

"I know a gay female who live down da block from me," Rona answered. "She kind a' cool, though. She be talkin' to me an' shit."

"Well," Porsche began, sitting slightly further back into her chair and crossing her arms in deep reflection. "I don't know y'all. I ain't sayin' I wanna be gettin' hollered at by no female. But we got a couple gay dudes 'round da way where I stay at." She smacked her lips loudly. "Ha ha!!! Feel me? Dey be singin' an' dancin' to Rihanna." The girls all giggled as Porsche continued. "Feel me? Dey be snappin' dey necks an' shit when dey seen me comin'. Like 'hey girl' and shit."

A couple of the girls laughed harder. Terri smiled endearingly.

"But dey coo'," Porsche concluded, "an we talk 'bout clothes an' boys an' shit. Dey awright. But all da boys in ma' hood be fuckin' wit' dem wit out fail."

"Oooohh nu-uh!" Rona exclaimed. "Da gay dude up on ma' block?!" she began, smacking her lips and wagging a wild finger over her head, "He be too ghetto!!! He a cut yo' ass wit da quickness!"

"Sheeit he a do yo' hair wit' da quickness!!" Shantel corrected. Shawn fought back laughter, this time almost successfully.

"Hey y'all hold up!! I ain't done," Porsche insisted, blowing everyone back into their seats. Venus particularly shrank back several inches. "Feel me? It be different gettin' hollered at by a female den by a dude. It like, wit' boys, you don't talk to 'em, an' some shit gonna go down." Three of the girls nodded sadly in commiseration.

Shawn frowned. *Wow, that's fucked up.* "Like what could go down?" he asked.

Venus glanced down furtively into her pocket, feverishly pressing buttons, trying hard not to be caught texting. Shantel stared hard into the floor at her feet.

"Da otha' day when I was at da movies wit' my sista," Gina began. "Deez boys wouldn't leave us alone for nothin'!!"

"Sheeit, dey a do anything!! Dey could come afta you, take yo' shit, knock you out, maybe worse," Porsche continued, almost in provocation.

Terri and Shawn stared back in interested silence.

Rona gazed off into the gray oblivion out the window, Johnny on her mind.

Shawn looked around the room in earnest. He'd never seen Shantel look so lost. Hands folded sadly in her lap, her dainty fingers intertwined. She was slumped over in her chair, staring blankly to the floor between her legs at something only she could hear and see and feel.

"Shantel, how are you over there?" Shawn wondered. Terri sat up and watched her closely.

"Fucked up!!!" Shantel whimpered, choking back tears. Many pairs of eyes searched for hers, saying nothing, feeling it with her as she began to cry in tears that gushed from her eyes and streamed down her cheeks. The silence was loud and total. Shawn's thoughts raced, words rose up and were rejected, not good enough.

Finally, Shantel continued and the group collectively hung on her every word. "I was out wit' deez dudes from da otha' side, ya know? And so we was kickin' it. Mobbin' up an' down da block, up on da boulevard up in a Lac', smokin', ain't doin' nothin'."

Everyone looked on in earnest, leaning over, trapped in suspense.

Shantel breathed in heavily, bracing herself to tell the rest of her story. "Den some shit go down wit' da boys we was' kickin' it wit' right?"

Venus nodded affirmatively.

Shantel shook her head sadly. "And den' later…" Stopping, another tear, another silence that felt much longer than it really was. "And den later, deez otha men in anotha car dey said dey was gonna kill me!!!" The sadness, the horror, the fright of it all overtook the room. Dreadful, ominous.

Shawn's mind was racing. *We have to do something! But what? Do I have to report this? Maybe I shouldn't… What should I…*

"Shantel, can you go to the police? Do you remember what the car looked like?" Terri inquired, a deep line of worry creasing her brow, her hands folded tightly in her lap. Shawn held his breath for long seconds. Some girls looked at Shantel, some down at the floor. Everyone in the room was gripped together, holding on above an abyss.

Shantel shook her head and scoffed disparagingly. "Dat jus' make shit worse. What dey gonna do?"

Gina looked up in earnest, as if wishing for something reassuring to say. Rona had shrunk further back into her chair, somewhere between having just arrived and wanting to leave. Porsche and Venus stared down in grim defeat, knowing what Shantel said was true.

"What about your parents?" Shawn inquired, already knowing the answer.

Shantel's eyes never left the floor. "Ain't nothin' I cou' do. Dey just gonna get me," Shantel croaked. "Dey crazy!! Dey seen me wit' dem boys, an' now dey figure dat I kick it wit' dat set."

"That you're in a gang," Terri reflected. Shantel nodded slightly, the sheer terror still holding the room tightly in its grip.

"Dey crazy like dat too," Shantel elaborated, eyes hollow and empty, her face long and deeply saddened. To her, her fate was sealed and it was only a matter of time before they got to her.

"Okay," Terri began, straightening herself back in her chair, "We need to figure out how we can help you stay safe. Can you go to school and come home with somebody else? Maybe one of your friends or one of your sisters? Can you take a different bus to get to school in the morning and to come home?"

Shantel nodded again, despairing and weak.

BRRRRRIIIINNNGGG!!!! A couple of long seconds passed before backpacks dragged off the ground, the girls blinking heavily in the stillness. They began wrenching themselves from their seats, but the weight of the world seemed to hold them fast. Slowly they trudged toward the door. Shawn could only sit and watch them walk out. He was deep in anguish and wished there was something he could do.

Assessment

This week's group work began long before the group actually started. The girls' initial resistance to coming to group could have meant any number of things. One hypothesis is that the girls' peers made fun of them because, in *The X,* mental health services were taboo and the girls resisted coming so as to "save face" with their peers. This hypothesis is supported by the fact that the girls disclosed the most significantly painful life experiences in the group that they resisted attending.

Another possible explanation for the girls' pregroup behavior might be that the group was reaching a deeper level of intimacy, so it was becoming scary for the girls to attend. They may have resisted coming to group because they were unconsciously trying to protect themselves. This was necessary because it had been their experience that emotional connection and vulnerability were sure to end traumatically.

It may have been particularly scary for the girls to reach a deeper level of emotional intimacy with me. They had learned to survive near-constant threats and attacks by men by hiding their inner vulnerabilities. The girls had learned to protect themselves from men by sexualizing themselves and behaving aggressively. These survival strategies were necessary because the men they typically encountered were often dangerous or threatening.

Some of the girls' risky behaviors were consistent with normal adolescent development and fulfilled their age-appropriate needs for excitement, risk-taking, the approval of peers, and experimentation. It is also possible that some of their behaviors helped them survive, even though those behaviors were self-defeating in the long run.

Venus's behavior in group is a particular example of this dichotomy. She often seemed preoccupied with whomever she was dating, which is a typical adolescent behavior. Venus was also one of the members who had survived the most significant trauma. Perhaps she did not discuss her trauma (and talked about boys instead) for the same reason that Gina said very little about the traumas she had survived: Each had learned to keep their traumas inside for the sake of emotional survival. It might ultimately help the girls to talk about what happened to them, but it was a good sign that they chose to divulge their painful experiences before they were ready to.

Trauma can overwhelm the neurobiological systems that usually help people contain themselves (J. Schore, personal communication, May 10, 2010). Trauma survivors who are quick to disclose painful traumas may do so because the trauma they survived damaged the affect regulatory systems that would normally support gradual exposure.

When trauma survivors disclose their traumas quickly, they typically detach from the emotional content that they need to feel and work through to heal. In past groups, it was productive for Shantel and Rona to share their traumas, because they had felt the emotions that related to the trauma and used the group's support to work through them. The group was effective both for the girls who disclosed and for the girls who listened.

Trauma survivors need to be able to explore and emotionally connect to their traumas when they feel safe enough to do so (Briere & Scott, 2006). If Gina and Venus were not yet at that point, it was a good sign that they did not disclose before they were ready. Gina and Venus might not have been exhibiting posttraumatic avoidance, but instead were coping and adapting in a socioculturally appropriate way.

All of the girls were doing what they had to do to survive in overwhelmingly harsh circumstances. In this regard, the group's primary purpose was to validate and respect the girls' distinct survival strategies and then provide them with experiences that would show them that their survival strategies were not always necessary. For example, they could sometimes be safe with a man even when they were vulnerable.

It would be an important developmental milestone for the girls to learn to use their survival strategies when needed rather than all the time. This would give the girls a positive experience with therapy so that, eventually, they might engage in the long-term individual work that would help them recover more fully.

EIGHT

Week 24

Porsche and Venus

Blaring rap music. Hands in the air. Marijuana smoke dancing in and out of the blue strobe lights, and waves of cheers from the crowd. Venus in the midst of it all, front and center. The world her entourage. Little Wayne on the stage and the spotlight shining down on her, dead center in the middle of the crowd. Just her and Little Wayne, although thousands of people were all around them. There he was, rapping to her, finger pointing, gold grill glistening like his sweaty muscles. Glorious. Nothing could be better.

"Venus, wake up!" blustered an intrusively shrill voice. Venus snapped up in that awkward just-waking-up kind of way, her half-closed eyes peering, brow furrowed. *Bitch ass mutha fucka! Now dat was a dream. Why he gotta fuck wit' me any damn way?!?! Ain't like we learnin' shit up in his punk ass class!*

A muffled, familiar giggle followed. "Ye-yeah! Wake up foo'!" Porsche pronounced, just loud enough for Venus's intruder to hear.

The teacher turned just enough for them to see his disapproving, and yet not scornful, frown. "Porsche mind your business! Take out your book and read, page 44," he ordered as he continued his rounds through the rows and rows of desks. One boy was drawing in pen on his desk while another looked on, eliciting a command from the teacher to focus on his work. Another boy by the chalkboard had just turned around complaining loudly, slapping away

213

at the back of his head, trying to remove the chalk dust another boy had just put there with a chalkboard eraser.

Porsche shook her head wearily. *Damn, deez foo's stupid! I mean, I ain't no goodie goodie o' nothin'. But I study and shit. Tryin' ta get myself up outta here one day an' go ta college an' make some real cash loot!!* Momentarily she eyed her half-sleeping girl with a disdainful chuckle, smacking her lips loudly, hand on her shoulder. "Feel me? You ma' girl right?! But, damn, yo! You hella lazy!"

Venus scoffed, pulling her hooded jacket tighter around her face as if trying to disappear into it. *Das fucked up. Dat foo' gonna come wake me up. I'm hella tired too.*

The classroom door swung open and blinding, golden sunlight flooded the floor. Several heads perked up from class work or chaos, blocking the sun with their arms and outstretched hands like vampires afraid of the light. The teacher looked up to locate the source of the interruption.

Into the classroom walked a shrouded figure, walking along the far wall as if hiding in the shadows. Face hidden in the hood of a dark blue jacket, her eyes fastened on the floor, shuffling steps from black Nike basketball shoes the only sound she made. She plunked her backpack down on the floor and plopped into her seat. Her lips were working their way around a Tootsie Pop that dangled out of her mouth.

"Who is that? Shantel?" the teacher inquired, hunching over at the waist so as to get a better look. He raised his thick gray eyebrows as if surprised to see her. "And where have you been?"

Shantel shrugged insolently. Her teacher shook his head. Shantel gave no sign of recognition or concern.

Porsche looked on in wonder. *Damn, ma' girl sometimes quiet… But, sheeit. Somethin' up.* Hunching over in her seat and beginning to open her mouth to find out for herself, she first peered around the classroom to see that the coast was clear. Yep, Mr. Justice was watching her.

Porsche smiled sweetly. "Hi, Mr. Justice!"

Mr. Justice smiled flatly. "Mmm-hmm. Back to work, Porsche."

Porsche scowled and pretended to return to the open textbook on her desk. "Uuuuhhh, I don't like dis class!!!"

"Yeah, well, maybe this class doesn't like you either," Mr. Justice retorted, turning his back and perfunctorily returning to his patrol of the room. Porsche watched him depart, making a rude gesture to his back.

Venus folded her arms on her desk, put her head on her arms, and observed Shantel. *Ma' girl look kinda fucked up. She be trippin'…* Glancing to the clock on the wall. *Uuuuhhh we gotta be here hella long. Dis class so hella boring!!!*

Porsche stretched her arms high over her head, smacked her lips loudly, and stole a glance at Venus, grinning mischievously. "Damn girl." she whispered, leaning over and giving her a playful shove, "Shantel comin' in all stank-a-dank-dank!"

Shantel didn't look up but gestured with her right hand and slung her backpack over her shoulder. She then simply got up and made her way to the door.

"Damn, hold up girl. I was jus' playin'?!' Porsche called out. But she was speaking to thin air. A few long strides and Shantel had reached the door.

"Hey, um, excuse me?!" Mr. Justice exclaimed frantically. "Shantel?! Where are you going? Hey, excuse me?!"

Wham! The door slammed, and Shantel was gone. He shrugged his shoulders, shook his head, and turned back to the student he had been talking to.

Venus felt bewildered. She looked at Porsche.

Porsche shrugged and smacked her lips, bouncing back in her chair, nonchalantly cocking her head to the side.

"Sheeit, Dalanna been all in da outs too! Don't talk ta nobady. Don't neva hang out on da block no mo'! Feel me?!?!"

Venus nodded affirmatively, thinking back on her last contact with either Shantel or Dalanna. *Has been hella long. My girls been trippin'…Dey ain't answer dey phones o' nothin'.*

BOOM! A chorus of young male laughter followed. Venus and Porsche looked up warily. Venus ducked her face into the palm of her hand, which she had been running through her hair. A tall, skinny, light-skinned male in a basketball jersey and holding a broken paper bag in one hand was towering over a formerly sleeping classmate, now lying on the floor. The class was roaring in glee.

"Wake yo bitch ass up!" the tall boy yelled into the face of the fallen boy.

"Darnell go to the office!"

"OOOOOH!'

"Damn foo'!"

"QUIET! Back to work!"

"C'mon, Mista Justice!!! I ain't even do nothin'!"

"Darnell I said go…"

"Ah man, das boo-shit!!! Black on black crime goin' on up in here!"

Venus sniffed in indignation, whispering to Porsche in a cupped hand. "Deez niggaz stupid!"

Porsche smacked her lips in agreement. "See das why I ain't tryin' ta even be fuckin' wit' all a deez lil' boys up in here. Who got some dollars like da ballers!"

Venus smiled widely, stretching her arms high over her head, her shirt rising slightly into the air, exposing her dark abdomen. Porsche took notice.

"OOO, wit' yo' black stomach!" she pronounced.

Venus lowered her shirt in embarrassment.

"Nah nah girl, you need ta pull dat shit on up! Feel me? Got some milk-shakes like DAMN!!" Darnell commented on his way out the door, backpack slung over one shoulder, a leering smile two feet from Venus. As he opened the door, he simultaneously pulled his pants up.

Venus folded her arms over her breasts, smacking her lips, and calling out over her shoulder, refusing to meet Darnell's eyes as they searched for hers. "Shut up!" she barked.

Porsche clicked her tongue insolently. *Why all boys gotta be like dat any damn way?!?! All lazy and crazy.*

"Mmm-hmmm," Venus began dreamily. "Feel me? Ma' nigga gotta have some papa, so he a' take me shoppin'. An' he better be coo' as fuck too. You know, hella funny? But like smart, too. Not like deez dumb ass niggas." She gesticulated for emphasis. Porsche nodded in agreement. Venus slid down slightly in her chair, beginning to twist a braid around her forefinger."Yeah!!! Mm-hmmm!!! Den he a' ride me around in a lil' Cadillac o' somethin'! Feel me? Stayin' fly!! 'Cuz YOU KNOW I stays fly!" Both girls laughed gaily.

Porsche's quick mind was racing. *She say a Caddi'. Dat remind me…matta fact…Oh shit!* Clapping her hands loudly. "Ooooh damn girl, das it! Rememba' dat night Dalanna had some shit go down wit' her mama?!"

Venus nodded, now beginning to connect the unmentionable dots.

Porsche's eyes grew wide and inquisitive. "She done took off wit' dat old man!!!"

Venus shuddered. "Uu-uhh!! He nasty, too!!"

"Porsche! Venus!! Get back to work!" blustered their teacher.

The girls looked up irritably at being interrupted. They pretended to read and waited until he was out of sight. They shook their heads in disgust, watching him walk off in those mincing, awkward steps. They had often remarked on his paunch, detectable from inside his too-small sweater vest. All of his clothes were caked with either chalk or lint and were faded far from their original color. His high-rising slacks and dullish dress shoes were a disgrace.

Porsche feigned a smile. "Sorry sir!" she hollered with more than a trace of sarcasm. "Ol' ass nigga ain't teachin' nothin' any damn way!" she muttered under her breath. She tried to resume her train of thought but had just a little trouble. "Okay now, wha' da' fuck I was talkin' bout?" she asked halfway to herself, bouncing back against the wooden frame of her desk and folding her arms across her chest in contemplation. A brief silence ensued.

"Dalanna," Venus offered. *Damn, ma' girl coo' as fuck, but she don't rememba' nothin'! But now, sheeit. Das some real shit! D ain't been 'round fa', like, hella long!* Clucking her tongue and glancing down at her feet. *Uh my kicks fucked up! I need ta go get one a' my niggas take me shoppin'.* Foot Locker and Champs Sports both looking good in her mind.

"Hey?!?! Pay attention foo'!" Porsche barked.

"Yee-ya, pay attention ho'!" agreed an uninvited male voice from several desks over.

"Don't be callin' me a ho' 'cuz, feel me? If I'm a ho, yo' mama' a ho!!" Venus hollered, raising her right arm high over her head and pointing sternly down at her accuser.

"OOOOO!!" chorused several onlookers.

"Hey hey!!!" their teacher intervened, taking several long, hurried steps back in their direction, pulling his pants slightly up to their usual position, two inches above the hips, as if to reinforce to himself that he was in control. "Any more noise out of this corner and you are all going to the office!"

Venus smacked her lips in dismay, scowling at the boy who had just interrupted her conversation. *Sheeit, he bes' ta watch his damn mouth 'fo he get da shit slapped out his ass!!!*

The girls buried their faces in the textbooks on their desks, pencils at the ready, feeling their teacher's eyes bearing down on them. Once he was satisfied that they were back to their studies, he returned slowly to his rounds.

Once he was several feet away, Porsche motioned Venus closer in. "But, feel me?!" Porsche began in a hushed whisper, "What happen ta dem hoes? I mean, my girls all AWOL an' shit! From dey mama's house too I heard! Watch!! Dey fitta be in hella trouble!!!"

Venus shuddered at the thought. *Mmm-hmm. Dat was me, my momma' prob'ly whoop ma' ass hella hard!!*

Porsche smacked her lips matter-of-factly. "Sheeit but dey prob'ly gettin' high AND paid too!! Feel me? I's like, yeah, dey be in trouble but den dey a' get off punishment sometime. An den on da while? Ridin' around in a fat ride wit' some 20s!! Fine ass mens!! Feel me?!"

Venus smiled. "Okay?" and they laughed triumphantly, but with a laughter that died hard. Porsche smiled grimly. *Don't look like dey havin' fun tho'. Look like dey need dey mamas.* The thought dredged up more memories of her mother than she cared to recall. She thought back to the nights her mother came home reeking of alcohol with scary looking men, speaking in gibberish, barely able to stand. The anger began to boil inside as she recalled the sour smell in the air whenever her mother was near. *Hmmm. Yeah, dey ain't da only one dat need a mama.*

Venus watched her closely, almost wanting to say something, but stayed quiet because she couldn't find anything that sounded right. For that moment, both of the girls began to see the truth. Although they wished things could go back to the way they once were, they knew things would never be the same. The giggles, the boys, the games on the schoolyard, the marches to the principal's office, the boys, they were all still there. But, all of a sudden, their lives were changed forever. Only now, in the silence, did they realize what it meant; their girls, Dalanna and Shantel, were gone. Though they would see them again, they knew they were never coming back.

Gina

Gray clouds hung in the sky. The streets were desolate. An empty soda can rolled down the street as if it were kicked around by ghosts. Despite the bleakness of it all, for Gina, the universe was rainbows, lollipops, and sunshine. The world had never been a better place. She could feel the seconds ticking away in her heart. She had spent her entire day at school alternating between reading the wall clock and looking out the window, almost as though she could will herself out there. She was practically jumping out of her skin. *Watchin' da clock only make it go slow.* 2:58 and 38 seconds, 39, 40, 41 . . . *One mo' minute and I'm HOME!*

And by home, she meant home, real home. No longer a foster child. No longer lost in a sea of unwanted girls at Kendra's, where she was just one among many. She had lived there, but she was never home. And now . . . stealing another glance at the clock. 2:59 and 20 seconds, 21, 22 . . . *Damn! When da fuck is dis class gonna be over so I can go HOME!* The thought of it was exhilarating. Home to her sister, to her family. It would be her first day coming home from school. She fingered the cold metal house key in her pocket, counting more seconds in her head.

She barely noticed the four boys in front of her pounding their fists on the table and rapping in rhythm or the young woman chasing a boy with thick natural hair with a hair pick sticking out of it. The hair pick was bouncing up and down as he ran as fast as his legs could carry him, a wide smile on his face. She kept trying to chase him down, a pink and white disciplinary referral in hand. He kept up the pace, around the desks, bobbing and weaving. His fellow classmates laughed hysterically, cheering him on.

BRRRRIIIINNNGGG!!! blared the bell overhead. Thirty plus bodies flew out of their chairs as if released from coiled springs and stampeded for the exit. Their teacher, a young white woman with bobbing blond ponytail and suede boots, plunked down in her seat behind her desk and sighed, folded her arms across the desk top, and put her head on her arms. Twenty-something going on 50. Gina, who was making sure that she had her key, noticed her teacher. Normally, she might have gone up to see if her teacher was okay. But not today. Out the door, backpack bouncing, eyes forward, mind going, new life just around the corner. It would be high times to come home to *home. Her* room and *her* sister.

Damn! Can't believe it! No mo' fosta homes! No Kendra tellin' me what ta do aauull da time! And all a' dem lil' girls takin' my stuff! Cussin' all loud an' shit. Thank G.O.D.!!! Mmm-hmm, neva' thought I see dis day!

She began weaving in and out of passing student traffic and went through the chain-link fence, back out into the world outside. She chewed her lip as she quickened her step. *Ooooohhh dat boy by da court was hecka' cute! Almos' forgot! I gotta tell Tarra! And Kendra punk ass!! Always tryin' ta fuck up my game. Matta fact, I'm a' tell Tarra dat too!*

Further down the boulevard, past traffic lights, past a pawn shop with a large African American man out front, wearing a pirate-style eye patch just below a shaved head, cigar dangling from his mouth, huge muscles, tattoos, dressed all in black, thick gold chain round his neck.

"What's up, lil' sista soldier?" he greeted Gina.

Gina nodded, murmuring a "whassup" in return. *Okay, so she jus' up da block. She said past da pawn shop, den hit a left. Around da corner. Oh, coo'. Here we go!*

A large blue apartment project loomed before her. *So dis home…* Girls on the nearby stoop were cursing loudly, hands clapping, interrupting one another and pointing fingers, arms raised, long and twisted nails pointing down for emphasis. Tight jeans, shirts several sizes too small, rolls of baby fat leaking out the side. *Look at dey muffin tops! Damn deez hoes ghet-to!*

One of the girls noticed Gina's wandering eyes, snapped her neck hard to the left, her crimped braids dashing to the side quick as wild fire. "Wha' choo lookin' at?!" she snapped as if hoping for a retort, her friends looking on in earnest.

Gina slightly slowed her pace, arched her eyebrows in surprise. "Um, nothing," she answered blankly. She had not expected to be "called out." She kept on walking by, not the type to go running scared but not about to go look-ing for trouble either. *Yeah, I jus' keep on goin' an' let it go. I gotta live here 'n I prob'ly see 'em again an' I don' wanna have no kinda problems.*

The girls on the stoop sized this up in a moment. Gina's antagonist fol-lowed her with her eyes. Gina kept her eyes forward so as to avoid further incident; the other girl scowling into the back of Gina's head. "Damn right nothin'!" she proclaimed, just loud enough for Gina to hear and for everyone in attendance to know she had heard.

Gina could feel the girl's eyes burning into her from behind as she continued on her way. *Sheeit, dey got problems 'round here. And I thought it was about to be a lil' mo' quiet up in here den up at Kendra's.*

Gina shook her head wearily and proceeded down the open hallway of the apartment complex to an iron-clad door with a palm tree floor mat. *HOME!*

BOOM! BAM! BAM! echoed a thump-thump-thump thump of one pair of footsteps being followed by another.

"Fo' real! You need ta jus' be a mutha fuckin' man!"

"'I'm bein' a man! You jus' trippin' all da god damn time!"

"Nu-uh, see?! You think you slick, but choo tryin' ta play me out. I smell da perfume! Why you can't jus' go an' admit it?"

BOOM! slammed a door from inside.

"Admit what? God damn! I ain't even do nothin'! Why you always gotta be stressin' me an' shit?!"

Shaking her head wearily, she realized the incongruity between what she expected and what was happening. *Damn, they goin' hella bad!!! An' I thought it was fit ta be a lil' mo' quiet and kick back up in here.*

"C'mon now! I ain't even tryin' ta hear dis shit right now! Jus' had a long ass day!"

"Long ass day? Now I know you's trippin'! Ain't even workin'! What you done had a busy day a' creepin' around the liquor store?!"

"LOOK NOW I DONE ALREADY TOLD YOU…"

Gina reluctantly began to reach for the doorknob and considered making a mad dash for the bedroom, but something inside her told her not to. She let her hand fall lifelessly at her side. *Sheeit. I ain't even tryin' to go up in der.* She started to walk in the other direction.

Breaking glass was followed by raucous female laughter and clapping. Gina sighed to herself. *Awright, I ain't goin' dat way neither.*

And so there she stood, there on the porch, hands jammed in her pockets, staring down at the floor mat at her feet. *There's no place like home,* it said.

"Tssshhh!!! Dis some boo' shit! Why every time I come home I always gotta hear dis shit?!?!"

"I a' tell ya' why, and you know is 'cuz…"

At this point, Gina drowned out the flurry around her. Leaning her backside against the wall beside the screen door with the heavy black bars, she slid down until she was firmly seated on the top stoop, elbows resting on her knees, hands propping up her head. *Mmmm, ain't even knowin' if I wanna come o' go.* The thought of it haunted her for a second longer. Smiling bitterly. *Sheeit, das da story a' my life.* Shivering slightly. *It be cold out here too! I ought 'a take my ass inside.*

"SEE NOW?!?! DAS WHAT I'M TALKIN' 'BOUT!"

"NAH-NAH...HOLD UP!"

"Cuz' when I walk up in the club, I'm a flirt! When I'm with my chick on the low, I'm a flirt! And when you see me, damn right I'm a flirt!" Gina had found some peace with her earphones in place, R. Kelly blaring. Tilting her head back and closing her eyes, she turned off her thoughts.

"So homie don't bring ya' girl around..."

"AWRIGHT BUT CHECK DIS OUT!"

Gina scowled mightily. "Damn why y'all gots'ta be dat loud?!" Gina demanded resentfully, louder than she would have been but for the blaring earphones in her ears.

"Gina? Dat you?" called a familiar voice from inside the house. Several hurried steps approached the door. The iron screen door opened slightly and Tarra, wearing a red and white scarf around her head, peered out from around the door. Gina irritably yanked one of her earphones out of her ear, letting it dangle loosely at her side.

"When I see ya' walk up in da club, I'm a flirt..."

"Yes Tarra," Gina answered irritably without looking up. *Y'all always be fightin' like dis! Sheeit I coulda kept my ass at Kendra's fa' all a' dat.*

"When I'm with my chick on the low, I'm a flirt..."

"YO' HO'D UP! DON'T BE WALKIN' AWAY FROM ME! I'M TALKIN' TA YOU!" bellowed an intrusive male voice.

"So homie don't bring ya' girl ta meet me, 'cuz I'm a flirt..."

Tarra glared back inside and rose purposefully to her feet. "Girl, hold up a minute." Gina opened her mouth to respond, maybe even protest. But Tarra was already gone back into the house, the screen door bouncing closed behind her.

Gina sighed to herself and went back to her former spot, folded her arms in resignation across the top of her knees, rested her face on her hands. She popped her other earphone back into place, and let R. Kelly carry on.

For that, Gina was grateful. He was often there for her when she was depressed. Even if it was only in spirit, he really helped when Gina was alone and in despair. Even if it was only for 3 minutes and 40 seconds of his latest hit single, he took her away. Gina nodded and listened, smiling slightly to herself. At least she had somebody.

Rona

BEEP! BEEP! BEEP! WHAM! The alarm seemed to blare through the morning almost immediately after Rona had fallen asleep. She let the alarm know how much she hated it by batting it away so it fell with a resounding thud, almost destroying its insides. Glaring into its battered face, she couldn't believe her eyes. *Damn! Fo' real?! 7:30 awready?! I ain't even been ta sleep yet.*

"Sheeit, god damn, mutha…" Still grumbling, she dragged herself upright, wiped the sleep from her eyes. With a deep breath, she climbed over piles of clothes, magazines, CDs and their empty cases all piled in heaps on the floor. Still, she knew where everything was. It just looked disorganized. Glancing out her bedroom window through half-closed eyes, she was disappointed. *Still dark outside an' shit.* Looking over her clothes, she tried to stay awake with sleepy mumbles and grumbles. *Why we gotta go to schoo' so damn early? Don't learn shit no how. All I be doin' is sittin' up in dat borin' ass class. Not even learnin' nothin' any damn way!!!* She smacked her lips at the thought. *Why I gotta go? Ain't even no point except…* Suddenly she remembered a certain somebody with thin-rimmed glasses and a wide chubby-cheeked smile she loved so dearly. Spinning mightily on her heels at the thought, her mind shifted gears. *OOOOOHHH! My man ova' der! Came up in da' class yestaday lookin' fine as a mug too! Wit' dat jersey?! OOOOOOHHH, he got some nice arms too!! Mmmm-hmm, I need ta get ready. Ain't about ta be late fo' school taday!!*

Smiling to herself, living in her fantasies all the way through a shower and primping up for the day, greasing her hair, finding her favorite outfit. She pulled on her jeans, a red tank top, and matching Michael Jordan basketball shoes. She slipped on bracelets and her gold chain with the little cross that dangled heavily above her breast. While brushing her teeth, she wondered what it would feel like to hold Johnny's hand. She imagined. Trey Songz latest love jam blaring overhead. It was all so real, it could come true.

Splashing cold water over her face, she gazed into the mirror. Her dreams were suddenly shattered by what she saw. She remembered what one of her peers had called her the other day: fat, black, and ugly.

"MAMA!!" Rona bellowed with her eyes closed in a rage.

"Girl stop yellin'!" her mother answered back irritably.

"SORRY MAMA! CAN I…"

"Girl open da do' when you talk an' stop hollerin'!"

Rona obliged, cracking the door open and poking her head out into the hallway, peering left and right.

"Mama, how you know I had da do' close'?" Rona inquired, ever amazed.

Her mother chuckled. "'Cuz momma' got game."

Rona grinned, poking her head further out the bathroom door, "Aw, here you go!!!"

Her mother laughed endearingly. "Yeah, mm-hmm. So what's all a' dat hollerin' about anyway?"

"I wanna get my hair did," Rona insisted, pulling down on her bangs, frowning at how nappy and coarse they were. She started considering possibilities. *Mama don't get paid 'til da end a' da week. Sheeit, she might say no.*

"Awright, now we could do dat," her mother answered.

Rona smiled wide and clapped her hands, her heart leaping for joy. Hopping up and down excitedly, seeing herself in long extensions, one green. Maybe she'd have her hair cut short and make it curl inward at the ends. *Mmmm, hell nah'! Dat a' make ma' face look fat.* She imagined long, intricately woven braids, tightly knit in a crisscross fashion, well-lined roots. *Yeah! Now das right! I'm gonna be up in da' class lookin' hella cute!! Get me some tracks, real long and fine, wit' tight braids. A lil' glue in da mornin'... Sheeit my man fa' sho' be swimmin'!!*

"I still ain't got da check from ya daddy though," her mother continued, almost reluctantly, strolling into the bathroom and looking over her daughter's shoulder.

Her mother looked at her own face in the mirror, opened her eyes wide, rubbed her lips with her index finger. "But I talk' ta him da otha' night and he said he had ta fix his car an' some otha' bills came in an'...."

Rona looked away, muttering something unpleasant. *Sheeit, mama believe wha' she sayin'?! Sheeit, prob'ly not. She prob'ly jus' sayin' all a' dat fa' me, but she know I ain't buyin' dat garbage neitha'.* She thought about giving voice to her thoughts but decided against it. *Nah, mama say she gonna get ma' hair did. I ain't tryin' ta mess dat up.*

Instead, she ducked out of the bathroom, stomped off in short, choppy steps. Her mother looked after her with concern; she knew talking about her father had upset her. She stood there wishing she could say something to make it okay. Okay for her daughter at least, but she had her own anger to deal with. Gazing back into the mirror, she was thinking bitter thoughts of her own.

Rona returned to her bedroom, where she played with her hair a little more and then began brushing her shoes spotlessly clean with an old toothbrush. She was trying to distract herself, to get her mind off of her daddy. That expensive-looking bottle of champagne, that woman who looked cheap and probably cost a bundle. *Car problems... Sheeit!!! He straight N.C.N... Yup, mmmm-hmmm, no count nigga!!!*

"Girl! You pretty as apple pie on da window sill!" her mother observed as she strolled by in a distracted hurry. "Now go ta schoo' an' don't be late." She tried to sound firm, but the endearment couldn't be hidden.

Rona nodded slightly in grim concession, wishing it were that simple. She took one last look in the mirror and frowned in disapproval. *Damn, I still ugly,* she thought, wishing her braids would grow on the spot, watching them do so in her mind. Long and fine and beautiful. She began smiling at the daydream. *Yeah, but I'm a' be hecka cute when I get my hair did and then I'm a' have my man!*

That particular thought made her smile even bigger, the surge of it giving her the energy to spin on her heels and head down the hallway. Quickening her pace, she started off to school.

Rona shivered inwardly and shook her head as she noted a homeless man on the corner being harassed by a group of boys in a black sedan. *Damn!! People round here got a lot goin' on!* Smacking her lips, looking up to the sky. *Mmmm, lord I need ta get up out a' here. Somewhere... Anywhere.*

She bounced down the block and around the corner, waving to the little old lady that smiled from her rocking chair, wearing the same blue and white striped dress she wore every day that Rona saw her. The woman smiled and waved back before going back to her rocking. Rona imagined where she was from. *She seem like such a nice lady. Maybe she was from down South. She prob'ly live in Atlanta. People der different, nicer and...*

Reality interrupted. Rona blinked in surprise, noticing a familiar chain-link gate and bustling kids her age in backpacks and heavy coats, all chortling with laughter. Cars pulled in and out of the parking lot. Boys a couple heads smaller than Rona were shooting baskets. She scowled. *Damn, I'm here already? Fuck, why I can't jus' go home?*

She walked past four boys hanging halfway up the fences, rattling the chain-links with one free hand, cat-calling out to young girls walking along the street. The girls yelling back, pointing, and making expressive hand gestures. The security guard was barking orders at a crowd of unruly smaller ones all dog piling on one another. Rona smacked her lips in disapproval. *Sixth graders... so immature! Don't got no kinda sense.* Shaking her head in disdain, she walked faster. She turned her thoughts to something more acceptable. *He so cute, dat stocky build in dat long orange basketball jersey.* Quickening her pace to get to first period, she looked out to the yard and noticed Shantel, Porsche, Venus, and Darrell and other familiar faces still lounging against the fences and tetherball poles. Part of her was there with them, but today she had other things on her mind. Her heart was bursting in her chest as number 23 made his way up a small row of steps and disappeared behind the closed door of a bungalow. Rona, some 10 yards behind, marched forward. Excited Latino boys dashed past her at breakneck speed, backpacks bouncing left to right, chattering in Spanish. Rona scowled irritably as one of them almost knocked her over.

"Watch out you mutha fuckas!" Rona barked over her shoulder. "Fuckin' Mexicans," she muttered. One of them called something over his shoulder in Spanish that sounded unpleasant. His companions laughed in a way that said it was something really unflattering. Rona muttered to herself as she made her way up the last stretch of schoolyard, up the steps, through the classroom door. She was grateful for the rush of warmth, but knew soon she would be almost dying of boredom. Science class was her long-standing nemesis. Not even 9:00 and she was already having a bad day, already in a foul mood. Throwing her backpack down on the floor in front of her seat with a thud, she sat and stared hard at her desk. She glanced at the clock, wishing her day was over. But it was only 9:01; one minute down, 5 hours and 59 minutes to go.

Her peers were mingling, whispering, taking pencils and notebooks out of backpacks, giggling, screeching desks closer to one another.

The classroom door suddenly swung open and a young African American man with a well-clipped mustache, short, waved hair, and thin-rimmed spectacles made his way into the class, shirt tucked in, khaki pants looking freshly ironed. As he closed the door behind him, he looked down at Rona and smiled. "Good morning Rona," he greeted pleasantly.

Rona didn't look up. *What's good 'bout it?* she said without saying.

"Yeah Rona, where yo' man Johnny at?" called a male voice from the far end of the classroom. Oooohhhs and aahhhhs and muffled laughter in the aftermath.

Rona was stunned in disbelief. Confused. Terrified. *Wait. Hold up.* Seeing red... *DEM BITCHES!*

"Alright class, settle down," the teacher encouraged gently but firmly. As he took his place at the head of the class, the laughter and other commotion slowly died down.

Rona yanked her backpack from the ground, dragging it behind her, taking long, stomping footsteps toward the doorway, never looking back. Her eyes were burning. She was determined to leave. Outraged. Violated. She had no idea where she was going or what she was doing. As she often felt at home, she wanted to blast off to anywhere but where she was.

"Rona can you have a seat, please?" her teacher called out to her, "Rona? Rona?" WHAM!!! The door slammed at her back. Traversing the yard, backpack bouncing behind her, she lurched forward in strong, angry steps, her mind a blank, stomach in knots, heart pounding in her ears. She was filled with an all-consuming, powerful rage, and nothing could stop her.

"HEY!!" bellowed a security guard from across the playground. "UH, UH, WHO DAT?!?! RONAAA!?"

Rona continued across the yard, pretending she didn't hear anything, clenching her fists. *OOOOHHHHH dat toy cop ass nigga best leave me alone taday!!!*

"HEEEEYYYY, ROOOOONNNNAAA!!!!" he called again, louder still.

Although his cry now rang in her ears, Rona didn't hear it. Down the slope of the yard, past the tetherball poles with no tetherballs, past the broken swings, the once teeming-with-life schoolyard now practically a cemetery. Furious and determined, she walked to the far end of campus, past the little office with a thick metal door, stopping across from the bungalows in a little corner of the school. For the moment she felt safe.

Shawn

Birds. Green lawns. College laughter down the street. A beeping horn from a red Toyota Camry. Shawn woke from a peaceful trance, having been captivated by the world around him. His mother smiling.

"Hello, my son," she greeted warmly. Admiring his snappy peacoat, t-shirt, and lightly faded blue jeans, she said, "You look cute."

Shawn straightened himself, smiling but a bit irritable. *Oh god mom.* "Don't you mean 'ready to heal the people'?" he corrected teasingly, buckling his seat belt. He stole a second look at two young Asian women in shorts and tank tops that didn't leave much to the imagination.

His mother noticed him noticing, shook her head and laughed to herself as the car pulled away from the curb and began to cruise down the street. *Some things will never change. Or will they?*

Shawn laughed in turn. "What?" he queried, knowing he was caught.

"Men! That's what!" she answered. Both lightly laughed as they sped up the street, through green lights at empty intersections; they had begun their trip early enough to avoid the traffic jams.

Older people were scuttling down the sidewalk, faces drooping, while younger professionals in sport coats or leather jackets with laptop cases or handbags seemed to hurry past them, off in various directions.

"These people all look depressed or something," Shawn observed, as he and his mother made further headway toward the highway.

"They're tired and determined to make it to the weekend," his mother offered.

"They're jaded," Shawn insisted.

His mother pulled the Camry sharply off to the right and onto the highway onramp.

"The girls are really funny ma," Shawn informed. "I wish you could have been there."

"Aren't they great?" his mother answered, smiling off into the distance, as if remembering a certain something of her own. "I mean, the kids always are. I don't know about the parents. When I taught seventh and eighth grade, the kids were great. But the parents... whew! Anyway, it's great that they have you to talk to. When I was their age, I never did."

Shawn began to grow irritated, uncomfortable. He always did when his mother took trips down memory lane. *Oh great, here we go again. Why does she always have to talk bad about grandma? I mean, they need to just get together and work it out.*

"I think you should give it another shot with grandma. I mean, she's not going to be around forever and you might wish you had at some point, but then it's too late," Shawn encouraged. His mother shook her head emphatically. Silence continued.

"It's been heavy lately though, with the girls," Shawn continued, noticing a school bus full of bouncing heads roaring by. Mother and son now began to work their way out of the college part of town and through the industrial half-way point. It was a kind of no-man's land. The smoking factories, chemical plants, and auto body shops seemed so desolate. Shawn took notice, knowing that meant they were getting close. *Yeah, they'd never have all this polluting shit in a white neighborhood, never.*

"I mean, one of the girls is getting beat up at home by her mom's boyfriend. I had to make a CPS report. That's my seventh one this year! Not on the girls, but on all the kids I work with." His mother looked over in concern, gasped a little, wanting to say something, but sensing her son needed to keep going uninterrupted. "I mean, now it's gonna get worse. Like, if they investigate? I don't know. What if she ends up being in a group home? Like, is that going to make it better or worse?" The questions he couldn't answer continued. The countless what-ifs.

His mother drove on and listened. She knew he was somehow sorting things out for himself, processing. She was smiling slightly, pleased that her son was so invested in these kids.

Shawn's mother shook her head in disdain as she turned past another stretch of empty lots. Homeless people on the sides of the road in front of closed up fast food joints and convenience stores, either sleeping with their mouths open atop brown cardboard mattresses or leaning back against gated fence ways, holding up signs advertising "hungry" or "I need a beer."

"Ma, one of the girls almost got shot. She said there's this gang that's out after her. And she was really freaked that we would say something. You know, like to the school or something," Shawn reported gravely.

"Will you?" his mother inquired in concern, almost wishing he would but knowing that he likely wouldn't do it. Telling him to would only make him balk.

"No, we don't have to," Shawn answered. Passing housing projects on their right, little kids were beginning to pack into cars while adults in heavy overcoats bustled off in various directions. "I thought we would have to, but I talked to my supervisor and she said we don't. We don't have to call the police or anything. And we can't because it's all confidential. But, I don't know. I mean, what if something does happen? And then I could have said something? I mean, she'd be really pissed and all. But, I don't know, like, what if she gets shot?" Shaking his head momentarily, wishing he knew what to do. "I mean, like, what if I knew stuff that I could have told the police? And, who knows? They could have stopped it. The girls don't think so. They all hate the police and won't go to them for anything. Shit, I don't know..."

The Camry pulled left at a traffic light, passing a boarded over liquor store on the corner and a bus stop out in front. A dozen or so people stood waiting, bobbing at the neck to blaring headphones, some sleeping with their faces in their hands. The sun was just beginning to creep up over the horizon, a beautiful candescent hue of yellows and oranges just beginning to color the clouds. For long seconds, mother and son said nothing, driving on in silence.

"Well, it's good that they have you to help them figure things out," his mother replied. She was worried about her son and how he would hold up under all of this pressure. She knew he hated feeling ineffectual. He would figure out a way to resolve this, eventually. She had faith in him.

Meanwhile, Shawn sat there quietly fuming. *Damn it. It's bullshit that all we can do is talk. It sucks that I can't do more. We have to do something, like, like, ... Shit, I don't know.*

"All right my son, we have arrived," his mother proclaimed. She stopped the car just outside a familiar chain-link fence, kids scattering in every direction at once. The girls chattering along the railings outside the bungalows, the boys shooting baskets. The parking lot packed to the brim with two-door sedans, gold-rimmed Cadillacs, Hondas, Chevys, and a couple of faded sports cars. Little kids ducking out of passenger side doors, giving hurried hugs, pulling jackets around their shoulders, scurrying off with bouncing backpacks. Volleys of rap music blaring from every direction at once.

Shawn smiled grimly, trying to get himself together for what was sure to be a long day ahead. "Bye, mama," he said, hugging her tightly for strength. She smiled, patting him reassuringly on the back. Shawn smiled a bit wider, always comforted when she did that.

The Group

As he closed the car door behind him, Shawn eyed the passing school scene. *It's kind a' peaceful in its own way, like, something you'd watch in a rocking chair out the window.* The kids were hurrying off, the excited chatter, the blaring rap music, a world unto its own.

He had no time. Glancing quickly at his watch. *8:37 a.m.; 23 minutes to go!* He tightened his grip on his book bag and began hurrying through a stretch of blacktop to the rusted doors on the far corner of the schoolyard. He found them unlocked and knew that Terri had gotten there before him. *Damn it, I should have been earlier.* He was irritated with himself as he made his way into the counseling office and closed the door behind him. *Now I don't have time to settle in! I hate having to jump into things.* He preferred to warm up slowly, to have a cup of coffee, to talk, and gradually get on with the day before him.

Suddenly, the doors flung open and bounced hard off the walls on either side, so hard that they might have come off the hinges, heavy as they were.

"MISTA REYNOLDS, I NEEEED TA TALK TA YOU!!!" demanded a familiar voice.

Shawn nearly doubled over, wincing at the urgency of the situation, but then he quietly composed himself, gathered his wits, and stood up to the challenge. "Rona, what's up?" he inquired, a hard line of concern creasing his brow.

"I ain't comin' to yo' class no mo'!" she proclaimed.

Shawn stared at her, dumbfounded, frantic. *Wait-what? Wait a second. What'd I say?* Shawn began to open his mouth but she cut him off.

"Dem girls 'posed ta keep dey mouths close'?!" Rona blared. "An' now everybady know I like Johnny!! Dey was like, yeah, mmm-hmm. We a keep era' thang on da hush. Now da whole schoo' know!!" Smacking her lips hard in exasperation, she glared at him.

Shawn nodded in concession. *No wonder she doesn't wanna come anymore. I would be pissed too!* "Oh Rona, I'm sorry. We need to do something," Shawn reassured. "That's not okay. We all agreed that what is said in the group stays in the group. We need to say something. What do you think? Can you bring this up with the girls today?"

Silence. Shawn waited. *I hope she comes back, I hope she comes back .*

But Rona just stood there, tense, livid, saying a lot by saying nothing.

"Rona, what do you think? Shawn repeated. "What they did wasn't okay. But it would mean more if this came from you. Can you tell them today?"

Rona breathed in heavily through the nose, staring hard at the floor, deep in thought. Shawn knew that she was considering possibilities. Then, she nodded affirmatively.

Shawn smiled in approval and relief.

Rona smacked her lips for emphasis, looking ready to seek revenge. Out for blood.

"Dey wrong!!!" she cried out in sorrow.

"Yes," Shawn agreed, nodding his head in affirmation. *This really hurt her. Wow. She needs to let them have it. Yeah, mm-hmm. I'm going to stay out of the way of this too.*

Rona looked up at him longingly, as if searching for solace. "Feel me? Dey scandalous!! Need ta keep dey mouth' shut!!! O' dem heffers!!!"

Shawn succeeded in fighting back laughter. *I gotta stop encouraging them. God, the girls call each other some awful names.* He realized he was smiling a little. "I'm sorry Rona, I'm not laughing at you, it's just that, well…"

"Yeeeeah, I know," Rona reassured him. She was ready and eager to do battle and kept her eyes on the door over Shawn's shoulder, waiting for her enemies to arrive, prepared to let them feel her wrath.

"Okay," Shawn conceded, straining to get himself and Rona back on the ground. "So we are going to address this. You're right. This isn't okay. They need to be held accountable. You know what I mean?"

Rona nodded affirmatively.

Shawn looked off to the doorway as well, beginning to feel a little anxious about what was sure to come. *Shit, I hope this doesn't turn ugly. Well, I don't know. Maybe it needs to get a little ugly so they appreciate the effect of what they did to her. But not too ugly.* He began thinking over all the girl fights he could remember over the past year, one of which had included Rona.

"Okay cool," Shawn continued. "They broke a promise to you and they need to hear from you that that isn't okay."

"YEAH!!!!" Rona agreed whole-heartedly.

"So how about I start with you first?" Shawn inquired, meeting Rona's eyes, their heads kind of leaned in as if in a huddle. "We'll start group and I'll ask who would like to start. Just like usual. And then you can tell them like it is, with no interruptions. You take as long as you need to. And we'll make the group safe for you to do that. We'll stop anyone who tries to interrupt or anything. We want to hear all of it."

Rona nodded slightly, staring hard at the doorway again.

Shawn breathed in heavily, hoping he was doing the right thing. He smiled grimly at Rona and looked up and around, over each shoulder, wondering how long they had been standing there talking. All of a sudden he noticed that Terri was gone. *How long has she been gone? Where'd she go? Must have gone to get the girls. Good move. I totally spaced that.* Glancing at his watch. *And we have less than a minute.* They heard the approaching footsteps on the blacktop, the familiar chatter in the distance. *Okay, just another second.*

"Rona, I'm really proud of you for doing this," Shawn encouraged in his final seconds. "It takes a lot of courage to face your accusers. You know what I mean?" Rona said nothing. "But this is good; it will be good for you and for them."

"I don't care 'bout dem!!!" Rona announced. The footsteps from outside were growing louder and louder until they were just beyond the confines of the heavy metal doors.

"Okay, but this will be good for you too. Don't worry, you can do this," Shawn insisted, as much for himself as Rona. He took his seat gingerly, tense in anticipation.

Rona plunked down hard in the chair across front of him, head down, tightly gripping either side of her chair as if holding on for dear life.

The door swung open and the girls piled in, making light chatter and pushing the buttons on cell phones along the way.

"Hey everyone, how are you?" Shawn greeted.

"A'ight," one or two of the girls responded. Gina took her seat next to Shawn, hands folded, deep in thought. A phone beeped loudly. Porsche quickly grabbed it out of her pocket while taking her seat next to Terri. Shantel sat next to Porsche and peered over at her phone.

"Phones away please," Terri ordered. A phone or two went back into the pockets.

Venus had watched the excited button pushing with great envy. "Ooohhh my mamma took ma' phone da otha' day," she exclaimed.

"Tsch…girl ma' mamma done did dat too!" Shantel related. "I ain't even do nothin'. Dey can't just be takin' nobody phone!!! Ooooh, dey doin' tooooo much!!!!"

Group topic, 'phone trauma,' Shawn thought, smiling at his little private joke.

"Okay everyone, where do we start?" Shawn inquired, slightly louder than the occasional giddy whisper in the room. The room grew slightly quieter, whispers dying down to bare murmurs.

"Okay, y'all let me tell y'all somethin'!!" Rona burst out, a hard frown creasing her brow, her eyes practically flaming. The girls all straightened up in their chairs, not a word in reply. "I got a problem, feel me?!" she began, smacking her lips for emphasis. "It s'posed ta be on da hush up in here. Y'all said you ain't gonna talk behind nobody back, right?" A face or two fell, eyes to the floor. None of them looked innocent. "Right?! It supposed ta be con-fa-dential!!" Gina looked up at Rona with worried eyes but leaned slightly away, almost as if she wanted to hug her and then run. Porsche and Venus stared hard at the floor, hands folded solemnly in their laps, as if they were at a funeral.

"Well y'all done told everybady dat I like Johnny!!" Rona declared. "And dat ain't coo'!!!! I ain't tell nobody secrets up outta here an' I trust' y'all. How y'all feel if I take all a' y'all bidness an' put it out in da street?!"

Shawn smiled slightly. *Go on with your bad self!! Get 'em!!*

But only a long silence answered. No one even moved. Somehow Shawn and Terri both knew it was a silence that they could not break. It needed to hang as long as it could.

Shawn gazed around at the girls intently. *I wonder who will crack first.*

Rona scoffed in disgust, rising sharply from her seat, yanking her backpack from the ground, taking a quick, lingering look around the room. The look on her face said, "My work is done. You're all pitiful." Saying nothing out loud because nothing more needed to be said, with several long, purposeful strides and a slam of the door at her back, she was gone. The rest of the girls did not look up, did not look at each other. Each was alone in her own thoughts.

Shawn waited and watched. The anxiety began mounting; a couple of the girls began fidgeting, directing glances over at Rona's empty chair. Shawn suppressed the urge to speak. Waited. Finally it was Gina who broke the silence.

"Can I use the bathroom?" she inquired. Shawn and Terri both nodded. They noted that Gina took her backpack along with her. She wasn't intending to return. Another long and uneasy silence prevailed.

An awkward, mumbling, fumbling chatter rose gradually, bringing the girls back to life. Venus and Porsche were back to business as usual. Boys, phones, fights, boys, need to lose weight, she's ugly, boys, stayed out late all night at that party, boys. Each taking their respective turn, Venus for 10 minutes, and then, "Okay it' my turn!" Then Porsche for her 10 minutes. Shantel was sitting back, looking at her shoes, frowning. The bell rang overhead. Shantel rose, slung her backpack over her shoulder and left quietly.

Shawn watched the remaining two girls breathe in heavily at the same time, gather their bearings, grab their book bags, and mumble goodbyes. None of the excited chatter on the way out the door that was typical. Today, the end was quiet and solemn. The end of group this time was not the end of the conversation each girl had most likely begun with herself after Rona had left.

Assessment

The way that the group handled the miscarriage of trust was clinically ideal. The breach of trust was unfortunate, but it provided an opportunity for the girls to work out a conflict in a healthy way. Rona's hurt feelings were understandable; to move on as much as possible, she needed to express her hurt feelings to her peers who had violated her trust and to have her peers hear her without defending themselves. This is what happened; this whole incident could not have worked out better. It would have been ideal if Rona and Gina had returned to the group so that they could continue with the therapy, although their abrupt departure may have helped the girls who had violated confidentiality to better understand the seriousness of what they had done. Youths in *The X* were tough and resilient; it was often the case that if an intervention was to be taken seriously it needed to be more direct and intense. It was good that Terri and I allowed this to play out naturally; Rona was able to express the full weight of her feelings, and the girls who had broken her confidentiality had to sit and take it. It was typical for an incident like this among young women in *The X* to lead to a fight. Gossip and rumor spreading was often a source of contention. Because Rona was able to say everything that she needed to, and because she left without anyone having defended or dismissed her feelings, the chances of a further incident were minimized. It is likely that there would continue to be tension between Rona and her peers in the future. Without this intervention, a serious fight could have broken out, one that might have resulted in injuries and suspensions. The ongoing tension as a result of the meeting might serve as a reminder to the girls that it is important to honor promises and to keep sensitive information confidential.

This experience modeled healthy methods of confrontation and expression of feelings for the girls. The next time there was a similar incident, they would have a frame of reference for how to talk out rather than act out their hurt feelings.

The healthiness of this interchange also demonstrates that the group was reaching a new level of intimacy. Corey (2002) noted that intimacy is a stage in group process that is marked by trust and safety among the members. Rona showed some trust in me by coming to me in a troubled time and taking my direction regarding how to air her feelings about her violated trust. The group members showed that they had reached this level of intimacy by being able to hold the space for Rona's hurt feelings. Although the group was dwindling in size, the work was getting deeper week by week.

NINE

Week 38

Porsche and Venus

White flecks. An endless stare. A deadening silence. The peacefulness of it all would usually be comforting. Venus liked the quiet. Lying there on her bed, head on her pillow, staring up into the ceiling. Usually, it helped her think. Only this time, the stillness, the nothingness, the silence had an eerily hollow feeling to it. Her mind was blank, but there was something unsettling about it.

What Percy doin' right now? Maybe he staring up at da ceilin' too. Hope he get out soon. Maybe ain't dat fucked up in der.

Her door flew open. "Giirrl what da hell you doin' up in here?!"

Venus breathed in heavily, letting her head fall effortlessly to the side, almost dreading having to face her mother. *Ooooohhh, leave me alone!!!!*

"Mmm-hmm, das what I thought," her mother continued scornfully, staring down at her daughter with a look of disgust, a judgmental contempt. "Just layin' up on yo' back. Not doin' shit. Thinkin' about yo' self. As usual!!" she harangued, shaking her head.

Venus stared right through her, waiting for her to go, counting the seconds until it happened.

"Girl ya' need ta get up an' do somethin'. See, das why you gettin' so biigg!" Her mother proclaimed.

Venus scowled, feeling her anger rise. *Sheeit look who talkin' wit' yo' 20 piece bucket a' thighs an' ass!!!* "Damn momma, why you gotta go der? I'm just chillin', feel me? I ain't even doin' nothin'!"

235

Her mother snorted disdainfully. "Yeah, mm-hmm, see now das yo' problem. You ain't neva doin' nothin'!" she retorted, smacking her lips in disapproval. "Feel me?! Ha! She laughed at her own joke. "Yeah, ain't dat wha' all yo' lil' ghetto ass smart mouth hoe ass friends be sayin' out here?!"

"My friends ain't no hoes!" Venus pouted, "An' you ain't even knowin' dem!!"

"Sheeit! I know da type," her mother replied, "and das a hell a' lot mo' den wha's worth knowin'!! Got da po-lice drivin' up an' down da block all da damn time. Got some old ass men comin' 'round here. An' one of 'em call da house last night at two o'clock in da damn mornin'. Da fuck is you doin' wit' yo' fast ass?! Sound like a grown ass man!!"

Venus' heart took a rushing leap. *Ooooohhhh who dat is?!?!* Calming herself as best she could, she tried not to sound too eager, tried to play it close to her chest. "Mmm, wha' dey wa'want?" *Mmmm, I wonder if das my nigga… Maybe he out a'jail. Damn, he bes' get out soon. Percy too.*

"Wha' choo think he wa'want?!?!" she said mockingly, shrugging her shoulders haughtily. "Prob'ly want yo' getting' around ass ta get on welfare so dey hoodlum ass could get out a jail next time dey in. Maybe wanna come by a house an' get you pregnant o' some shit. How da fuck I'm s'posed ta know?!"

Venus smacked her lips insolently. *Sheeit, you ain't knowin' nothin' 'bout my man. He ain't even like dat. Tryin' ta get me on welfare?! Nah. My man paid like a motha'fucka'!!! Da fuck you know?* She grinned in satisfaction at her private little retorts.

"Yeah mmm-hmm," her mother continued, rolling her neck sharply. "Awright den." Clicking her tongue in feigned sympathy, she looked out the bedroom window. "You just go on an' do what you do. An' when you up in da fuckin' projects wit' four o' five baby daddys? Don't you be sayin' ya' momma didn't try an' tell ya'!" She watched for her daughter's reaction.

Venus just rolled her eyes wearily. *Damn, why I always gotta hear dis shit?! Is you done yet?*

"An' don't be rollin' yo' eyes at me neitha'!!" her mother roared, pointing a long, jagged finger down at her daughter.

Venus sighed, wondering when it would ever end.

"Hear me? You neeeeeed to get yo education. Go to class an' stop all a' yo' lil' shit. Hear me talkin' to ya'?!"

Venus nodded resignedly. *Awright, awright. Damn!! Leave me alone. Ol' raggedy bitch. Ain't no real motha' no how.* Counting seconds on her invisible clock, feeling that her dressing down was almost over, she had long ago learned the signs that her mother was wearing herself out. "Hear me talkin' to ya" let Venus know that the end was near.

"Good. 'Cuz you don't clean up yo' act? You gonna end up like all a' deez otha' lil' heffers out here. Yo' lil' friends fit ta be pregnant quick an' down at welfare beggin' dem white folks fo' money. Mmm-hmm. Yeah, das right. Why doncha think 'bout dat fo' a minute!"

Venus nodded in concession, her mother grunting reluctant approval. She turned on her heels and made her way back out the door, not bothering to close it.

Venus groaned irritably. *Damn, what's yo' problem? Can't just close da...*
SLAM.

Her head was aching, as if there was just too much in there and it was all trying to bust out. She grasped the sides of her head and squeezed. Stomping her way back to her bed, she flopped down and gazed out the window. The wind was blowing through the trees. Faint laughter was emanating from somewhere near the sidewalk. An SUV rumbled by with blaring rap music, packed to the brim with young men looking for a night of trouble. A siren wailed in the distance. It didn't take Venus another second to decide what to do.

Glancing into the vanity mirror over her desk, she began pulling her long braids over her right side, the bright purple one over the others. She went to her dresser and changed her comfy t-shirt for something a little more "fitting," then donned some short shorts with "Juicy" written across the backside. She then pulled on a pair of bright golden sandals and observed herself in the mirror with a slight satisfied smile. *Oooh, I look hecka cute. Now I gonna see what's on an' crackin' up in dis bitch!!* Her heart began to race in excitement, the fear of getting caught upping the stakes. Taking delicate steps to her bedroom door, pressing her ear cautiously to it, she figured the coast was clear. *Coo'!! Das it. I'm out.*

Before climbing out the window, she stopped to place pillows underneath the sheets, arranging them lengthwise so that they might resemble something like her sleeping form. She stood and considered, then pushed up the pillows where her rear end would be. She nodded half-heartedly. *Not exactly, but gettin' der.* Delicately, she raised the window, unlocked the black-barred screen with a screwdriver that was placed conveniently nearby, and the stepped over the ledge and out into the garden just outside. Gently pulling the window most of the way closed behind her, latching the black bars back in place, glancing hard to the left and right before hiding the screwdriver in a nearby bush, she looked behind her. *Awright, coo'. Ain't tryin' ta have none a' deez crack heads up in my room, stealin' all a' my shit.*

Beginning to edge out over the lawn toward the sidewalk, listening closely to make sure that her narrow escape was going undetected, she stopped momentarily. She heard nothing but some soft laughter from the television sitcoms in the living room. Smiling to herself in victory, she started creeping out over the last stretch of lawn, ducking out onto the sidewalk. Excitement rushed through her pores. *Okay. I'm coo' now. Yeah, now what I'm gonna do?! Sheeit, der best be some cute boys out here, maybe smoke a lil' somethin', o' like…*

"WHHHHHOOOOO-WEEEEEE!!! WASH YO' NAME LIL' MAMA?!?!" slurred a deep and gurgling male voice from somewhere in the shadows.

Venus doubled several steps back, almost all the way into the street. Scowling, she made her way past the slovenly form leaning heavily against a wooden fence, halfway asleep, brown paper bag in hand, smelling like wine in a box mixed with peanut butter.

"Damn shut up nigga!" she hissed, "You 'bout ta get me caught up!" Stealing a hurried look over her shoulder at the living room window, she was relieved to see that no one had heard. *Sheeitt, momma' be out here wit a straight ass whoopin' if she heard dis foo'!!*

The homeless man looked unconcerned, shrugging his shoulders and smiling wide in a drunken stupor. Raising a rickety arm in protest, mumbling something unintelligible, he sauntered toward her, but Venus was soon halfway around the corner. She strode up the block past barred windows and dying lawns, housing project homes that looked exactly alike. A grandmother on a porch in a rocking chair was watching Venus make her way down the street.

"Girl, where you goin' to by yo' self?" the woman inquired concernedly.

Venus smacked her lips haughtily. "My frien' house," she replied without looking back. *Damn!! Why deez old ass men always gotta be tryin' ta holler at me?!?! Wit' dey old asses. Bunch a' damn child mo-lesters.* Shaking her head wearily, she felt exhausted. *Lord help me! Can't take much mo' a' dis shit. Ol' woman should mine her own bidness, too.* She picked up her pace as she passed more project homes with music blaring, men and women laughing, gossiping, smiling, scowling, drinking, lounging beneath the moon now beginning to make its way up into the azure sky.

Venus awoke from her thoughts to the faint sound of crying nearby. "Damn Po-po, wha's wrong?" she called out to a familiar face on a nearby stoop.

Porsche sat there, face buried in crisscrossed arms laid heavily atop her knees. Almost painfully, she straightened up a little, wiping away tears with the back of her hand. *Ain't nobady gonna see me cry.* Porsche didn't look up. Venus watched and waited, but then Porsche bounded to her feet and began to walk off briskly, her white sandals making clip-clop sounds against the sidewalk.

Venus caught up to her and tried to keep pace. A loud boom resounded in the distance followed by clapping hands and uproarious male laughter. Venus shook her head wearily. *Damn, deez niggas out here crazy as hell!*

"I hate dat bitch!!!" Porsche proclaimed, wrapping her arms tightly around her torso as she pushed onward.

Venus looked over at her in deep concern. "Who? Yo' auntie?"

"Yeah ma' nigga!" Porsche retorted, snapping her head around in a hard half-circle to the right.

Venus winced. *Damn what da' fuck I do. Sheeit?!?! Don't gotta be taking yo' shit out on me, shoot!*

The girls rounded a corner and began to navigate their way through a crowd of nine or 10 females lounging in front of a stop sign. Girls in short shorts and half shirts despite the cold, muffin top mid-sections hanging over tightly pulled belts, long hair extensions. Behind them, some boys in bright down coats, baggy jeans, gold chains, and nylon wave caps were standing before a dimly lit apartment building. They were passing marijuana joints. All were dressed in red and gold.

Venus took careful notice. *Damn!!! Hella niggas out here posted up. Look like some gang bangers too.* She was getting that dreadful feeling as they made their way past the crowd.

Porsche snorted mightily. "I can't be takin' dis much mo'. Feel me?!?! My auntie was talkin' hella shit!!!"

"YEAH I HEARD SO WAS YO' ASS!!" intruded a female voice, as unfamiliar as it was uninvited, just as the girls were almost past. Muffled laughter and ooohhhss and ahhhsss ensued at the gauntlet that had been thrown down.

Rising to the challenge, Porsche spun on her heels, her twin braids swinging around behind her, left eyebrow high on her forehead. Raising her arm high over her head and pointing down at her nemesis, she was ready for battle. "WHO DA FUCK IS YOU?!" Sizing up her accuser with a watchful eye, she stood her ground solidly. *Ooooohhh I know dis bitch ain't tryin' ta talk shit. Not tanight. Oh hell naw!! Watch, she stay out a' line den I jus' might have ta whoop her ass. Bitch don't even look like she cou' fight neitha'. Lil' skinny ass bitch!!* She was a girl maybe Porsche's age or so, dark skin, a little taller, scowling, wearing a cropped belly shirt and matching skintight stretch pants and high-top basketball shoes. Her braids were pulled back into a bun. Several had been dyed fiery red. Her companions parted to the left and right to make way for the show, looking on in anticipation.

"BITCH WHO DA FUCK IS YOU?!" the girl retorted, taking a long step into Porsche's path, their faces now inches apart. Eyes blazed, tension built as they sized each other up.

Porsche looked her up and down in disdain, stepping further in. "Ooooh na-uh, you bes' ta watch who da fuck you callin' a bitch!" she warned, "'Cuz you ain't even knowin' wha' da fuck you talkin' 'bout!!"

"Yes you did!!" the girl in red roared back, raising her arm high and pointing a wagging finger of her own down at Porsche. "You got all up in ma' cousin Rona bidness an' runnin' yo' mouth 'bout it!! An' you bes' ta watch it fo' you fit ta get knocked da fuck out fo' it!!!" Another round of ooohhhhsss and ahhss was followed by hands clapping, cheering her on in excitement.

Venus's heartbeat raced a mile a minute. *Nu-uh, deez girls crazy.* Looking left and right, hoping an escape was possible if need be, she realized she had nowhere to go.

Porsche shoved her accuser hard with both hands, sending her reeling backward. "Go on an' do somethin' den ugly ass bitch!!"

The girl in red came back swinging, lefts and rights flying through the air in tandem, one glancing off the side of Porsche's head before she instinctively ducked low and to the left, firing back with a right of her own to the girl's midsection, landing it with a satisfying thud. Oooohhs and aaahhhs and cheers and whistles rang out.

"Ooooohhh shit!!" a boy from the nearby crowd chortled in earnest, cupping his hand around his mouth and making a loud caw-cawing kind of sound. Venus looked up his way without intention, but then noticed that he looked vaguely familiar. Tall and skinny, milk chocolate skin, scrubby mustache, and glistening muscles in a tank top with a heavy gold chain hanging down from his neck, he quickly drew a cell phone from inside the pocket of his baggy jeans, jeans that hung down well below his waist. Holding the phone away from his face so that its built-in camera faced him, he said "Yeah, yeah ma' niggas dis how it goin' down up in dis bitch!!! Bout ta put dis shit up on *YouTube*, feel me?" He then kissed a much older woman in a mini-skirt and tube top, kissed her long on the lips and turned his phone outward so that he could film the fight. Meanwhile, Porsche and her nemesis were scratching and ripping clothes and shouting four-letter words.

"Yeah-yeah!!!" the boy with the camera phone announced. "Whoop dat bitch ass!!!"

Venus eyed his smiling face, almost jumping in revelation. *Das dat foo' Shantel messin' wit' at da party da otha' night!!!! Ooooohhh das fucked up. He kissin' up on dis other female. OOOHHHH!!!! She hecka' old too!!! I ought a' tape dat shit right there.* Venus turned her attention back to Porsche to see how she was doing.

Porsche landed a deafening blow to the side of the girl's temple, sending her wincing backward. Porsche stopped to grin and puff her chest out triumphantly, but it took only that split second for the girl to recover, regain her footing, and plow forward with her head down like a bull. She knocked Porsche over, but Porsche got up and landed a jab to her face. It seemed to make her angrier, fueling a hard body shot that nearly sent Porsche doubling over. Each of the girls was beginning to breathe hard. Drops of blood had spattered the pavement. The crowd cheered on.

Venus frowned hard in concern. *Damn, c'mon girl! Whoop her ass. Don't let her do all a' dat to you... damn... hope she okay... she look hella bad.* Eyeing Porsche's swollen lip and torn clothes, Venus hoped this blood bath would be over soon.

Shantel's Darrell, the young man with the camera phone turned inward, was filming himself with the fight in the background. "Das right all you bitch ass niggas! Das how we do up in da X, feel me?" He slapped hands with his friends who crossed their index fingers mightily over their chests and roared their approval. "Watchin' deez bitches whoop each otha ass. Blood on da ground. An' ain't no bells up in dis bitch, feel me? Da mutha fucka ova' when somebady life ova'! So you bes' ta know wha's up 'fo you come up in da X, feel me ma' nigga?" Darrell continued with a sinister smile. "Dis big Darrell from da X up in dis bitch kickin' dis shit fa' y'all, y'all got it? Fit ta get yo' ass whooped fo' tryin' ta bang dat weak ass shit up in here, nigga!!" Slapping hands with his comrades again. Whisking the camera phone over the crowd, each member pumping a fist in the air, flashing hand signs, smiling gold grills, blowing marijuana smoke into the camera.

Darrell leered over hungrily, pulled his older lady friend in front of the camera with him, his hand wrapping tightly around her waist and squeezing her rear, shaking it up and down, pulling her waistband down to expose thong underwear, pulling the camera back just a bit so that it was sure to catch his hands on her body. His friends were shouting curse words and waving hand signs triumphantly in the air, taking long swigs out of bottles in brown paper bags, laughing uproariously, swearing love for their allies and death to their enemies. A loud ripping of clothing and a resounding thud diverted the camera's attention back to the fight where Porsche had just landed a series of solid blows to her opponent's face and temple, sending her reeling back against a nearby tree.

Darrell laughed like a maniac. "Yeah, whoop dat bitch ass!!" Raising his arm high and pointing down gloriously at his lady friend as she danced for the camera. His partner smiled wide in excitement, pumping her arms high in the air and wiggling her hips like she was in a wrestling ring entertaining the crowd between rounds. Darrell grabbed her and kissed her on the chest, holding his arm out so the camera could catch it.

Venus looked on in disbelief. *Das fucked up. He jus' up on my girl da other night. Now he up on dis otha' female??! Mmm-mm... Ma girl like dat boy too... Oooohhh she be hella mad when I tell her!!! But den...* The girl in red had just yanked Porsche hard by the collar of her shirt, tearing it at the seam and sending her careening backward. Now she was continuing her march forward, with rights and lefts flying. A blow landed squarely on Porsche's nose, sending blood splattering to the concrete on all sides. The crowd roared.

Venus wanted to turn away. She couldn't bear to watch further, but she made herself stay and stand tall. *Don't be lookin' spooked, den dey a turn on me next.* She started considering that seriously for the first time and stole a glance at the crowd. Darrell and his lady friend were tongue kissing for the camera; the other girls were cheering, advising, instigating. *Awright, coo'. Dey ain't even thinkin' about all a' dat. Dey can't be goin' on much longer. Both a' dem look half dead!! Dis a be ova' soon. Den I cou' go home.* Seeing her bed in her mind, almost feeling the covers around her body, the soft pillow where she would lay her head and drift off into eternity, she looked down at her shoes. It sounded so good she almost wanted to turn and bolt, to run home as fast as her legs would carry her. But she would never leave her girl like that. *Hell, deez bitches might try ta jump in. Den she need me.*

Taking a moment to size the other girls up, assessing who she could take on and who might be trouble, her eyes went left to right. By the time she reached the end of the procession, she found a pair of eyes waiting for hers.

"'Da fuck is you lookin' at bitch?!" taunted a girl about Venus's age and build. Lighter skinned with almost hazel eyes, big gold hoop earrings and gangster baggies, a red bandana wrapped tightly around her head and tied up backwards so that the knot lay across her brow, she frowned at Venus, cocked her head to one side to emphasize the question was not a question.

The crowd turned their attention to Venus, calls and shouts and whistles following. Venus began to tremble, feeling her blood beginning to boil, now really wanting to turn on her heels and run. She fought the urge and instead reared back into a fighting pose with clenched fists, up on the balls of her feet, chest puffed out. The girl with the bandana stared her down. Venus scowled right back.

"Wha'?! You got somethin' ta say?! Ol' fat ass heffer" the girl goaded. The crowd howled, slapping each other on the arms or backs, pointing and cheering them on.

Venus swallowed hard, looking left and right. Seeing that there was nowhere to go, she felt like a cat surrounded by Rottweilers; the only way out was to fight. Swallowing a heavy lump in her throat, she considered the situation. *Damn, she hella big, I ain't wanna fight her. But, oh well shit. Can't do nothin' else!! Sheeitt I whoop her ass any damn way!!* Taking a first step forward, ready to do battle, she pursed her lips and held up her right hand, motioning the other girl forward. "Com' up den bi…"

A loud, high-pitched siren interrupted her challenge, rippling through the mass of shouts and cheers and whistles, thuds, and smacks. A police car came tearing alongside the fighters, engine roaring. Burly white officers barreled out and slammed their doors hard behind them. Night sticks drawn, they charged forward. "All right, all right, stop this…everybody…"

The onlookers and Venus scattered over chain-link fences, ducking through backyards and alleys, around corners, down endless boulevards. The police watched them retreat as they pulled Porsche and her combatant apart with night sticks and choke holds, the girls kicking and screaming, swearing the other was dead, out for blood, promising revenge.

As she tore down an alley, Venus looked over her shoulder to see if she was being pursued. She saw a familiar pale face with scrubby beard, fair skin, short blond hair, and dark sunglasses. The trademark look of a police officer. Venus wasn't sticking around to find out if that one was *him*. Turning sharply on her heels and tearing away at breakneck speed, eyes closed, chest heaving, arms pumping, never having run like this before in her life, she bolted down the last stretch of alley way, narrowly sidestepping garbage cans and a sleeping homeless man. Around another corner as fast as her legs would carry her, blasting full throttle until her chest burned mightily and sweat poured down her forehead. Then she ran faster. Around another corner, almost knocking an old woman down who glowered disapprovingly, clutching her half fallen shopping bags. "Ya oughta be mo' carefo'" she shouted resentfully, but Venus was already around the corner. Tears welled up in her eyes, trickled heavily down her face as she gasped for breath. She tried to fight them off but by now they were gushing. Powerful emotions began to swell inside her. Rage and terror and deadness and a longing wish that God would take her. Barreling further still through *The X,* her breath was becoming shallow and raspy, her throat was dry, and her head was growing dizzy; she felt as if she were about to faint from exhaustion. But nothing could stop her.

She slowed to a jog as she rounded one last corner barricaded by familiar shrubbery and a white mailbox. She slowed to long strides as she headed up the winding walkway to the bars on the windows, her mother clutching herself tightly on the porch, eyes dry and red from having run out of tears. When she saw her daughter, who had found a way to run when she couldn't run anymore, her mother cried again.

The porch light guided Venus. On seeing her, her weeping mother opened her arms wide as if she had never expected to see her daughter again. Once she held her, she hung on as though she would never let her go. Her eyes widened, barely able to believe Venus was really there. There was so much she wanted to say, but nothing came out. Before she could say a word, Venus looked up. They looked at each other and then just held on tighter. At last, mother and daughter were together again. For just a moment, Venus wanted to yell and pull hair and cry and demand an explanation, demand to know where she had been, sensing that her mother was on the verge of demanding to know the same. But togetherness prevailed. Without another thought, Venus just laid her head in her mother's lap, soft as a pillow.

Shawn

Closing the door tenderly behind him, Shawn began to make his exit. On a usual day, he would exit from his cozy, sometimes lonely apartment, proceed to the elevator, and find his way downstairs and out to the sidewalk that led to the nearby college campus. Then he would begin counting the minutes until his class was over so he could call the girl he had met the other day, plunk down in front of the television with popsicles and soda, and call his mother and tell her everything on his mind.

Today was different. He felt a weighty sense of responsibility, heaviness in his heart, with no suitable words to help him organize and understand what was bothering him. Stepping into the elevator almost reluctantly, Shawn stared down at his feet, hands digging into his pockets, wishing he had someone to explain what was going on inside him. *It's almost the end of the year, and I won't ever see them again. Fuck, I'm really going to miss them.* The thought of it made him want to cry. Approaching the lobby floor, he had to push down the tears coming and these stupid feelings. *It isn't supposed to be like this. I always thought I was supposed to be a little distant, detached. Objective, not so, hmmm, I don't know … not so, all up in it.*

But the pain was inevitable. Although he wouldn't let himself cry, there was no escape, nowhere to run as the elevator opened at the ground floor and he began to make his way to the rest of his life. Through the glass double doors of his apartment lobby and out into the dimly lit courtyard in front of the building, he sidestepped an unobservant crowd of hysterically laughing, half-drunk college students, pitching in several directions at once. Making a miserable attempt at an apology, one of them careened sideways and sent him into the railing that led to the front door. Shawn scoffed and continued on his way while they cheered mightily at who knows what, pumping their fists triumphantly in the air, cheering loudly as if they were accomplishing a mighty feat.

Shawn was shaking his head as he made his way, dumbfounded. *Fucking idiots, what are they so happy about? I still don't get it … that would be an ass kicking in The X for sure.* He smiled at his little private joke, but it was a smile that quickly grew bittersweet as he acknowledged again the goodbye that was just around the corner.

By the time he reached the campus and the 10-story, sand-colored building, he had somewhat settled; termination was inevitable, and he would just have to accept it. Pictures of smiling professors and academic forms lined the walls of the Social and Behavioral Sciences building. Students, grads and under-grads, mingled in the hallway, rushing to classes, checking their cell phones. *They look beat. Yeah, I know what that feels like.* He was a little surprised that he was only noticing this now, realizing how tired he was as he made his way down the corridor and around a corner. The Wednesday 7:00 p.m. class always zapped his last bit of energy, making going home and curling up in front of the television with junk food afterward seem like nirvana. Turning fast around a sharp corner, savoring the smell of old electrical charges and textbooks, know-ing this long walk would be one of his last, it now definitely registered that this was the end of the semester. *Mmmm, that's almost it. There'll be a day when I miss this.*

A woman about Shawn's age flew around the corner and almost ran into him, catching herself before a head-on collision. She smiled apologetically and pushed up her thick, librarian-like glasses, clutching her books to her chest, continuing on her way. Shawn muttered to himself, the heaviness on his mind leaving him with no patience. He pulled open the door to room 107 where his night class was already going full blast.

His professor was lecturing on social policy. Half the students were atten-tive and focused. The other half were trying to look like they were attentive and focused. Shawn slid into a seat, all of a sudden tired, trying to clear the cobwebs and get down to business. This subject was normally one of his favorites; but tonight, the words coming from the lecturing professor sounded almost like those of Charlie Brown's teacher. *Wah Wah Wah . . .*

Dropping his bag to the ground, squinting into the face of his professor who talked with his hands, he smiled broadly, obviously ready to go. *Awright, can I just go home. Shit, I mean, this is normally good stuff, but, I don't know.* He folded his hands on his desk, his head on his hands. Soon he was drifting off into nothing. The next few hours flew by. He began thinking hard about the day of goodbye. *Yeah, that's it. That's the end. And it's not even that far away. Shit. It's tomorrow!* Glancing around, he spotted the pretty African American girl he had noticed more than once. He admired her intricately braided hair. *Looks like Shantel's hair.* Shawn glanced out the window into the night, to the moon and the stars set in a deep blue sky. He was seeing and hearing the girls in his mind. *I wonder what they're doing right now.* He started picturing wild parties and fist fights and loud talking and marijuana joints. *Life should be better than that for them. But it isn't. That's just the truth.*

The Group

Beep! Beep! Beep! WHAM! Shawn's alarm clock had once again got what it deserved for waking him up so early. It now lay there quietly blinking at him from the floor beneath his bed. He lay back, the back of his forearm on his forehead, sighing and frowning a little. *Damn, it's the last day. Today is goodbye.* Dragging himself out of bed, he peered out the window into the dark of morning. Sometimes at this early hour, it felt like he was the only person awake in the world. He shuffled into the bathroom and made himself shower and shave. He wished there were a way to make this day go slower, keep the end from coming. *Maybe I can stay on next year, like, maybe I can come back and volunteer a couple of hours a week, maybe... Um, fuck, I don't know. Who am I kidding?* After drinking some coffee, he dressed and prepared for the inevitable. *This sucks; we just barely got going too.* Down the elevator and out the front door, the sky was still almost pitch black. Shawn marched solemnly and with determination to the bus stop, eager to get out of the cold, having declined a ride from his mother this time around. Normally he appreciated her company, but this time, he needed to go it alone. It was this feeling of alone that owned him all the way to the school that morning.

Once seated on the bus, he tried to ignore the raucousness of school kids yelling, blaring music, disturbing two elderly people shaking their heads disapprovingly. He opened his backpack and took out his favorite book, *8 Ball Chicks* by Gina Sykes, a compilation of stories about teenage girls in gangs. Normally, he would be enthused to be so immersed in it, hanging on the words from page to page, the tales of drive-bys and drug deals having him on the edge of his seat. The immediate world around him would drop several octaves in volume. Only this time, it didn't work. The first couple of times he had read this book, he had been able to conjure up his own images of what the girls in the stories looked like; sometimes they were tall and skinny wearing gangster baggies. Other times they were dark-skinned and chewing Tootsie Pops on basketball courts. Only this time, he saw Porsche and Shantel, Venus and Rona, Gina and Dalanna. Their faces were too real to deny. He quickly put the book away and settled back in his seat, staring long out the window.

When he had taken the bus to *The X* on previous mornings, he had almost always enjoyed the long ride that had let him sleep or relax or think or read, but this time the ride went particularly quickly. Glancing out the windows left and right, he saw some familiar faces, bouncing backpacks, immaculately matching basketball shoes and tank tops, gold chains, a man spitting in the gutter, a woman pushing a shopping cart, a guitar poking out from under the plastic garbage bags. He noted the corner liquor store owner once again out in front, bending over his broom, sweeping cigar and cigarette butts into his dust pan. He stood up for a minute, pushed his thick glasses back up into position. Shawn kept watching as he rose from his seat, preparing to make his descent into his last day in *The X. Wow, he must have been here for, like, ever! Probably has run this store his whole life. I wonder what it'd be like to live here.* He let his mind run off with that idea. He started to imagine how it would be if he took a job at the school, dropped out of his grad program, started working with crop after crop of kids out here. He could watch the little kids get big and the big kids get bigger. They would then move on to make way for the next group, on and on, forever. He then realized he was smiling at the thought. *Yeah, I'd be happy here. I know it.* Breathing in heavily, he dragged down the aisle and down the steps, waving goodbye to the driver on his way.

He walked across the street, passing houses with bars on windows and dogs barking behind fences, signs that warned "keep out." He heard the rumbling of old luxury sedans and SUVs blaring rap music. Little kids were crossing the street carrying backpacks practically as big as themselves, puffy coats zipped up, packs of them bustling through crosswalks. Some of them were laughing and playing while others moved as if they were wading in water up to their necks. Two girls talked rapidly into their cell phones, chewing gum, waving their hands. Shawn smiled as he watched them. He would miss this all.

Up the cracked gravel sidewalk, past at least 20 kids playing basketball on a half court. Mrs. Trenton saw him, smiled, and waved as she made her way down the yard to the bungalows. Shawn smiled back at her, waved, and headed off in the opposite direction on his way to the counseling office. Three boys were sharing music on their headphones while a couple of girls sat and chatted, legs crossed, chins cupped in the heels of their hands, nodding at each other, shaking their heads, frowning at the boys. It reminded him of the way the girls, some of them anyway, would talk about boys. *The girls have a way of shaking their heads, smacking their lips when talking about boys their own age. They don't exactly disdain them. In a way, it's as though....*

BRRRRRIIIINNNNGGG!!! The warning bell blared over head from every direction on the schoolyard. Shawn looked up from his reflections, came back in time. *Five minutes...Damn, what am I going to say to them?* Shaking his head slightly, he frowned, looked down at his feet carrying him to the office.

"Whassup Mista Reynolds?!?! Why you sad?!?!" piped an inviting and yet concerned little voice from somewhere down below. Shawn shook himself back to reality. *Johnson. Now who is counseling who?* Working up a smile. *God, I'm that obvious?* "Oh no, it's nothing, I'm okay, just tired," he demurred. "How you doin'?"

Johnson frowned and cocked his head a little, not looking convinced in the least. He was looking like he wanted to ask again but then brightened up quickly, smiling wide and inviting. He followed Shawn on his way to the far end of the schoolyard, past the basketball game that had dwindled, the raucous players dragging their backpacks from the ground at their feet, making their way to classrooms in every direction, stopping only long enough to yell through cupped hands and take advantage of the last minute opportunity to antagonize each other just a little more.

"Mista Reynolds, can I go to yo' class?" Johnson inquired hopefully.

Shawn laughed and shook his head emphatically, trying to get the words out. *God, I'm gonna miss him too. No more Johnson either.* Staring at him for a second, his sparkling little eyes, his dentist's office magazine cover smile. "No, you have first period. And I have a group to do."

Johnson hopped slightly up and down, his happiest of little smiles falling into a pouting frown. Slowly, he turned and disappeared into the crowds bustling in every direction. Shawn watched him disappear. *Damn, that might be the last time I see him...*

"Mista Reynolds, it's time ta start yo' class right?" a familiar female voice inquired from behind.

Shawn turned on his heels to find Porsche and Venus standing there before him, eyes focused and attentive. Ready to go. Porsche was looking up at him, with long, freshly braided extensions pulled back into an off-center ponytail. She wore an orange-striped polo shirt, form-fitting white jeans that matched white high-top basketball shoes with orange trim. Shawn took notice of her stylish ensemble. *Some of the kids dress so well here. Makes me think I got work ta do.* Venus smacked her lips loudly, standing beside Porsche in a heavy parka with the hood pulled up and over her face, staring down into the ground at her feet, hands jammed into her pockets.

Shawn smiled, waved them onward, led them across the last stretch of schoolyard. He was still trying to figure out what it all meant. *Wow, uh, okay. This is weird. I usually go get them. Oh well, maybe this is a good thing.* They walked on in silence. *What's going on?*

Shawn was quiet. The schoolyard was fairly deserted except for the three of them and the security guard standing under the overhang near the main office. *This is it.* All he could do was continue on, lead the little parade, keep moving until they got to the room where so much had happened to all of them. *This is it, the end. Damn!*

For some reason, he found himself growing angry. *What am I going to say? Damn it, I need more time with them.* His mind began racing for ways that he could make it more palatable. No matter what he said, it was soon to be over. This was to be his last walk with them across the yard to his office, the last time he would hear the initial silence gradually give way to idle chatter as soon as they forgot he was there.

Turning the squeaky doorknob of the counseling office, he held the door open for the girls who trudged in slowly. Shawn followed them in and almost immediately started the group with an energetic salutation, much quicker than usual.

"Hi you guys," he began, smiling. Silence followed. Terri smiled as if to encourage them to begin. An eerie quietness for a few seconds and then....

"Okay, ma' turn first!!!" Porsche announced excitedly. "Ooohhh my auntie been doin' toooo much! Ol' nasty heffer !!"

Shawn smiled. *I shouldn't be encouraging them, but, oh well. Ta hell with it.*

Venus stared at her feet, looking like she might be listening, but waiting for her chance to speak.

"I swear to G-O-D, I hate her!!!" Porsche continued, smacking her lips loudly for emphasis, stopping only for a second to reflect, shaking her head in disgust at whatever she was thinking. "Like, I be comin' home, mindin' my owwwnnn bidness, not doin' nothin', don't be botherin' nobody. An' she be yellin' an' shit, callin me out ma' name. OOOHH!!!"

Terri frowned in concern. "Wow, she's really mean to you sometimes."

"Yeah!!" Porsche agreed. "She don't do nothin' neither! Always lying up on da couch, watchin' TV. Some bootsy ass shit too!!! She only have me 'round 'cuz den she get a check. She don't care 'bout me."

A long silence prevailed. Everyone present felt the sorrow within her.

Porsche stared hard through the wall above Shawn's head, fuming at something only she could see. "An' I ain't playin'. One a' deez days," she resumed ominously. "I ain't 'bout ta be in da mood, an' den, mmm-hmmm, yeah!!"

Venus shifted uncomfortably in her seat, breathing in heavily, feeling some weary resignation, even utter hopelessness. *Her auntie be fuckin' wit' her wit' no let up. I mean, yeah...ma' girl do be doin' too much, doin' thangs ta make her mad, but she be fucked up too. An' her mama?*

Venus remembered Porsche's mother. What was it about her? She recalled their late-night phone conversations, hearing thuds and shrill yelps and screams from Porsche's mother. A man's rumbling bellows. Porsche having to get off the phone quickly. Never wanting to talk about it the next day, but the look on her face said it all anyway.

Then there was another day that Venus suddenly remembered, while Porsche continued her tirade about her aunt. Venus remembered Porsche bounding down the steps, nose high in the air, slamming the door behind her.

Long, defiant strides down the walkway were followed by her aunt still roaring obscenities from behind the closed door. Porsche had briskly passed Venus by, and Venus had to nearly double over to keep up. Porsche had then begun to make small talk about boys and parties as if nothing mattered. They both decided they were going to McDonald's first thing.

Now, Venus was beginning to add it up. *Mmm-hmm, I been knowin' dat shit fuck ma' girl up. Her auntie hella mean! An' she be actin' like it don't matta. But I thought it did. Now, sheeit. Now I know it did!!*

Porsche continued airing her grievances about her aunt's latest atrocities. Meanwhile, Venus continued to remember.

They had headed to the McDonald's on the corner, walking in hurried steps, talking of boys and parties and hating school. Out of nowhere, a flurry of "bitch" and "hurry-ups" came from somewhere behind them. The girls had turned around in earnest, and Venus recalled feeling particularly frightened. *Ooohhh, dey soun' like dey gonna flash!! Yup, mmm-hmm…*

The yelling was coming from a small crowd that was gathered on the sidewalk ahead of them, a motley collection of thin, hunched-over figures with holes in their shirts, grey slacks, a lifetime of shaggy grey and black beard growth. The girls avoided the hollow and soulless eyes of these crack heads. Venus clicked her tongue. *Damn, deez niggas crazy out here!!* She paid them no mind as the men parted enough to allow them to pass. Then Venus noted a familiar female face in the crowd. Withered, decaying, red-eyed. Venus covered her mouth with a heavy hand and almost stopped in her tracks. *Damn, dat ma' girl mama!*

Porsche's mama was huddled over in a short skirt. Her legs were bruised, and her face was pale and dry from sleepless nights. Her lips were chalky, and her red eyes were sunk deep into the back of her skull. A shell of a human being. A zombie walking the graveyard. Porsche saw her too and turned away; she couldn't bear to watch. Venus looked on in shock and dismay. Porsche's mother was taking a wad of bills from one of the men. He was ordering her toward the back of a house, his companions looking on in feverish anticipation, one of them beginning to undo his pants.

Porsche opened her mouth, a thousand words at the ready. But she turned on her heels and ran. She was running hard with long strides and pumping fists. In seconds, she was gone. Venus could only watch her run off into the distance. After that day, she had often wondered just where Porsche had run off to.

Venus now sensed the room had gone quiet, but for how long, she wasn't quite sure. "Okay, it's my turn," she began almost hesitantly, turning in her seat so she could face Porsche. "Yeah, I know wha' choo sayin'."

Porsche looked up from her dismal spot on the floor, catching Venus' eyes for a second. She was smiling slightly.

"See, I's like dat wit' ma' mama too," Venus continued, sitting up a little straighter in her chair. "See I be tryin' ta jus' be like, yeah, whateva'. Feel me? Like, when ma' mama be callin' me fat, callin' me out ma' name. An' like, feel me? I ain't even do nothin'. I just be up in ma' room, talkin' on da phone o' somethin'. An' she jus' come up in there like dat. It hurt my feelin's."

Porsche nodded hard, knowing exactly what she meant.

Shawn and Terri looked on in deep concern, leaning forward in their chairs, hanging on every word, feeling the heavy sadness all around.

Porsche stared down at the floor between her legs crossed at the ankle, folded her hands solemnly in her lap. *Sheeit, dat soun' jus' like ma' auntie. I ain't got no real fam'ly neither! An ma' girl tellin' da truth too. Her mama do be on her ass fa' no reason. An' she say some fucked up shit!!!*

"I jus' be like, feel me? Talkin' to my many mens you know? Like, Tyrone, oooohhhh!!! He hecka cute. But he jus' like, you know, on da side. Den Jerome, he like, mm-hmm. Das like, ma' main man." She looked out of the corner of her eyes at Porsche. "Oooohhh he got hella money too. Fat ass bank roll like dis!" She was holding her thumb and index finger up and about two inches apart. "Sheeit, he best be take me shoppin' o' somethin' soon. Feel me?" Porsche and Venus laughed gaily.

Shawn began to grow irritated as their laughter trailed off. Fleeting thoughts of women he had once dated. Had they been using him?

Meanwhile, Porsche began to pick uncomfortably at a fingernail. *Damn, dey jus' be linin' up fo' ma' girl. She lucky. Don't know how she do it. But, damn! Dey jus' on her like dat!*

Terri watched and waited.

"Yeah…But, den, ooooohhhhh!!" Venus proclaimed. "She be comin' up in ma' room!! Don't be knockin' o' nothin'!!"

Porsche shook her head wearily. *Yeah, her mama trippin' hard sometimes. An' she ain't do shit neitha'!*

"She be doin' toooooo much. Feel me?!" Venus continued, smacking her lips and folding her arms haughtily across her chest, crossing her legs, and leaning back in her chair in a humph. *Mm-hmm, I ain't got no real mutha. She don't give a fuck 'bout me. I ought a' just run away. Go down to L.A. o' some shit. She don' even miss me.* The silence was growing loud and powerful.

Shawn searched for something to say, something that would make everyone feel better. Finding nothing made him angry.

"Venus you were saying that she makes you really angry and you usually try just to let it go?" Terri inquired.

Venus nodded affirmatively. *Tryin' to anyway. But she on my ass all damn day an' night.*

Shawn sat up slightly in his chair. *Yeah! I see where she's going.*

Porsche glanced longingly out the window.

"Why is that?" Terri continued.

Venus shrugged.

"Her mama scandalous!" Porsche supplied.

Venus snickered. Shawn laughed hard. Terri smiled.

"See what I'm sayin'?" Porsche elaborated. "If dat was me? I be quick to cuss her ass out!!" She smacked her lips loudly. "Mmm-hmm, b'lieve dat, feel me?!? It a' be on!!!"

All in the group watched her closely, locked eyes urging her to continue.

"But…yeah…" Porsche admitted. "All a dat prob'ly why I be doin' too much. Feel me? Like, why I be wilding out sometimes?"

Venus looked up in wonder. *Damn, ma' girl don't be gettin' deep like dis.*

Shawn smiled approvingly. *Wow, that's a great insight.*

"Like, I know people be thinkin' dat I'm jus' like, you know?"…like…"

Venus chuckled. "Doin' too much?"

Porsche grinned. "Yeah, an' das how it is too. Everybody think I just do too much, but, den, like…Feel me? Like, dey be thinkin' I'm crazy."

Venus smiled. "'Cuz you is," she muttered just loud enough for everyone to hear. Everyone laughed—Porsche laughed the hardest. "Yea…" she conceded, taking a second longer to figure out what she wanted to say. Sitting upright in her chair once she was sure of herself, she continued. "But dat ain't all it is, feel me?" *Hmmm, I ain't even think about it like dat. But it kind a' fucked up dat nobady even know me.*

Shawn nodded. *That's right. You know, you're much more than that.* He took a split second to think how much more all of the girls were than that. So much more than even they probably knew. *That's all a lot of people prob'ly think of them. But that isn't even the half.* He raised his eyebrows, almost wanting to laugh at himself. *God, I'm thinking in the way they talk!!*

Porsche breathed in heavily, bracing herself for what she had to say next. "Feel me? I be like, mo', wha's dat word? Sensitive!! Like, when dey say thangs dat hurt my feelin's? I don't be trippin' on da outside…" Silence. More silence. Everyone waited patiently.

"But on da inside," Venus finished. *Yeah, dat shit hurt like hell.*

"Yeah," Porsche readily agreed, exhaling heavily through her nose and sitting back in her chair, crossing her legs, jamming her hands into her pockets, looking off into an inconspicuous spot on the wall, opening her mouth to say more. No words came. There was nothing more to be said. Closing her lips, sitting back a little further, savoring the moment. Looking as if her mind had caught up to what she had been saying.

Shawn watched her closely. *Maybe this is the therapy.* Soon, it began to feel uncomfortable.

"All right you guys," Terri began. "So we're almost out of time and this is our last day together. Is there anything you want to say?"

Shawn thought of so many things he wanted to say that nothing came out.

Meanwhile, the girls shrugged, looking to Shawn and Terri, to each other, and then back to arbitrary spots on the floor or along the walls.

"So, how was this for you guys?" Terri continued.

"Okay," each murmured.

Porsche laughed. "Okay! But I be real wit' y'all. You know how we used ta hide an' be actin' like we ain't wanna come ta yo class? Yeah, we was lyin'. We kind a' like all dis."

Shawn and Terri both smiled approvingly.

"Do you think this helped you?" Terri inquired.

Porsche shrugged.

"Yeah," Venus conceded. "We was talkin' about everythang dat was goin' on up in here an' then we ain't get in dat much trouble fo' talkin' in class."

"How did this help?" Shawn wondered.

"We done talked about everythang in here so we ain't got nothin' left ta talk about in der," Porsche elaborated, pointing to the classrooms across the way.

Shawn smiled, comforted.

BRRRRINNNNGGGG!!!! clamored the bell from overhead. The girls stayed sitting for a second longer than they had to, almost hesitating to go. Slowly they reached down to pick up their bags.

"All right you guys," Shawn began. "Take care of yourselves. I'm going to miss you." He was feeling sadness coming upward from deep within, so he began pushing it back down again with the hardest inner willpower that he could muster.

Porsche smiled without looking back. "Yeah, peace out Mr. Reynolds!" Looking over her shoulder and meeting his eyes before grabbing her backpack, she smiled slightly. Venus followed, smiling at Shawn and Terri. "Yes, thank you guys, thank you for coming," Terri called out to them. A soft kind of sadness was in her voice. She sounded exactly like Shawn felt. Together they watched the girls walk out the door.

For a long while after the girls had left, neither Shawn nor Terri said anything. They just stood there in the nothingness, looking at their backpacks and folders, sensing the emptiness that was left. All they could do was watch out the window as the girls stepped forward, across the blacktop, off to class and the rest of their lives.

Shawn smiled, wishing he could have had just a few seconds more with them. He began wondering if this wasn't the best way to feel at the end. *Missing them wouldn't quite cover it.*

Assessment

In this week's group, each member grieved in his or her own way. My feelings were particularly intense, despite my understanding that therapists are not supposed to get so attached to their clients. This is somewhat common for younger therapists. In fact, it is this deepest of bonds that is the most necessary for healing to occur. In termination, it is often the case that the weight of the love is equal to the weight of the loss.

Everyone present expressed mutual feelings of loss and the uncertainty about moving on, more in terms of what they did than what they said. In this last week of group, there was less talking about the grieving and more feeling the grieving.

It was particularly noteworthy that, in this last week of group, both girls present became significantly more vulnerable than they had in past weeks. It is sometimes the case that this is what happens: Clients may begin to disclose more emotionally sensitive material toward the end of a session or begin to open up emotionally toward the end of the therapy. As discussed in attachment literature, a normal response to loss is to protest it in various ways. When infants are separated from their mothers, they tend to cry. In the case of this last week of the girls' group, their more sensitive disclosures toward the end of the last session may have been their way of protesting their loss of the group.

In any case, it was important for them to have an opportunity to express their feelings about the group and the termination process. It was just as important for Terri and me to make the therapeutic space safe to do so and to then respect how much or how little the girls wanted to say about the group ending. It was also important for the girls to hear, from Terri and me, that we were also grieving. This was important because the mutual expression of loss provided the girls with an experience that modeled a healthy goodbye. It contrasted with the girls' typical experience with saying good-bye, which was usually more abrupt or traumatic, such as someone being taken away to jail or to foster care. This last week of group gave them the chance to probe their feelings concerning the losses and to say what they needed to say before moving on.

This was also an important developmental experience for me as a younger clinician. Like the girls, I needed to have a more emotionally intense termination with clients I felt close to so that, in future clinical work, I would be better prepared to handle these understandably painful experiences with professional decorum and boundaries.

The end result was that everyone went through a range of emotions: anger and fear, sorrow, relief, happiness, and grief. And they survived them together. Although they moved on and were never in the same room again, somewhere deep inside, they would always be a part of one another.

TEN

Graduation Day

A long stare into the mirror two inches in front of his nose, turning left and right, inspecting both the good and the bad side. Pulling his face down and up, scanning for blemishes. Tightening his jacket around his shoulders, straightening the shirt underneath. Tussling loosely combed hair into a satisfying off-center part. Finally, a smile. Shawn was satisfied and ready to go.

He looked at his watch. 4:40 p.m. *Shit I'm gonna be late. Graduation starts in an hour and a half and my bus leaves in 10 minutes!* Flicking off the light switch and bolting out the door, then going back to lock it behind him, he tore down the hallway to the elevator and then, once inside, he pushed the lobby button at least six times more than he needed to. He waited and watched as each floor number lit up slowly, mockingly. Floor 4. *Shit, c'mon let's go! What the fuck is taking so long?!* Floor 3. Nervously, he began tapping his right foot, trying not to envision the worst of the worst possible outcomes as the elevator finally reached the ground floor.

He imagined kids in immaculate single file lines walking onto the stage, purple gowns, hats with tassels, parents and grandparents taking pictures with hands on their hearts, the classic graduation song blaring overhead. And then Shawn would arrive, throwing open one of the double doors that led into the auditorium. A record scratching hard, every head would be turned backward, scowling faces straining to determine the identity of this vilest of intruders. Shawn would be standing there in the back of the room, all angry eyes on him. Nothing to do but to stand frozen, feeling frightened and small. It was this horrific fantasy that propelled him out the front door and down the block at breakneck speed. *Okay okay, whew!! I need to get in better shape. Awright, the bus stop is just a few blocks down. Uuuhhhhh!!! Maybe I can make it.*

Past grungy young men in beanie hats sitting on their front stoop, two days' worth of facial hair, wrinkled t-shirts, one of them with holes in his socks. College students. *God, they all look homeless or some shit!* He smiled at this fleeting connection as he tore up the final stretch of walkway to a familiar green bench at the top of the hill. Stopping just short of it, dropping his book bag down to the ground, hands on his knees, starting to heave, he recovered quickly and then paced back and forth in heavy steps. *Damn it!!! I'm gonna be late. It's going to be all bad. The bus probably already showed up and now it's going to another…No…Wait. That's it right there.* Looking at his watch. *4:48. I still have some time, just might make it, but it's gonna be close.* The bus came to a stop and Shawn gladly mounted the steps. He paid his fare and slumped down into a nearby seat, relieved that, at least for the next little while, everything was out of his hands. *That was too close.* The bus picked up speed and veered onto the highway, a nearly empty road ahead. Shawn settled further into his seat and began wrestling around to get comfortable. Popping in his earphones, turning on his iPod, grateful to hear R. Kelly, he began relaxing about 10 minutes into the ride. Glancing off to the horizon where the sun was just beginning to set, he once again envisioned the day. *Wow, they are going to graduate! I hope they'll all be there. Maybe.* He felt a buzzing in his pocket, pulled out his cell phone.

"Hey mama," Shawn greeted, glancing out the window at passing bill-boards, a semi-truck barreling past in the far left-hand lane.

"Hello son," his mother replied, sounding like she might be doing two things at once. "How are you?"

"I'm okay," Shawn answered, the bus stopping briefly, an elderly couple making their way slowly and gingerly up the steps. Shawn watched, wishing they would hurry up, feeling guilty for his wish, knowing they were elderly and couldn't help it. "I'm going to the kids' graduation. Today is the day. Like, no more after this, you know?" The thought made him sad.

His mother's smile could be heard through the other end of the phone. "Awwww!!!"

Shawn grew irritated, glancing out the window again. *How far away are we?* The advertisement banners and office buildings were rapidly coming to an end. Smoking factories and vacant lots were taking their place. *Yeah, no man's land. That's what the kids call it. When I get to the industrial stuff where all the big factories are and shit, that's when I'm close. They'd never put all that stuff where I live.* He had to think about that for a minute, wondering how it all added up.

"You there?" his mother inquired. The bus suddenly lurched to a stop, the double doors flying open, a crowd of younger black guys scurrying on in groups of fours and fives.

"Yeah, I'm here ma, I gotta go," Shawn answered quickly. He began trying to conceal his cell phone in the inside of his pocket and then stopped himself. *I wouldn't do that if they were white.* Now really wondering how it all added up. Not quite able to think clearly, but knowing he was on to something. Thinking hard, feeling a little guilty, wondering, searching for an answer that seemed just out of reach.

The bus pulled off and to the right, halting at a familiar corner. The woman who was driving looked off and to the right, just enough so Shawn was in the corner of her eye. Waiting? Shawn shook his head. *Naw, I'm imagining things.* Jolting himself back to reality, grateful to see that he was just in time, he looked out the windows left and right, seeing liquor stores with barred windows, trash blowing through the streets, patrolling police cars, lawns with no grass. *I'm here already?* It always amazed him that it could happen so quickly. Glancing again at his watch. *5:59. Shit!* He snapped to his feet and strode quickly down the aisle, waving goodbye to the driver, the same woman who was always there. She was smiling and waving goodbye as Shawn made his last exit.

Shawn momentarily noticed it. *Hmmm, she sure came around.* Down the steps and out onto the sidewalk. *Or maybe I did.* The thought stayed with him for a good minute. Looking both ways, he waited as a lowrider truck rumbled by with blaring rap music. Seeing that the coast was clear, he made his way across, stopping momentarily to pull his pants up so the cuffs didn't drag on the ground. *I like this little walk... God, lot's changed. I remember the beginning of the year I used to tear off down the street, eyes forward, the whole bit. Like there was no tomorrow. Hmmm, I've been a lot more comfortable here in The X the last few weeks. Yeah, maybe I came around.* The thought made him smile slightly. He wasn't quite sure but something had changed, and what had happened to him at this school in *The X* would never leave him. That was a good thing that he would cherish always.

Feeling this way all the way up the street past barking dogs and sprinklers, he saw a grandmotherly woman rocking on the porch, her eyes waiting for his when he looked to her. Each smiled and waved at the other. He marveled at the familiarity he felt with this place, the people he had grown accustomed to and those who had become accustomed to seeing him. He recalled what his mother once said about how he sure had invested a lot of himself in his work this year. Now he realized how true that actually was.

"Hey now, Mr. Reynolds!" greeted a familiar deep, male voice as he entered the school grounds.

Shawn smiled wide, trying to look like he had been paying attention. "Hey, Mr. Justice. You know where we're going?" he asked as their strides through the playground gradually came into synch.

Getting a better look around, he could see kids in caps and gowns bustling to and fro with moms and dads and brothers and sisters and grandmothers, grandfathers, aunts or cousins. *It's so cool that they all show up like this with hella people.* Mr. Justice smiled and raised his palm high in greeting, peering inquisitively through the crowd as if he were looking for someone. "I think we're out this way," he said, motioning far off to his right, toward the auditorium where kids and their families were slowly filtering in.

Shawn had to laugh at himself. *Wow, that was pretty unobservant. He must think I'm an idiot. Where they had to go was practically right in front of my face.* Walking alongside Mr. Justice, across the basketball courts, past the jungle gym, Shawn observed kids in bright gowns with hoods and tassels standing with proud parents, restless little ones, and grandparents, leaning heavily on canes and walkers; he found himself taking a good look. *Yeah, they get the bare minimum. I swear, kinda blows my mind sometimes. No senior centers or anything. I haven't even seen a hospital now that I think about it.*

"What's that, Mr. Reynolds?" Mr. Justice inquired knowingly. "Got something on your mind?"

Shawn shook his head, purposefully denying Mr. Justice's perceptiveness.

Mr. Justice nodded understandingly but looked unconvinced.

Shawn admired him. *He's so observant. Everyone is here. They notice everything. Wish I had that.* As they began to quicken their pace, they narrowly sidestepped a group of smaller boys tearing past in a single file run, each one seeming to chase the other in front. Four of them, with mischievous smiles and outstretched arms, determined to catch each other.

Shawn laughed as he watched. *Damn, I'm gonna miss this place hella bad.* Then he caught a glimpse of Porsche and Dalanna in high heels, ornate hair styles, and immaculate makeup chatting several yards away. They were looking around, wondering where their parents were.

Shawn turned his body back toward Mr. Justice as they walked on. "Yeah, I'm fine," he confirmed.

Mr. Justice smiled bitterly, eyeing some of the older, sickly looking people. "Yup aren't we all." He was the first to walk through the double doors, and Shawn followed him into the gymnasium where crowds of young matriculating students and their families bustled in, some taking their seats, some leaning heavily against nearby walls, removing coats, placing them over chair backs, careful not to intrude on the spaces next to or in back of them.

Shawn saw Venus walk up toward center stage, looking eager to get on with it, her hair pulled up into a twisting and curving bun, long fingernails, a little makeup, holding her graduation mortarboard in hand, obviously not wanting to mess up her hair by putting it on. Five or six adults were there with her. A teenage boy who was a head taller stood to her right. The others were much older. To her left stood a stern and proud-looking couple. Dark-skinned, straight-backed, classily dressed, expensive shoes.

Shawn looked on in earnest. "Wow, so this is it. The last day."

"Are you coming back next year?" Mr. Justice inquired, hopefully but half expecting a no.

Shawn looked down sorrowfully at his feet, shaking his head emphatically. "No, my internship is up."

Mr. Justice's eyed the floor, too.

Shawn smiled, the tenderness of it bittersweet. *Nice that someone wants me to stay.* "I wish I could though. I wanted to stop my program and just work here."

Mr. Justice nodded, smiling grimly, motioning him to a couple of open seats near the back. They took their seats and looked around the room.

As if to say, "perfect timing," a loud screech of microphone feedback ripped through the whispers and scraping of feet against the gymnasium floor, bringing everyone to a hushed silence. Shawn looked up to see Mrs. Trenton on stage.

"Good afternoon, everyone," she began. "Please take your seats so we can get started." Shawn detected that same, stern-but-polite finality in her voice. Everyone was waiting for the hustle and bustle to dissipate. Mrs. Trenton knew better than to wait for total attention in this circumstance as she continued her introductory remarks.

"We are gathered here today to celebrate this year's graduating class!"

"Whoo-hoo!!" "Yeah!" and a roar of applause broke out. The kids who were lined up along the wall and down the steps that lead onto the stage whooped and hollered triumphantly. All were smiling wide, throwing hands signs in the air, doing little dances. Shawn smiled sadly, shaking his head, laughing a little. He would surely, dearly miss these kids.

He watched each kid take his or her turn walking the stage, some smiling nervously and marching hard to receive their diplomas and then turning to go back down off the stage on the other end, as if wanting nothing more than to get it all over with. Others threw up their hands, making gestures high over their heads, yelping and stirring up the crowd. Johnson cupped one of his little hands over his mouth, caw-cawing through the funnel like a rooster. Porsche, Dalanna, and Gina each took their diplomas with wide smiles. Venus marched across the stage gracefully in high heels like a model on a runway, head held high.

Shawn was mentally taking roll call as each of the girls passed. An hour or so later, there was still no sign of Rona or Shantel. Shawn frowned in worry. Glancing left and right and up and over the crowd expectantly, he knew the ceremony was almost over as the crowds were beginning to thin out. Still, no sign of either of the final two. *Maybe they just got here late, or maybe they're up to some shit out behind the school.* He began watching what could be happening in the parking lot in his mind. The loud talking, the gestures, the hands clapping, the little dances. He smiled to himself. *Yeah, I'm gonna miss them bad.*

"What's up, Mista Reynolds?!" A familiar voice inquired, jolting Shawn back to reality. He shook himself slightly, focusing, again attentive.

"Hey, Dalanna," he greeted. She looked breathtaking in an ornate hairstyle with freshly dyed streaks of natural red, a little flashy but definitely not what the girls would call *ghetto*, not too outrageous or extravagant. She wore high heels and elegant ebony and gold jewelry.

Shawn smiled broadly. "Congratulations!!! Wow, right?! No more of all this! On you go!"

Dalanna beamed. "Mmm-hmm...So where yo' class gonna be next year?"

Shawn smiled slightly, flattered, and then suddenly remembered the totality of the truth. "That's it, Dalanna. We're all done. I'm only here for one year."

Dalanna looked momentarily dumbfounded. "What? Where you goin'?"

Shawn had to think about it for a second. *Shit, good question.* "Well, I don't know yet. But I'm going to work somewhere else next year. You know. I'm in school too."

Dalanna's quick mind considered the possibilities. "Where you stay at?"

Shawn found himself reeling, but in an excited, flattered kind of way. *She wants to stay in touch. That sounds great! I mean, it's probably good for her. I mean, it sounds like it's so shitty for them out here. It would be cool for us to talk sometimes.* "I stay out by the college on the other side of town." The answer was hopefully vague enough.

Dalanna nodded. "Can we trade numbas?"

Shawn fumbled about a bit. *Uh oh, wait a second, this isn't what I had in mind.* "N-no, we can't do that I..."

"You got a My Space? We cou' do a My Space' sometime," she suggested hopefully.

Shawn looked off to the horizon, thinking, wondering, hoping. *That would be nice, I mean, that couldn't hurt. Well, I don't know. She might get the wrong idea. But then, they need to have adults around who are helpful and kind. Maybe, yes, that would be okay. Well, no.* "Dalanna, let me look into this okay? Can you hang tight for a second?"

"Yeah," Dalanna conceded.

Shawn nodded in gratitude and then went hurrying off into a corner several feet away, just out of ear shot, springing a phone from his inside jacket pocket, excitedly pushing buttons. Pressing the phone hard against his ear, hearing it ring, he waited for his supervisor to answer, although he was pretty sure what she would say. *C'mon pick up!!!!*

"Hello?" answered a familiar female voice.

"Hey Kristine," he replied. "It's Shawn. How are you?" Beginning to pace nervously in anticipation, he moved slightly back and forth, back and forth, wrapping his free arm tightly around his rib cage, bracing himself for the discussion.

"I'm good. So what's up?" Kristine inquired.

Shawn breathed in heavily in anticipation, trying to calm down. *Damn, she's going to say no, I know it. Well, no, she might say it's ok if I...* "Well, I was going to go ahead and do this, but then I figured I should call my supervisor and make sure."

"Mmm-hmm, good," Kristine affirmed, already able to tell that she would be telling him no to whatever he was asking about, hearing the eagerness in his voice, sensing that something was up. She was relieved that he had called her first.

Shawn breathed in heavily again. *Alright, shit, I just need to ask. Fuck it, here goes nothing.* "Well, Dalanna just came to see me. I'm at the kids' graduation and she wants to stay in contact. Nothing real heavy, like, just like an e-mail every now and then."

He felt a little guilty. *Well, okay, shit, that's not exactly what she had said. But it would be good if she had a guy to talk to that wouldn't try to hook up with her. I mean, she's probably never had that before!* "I mean, I know it's the end of the year and all. But she doesn't have anyone to talk to really, you know? I think it would be nice. What do you think?"

"No," Kristine answered quickly. "A couple of things. You're right, it would be nice for her. But what is more important is that she needs to learn how to end relationships in a good way, and so do you. I mean, well, it would be different if she were a boy, but even then. No, you have to end things here. Termination needs to happen."

Shawn found his spirits sinking rapidly, knowing the end was no longer around the corner, it was now. He felt the anxiety mount, rushing in long and frantic waves.

"I know this is hard," Kristine reassured. "But Shawn, this has to happen. I mean, what if you kept in contact with every kid you worked with? You would have no space to work, no free hours. This has to be."

"What if it was just her?" Shawn insisted enthusiastically. "And I could be really clear what this is about and that, you know, like, nothing is going to happen. It would be good for her, and it would probably make it easier."

Kristine smiled in compassion. She knew what she had to say, and Shawn knew it too. Shawn could feel that sympathetic smile from the other end of the phone. "You've done a lot for them Shawn. And they will remember you," Kristine comforted.

Shawn's spirits sank. That was it. No meant no.

Kristine then rose to the occasion. "Don't worry. They'll be okay. And so will you. But no. You have to do this. You need to terminate with your clients."

Shawn smiled bitterly, murmuring an okay and goodbye into the receiver and then started trying to brace himself for what he knew he had to do. *This sucks! Why do I have to do this? I'm tired of these bullshit therapy rules. I mean, this is stupid. The group was great. And she wants to keep talking! It's not like anything is going to happen. She already knows we're not hooking up or anything. She just wants to have someone to talk to. This is fucked. I, I, I don't know.*

"Dalanna?" He called out bitterly, resigning himself to get it over with. *God, I don't want to do this. But I gotta. Like Kristine said. There's no other way. But that doesn't mean I have to like it either!*

Feeling the anger rise to a boil as Dalanna made her way to him, heels clip-clopping across the gymnasium floor, he could see as she approached that she sensed what was to come by looking at Shawn's face. Shawn could sense that she knew, even before he opened his mouth to say goodbye. She wore that look of cautious confusion. A frown was etched on her brow and she avoided his eyes.

"Dalanna, I'm sorry. We can't correspond. As much as we would like to stay in contact, we both have to move on," Shawn informed.

Dalanna breathed hard through her nose. "Why?" she demanded.

Shawn shook his head. *For no fucking good reason.* "Because you need to have a good-bye that isn't so sudden and traumatic, you know, like shootings and people disappearing and shit, you know?"

Dalanna looked off into the crowd, a look that conveyed disappointment but some understanding. "But, like, why not jus' a My Space, feel me?!"

"No, I'm sorry we can't, I..."

Shawn began again to try to explain, but he was already speaking to thin air.

Dalanna had whirled on her heels and stomped away in long, powerfully strides. Indignant, contemptuous, dismissive.

"Dalanna, wait. I…" Shawn protested, taking a step in her direction, but he realized that she was already lost in the crowd. He knew exactly how she felt, but he knew that he needed to let her go. Watching her walk away, beautiful, determined, ready for the world, he knew that she would be okay and began thinking that he would be too. Watching the door close at her back, it was done.

After a while, he realized that he was alone. The procession had ended, everyone was outside in the parking lot, speaking in whispers among themselves, just a few excited chatters barely audible. He rose and stood there in the center of the gym, breathing in heavily, feeling like the last person alive in the world. Smiling bitterly and wiping a few tears from his eye, he sighed. *Well, that's it. It's all over. They're gone. But they'll always be My Girls.*

References

Ainsworth, M., Blehar, M., Waters, E., & Wall, S. (1978). *Patterns of attachment: A psychological study of the strange situation.* Hillsdale, NJ: Lawrence Erlbaum.

American Psychiatric Association. (2000). *Diagnostic and statistical manual of mental disorders* (4th ed.). Washington, DC: Author.

Barak, G., Flavin, J., & Leighton, P. (2001). *Class, race, gender, and crime* (1st ed.). Los Angeles: Roxbury Publishing.

Bowlby, J. (1960). Grief and mourning in early infancy and childhood. *Psychoanalytic Study of the Child, 15,* 9–52.

Bowlby, J. (1963). *Child care and the growth of love.* Baltimore: Penguin Books.

Bowlby, J. (1969). *Attachment and loss: Vol. 1.* Lubbock, TX: Hogarth Press and The Institute of Psychoanalysis.

Briere, J., & Scott, C. (2006). *Principles of trauma therapy: A guide to symptoms, evaluation, and treatment.* Thousand Oaks, CA: Sage Publications.

Cassidy, J., & Shaver, P. (2008). *Handbook of attachment: Theory, research, and clinical applications* (2nd ed.). New York: Guilford Press.

Corey, M., & Corey, G. (2002). *Groups: Process and practice* (6th ed.). Pacific Grove, CA: Brooks/Cole Thomson Learning.

Duncan, L., & Johnson, D. (2007). Black undergraduate students attitude toward counseling and counselor preference. *College Student Journal, 41,* 696–719.

The East Bay Community Recovery Project. (2009, October 12). *African-American women's panel.* Unpublished Proceedings, Hayward, CA.

Ellensweig-Tepper, D. (2000). Trauma group psychotherapy for the adolescent female client. *Journal of Child and Adolescent Psychiatric Nursing, 13*(1), 17–31.

Evans, K., Kincade, E., Marbley, A., & Seem, S. (2005). Feminism and feminist-therapy: Lessons from the past and hope for the future. *Journal of Counseling & Development, 83,* 269–277.

Freud, A. (1966). *The ego and the mechanisms of defense* (Rev. ed.). London: Hogarth Press.

Freud, S. (2007). *Collected works of Sigmund Freud.* Charleston, SC: Biblio Bazaar.

Gregory, M., & Leslie, L. (1996). Different lenses: Variations in clients' perception of family therapy by race and gender. *Journal of Marital and Family Therapy, 22,* 239–251.

Harwood, I. (2003). Creative use of gender while addressing early attachment, trauma, and cross cultural issues in a cotherapy group. *Psychoanalytic Inquiry, 23,* 697–712.

Herman, J. (1996). *Trauma and recovery: The aftermath of violence—From domestic abuse to political terror.* New York: Basic.

Hughes, D. (2006). *Building the bonds of attachment, awakening love in deeply troubled children* (2nd ed.). Lanham, MD: Rowman & Littlefield.

Kimmerling, R., Ouimette, P., & Wolfe, J. (2002). *Gender and PTSD.* New York: Guilford Press.

Kozol, J. (2005). *The shame of the nation: The restoration of apartheid schooling in America.* New York: Three Rivers Press.

Lieberman, A., & Van Horn, P. (2008). *Psychotherapy with infants and young children: Repairing the effects of stress and trauma on early attachment.* New York: Guilford Press.

Leon, S., Martinovich, Z., Lutz, W., & Lyons, J. (2005). The effect of therapist experience on psychotherapy outcomes. *Clinical Psychology and Psychotherapy Journal, 12,* 417–426.

Lester, P., Wong, S., & Hendren, R. (2003). The neurobiological effects of trauma. *Adolescent Psychiatry.* Retrieved from http://findarticles.com/p/articles/mi_qa3882/is_200301/ai_n9209872

Lum, D. (2003). *Social work practice and people of color* (5th ed.). Florence, KY: Wadsworth.

Main, M., & Solomon, J. (1986). Discovery of an insecure disorganized/disoriented attachment pattern: Procedures, findings and implications for classification of behaviour. In M. W. Yogman & T. B. Brazelton (Eds.), *Affective development in infancy* (pp. 95–124). Norwood, NJ: Ablex.

Mitchell, S., & Black, G. (1995). *Freud and beyond.* New York: Basic Books.

Sable, P. (2000). *Attachment and adult psychotherapy.* Lanham, MD: Rowman & Littlefield.

Siegel, K. (1980). *Group treatment for adolescent girls in incestuous families.* Paper presented at the annual convention of the American Psychological Association, September 1–5, 1980, Quebec.

Spitz, R. A. (1951). The psychogenic disease in infancy—An attempt at their etiologic classification. *Psychoanalytic Study of the Child, 6,* 255–275.

Springer, C., & Padgett, D. (2000). Gender differences in young adolescent's exposure to violence and rates of PTSD symptomology. *American Journal of Orthopsychiatry, 70,* 370–379.

Sykes, D. (1987). An approach to working with black youth in cross cultural therapy. *Clinical Social Work Journal, 15,* 260–270.

Sykes, G. (1992). *8 ball chicks: A year in the violent world of girl gangsters.* New York: Anchor.

Wallin, D. (2007). *Attachment in psychotherapy.* New York: Guilford Press.

Wood, G., & Roche, S., (2001). *Representing selves, reconstructing lives: Feminist group work with women survivors of male violence.* London: Haworth Press.

Index